INSIGHT GUIDES

CALIFORNIA

APA PUBLICATIONS

Part of the Langenscheidt Publishing Group

INSIGHT GUIDE
CALIFORNIA

Editorial
Editor
Martha Ellen Zenfell
Picture Manager
Steven Lawrence
Series Manager
Rachel Fox

Distribution
North America
Langenscheidt Publishers, Inc.
36–36 33rd Street, 4th Floor
Long Island City, New York 11106
orders@langenscheidt.com

UK & Ireland
GeoCenter International Ltd
Meridian House, Churchill Way West
Basingstoke, Hampshire RG21 6YR
sales@geocenter.co.uk

Australia
Universal Publishers
1 Waterloo Road
Macquarie Park, NSW 2113
sales@universalpublishers.com.au

New Zealand
Hema Maps New Zealand Ltd (HNZ)
Unit 2, 10 Cryers Road
East Tamaki, Auckland 2013
sales.hema@clear.net.nz

Worldwide
Apa Publications GmbH & Co.
Verlag KG (Singapore branch)
7030 Ang Mo Kio Avenue 5
08-65 Northstar @ AMK
Singapore 569880
apasin@singnet.com.sg

Printing
CTPS - China

©2008 Apa Publications GmbH & Co.
Verlag KG (Singapore branch)
All Rights Reserved
First Edition 1984
Seventh Edition 2003
Updated 2008
Reprinted 2010

CONTACTING THE EDITORS
We would appreciate it if readers
would alert us to errors or out-
dated information by writing to:
Insight Guides, P.O. Box 7910,
London SE1 1WE, England.
insight@apaguide.co.uk

www.insightguides.com

ABOUT THIS BOOK

The first Insight Guide pioneered the use of creative full-color photography in travel guides in 1970. Since then, we have expanded our range to cater for our readers' need not only for reliable information about their chosen destination but also for a real understanding of the culture and workings of that destination.

Now, when the internet can supply inexhaustible (but not always reliable) facts, our books marry text and pictures to provide those much more elusive qualities: knowledge and discernment. To achieve this, they rely heavily on the authority of locally based writers and photographers.

How to use this book

Insight Guides have been structured to convey an understanding of a region and its culture, and to guide readers through its best sights and activities:

◆ The **Best of California** section at the front of the guide helps you to prioritize what you want to do.

◆ The **Features** section, indicated by a yellow bar at the top of each page, covers the natural and cultural history of California and includes illuminating essays on food, car culture, Hollywood and the Great Outdoors.

◆ The main **Places**

convey its cultural diversity. Visitors instinctively understand the word "Eureka," California's state motto, when they first discover this rich region. The word means: "I have found it" in Greek. With its mountains, redwood forests, beaches, cosmopolitan cities and varied lifestyles, California is one of the world's most exciting travel destinations.

The contributors
This edition was supervised by London-based, American-born **Martha Ellen Zenfell**, and builds on the previous version edited on-site in California by **John Wilcock**, a graduate of the *New York Times* travel desk and project editor of several Insight Guides. **Laura Martone** updated the Southern California section of this edition, while **Alison Brick** of San Francisco did the same for Northern California.

Skilled contributors to previous editions include local residents **Erika Lenkert, Jeffrey Davis, Sean Wagstaff, Tom Cole, Joan Talmage Weiss, Karen Klabin, Dennis Pottenger** and **Jessica Cunningham, John Eldan, Howard Rabinowitz** and **Julie Petersen**. A very special thanks to **Jon Carroll, Tracey Johnston** and **Ben Kalb**, who created such a solid first edition.

Adding enormously to the look of the book are the photographs by **Catherine Karnow**, who was also the principal lensperson on *Insight Guide: Las Vegas* and *Insight Guide: Los Angeles*, and by **Doug Traverso, Kerrick James, Bret R. Lundberg, Glyn Genin** and **Richard Nowitz**.

section, indicated by a blue bar, is broken down into Northern and southern California and forms a complete guide to all the sights and areas worth visiting. Places of special interest are coordinated by number with the maps.
◆ The **Travel Tips** listings section, provides full information on transportation, accommodations, eating out, activities, and an A–Z section of essential practical information. An easy-to-find contents list for Travel Tips is printed on the back flap, which also serves as a bookmark.
◆ The **Photographs** are chosen not only to illustrate the beauty and glamor of California, but also to

Map Legend

– – – ··	International Boundary
– – – –	Province Boundary
– · – ··	National Park/Reserve
– – – –	Ferry Route
⊖	Border Crossing
✈ ✈	Airport: International/Regional
🚌	Bus Station
Ⓜ	Metro
❶	Tourist Information
✝ ✝ ✝	Church/Ruins
✝	Monastery
∴	Archaeological Site
∩	Cave
⚊	Statue/Monument

The main places of interest in the **Places** section are cross-referenced by letter or number (e.g. ❶), with a full-color map, and a symbol at the top of every right-hand page tells you where to find the specific map.

CONTENTS

Introduction

History

People and Culture

A golden day
by the bay,
San Francisco

Travel Tips

Places

Insight On...

Information Panels

THE BEST OF CALIFORNIA

From unique attractions to top beaches and museums,
here, at a glance, are our recommendations, plus some
tips and tricks even the locals won't always know

BEST BEACHES

- **Huntington Beach**
  Ever wonder where "Surf City USA" is? You just found it. *See page 308.*
- **Cabrillo Beach**
  Cabrillo has windsurfing, scuba diving, whale-watching, a good aquarium and views of Catalina. *See page 308.*
- **Malibu Beach**
  Popular with surfers, this beach has wetlands, flower gardens, tide pools and terrific bird-watching perches. You can spot celeb houses from the sand, too. *See page 271.*
- **Point Vicente**
  At the tip of the Palos Verdes Peninsula, this is an ideal place to watch passing whales. *See page 307.*

- **Venice Beach**
  There's terrific people-watching potential here, from hippie artists to muscle-bound men. *See page 275.*
- **Santa Cruz** has three beaches: Main Beach has the boardwalk, Cowell Beach is for beginning surfers, while Steamer Lane is for experts and their boards. *See page 159.*
- **Santa Monica Beach**
  The soft white sand on either side of Santa Monica Pier is a wonderful place to enjoy Pacific sunsets. *See page 272.*
- **Stinson Beach**
  The most popular beach in the East Bay, the chilly water does not deter hearty San Franciscans. *See page 172.*

BEST CULTURAL ATTRACTIONS

- **Walt Disney Concert Hall** The home of the LA Philharmonic is a gleaming modern design by noted architect Frank Gehry. *See page 254.*
- **Hollywood Bowl**
  Music lovers come to this amphitheater for classical music and jazz concerts. *See page 261.*
- **Museum of Contemporary Art**
  This San Diego facility with its fantastically sited oceanside La Jolla branch celebrates the best of modern art. *See page 333.*
- **Civic Center**
  San Francisco's arts complex includes the

Asian Art Museum, the opera house, and symphony hall. *See page 131.*
- **SF MoMA**
  Northern California's premier art collection, displayed under a five-story glass-roofed staircase. *See page 133.*
- **San Jose Museum of Art** houses nearly 1,500 works of art, including glittering blown-glass sculptures by Dale Chihuly. *See page 154.*

ABOVE: surfing champs.
RIGHT: a good way to spend a day in San Jose.

ONLY IN CALIFORNIA

- **Alcatraz** A high-security prison may seem like an unlikely attraction, but "The Rock" is both haunting and fascinating. The ferry ride across the chilly water is an adventure, too. *See page 124.*
- **Cable Cars** Most tourists wait for hours at the base of Powell Street for a trip; be different and start at California and Van Ness for the same thrill. *See page 128.*
- **California Cuisine** Think of the freshest ingredients, a menu

- **Grauman's Chinese Theatre** This 1920s-era LA movie palace has a forecourt of famous hand- and footprints. *See page 260.*
- **La Brea Tar Pits** Since the 1900s, these bubbling pools of asphalt yielded prehistoric fossils. *See page 257.*
- **Silicon Valley** When the world was catapulted into the electronic age, Silicon Valley was manning the keyboard. *See page 155.*

BEST FESTIVALS AND EVENTS

For more festivals see Travel Tips, page 380.
- **Bay to Breakers** This San Francisco footrace occurs every May and covers the city from the east side to the west. Most participants wear outrageous costumes; some wear nothing at all. *See page 132.*
- **Chinese New Year** This parade in San Francisco's Chinatown is the largest outside Asia. *See page 120.*
- **Halloween Costume Carnaval** America's largest Halloween street party lures outrageous folks to West Hollywood. *See page 261.*

- **Kinetic Grand Championship** Transportation meets art in this zany, three-day race through Humboldt County. *See page 225.*
- **Monterey Jazz Festival** One of the most significant events on the international jazz calendar happens here every September. *See page 381.*
- **Pride Week** A June gay-fest in SF's Castro climaxes in the world's biggest Pride Parade. *See page 137.*
- **Rose Parade** Flower-covered floats and bands strut through Pasadena to celebrate the Rose Bowl football game. *See page 286.*

that changes, often daily, to accommodate the farmers' produce, and you've got the message. *See page 68.*
- **Car culture** Where else could the coming of age be marked by the ability to obtain a car? *See page 99.*
- **Golden Gate Bridge** Take a walk across this most famous of landmarks. Sunny or foggy, you won't regret it. *See page 141.*

- **Wine Country** Take your pick: Napa or Sonoma counties. Both are just an hour and a half north of San Francisco, but eons away in pace and landscape. *See page 177.*
- **Santa Catalina Island** With two-thirds of its interior protected land, Catalina is calm and practically car free. Plus, you can visit in a day. *See page 313.*

ABOVE: runners in San Fran's Bay to Breakers race.
LEFT: a peaceful afternoon in California Wine Country.
BELOW: cruising through the canyons of Los Angeles.

BEST FOR KIDS

- **Disneyland**
Mickey Mouse isn't the only attraction: families flock here for Space Mountain, the Fantasmic! night-time show and the rides at California Adventure. *See page 299.*
- **Universal Studios**
Attractions based on *Back to the Future*, *Jurassic Park* and *Shrek* are winners for kids – and adults, too. *See page 282.*
- **Knott's Berry Farm**
America's first theme park delights with gunfights, Camp Snoopy musicals and fried chicken dinners. *See page 302.*
- **Calico Ghost Town**
Not far from the Mojave Desert, an 1880s silver-mining town is now a theme park. *See page 344.*
- **Great America**
Think thrill rides, family rides and kids' rides in the Bay Area's Santa Clara Valley. *See page 154.*
- **Monterey Bay Aquarium**
Spectacular sanctuary by the sea with over 350,000 specimens. Don't miss feeding time. *See page 160.*

- **Tech Museum of Innovation**
Want to create your own virtual roller-coaster ride? Interactive exhibits highlight the latest in Silicon Valley tech. *See page 154.*
- **San Diego Wild Animal Park**
Giraffes, zebras, lions and tigers – what more does a kid need? *See page 310.*
- **Pier 39** Fisherman's Wharf's Pier 39 has bumper cars, an aquarium, street performers and sea lions. *See page 122.*
- **SeaWorld**
Watch irresistible dolphins, "killer" whales, sea lions and all things finny in this San Diego water park. *See page 331.*
- **Six Flags Magic Mountain** X-treme roller coasters are the attraction at this theme park near the Mission Hills in Valencia. *See page 284.*
- **San Diego Zoo**
Visit lush Balboa Park and see giant pandas and other animals in naturalist settings that use moats, not cages. *See page 334.*

ABOVE: Marilyn pouts and poses on the Walk of Fame.
BELOW: a panda catches some shut-eye at the San Diego Zoo.

BEST ICONIC SIGHTS

- **Haight-Ashbury**
Popular in 1967's Summer of Love, the street is a magnet for fashionistas and hippie "freaks." *See page 138.*
- **City Lights**
The San Francisco bookstore of choice for 1950s Beats. *See page 122.*

- **Hollywood Walk of Fame**
Over 2,000 star-shaped plaques on Hollywood Boulevard are emblazoned with celebrities' names. *See page 259.*

BEST TOURS

- **Hearst Castle**
Several different tours are available to this castle in the sky. *See page 166.*
- **Paramount Studios**
The only major studio still in Hollywood lets you go behind the scenes. *See page 258.*
- *Queen Mary*
History and ghostly legends in this famous ship. *See page 308.*

- **Kodak Theatre**
See where the stars sit during the Oscars ceremony at the Hollywood & Highland complex. *See page 260.*
- **Winchester Mystery House** Every Friday the 13th, there are flashlight tours to this kid-friendly and spooky home. *See page 154.*

CALIFORNIA FOR FREE

- **Getty Center**
  This LA clifftop complex draws art, architecture and garden enthusiasts who can explore the beautiful setting free of charge. *See page 268.*
- **Getty Villa**
  The Malibu museum is devoted to the culture of ancient Greece, Rome and Egypt. Admission is free, but there is a fee for parking. *See page 271.*
- **Mission Dolores**
  The oldest building in San Francisco has the distinction

of having the only mission chapel that is still intact. Immortalized in the Hitchcock film *Vertigo*, a serene cemetery holds the remains of some of the city's first leaders. *See page 137.*

ABOVE: Yosemite National Park.
BELOW: Mission Dolores in the sunshine.

- **Santa Monica Pier**
  100 years old, this famous pier has free activities like juggling acts, film screenings and summer concerts. *See page 273.*

BEST SCENERY

- **Big Sur** Highway 1 south of San Fran may be the most spectacular route in America, hugging the coast in razor-sharp switchbacks. *See page 164.*
- **Death Valley** Despite searing temperatures, 900 different types of plant grow here. *See page 347.*
- **Lake Tahoe**
  Go snowboarding or skiing in the winter and hiking, biking or fishing in the summer. *See page 217.*
- **Yosemite National Park** Its fame is exceeded only by its beauty; just avoid the summer. *See page 197.*
- **The High North**
  A remote domain of mountains, valleys, volcanoes, rivers, canyons and basins. *See page 231.*
- **Muir Woods** San Francisco in the morning; giant sequoias in the afternoon. Stop at the Pelican Inn at Muir Beach for a spot of ale. *See page 171.*

MONEY-SAVING TIPS

National Parks Pass Frequent visitors to California's national parks should buy an "America the Beautiful" pass, which admits the holder, a vehicle plus any passengers to most parks and national recreation areas. Even better, 90 percent of the profits goes back into supporting the parks. Visit http://store.usgs.gov/pass/

Attractions cards Two companies offer visitor cards that give discounts up to 25 percent off admission to

attractions. The **Explorer Pass** allows visitors to create their own itinerary within a 30-day limit and a specific area. The pass to California Wine Country includes tastings as well as entry into wineries, while the Explorer Pass to Hollywood and San Francisco includes museums, tours and high-energy activities. Go to: www.explorerpass.com.

CityPass is a similar scheme for visitors, except that tickets must be used within 9 days (cities) or 14 days. The Southern California pass is particularly good for families, as it allows admission into five theme parks and cuts down enormously on waiting in lines. Go to CityPass.com.

CALIFORNIA HERE I COME

The California Dream has been described as "a love affair with an idea and a surrender to a collective fantasy"

For more than a century, since the arrival of the transcontinental railroad, California has been the last stop on the line for Americans heading west in search of a new life. James J. Rawls, author of the above description, said that California's promise raised the expectations of the millions who came to the state hoping that their lives would be better than the one they left behind. "California is to them their best – or perhaps their last – chance for success."

Even if for many long-time residents the dream has soured in the reality of traffic-clogged freeways, social unrest and blue skies too often filtered through man-made clouds, there are always new dreamers arriving – many from lands where a little smog seems a small price to pay for the freedom that goes with it. Truth to tell, California is a highly enticing and fascinating place; America "only more so," as Wallace Stegner put it, "the national culture at its most energetic end. In a prosperous country, we are more prosperous than most… more mobile… more tasteless… more energetically creative… more optimistic… more anxious."

Twenty-five years after writing that, Stegner said he hadn't changed his view, but he was regretful about "the excesses of wide-open opportunities and uncontrollable growth." And mainly over water, he said, referring to the age-old battle between the north and south, it had split itself politically in two.

A curious thing, this split, with Northern California centered around its nominal "capital" of San Francisco, and Southern California beholden to Los Angeles. It's going a bit too far to state that they hate each other, but physically and temperamentally they are very different. From a visitor's point of view that's all to the good: two very different destinations on the same coastline, and both in the same state.

Most trips in this book begin from one or the other, with the dividing line roughly at San Luis Obispo. Although this is about halfway between Los Angeles and San Francisco, it's not, strictly speaking, the halfway point of the state's coastline. California stretches for at least another 300 miles (480 km) beyond the latter, all the way north to the Oregon border. We deal with that in the chapter named "The High North." It's sparsely populated up there, but of course some people prefer that.

Movie stars to the south; majestic solitude to the north. Can you blame anyone for thinking California was their best possible chance for success? ❑

PRECEDING PAGES: a San Francisco fog envelops the Golden Gate Bridge; Los Angeles by night – one of the world's biggest consumers of electricity.
LEFT: a mad-hatted welcome to San Francisco at *Beach Blanket Babylon*.

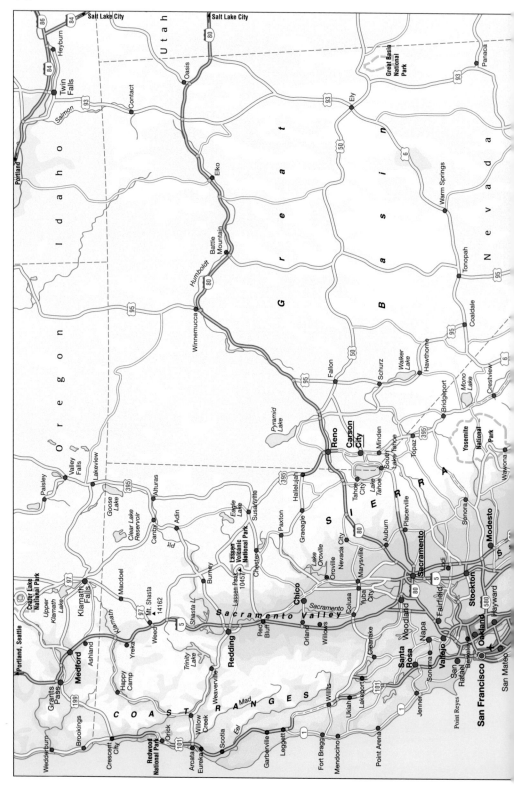

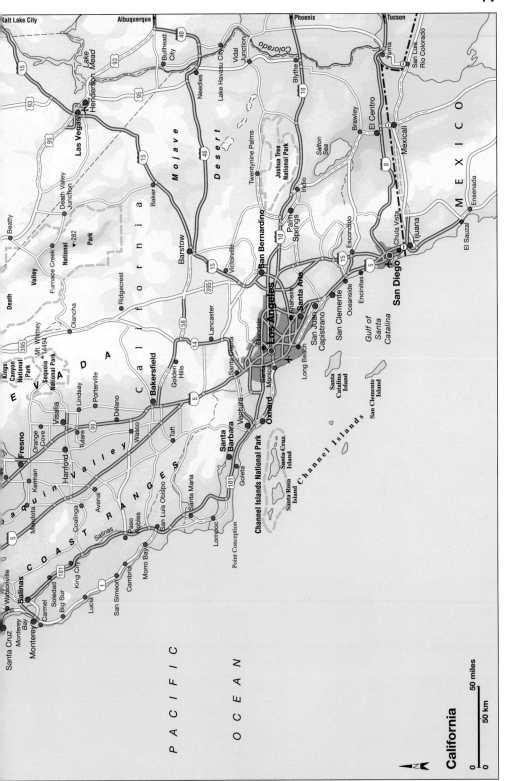

California

History Timeline

Circa **9000 BC** The first nomads reach what is now California.

AD 500 Miwok tribes settle in the San Francisco Bay region.

1579 Sir Francis Drake anchors the *Golden Hind* on the northern coast where a controversial brass plate was discovered more than 350 years later.

1769 Adventurer Gaspar de Portolá discovers the small Indian village of Yong-na.

1770s The Spanish found a *presidio* (military garrison) and mission near San Francisco Bay.

1781 Don Felipe de Neve marches from the San Gabriel Mission with 11 Mexican families to found what is to become Los Angeles.

1769–1823 Spanish padres found 21 missions along the Royal Road *(El Camino Real)* between San Diego and Sonoma.

1804 The Mexican territory of California is divided into a northern and a southern section, reflecting the land's differences.

1820s Mexico breaks away from Spain.

1846 The US declares war on Mexico and captures California.

1848 Gold is discovered at Sutter's Fort in the Sierra foothills and within three years 200,000 prospectors have flooded Northern California.

1850 California becomes the 31st state.

1850s Under successive treaties with the Federal government (but never ratified by the Senate) Native Americans sign away up to 90 percent of their lands.

1858 The Butterfield Stage Line delivers Los Angeles' first overland mail.

1859 The discovery of the Comstock Lode turns San Francisco from a frontier town into a prosperous metropolis.

1860s Constructon of railroads to link the East and West Coasts of America begins.

1869 The first transcontinental railroad is completed, with a terminus at Oakland.

1873 The world's first cable car runs between Kearny and Jones Street in San Francisco. The first navel orange trees begin to thrive at Riverside.

1876 The Southern Pacific Railway arrives in Los Angeles, nine years before the Santa Fe.

1886 Harvey H. Wilcox opens a subdivision that his wife names Hollywood.

1892 Edward Doheny and C.A. Canfield strike oil near the site of today's MacArthur Park in downtown Los Angeles.

1905 Abbott Kinney opens his Venetian-style resort with canals and gondoliers near Los Angeles' coastal Santa Monica.

1906 A massive earthquake measuring 8.2 rocks San Francisco. At least 250,000 people are left homeless, but rebuilding begins immediately.

1908 Filmmaker Francis Boggs completes *The Count of Monte Cristo,* Southern California's first commercial film.

1911 Hollywood's first movie, *The Law of the Range*, is filmed inside a former tavern in a city gone "dry."

1913 Water from the eastern Sierra Nevada mountains reaches Los Angeles via the Owens Aqueduct.

1926 Second-string studio Warner Bros adds sound to its feature *Don Juan* and the following year gives Al Jolson some dialogue in *The Jazz Singer.*

1929 The first American Academy of Motion Pictures awards, or, as they are better known, the Oscars, are presented.

1932 The Olympic Games are staged in what is then the world's largest stadium, LA's Coliseum.

1933 Construction begins on San Francisco's Golden Gate and Bay bridges.

1933 An earthquake (measuring 6.3 on the Richter scale) kills 120 people in Los Angeles.

1937 The Golden Gate Bridge is opened to an uproarious reception, six months after the Oakland Bay Bridge.

1939 LA's Union Station, the last of the great railroad terminals, opens.

1945 The United Nations Organizaton is born in San Francisco with 50 countries agreeing to sign its Charter.

1947 The California legislature passes a law against smog.

1953 Lawrence Ferlinghetti opens City Lights bookstore in San Francisco's North Beach which becomes the hang-out for a new youth movement, the "Beats" or beatniks.

1955 Disneyland opens at Anaheim.

1960s Hippies, leftists and idealists are drawn to San Francisco's Haight-Ashbury district and, in 1967, celebrate the Summer of Love.

1963 California's population exceeds that of every other state.

1965 Rioting in the Watts area of Los Angeles kills 34 people.

1968 Presidential candidate Robert F. Kennedy is shot and killed in Los Angeles.

1971 An earthquake measured at 6.6 on the Richter scale claims the lives of 64 Southern Californians.

1974 Oil tycoon J. Paul Getty donates his Los Angeles home as a museum. BART (Bay Area Rapid Transit System) starts a regular transportation service.

1978 San Francisco mayor George Moscone and supervisor Harvey Milk are assassinated by a deranged former supervisor.

1980 Former actor and governor of California Ronald Reagan becomes the 39th president of the United States.

1980s Phenomenal growth in the computer industry, particularly in the Northern California region, puts Silicon Valley on the map.

1989 An earthquake (7.1 on the Richter scale) collapses a freeway and causes death and destruction in the San Francisco Bay area.

1991 Berkeley Hills fire kills 25 and destroys over 3,000 homes.

1992 The acquittal of LA police officers charged with beating a black motorist starts riots that kill at least 50 people.

1993 LA's first subway opens, with a route running between MacArthur Park and Union Station.

1994 An earthquake (6.7 on Richter scale) in the San Fernando Valley kills over 60 people.

PRECEDING PAGES: Central Pacific Railroad, 1867.
LEFT: native tribes settled as early as AD 500.
RIGHT: California's movie industry, which began *circa* 1910, had an impact around the world.

1995 The opening of the Museum of Modern Art in San Francisco's SoMa (South of Market Street) district spearheads a downtown building boom.

1995–97 The trials of football star O.J. Simpson, accused of two murders, enthrals the nation.

2000 Completion of the Anaheim Convention Center and campus near LA. Completion of the Pac Bell Park baseball stadium in San Francisco.

2001 California is hit by "rolling blackouts" due to electricity crisis.

2003 The Asian Art Museum opens in San Francisco's Civic Center. Movie star Arnold Schwarze - negger becomes the state of California's governor in an historic recall election.

2004 Ronald Reagan dies at 93. The *USS Midway* opens to the public as the San Diego Aircraft Carrier Museum. San Francisco mayor Gavin Newsom authorizes the city clerk to issue marriage licenses to same-sex couples, sparking a national debate.

2005 George Lucas moves his movie studio to San Francisco's Presidio; the de Young Museum reopens in San Francisco's Golden Gate Park.

2006 The Amgen Tour, an eight-day bicycling race from San Francisco to LA, makes its debut.

2007 Wildfires from Santa Barbara to San Diego kill 12 people and destroy 1,500 buildings. One month later, 50 buildings burn in Malibu.

2008 The Writers Guild of America strike disrupts LA's awards shows and delays TV broadcasts. ❏

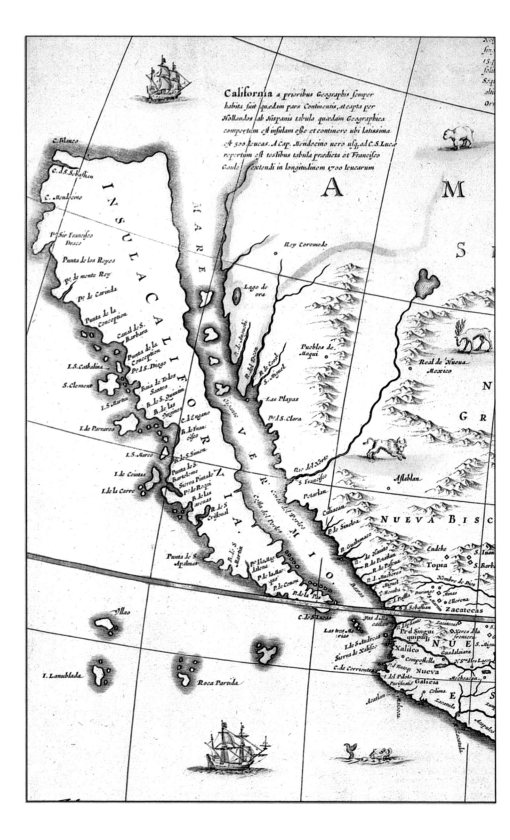

California *a prioribus Geographis semper*
habita fuit quædam pars Continentis, at capta per
Hollandos ab Hispanis tabula quædam Geographica
compertum est insulam esse et continere ubi latissima
est 500 leucas. A Cap. Mendocino uero usq, ad C. S. Lucæ
repertum est testibus tabula prædicta et Francisco
Gauldi extendi in longitudinem 1700 leucarum

C. Blanco

C. d. S. Sebastian

C. Mendocino

P.ᵗᵃ Sir Francisco
Drake

Punta de los Reyes

P.ᵗ de monte Rey

P.ᵗ de Carmela

Punta de la
Concepcion

Canal de S.
Barbara

Ponta de la
Conception

I. S. Catalina

S. Clement

I. S. Martha

I. de Pxnaros

I. S. Mateo

I. de Ceuitas

I. de la Carro

Punta de S.
Apolimar

Yllao

I. Lanublada

Roca Parida

INSULA CALIFORNIA

MARE VERMEIO

Rey Coronado

Lago de
ora

Pueblos de.
Maqui

Real de Nueva
Mexico

Las Playas

P.ᵗ d. S. Clara

Astablan

Culiacan

NUEVA BISC

Topia

Nombre de Dios

Zacatecas

C. de S. Lucas

Las tres Ma-
rias

I. de S. Andres

Sierra de Xalisco

C. de Corrientes

Xalilco

Nueva
Galicia

Acatlan

A   M

S

N

G R

N U E

E

S

NATIVE TRIBES AND EUROPEANS

California tribes thrived and prospered for 10,000 years.
Then the white man brought disease and religion

The first tenants of the rich land that became California were the tribes that, through the centuries, crossed the land bridge of the Bering Strait and slowly filtered down into the North American continent. So many native people died soon after Europeans arrived that anthropologists have had to rely on patchy mission records for their estimates – a reasonable guess being that 230,000 Native Americans originally inhabited the northern region.

California tribes led a simple life, their igloo-shaped homes of reed providing breezy shelter in summer, while deer-skin roofs afforded protection during the rainy season. When it grew cool, open fires were built in the homes, with holes in the roof allowing the smoke to escape.

In warm weather, the men and children were naked except for ornamental jewelry such as necklaces, earrings, bracelets and anklets. They kept warm when needed with robes of yellow cedar bark or crudely tanned pelts. Some groups practiced tattooing. The women wore two-piece aprons made of deer skins or reeds.

Tribal identities

Customs, talents and preoccupations varied from tribe to tribe, each with separate identities and distinct languages. The Miwoks and Ohlones around San Francisco Bay moved in short nomadic spurts, sometimes trekking from their ancestral shell mound up to the oak groves on what are now the Berkeley Hills. Here they ground acorns into rich and oily meal, and socialized warily. Then they would pack up for the meadowland and its rich harvest of deer and elk, at each stop along the trail being greeted and heartened by ancient landmarks: a venerable oak tree, a mossy boulder, a lively stream, a soft meadow.

The land around the Bay probably supported more humans than any other California locale, but one area that was not much frequented was that where the city of San Fran-

cisco now stands. It was a sandy, windy, desolate place compared to the lushness of the Berkeley Hills, the mild slopes of Mount Tamalpais, or the woods of the southern peninsula. San Francisco today, in fact, has more trees and wildlife than at any time in its history.

In the south, the Chumash tribe, living in

habitants de Californie

what is now Santa Barbara, were adept fishermen who used seashell hooks, basket traps, nets and vegetable poisons, even catching fish with their bare hands. The tons of shellfish eaten over the course of centuries have left us with mounds of discarded shells, which can now reach 20 ft (7 meters) deep.

Canoe-making was usually with easily worked timbers such as red cedar and redwood. The canoes were distinguished by their symmetry, neatness of finish, and frequent decoration. All of this was achieved with limited tools, the principal ones being chisels, curved knives, abrasive stones, wedges and sharkskin. The Chumash in particular were expert boat-

LEFT: map by Dutchman Joannes Jansson, 1638.
RIGHT: early painting of Californian natives.

builders. One of their elegant vessels can still be admired today at the Santa Barbara Museum of Natural History

The California tribes' lifestyle continued and prospered for 10,000 years with few major changes and, by our standards, few possessions. The arrival of white people bewildered them but their acquisition of manufactured articles such as guns, metal utensils, axes, knives, blankets and cloth led inevitably to a decline of the native arts and crafts. With the coming of the immigrant wagons and the encroachment of white settlements, warfare became a unifying force.

Tribes that had been enemies often united

against the intruders. But even this did not save them and, in the end, they were overwhelmed. The culture of all Native Americans was radically changed and remains so today. They had survived regular earthquakes and droughts, but the white man proved too strong for them.

Hernando Cortés, the Spaniard who conquered Mexico, sailed up the west coast of North America. Stumbling upon a "peninsula" which stretched down between the sea and a gulf, he believed he'd found a long-lost fabled island, and he named it "California." But the discovery of the state of California is officially credited to Juan Rodríguez Cabrillo, Portuguese commander of two Spanish caravels, who is thought to have embarked from the Mexican port of Navidad in June 1542. He explored most of the coast of what is now the state of California, entering San Diego harbor in September 1542 and labeling it "enclosed and very good."

Sir Francis Drake, sailing around the world in 1579 in the *Golden Hind,* passed by the entrance to the bay of San Francisco without noticing an opening. But his log shows that he did anchor just north and sent several landing parties ashore. For over 65 years it was believed that one of these groups may have left behind a small brass plate that was discovered in 1936 near what is now Drake's Bay. But in 2003 it was declared an elaborate hoax.

Twenty-three years later, Sebastian Vizcaíno arrived in the south, searching for suitable ports of call for his Manila galleon on its annual return to the Philippines. What Spain most needed was a safe haven from marauding Dutch and British pirates for the treasure ships en route to Spain with the riches from their empire as far afield as the Philippines. But the canny and ambitious Spanish king, Charles III, was also keenly aware of Russian incursions from the north, where otter-hunting had reached as far south as Bodega Bay.

Vizcaíno gave lasting names to several California sites, such as San Clemente Island, San Diego and Santa Catalina Island. Of more importance was his glowing report on the virtues of the California coast that urged Spain to colonize the state.

Converting the natives

What followed was another 150 years of lassitude until the overland arrival in 1769 of Gaspar de Portolá from Baja. Crossing the Santa Ana River and exchanging gifts with friendly tribes, de Portolá's band passed by the bubbling tar pits of La Brea, through the mountains at Sepulveda Pass to Lake Encino and headed northwards to open up the route to Monterey.

"The three diarists in the party agree that the practical discovery of most significance was the advantageous site on the Los Angeles River," noted John Caughey in a volume published by the California Historical Society to mark the city's bicentennial. "Equally important were the numerous able-bodied, alert and amiable Indians because Spanish policy looked towards preserving, Christianizing, hispanizing and engrossing the natives as a major element in the Spanish colony now to be established." Over the centuries, Spain had developed a standard method for settling new territory, using the sword to cut down any opposition from the natives and pacifying the area with the introduction of Christianity. This was the approach used in California, where between 1769 and early in the following century a chain of 21 Franciscan missions was established between San Diego and Sonoma. These missions enslaved hundreds of coastal Indians into an endless round of work and prayer.

EARTHLY PARADISE

Hernando Cortés believed he had found the fabled paradise island "California."

Indian men were taught to tend cattle, and the women were taught to sew.

White diseases, such as measles and chicken pox, killed thousands and as a result, the Native Americans developed a mortal fear of mission life. But benevolent despotism kept thousands in the missions and it was their labor that made the system successful. Not until the Mexican Government's secularization decrees of 1834 were the native people freed – only to exchange their status for that of underpaid peons on the vast ranches.

As early as 1775 the natives rebelled: in an uprising at the San Diego mission one of the Franciscans was killed. But abolishing age-old tribal customs and introducing a complex religious structure centered around endless work eventually converted the natives into obedient servants. The object of every mission was to become self-sufficient, to which end its subjects became cooks, blacksmiths, farmers, tanners, vintners or underpaid laborers. The

In theory, the Secularization Act of 1834 gave lay administrators and Native Americans the right to ownership of the missions and their property; a potential ranchero could ask for as many as 50,000 acres (20,200 hectares). In practice, the acts were barely observed: tribes were driven out into the world of poverty and helplessness, ill-equipped to deal with white men's laws.

Some returned to the hills, others indentured themselves as ranch hands or turned to drinking and gambling. Meanwhile, the orange groves and the productive gardens were cleared or ploughed under, and the so-called "string of pearls" – the missions – transformed into a patchwork quilt of ranches. ❏

LEFT: California Indian tribes prospered for nearly 10,000 years – until the white man came.

ABOVE: Sir Francis Drake (left) in his ship the *Golden Hind* (right) sailed past San Francisco Bay in 1579.

THE MISSIONS OF OLD CALIFORNIA

The "string of pearls" – the 21 Franciscan missions spread out along California's coast – offer a serene look into California's history

Heading north from their Baja California settlement in 1769, Franciscan missionaries led by Father Junípero Serra established 21 missions during the subsequent 54 years. Most now lovingly restored, the missions form a uniquely serene look at California's past. Each mission lies roughly a day's journey apart in a line (the "string of pearls") that stretches between San Diego and Sonoma, 600 miles (965 km) to the north. Following the Secularization Act of 1834, the missions fell into disuse and were abandoned for almost half a century. Interest was sparked again with a series of magazine articles by Helen Hunt Jackson in the 1880s that brought attention to the plight of former mission Indians, many of whom had been used as slave labor in the construction of the buildings.

Each of the timber and adobe missions has some architectural or historical distinction, although all feature the thick walls, small windows and elegant bell towers usually associated with Mexican churches. A few had specific functions: the northernmost mission, San Francisco Solano (1823), was there to discourage the Russians – who for the previous decade had garrisoned Fort Ross on the northern coast – from occupying any more of the still-sparsely populated country. Solano, one of the last missions to be built, and to which at one time 1,000 Indians were attached, was to have a short life as a religious center, for barely a decade later secularization led to its abandonment. A highlight of Solano's museum today is a collection of 60 watercolors of the other missions, painted by Chris Jorgensen in 1903.

For more information on missions see the relevant chapter: ie, Santa Barbara p293 or San Diego p331.

△ **MISSION DOLORES GLASS**
In reality called San Francisco de Asís, its name derived from its location beside the Laguna Dolores. The mission was opened in 1776 by Father Serra, whose biography was written here by Father Palou.

▷ **MISSION SAN GABRIEL**
This 1832 work by Ferdinand Deppe is one of the earliest paintings showing a mission. San Gabriel was very prosperous, with over a million acres (405,000 hectares) and 40,000 head of cattle. At its peak, almost 2,000 Indians lived here.

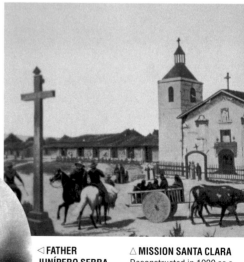

◁ **FATHER JUNÍPERO SERRA**
A tireless zealot and a mere 5ft 2ins (1.6 m) in height, Father Serra was responsible for establishing the chain of missions along the coast.

△ **MISSION SANTA CLARA**
Reconstructed in 1929 as a faithful copy of the mission of a century before, it sits on the campus of Santa Clara University, surrounded by gardens as lush and splendid as the original grounds.

⊲ **SAN JUAN CAPISTRANO**
Behind Father Serra's statue is a tiny stone chapel (the only one remaining) in which he celebrated mass. The oldest building in use, it houses a magnificent 350-year-old altar.

△ **MISSION SANTA BARBARA**
Replacing the earlier adobe destroyed by an earthquake, the present "Queen of the Missions" – the most visited in the state – was completed in 1833 based on a design of the Roman architect Vitruvius.

THE SWALLOWS OF CAPISTRANO

The fame of Orange County's Mission San Juan Capistrano has spread around the world: each year on March 19 – St Joseph's Day – a flock of swallows returns to roost here. Legend says the influx began back in the mists of time when the original brood took refuge in the mission's eaves after a local innkeeper destroyed their nests.

The birds have been coming here for at least two centuries, building their nests out of mud in the tiled roof *(see above)* and, after a summer in California, heading south again in the fall. The arrival of the swallows, although not always on the exact day, is celebrated with a festival.

Another legend that is associated with the mission – described as "an American Acropolis" – is that of a woman named Magdalena whose penance was to walk up and down the church aisle with a lighted candle to atone for disobeying her father by courting a man of whom he disapproved. On occasions, it is said, her candle can still be seen shining among the ruins of the cruciform Great Stone Church in which the poor unfortunate perished during an earthquake.

The Great Stone Church, one of the oldest sections of the mission still standing, has recently been restored to its former glory.

For more information on Mission San Juan Capistrano, see p309.

CALIFORNIA.

Golden Regions.

EMIGRATION TO

CALIFORNIA !

Do you want to go to California? If so, go and join the Company who intend going out the middle of March, or 1st of April next, under the charge of the California Emigration Society, in a first-rate Clipper Ship. The Society agreeing to find places for all those who wish it upon their arrival in San Francisco. The voyage will probably be made in a few months.— Price of passage will be in the vicinity of

ONE HUNDRED DOLLARS !

CHILDREN IN PROPORTION.

A number of families have already engaged passage. A suitable Female Nurse has been provided, who will take charge of Young Ladies and Children. Good Physicians, both male and female go in the Ship. It is hoped a large number of females will go, as Females are getting almost as good wages as males.

FEMALE NURSES get 25 dollars per week and board. SCHOOL TEACHERS 100 dollars per month. GARDNERS 60 dollars per month and board. LABORERS 4 to 5 dollars per day. BRICKLAYERS 6 dollars per day. HOUSEKEEPERS 40 dollars per month. FARMERS 5 dollars per day. SHOEMAKERS 4 dollars per day. Men and Women COOKS 40 to 60 dollars per month and board. MINERS are making from 3 to 12 dollars per day. FEMALE SERVANTS 30 to 50 dollars per month and board. Washing 3 dollars per dozen. MASONS 6 dollars per day. CARPENTERS 5 dollars per day. ENGINEERS 100 dollars per month, and as the quartz Crushing Mills are getting into operation all through the country, Engineers are very scarce. BLACKSMITHS 90 and 100 dollars per month and board.

The above prices are copied from late papers printed in San Francisco, which can be seen at my office. Having views of some 30 Cities throughout the State of California, I shall be happy to see all who will call at the office of the Society, 28 JOY'S BUILDING, WASH—INGTON ST., BOSTON, and examine them. Parties residing out of the City, by enclosing a stamp and sending to the office, will receive a circular giving all the particulars of the voyage.

As Agents are wanted in every town and city of the New England States, Postmasters or Merchants acting as such will be allowed a certain commission on every person they get to join the Company. Good reference required. For further particulars correspond or call at the

SOCIETY'S OFFICE,

28 Joy's Building, Washington St., Boston, Mass.

FROM RANCHOS TO STATEHOOD

It started as a simple war with Mexico. But it ended by transforming a wild and savage wilderness into the 31st state of the Union

After three centuries of Spanish rule, Mexico finally broke away in 1821 and, on September 27, declared itself a republic; coincidentally, secularization of the missions was sought by Spanish-Mexican settlers, known as the Californios. Eight million acres (3.2 million hectares) of mission land were fragmented into 800 privately owned ranches with some governors handing out land to their cronies for only a few pennies per acre.

Soldiers who had finished their time in the army often stayed on in California rather than return to Spain or Mexico. Under Mexican law, a ranchero could ask for as many as 50,000 acres (20,200 hectares) and native slave labor became part of the plunder.

The *vaquero's* values

Orange orchards were cleared for firewood and herds were given to private hands. The predominant lifestyle quickly changed to that of an untamed frontier-style cattle range, although cattle ranching in this part of the world made few demands upon its owners. With no line fences to patrol and repair on the open range, and no need for vigilance because of branded stock, the *vaquero* had little to do but practice feats of horsemanship to improve his masculinity and impress the *señoritas*.

His sports were violent, including calf branding, wild-horse roundups, bear hunts, cock-and bullfights; his entertainment included dances, such as the Spanish fandango and the Western waltz, and at his fiestas he was bedecked in gold-braided clothes dripping with silver. Crops and game were plentiful; wildlife included badgers and coyotes; the lordly condor circled overhead and grizzly bear, deer, gray wolves, mountain lions and wildcats roamed the hills.

Author Richard Henry Dana, who visited the state in 1835, called the Californians "an idle thriftless people," an observation lent considerable weight by the lifestyle of so many of the rancheros, who found it a simple matter to maintain and increase their wealth. The sudden influx of prospectors to the north created an immense demand for beef which the southerners were readily able to supply.

In his novel, *Two Years Before the Mast,* Dana

described how cattle hides and tallow in 500-lb (227-kg) bags were thrown from the cliffs to the waiting ships. Accepted as a basic unit of barter, these hides were turned into rugs, blankets, curtains, sandals, chaps and saddles. Rawhides were twisted into *reatas* (used for roping cattle) or used to lash timbers together. Edible meat not eaten immediately was sun-dried as beef jerky or pickled for barter with trading ships. All fat was rendered into tallow, the basis for candles and soap.

Yankee trading ships plied up and down the coast, operating like floating department stores offering mahogany furniture, gleaming copperware, framed mirrors, Irish linen, silver candle -

---

LEFT: enticing New Englanders to join the migration.
RIGHT: an 1842 portrait of Richard Dana, author of the influential *Two Years Before the Mast.*

sticks and cashmere shawls. For many of the native-born Americans, these were their first amenities from the civilized world. Sometimes the trading ships, which had survived the pre-carious Straits of Magellan, would stay an entire year, working up and down the coast.

A genteel contraband soon developed. To reduce import taxes, ships worked in pairs to transfer cargo from one to the other on the open seas. The partially emptied ship would then make port and submit to customs inspection. With duties paid, it would rejoin its consort and reverse the transfer. Sometimes the Yankee traders used lonely coves to unload their car-

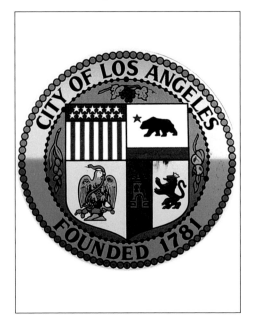

goes which were eventually smuggled ashore. Both sides fared well: the Yankee traders sailed south with full holds and the rancheros dis-played their new finery with yet another fiesta.

The weather remained temperate except for the occasional hot, dry, gale-force wind the Native Americans called "wind of the evil spir-its." The Spaniards called them *santanas*, a name which today has become corrupted to Santa Ana winds. Now and again an earthquake rumbled down the San Andreas Fault. The rancheros spent their energy rebuilding damaged hacien-das, made from red-tile roofing set on white-painted adobe brick walls, while allowing the missions to fall into ruins. Restoration of the

missions began only in the 20th century after they were declared historical landmarks.

In 1834, Governor Figueroa issued the first of the Secularization Acts, which in theory gave lay administrators and Indian neophytes the right to ownership of the missions and their property. Having been first introduced to the "civilized" world and then enslaved, the natives were dis-oriented. At the height of the mission era, as many as 20,000 Indians had been tied to the sys-tem as unpaid laborers, and many were worked to death. Like other slaves, they were psycho-logically ill-prepared to cope with freedom.

Official Washington soon became aware of this land of milk and honey on the Pacific coast. President Andrew Jackson sent an emissary to Mexico City in the 1830s to buy California for the sum of $500,000. The plan failed.

The Mexican War

When James K. Polk took office in 1845, he pledged to acquire California by any means. He felt pressured by the English financial interests which plotted to exchange $26 million of defaulted Mexican bonds for the rich land of California. On May 13, 1846, he surprised no one by declaring war on Mexico. News of the war had not yet reached California, however, when a group of settlers stormed General Mar-iano Vallejo's Sonoma estate. Vallejo soothed the men with brandy and watched as they raised their hastily sewn Bear Flag over Sonoma.

The Bear Flag Revolt is sanctified in Califor-nia history – the flag now being the official state flag – but, for all its drama, it was immaterial. Within a few weeks Commodore John Sloat arrived to usher California into the Union.

Most of the fighting in the War of American Conquest took place in the south. The war in the north effectively ended on July 9, 1846, when 70 hearty sailors and marines from the ship *Portsmouth* marched ashore in Yerba Buena vil-lage and raised the American flag in the vil-lage's central plaza.

The bloodiest battle on California soil took place in the Valley of San Pasqual, near Escon-dido. The Army of the West, commanded by General Stephen W. Kearney, fought a brief bat-tle during which 18 Americans were killed.

Kearney's aide-de-camp was US naval offi-cer Robert F. Stockton. Together they skir-mished with Mexican-Californians at Paso de Bartolo on the San Gabriel River. The Californios, however, soon readily capitulated to the Americans and California's participation in the Mexican War ended at last with the Treaty of Cahuenga, signed by John Fremont and General Pico.

The treaty, which came into force on July 4 (US Independence Day), 1848, ended the War with Mexico. By the Treaty of Cahuenga, California became a territory of the United States of America. Only through fierce negotiation was San Diego saved from being on the south side of the Mexico-California boundary.

BEAR FLAG

The state flag of California commemorates the Bear Flag Revolt of 1846.

Alta California in 1848 following its war with Mexico, Los Angeles remained a predominantly Mexican city infused with a Latino culture and traditions. But the arrival of the Southern Pacific Railroad triggered a series of land booms with the subsequent influx of Anglo-American, Asian and European immigrants eventually outnumbering Mexicans 10 to 1.

Next to suffer from marginalization and racist attitudes were the Chinese, thousands of whom had poured into Northern California from the gold fields and, later, into Los Angeles after

1822 MEXICAN RULE

From 1850 onwards the Federal government signed treaties (never ratified by the Senate) under which more than 7 million acres (2.8 million hectares) of tribal land dwindled to less than 10 percent of that total.

Apart from being denied legality and having their labor exploited and their culture destroyed, the Native Americans themselves had been fatally exposed to not only alcoholism, but to all manner of dreaded foreign diseases.

For three decades after America had acquired

LEFT: the historic seal of the city.
ABOVE: a Southern Californian mural shows the transition of California to Mexican sovereignty.

their (mostly unappreciated) building of the railroads had been completed. In one notorious incident in 1871 during an economic slump that had led to widespread unemployment, a mob of frustrated whites descended on LA's Chinatown and killed a score of its residents.

California was rushed into the Union on September 9, 1850, as the 31st state, only 10 months after convening a formal government. But it had already drafted a constitution which guaranteed the right to "enjoying and defending life and liberty, acquiring, possessing and protecting property, and pursuing and obtaining happiness," with hindsight a typically Californian mix of the sublime and the practical. ❏

THE CALIFORNIA GOLD RUSH

Gold and silver were the stuff of dreams. They made millionaires out of mountain men and, sometimes, paupers out of millionaires

Gold was discovered in Placeritas Canyon, north of Mission San Fernando, in 1842. Francisco Lopez, rounding up stray horses, stopped to rest beneath an oak tree. He opened his knife to uproot some wild onions, and their roots came out attached to something gleaming bright in the sun – a nugget of gold. Six years later, gold was discovered in quantity at Sutter's Mill near Sacramento in Northern California. Word quickly spread east and the stampede began. Soon a torrent of gold-dazzled prospectors was running through the Sierras to California. Entire parties in covered wagons made their way west. When they encountered the sheer cliffs of the Sierra Nevada, they winched up the wagons or took them apart and lowered them down the steep precipices.

Population explosion

Nowhere was the Gold Rush's magic more powerful than in San Francisco. When storekeeper Sam Brannan ambled down Montgomery Street with a recently prospected vial of gold, the town's population was less than 1,000. By early 1850, when the madness was in full swing, the population topped 30,000. Brannan, who had recently settled in San Francisco heading a group of Mormons, saw the potential of this future city (and the success of his own store), and he excitedly spread the word.

Bayard Taylor, a reporter for the *New York Tribune*, described the atmosphere as a "perpetual carnival." What he found when he returned from four months at the diggings was not the town of "tents and canvas houses with a show of frame buildings" that he had left but "an actual metropolis, displaying street after street of well-built edifices... lofty hotels, gaudy with verandahs and balconies... finished with home luxury and aristocratic restaurants presenting daily their long bills of fare, rich with the choicest technicalities of Parisian cuisine."

By the end of May, the word had spread all

LEFT: gold miners drawn by William McIlvain.
RIGHT: Pony Express rider brings the news.

over California: stores closed, city officials left their offices, soldiers deserted, sailors jumped ship and the exasperated editor of the *Californian* announced the suspension of his daily newspaper because the staff had walked out. "The whole country from San Francisco to Los Angeles and from the sea shore to the base of

the Sierra Nevada," he wrote, "resounds with the sordid cry of gold! GOLD! GOLD! – while the field is left half-planted, the house half-built and everything neglected but the manufacture of shovels and pickaxes." Before the year was out more prospectors arrived in California from Oregon, Mexico, Peru and Chile.

The first big discovery of gold took place at a sawmill beside the American River in the Sierra Nevada foothills. (Today a recreation of the fabled mill stands at Coloma, 50-odd miles/80 km east of Sacramento.)

The mill was the idea of John Augustus Sutter – a man, one contemporary wrote, with a disastrous "mania for undertaking too much." Born in Switzerland in 1803, Sutter arrived in San Francisco in 1839. Despite a disorderly career as a Swiss Army officer and dry-goods merchant, he somehow impressed Alta California's authorities enough to offer him the largest possible land grant, nearly 50,000 acres (about 20,000 hectares) of the Central Valley. Naming his land "New Helvetia" and using Native Americans as serf labor, Sutter set out to create his own semi-independent barony.

Sutter's Fort, at what is now Sacramento, was often the first stop for bedraggled overlanders

GOLD FEVER

"Gold! Gold! Gold on the American River!" he shouted.

applying "every test of their ingenuity and the *American Encyclopaedia*," decided that it was indeed gold. They raced back up to the sawmill, poked and panned awhile, and found quite a bit more.

Realizing that New Helvetia would be overrun if word of the discovery leaked out prematurely, Sutter swore his mill hands to secrecy. But nuggets kept popping up in bars and stores all over the region. "As a lumber enterprise, the mill was a failure, but as a gold discovery, it was a grand success," said a later report. And when Sam Brannan strolled

after their harrowing Sierra to the valley crossing. Sutter gloried in providing comfort and goods (at a price) to California's new settlers. He planted wheat and fruit orchards, bought out the Russians at Fort Ross, lent his aid to several of Northern California's jostling factions, and, in 1847, decided to build the sawmill that was his ultimate undoing.

James Marshall, who had been hired to oversee the mill's construction, peered into the millrace on January 24, 1848, and noticed a bit of shiny material, one of the millions of smithereens of gold that had been tumbling down the streams of the Sierra for millennia.

He took the nugget to Sutter and the pair,

down San Francisco's Montgomery Street shouting "Gold! Gold! Gold on the American River!" the secret was well and truly out. The Western world had been waiting for the myth to come to life for centuries. The Spanish had uprooted and discarded more than one civilization in their search for the country of gold. The myth had eventually grown into a prophecy.

The news spread as rapidly as the times allowed. San Francisco was left nearly deserted, its shops stripped of axes, pans, tents, beans, soda crackers, picks and whatever else might conceivably be of use. Monterey, San Jose, all of Northern California's mission towns and farms joined in the scramble. Gold fever worked its way to the states of Utah and Oregon, where "two-thirds of the able-bodied men were on their way to the diggings."

Ships in the Pacific spread the word to Peru, Chile, Hawaii and Australia. Lieutenant L. Loeser carried a "small chest... containing $3,000 worth of gold in lumps and scales" back to Washington DC, where it was exhibited at the War Office, increasing greed in the capital. On December 2, President Polk told Congress that the "extraordinary accounts" were true. A few days later, the *New York Herald* summed it up: "The El Dorado of the old Spaniards is discovered at last."

Hundreds of thousands of reveries were fixed on the fabled Mother Lode region, which ran for 120 miles (190 km) from north of Sutter's Mill to Mariposa in the south. Forty-niners (as the Gold Rush miners were known) first worked the streams of the Klamath Mountains in the far north: later, the southern deserts had their share of boom towns. But the Mother Lode's wooded hills and deep valleys were the great centers of the raucous, short-lived argonaut civilization.

How claims were staked

Gold Rush mining, especially in the early days before the streams were panned out, was a simple affair. The Mother Lode was owned by the federal government, and claims were limited to the ground a man and his fellows could work. Stockpiling claims was impossible and hiring a workforce was unlikely. There was scant reason to make another man rich when one's own wealth-spouting claim was so easily achieved.

There was money to be wrung out of those hills. The problem lay in keeping it. In 1849, $10 million of gold was mined in California; the next year, four times that amount. In 1852, the pinnacle of the Gold Rush, $80 million wound up in prospectors' pockets.

The Sierra streams did much of the miner's work for him. The rushing waters eroded the hillsides and sent placer gold (from dust to nugget size) rushing downstream. A miner crouched by the streambank scooped up a panful of gravel, shifting and turning his pan as the debris washed out and the gold sank to the bottom. Later, sluices were built and holes were dug. Finally hydraulic mining took over,

LEFT: a 19th-century illustration of mining life.
RIGHT: pre-Gold Rush Yerba Buena.

although this was banned in 1884 after causing dramatic ecological damage to the foothills.

The endless disputes over water rights, which continue to this day, mostly date to the days of the gold prospectors when miners, whose claims were far from stream beds, collaborated to build ditches funnelling water from sources whose "riparian rights" (that is, owning the adjoining land) were in conflict with "appropriation rights." The introduction of hydraulic mining bringing streams of water to bear on hillsides intensified the problem. The extensive network of canals and flumes which eventually brought water a long way from its original

source came to be worth more than the claims it served, but the conflicting arguments over who had a prior right to the water were never entirely solved. (However, as the mines petered out, the agribusinesses of the state's central valleys gained the lions' share.)

As easy as it was to find, the Mother Lode's gold was easier to lose – to rapacious traders, in the gambling halls and bawdy-houses, to the simple unwiseness of young men. But for most prospectors it was a grand adventure. Many returned home sheepishly but full of stories for their grandchildren. *California as It Is and as It May Be, Or, A Guide to the Goldfields* was the title of the first book to be published in San

Francisco (in 1849). In it, the author F.B. Wierzbicki wrote that the city looked like it had been built to endure for only a day, so fast had been its growth and so flimsy its construction.

"The town has led the van in growth... there is nothing like it on record. From eight to 10 thousand may be afloat on the streets and hundreds arrive daily; many live in shanties, many in tents and many the best way they can... The freaks of fortune are equally as remarkable in this place as everything else connected with it; some men who two years ago had not a cent in their pockets, count by thousands now..."

For most of the '49ers it was rough and

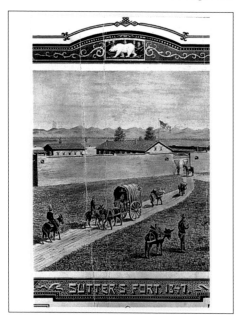

SUTTER'S FORT 1847.

expensive. Eggs from the Farallone Islands sold for $1 apiece. Real-estate speculation was epidemic. Each boatload of '49ers represented another batch of customers. As the city burst from the boundaries of Yerba Buena Cove, "water lots" sold for crazy prices on the expectation they could be made habitable with landfill. Much of today's downtown San Francisco is built on landfill.

Most of California's new tenants had little desire to lay the foundation for the orderly society that would surely follow the Gold Rush. The popular conception was that the foothills were crammed with gold. "Ages will not exhaust the supply," Bayard Taylor wrote. In the end, the

winners in the great money-scramble were those who took the time to sink roots by establishing businesses and buying land, taking advantage of the '49ers' disdain for tomorrow. Each fire was an opportunity for the arising bourgeoisie to build anew.

In 1853, the Gold Rush began to wind down. Real-estate values fell 20 to 30 percent. Immigration slowed to a trickle and merchants were cornered by massive oversupplies ordered during the heady days. The men who started the Gold Rush, John Sutter and James Marshall, were only two of the many losers in the great game. Marshall ended his days in 1885 near the site of his discovery, broken-down, weepy, shaking his fist at fate. Sutter, whose barony was overrun just as he'd feared, kept a brave front for some years. But history had swept him aside, too, and he died in 1880 after years of futile petitions to Congress for restitution.

Robberies and the Silver Rush

None of California's new towns, much less San Francisco, was built with much care or foresight. Pre-Gold Rush street plans, based on tight grids, were expanded out from flat Yerba Buena Cove with a flick of pen on ruler, jauntily ignoring the city's hills – which is why San Francisco's streets barge up and down those hills, rather than gracefully following their contours. Most buildings were hasty wooden edifices and, between 1849 and 1851, six major fires ravaged San Francisco. Sacramento, smaller, marginally quieter, also had its share of blazes.

In San Francisco, hoodlums (a word coined in late-19th-century San Francisco) had organized themselves into gangs like the Sydney Ducks and the Hounds. At least some of the city's fires were set by these gangs, in addition to routine robberies, beatings and generally ugly behavior. In 1851, the forces of social stability asserted their constitutional right to "acquire, possess and defend property" by warring against the criminal elements in the community.

The robbery and beating in early 1851 of a merchant named C.J. Jensen inflamed the righteous, especially Sam Brannan – a man who, according to historian Josiah Royce, was "always in love with shedding the blood of the wicked." Newspapers like the *Alta* brought up the specter of lynch law, and Brannan shouted that the time had come to bypass "the quibbles of the law, the insecurity of the prisons, and the laxity of those who pretend to administer justice." A Committee of Vigilance was formed; soon a Sydney Duck named John Jenkins was hanged for stealing a safe. Within two weeks Sacramento also had its vigilante corps and other California towns followed its lead. California's first bout of vigilantism put a damper on crime only for a while. Whatever chance California had of becoming placid was swept away in 1859 by yet another torrent of riches flowing down the Sierra slope. This time it was silver, not gold, that geared up the rush.

One of the most comfortless outposts of the Gold Rush had been centered around Nevada's Sun Mountain on the dry eastern slope of the Sierra near Lake Tahoe. There was a little gold up in the Virginia Range, but eking a living out of the area's irritating bluish clay was wicked work. In June, 1859, a sample of that "blue stuff" found its way to Melville Atwood, an assayer in Grass Valley. Examining it closely, Atwood found an astounding $3,876 worth of silver in that sample of ore.

At first it appeared that the Silver Rush would mimic the Gold Rush of a decade earlier. "Our towns are near depleted," wrote one spectator. "They look as languid as a consumptive girl. What has become of our sinewy and athletic fellow citizens? They are coursing through ravines and over mountaintops," looking for silver.

Mark Twain as prospector

One of the athletic young men who rushed up to the Virginia Range was Mark Twain. In his marvelous book, *Roughing It*, he describes how he and his fellow almost-millionaires "expected to find masses of silver lying all about the ground." The problem for Twain and the thousands like him was that the silver was in, not on, the steep and rugged mountains. And getting it out was no matter of poking and panning.

The Silver Rush, it turned out, was a game for capitalists, men who possessed the money to dig tunnels, purchase claims, install the expensive machinery and mills that transformed the "blue stuff" into cash. They were men like William Ralston of the Bank of California in San Francisco, and the four legendary "Bonanza Kings" – James Flood and William O'Brien, former

saloon-keepers; and James Fair and John W. Mackay, old miners whose Consolidated Virginia regularly disgorged $6 million a month.

As usual, the treasures of the Comstock Lode flowed from the boomtown of Virginia City to San Francisco. By 1863, $40 million of silver had been wrestled out of the tunnels, and 2,000 mining companies traded shares in San Francisco. Fortunes were made and lost in moments and at one time, more speculative money was wrapped up in Comstock mining shares than actually existed on the whole Pacific Coast. The Comstock Lode lasted until the 1880s, plumping up California's economy with

the $400 million that the Virginia Range yielded. In San Francisco, Billy Ralston, the Comstock's greatest mine-owner, had taken over from Sam Brannan as the city's top booster. (But Sam was going broke trying to make his resort at Calistoga into "the Saratoga of the West" and died, dollarless, in 1889.)

Ralston rebuilt America's largest city hotel; he bought sugar refineries, lumber and water companies; and as the 1860s drew to a close, he happily made confident preparations for what he and his fellow plutocrats thought would be the capstone to the state's greatness – the long-awaited completion of the Transcontinental Railroad in 1869. ❏

LEFT: gold was first found on John Sutter's property, but Sutter himself lost a virtual fortune.
RIGHT: panning and posing for the camera.

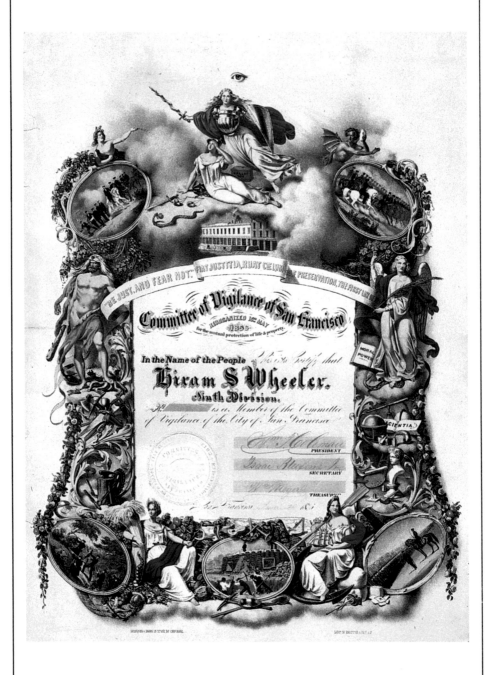

BOOM AND BUST YEARS

After enjoying immense wealth, the state was hit by massive unemployment.

But California was too rich to suffer for long

Plans for a railroad linking the coasts had been floating around for many years. When the American Civil War broke out, Congress, intent upon securing California's place in the Union, at last stirred itself. In the winter of 1862, the Pacific Railroad Act granted vast tracts of western land, low-interest financing and outright subsidies to two companies – the Central Pacific, building from Sacramento, and the Union Pacific, building from Omaha, Nebraska, in the Midwest. As it happened, the Civil War largely bypassed California, but it nonetheless prompted the building of a railroad that brought unexpected havoc to the residents of the state.

In his regarded and widely read book, *Progress and Poverty*, Henry George, a journeyman printer and passionate theorist, had warned that the increasing dominance of the railroads would prove to be a mixed blessing. He predicted that California's immature factories would be undersold by the eastern manufacturing colossus and that the Central Pacific's ownership of vast parcels of land along its right of way would drive prices of agricultural land shamefully high. George even foresaw the racial tensions that would result from the railroad's importation of thousands of Chinese laborers. "Crocker's Pets," as they were called, flooded the state's job market in the 1870s.

Railroad woes

George's prophecies began arriving with the first train. In San Francisco, real-estate dealing of $3.5 million a month fell to $1.5 million a month within a year. "California's initial enthusiasm soon gave way to distrust and dislike… an echo of the national conviction that the railroads were responsible for most of the country's economic ills," was the assessment of historian John W. Caughey in his book *California*. "The railroad became a monster, the Octopus. It was

a target for criticisms by all those made discontented and bitter by the hard times of the Seventies." The genius of the Central Pacific was a young engineer named Theodore Dehone Judah who had built California's first railroad, the 22-mile (35-km) Sacramento Valley line, in 1856. He spent years crafting the crucial route across

the Sierra at Donner Pass. Unfortunately for Judah, the Central Pacific's other partners were uncommonly cunning and grabby men.

Charles Crocker, Mark Hopkins, Collis Huntington and Leland Stanford, who became known as "The Big Four," had been lured west by the Gold Rush. They were Sacramento shopkeepers when they invested in Judah's scheme. Shortly after Congress dumped its largesse in their laps, they forced Judah out of the Central Pacific. He died, aged 37, in 1863, still trying to wrest back control from his former partners.

The Central Pacific made the Big Four almost insanely rich. The government's haste to get the railroad built, and Stanford's political maneu-

LEFT: a vigilante committee membership certificate.
RIGHT: the domination of the railroad by the "Big Four" was a target of indignant press protest.

vering, made the Central Pacific the virtual dictator of California politics for years. Between them, the railroad barons raised private investment, earned government subsidies, acquired bargain-priced land, imported cheap labor from China and by their exploitative and monopolist practices made themselves multi-millionaires.

As the biggest landowners and biggest employers, the immensely rich railroad barons were able to manipulate freight rates, control water supplies, keep hundreds of thousands of productive land acres for them-

JOINING OF THE RAILS

In 1869, the Union Pacific and the Central Pacific met at Promontory Point, Utah.

a firm and fabulous prosperity to California.

In April, 1868, five years after construction had begun on Sacramento's Front Street, the first Central Pacific train breached the Sierra at Donner Pass. Where, on May 12, 1869, the Golden Spike was driven at Promontory Point, Utah, the coasts were finally and irrevocably linked. "San Francisco Annexes the Union" read one San Francisco headline. But the rush of prosperity failed utterly to materialize. Only a few deep thinkers – none of them ensconced in boardrooms – had

A NEW AND MAGNIFICENT CLIPPER FOR SAN FRANCISCO.
MERCHANTS' EXPRESS LINE OF CLIPPER SHIPS!
Loading none but First-Class Vessels and Regularly Dispatching the greatest number.
THE SPLENDID NEW OUT-AND-OUT CLIPPER SHIP
CALIFORNIA
HENRY BARBER, Commander, AT PIER 13 EAST RIVER.
This elegant Clipper Ship was built expressly for this trade by Samuel Hall, Esq., of East Boston, the builder of the celebrated Clippers "SURPRISE," "GAMECOCK," "JOHN GILPIN," and others. She will fully equal them in speed! Unusually prompt dispatch and a very quick trip may be relied upon. Engagements should be completed at once.
Agents in San Francisco, Messrs. DE WITT KITTLE & CO.
RANDOLPH M. COOLEY, 88 Wall Street, Tontine Building.
NESBIT & CO., PRINTERS.

selves and with their wealth subvert politicians and municipalities. It was years before state regulation of the railroads became the norm; when Frank Norris wrote *The Octopus* in 1901, no one had to guess at the reference: the Southern Pacific (as it was renamed in 1884) had its greedy tentacles in every corner of the state.

In the beginning, at least, carping at the Big Four's use of the railroad's treasury as a kind of private money preserve was a game for malcontents and socialists. In the mahogany boardrooms of San Francisco's banks, on the editorial pages of its newspapers, in the overheated stock exchange, up and down Montgomery Street, the verdict was the same. The railroad would bring

understood the financial calamity the railroad would bring. In the winter of 1869–70, a severe drought crippled the state's agriculture. Between 1873 and 1875 more than a quarter of a million immigrants came to California. Many were factory workers and few could find work. The "Terrible '70s" had arrived which certainly for William Chapman Ralston were a calamity. As head of San Francisco's Bank of California, he had presided over the boom mentality that was a legacy of the Gold Rush.

The mid-Seventies saw the depression at its deepest. On "Black Friday," April 26, 1875, a run on the Bank of California forced it to slam shut its huge oaken doors at Sansome and California streets. Driven into debt by Comstock mining losses and by the failure of the railroad to bring prosperity, Bill Ralston drowned while taking his customary morning swim in the Bay.

Ralston's death signalled the end of California's booming affluence. Those hurt most by the great shrinkage of capital in the 1870s were the state's working people. During the Gold and Silver rushes, California's laborers had enjoyed a rare freedom to move easily from job to job and to dictate working conditions. Now, however, with mas-

BLACK FRIDAY

On April 26, 1875, a run on the Bank of California forced it to slam its doors.

minerals, the state developed its agricultural lands as never before. In the Central Valley, wheat, rice and cotton became major cash crops. The splendid Napa Valley began to produce fine wines in earnest in the late 1870s.

Sometime between 1873 and 1875, two or three orange trees were sent from the Department of Agriculture in Washington to Eliza and Luther Tibbetts in Riverside, not far from San Diego. The young trees had been budded from a seedless orange whose origin was Bahia, Brazil. The Tibbetts planted the trees, lit-

sive unemployment, unionization began to take hold. For the next 60 years California suffered recurrent bouts of labor strife.

The depression was slow to disappear, but California was too rich to suffer permanently. In the next few decades, it slowly built its industrial strength up to the point where it could compete with America's prosperous East Coast. After decades of depending on the land to deliver riches in the form of gold or silver or

tle knowing that a decade later navel oranges would dramatically alter the agricultural, economic and social patterns of the entire region. The Washington navel orange, as the seedless and sweet fruit was officially known, became (in the words of Charles F. Lummis) "not only a fruit but a romance."

Durable enough to survive long-distance shipping, this citrus fruit hit its prime in 1889 when more than 13,000 acres (5,260 hectares) of land in the six southern counties were devoted to its cultivation.

Growers formed a marketing cooperative, the California Fruit Growers Exchange, famed for its ubiquitous trademark, Sunkist. In a mere 18

LEFT: canny 19th-century travel agents encouraged migration to the West by sea.

ABOVE: the railroad was built in large part by imported Chinese laborers, many of whom settled in the state.

months, Horace Greeley's "Go West, young man" philosophy became a reality. Many boomtowns took root and soon the population of the south equalled that of the north.

This vast semi-tropical, often desert-like land reached its potential. Thousands of acres of good farmland sold by the railroads at low prices were planted with wheat, oranges, grapes, cotton, tea, tobacco and coffee. Irrigation converted vast tracts of this arid waste to fertile land bearing fruit and field crops. Agriculture, crucially boosted by rail transportation, became the backbone of Southern California's economy.

Well before the new century began, the enter-

prising Edwin Tobias Earl had made a fortune from his invention of the refrigerated railroad car. Meanwhile San Francisco's boomtown mentality may have taken a beating, but as the century wore on, the city's historic predilection for high living remained. Rudyard Kipling, visiting during the Gilded Age at the end of the century, called it "a mad city, inhabited for the most part by perfectly insane people whose women are of a remarkable beauty." San Francisco's society had "a captivating rush and whirl. Recklessness is in the air."

The city by the Bay reached a peak in the 1870s, a now-graceful community whose 1,700 architects were perfecting the characteristical-

ly Victorian and "Queen Anne"-style homes which still predominate in at least half a dozen neighborhoods today. Hundreds of others, however, failed to survive the 1906 earthquake.

The rise of the south

Los Angeles, too, was now growing fast: in every decade from 1870 onwards it doubled its population. Before the end of the 19th century, the *Los Angeles Times* with Charles Lummis, a man who had hitchhiked across country from the Midwest on the way to becoming the newspaper's city editor, was proclaiming that it was no place for "dudes, loafers, paupers… cheap politicians, business scrubs, impecunious clerks, lawyers and doctors."

It is hard to imagine what they had against the last-mentioned category, especially in a city growing so sophisticated that by 1897 it boasted the first orchestra to be established west of the Rockies. Eight years later, Abbott Kinney's ambitious reconstruction of Venice on coastal marshland added an international touch, although his initial high-minded attractions soon gave way to motor racing and carnival events.

The pueblo of Los Angeles had become a prosperous community, facing its perennial problem: a shortage of water. To assure a steady water supply, the city fathers made plans for a lengthy trench running from the river and hired a Vermont-born shopkeeper, Ozro W. Childs, to dig this *Zanja Madre* or Mother Ditch, paying him off with land instead of scarce city funds.

The land, a tract bordered by today's 6th & Main streets and Pico Boulevard and Figueroa Street, eventually made Childs so prosperous that, in 1884, he spent $50,000 to build an 1,800-seat opera house. At the ocean, frontage at Santa Monica owned by Southern Pacific Railroad magnate Collis P. Huntington almost became the Port of Los Angeles, but intensive lobbying by rival Santa Fe railroad chiefs won out and San Pedro was chosen instead. Already the region was annually producing almost 5 million barrels of oil, the exporting of which was greatly facilitated by the subsequent opening of the Panama Canal.

The new sales pitch

Southern California's growing reputation as a health resort was responsible for the next big wave of newcomers, enticed by the climate, the abundance of thermal and mineral springs and the boosterism of such communities as Pasadena, Riverside, Ojai and Palm Springs. The state was already first in honey production; vineyards, citrus and walnut groves blossomed over thousands of acres. "Buy Land in Los Angeles and Wear Diamonds" was typical of the slogans that lured newcomers into the area where they were met straight from the train with bands, barbecues and fast-talking salesmen.

The increasing use of the refrigerated railroad car not only escalated freight shipments of oranges throughout the country but spread even more widely the appeal of this fruitful land. In Califiornia's vast deserts and verdant valleys,

Wilcox's death, his widow sold a plot of land on Cahuenga to a French flower painter named Paul DeLongpre and it was his palatial house and floral gardens that became the area's first major tourist attraction.

Hollywood signs up

That same year, ground was broken at Hollywood and Highland for the soon-to-be-famous Hollywood Hotel and also for Whitley Heights, an elegant hillside community that became for early movie stars what Beverly Hills was to become in later years. Planned as a completely separate community, Hollywood was obliged in

figs, rice, vegetables and cotton became profitable. The balmy climate encouraged dairy farming, livestock and poultry raising. And, from the turn of the century, in this already bountiful land oil production became the most profitable of all.

Due to early huckstering by the big railroads, whose salesmen had gone to such lengths as spiking thorny trees with oranges to sell worthless land, real-estate had long been big business. In 1886, Harvey H. Wilcox had given the name Hollywood to his new sub-division. After

1903 to join up with the city of Los Angeles, along with so many neighboring communities, to obtain an adequate water supply.

Since 1854, California's capital had been Sacramento, but it was San Francisco that ruled a rapidly coalescing state. Agriculture in the Central Valley had grown in response to the needs of the exploding population; in the decade of the 1850s, California's cattle herds grew from 262,000 to more than 3 million. Towns like Stockton and Monterey were thriving as '49ers set up shops and sank roots. The Gilded Age, with its extravagance and corruption, continued right up to that fateful morning in 1906, after which nothing was the same again. ❑

LEFT: tropical fruit became an early industry in sunny Southern California.

ABOVE: the first map of Hollywood, *circa* 1900.

THE EARLY 20TH CENTURY

The Great Earthquake of 1906 had immediate devastating consequences for

San Francisco. It also helped Los Angeles inch ahead in popularity

Southern California mushroomed from an agricultural community to an industrial complex spurred on by the discovery of oil in 1892 in what is now the Westlake area. It made Los Angeles aware it was sitting on a fat reservoir of wealth. The "Salt Lake Field" in southwestern Los Angeles was developed, followed by fields in Huntington Beach, Santa Fe Springs and Signal Hill. Oil derricks sprouted from the hills to the sea. Even Venice, constructed with canals rather than streets and sporting gondolas like its Italian counterpart, became an oil city. Fresno struck oil in 1899 and began steady oil refining, as well as producing cotton, alfalfa, potatoes and fruit.

Trains and trolley cars

Downtown LA was linked to Pasadena and Santa Fe by an urban railway. But, not to be outdone, the Southern Pacific's Collis P. Huntington had, in 1901, devised a vast inter-urban network of electric trains to blanket the entire area. "I will join the whole region into one big family," he promised, adding that Los Angeles was "destined to become the most important city in the country, if not in the world. It can extend in any direction, as far as you like." Within a decade, his trolley cars on which passengers could ride 20 miles (32 km) for a nickel stretched everywhere from a city whose population had tripled to 300,000.

"The whole area within a radius of 70 miles of the city took on a new life," wrote Huntington's biographer, Isaac Marcosson, in 1914. "Villages became towns; towns blossomed into miniature cities." When the author Henry James came by on a lecture tour in 1905, he said he'd never seen such an efficient transit system in all his worldwide travels.

But within five years, the *Times* noted that "with thousands of motor cars passing and

repassing, the traffic question has become a problem." A transportation expert brought from back east to anticipate transit needs for the next decade (during which the population was expected to triple again) urged the creation of a planning commission "to replace the present haphazard system of growth." When Los Angeles held its

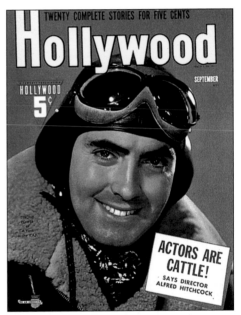

second annual motor show in 1909, it had more cars on its streets than any other city in the world.

The Big One

An earthquake measuring 8.25 on the Richter scale preceded the fire that first shook Northern Californians from their beds at 5.12am on April 18, 1906. When the deadly San Andreas Fault lurched that morning, it sent terrifying jolts through an area 210 miles (338 km) long and 30 miles (48 km) wide, from San Juan Bautista in the south to Fort Bragg in the north. Other towns, like San Jose and Point Reyes Station near Drake's Bay, suffered more from the initial shock than San Francisco. Church bells jan-

LEFT: Los Angeles as a transportation hub: at its second annual motor show in 1909, the city had more cars on its streets than any other place in the world.
RIGHT: Hollywood hunk smolders happily.

gled chaotically, dishes fell, windows shattered, dogs barked, Enrico Caruso (appearing locally in the opera *Carmen*) was scared voiceless and San Francisco's new City Hall crumbled. In 48 seconds, it was all over but the city lay in ruins.

The subsequent fire destroyed 28,000 buildings over an area of more than 4 sq. miles (10 sq. km). It killed 315 people; the bodies of 352 more were never found. The city had experienced many earthquakes before, but none on this scale, and in a city that hosted more than 40 per-

EARTHQUAKE AFTERMATH

The 1906 earthquake and fire killed more than 300 people, destroyed 500 square blocks and 28,000 buildings.

and improvisations by the commandant of the Presidio, Brigadier General Frederick Funston – who had leaped in unauthorized to fill the gap in authority – served only to destroy scores of beautiful Victorian mansions along Van Ness Avenue and to spread the fire still further.

Hundreds were dead or still trapped in smoking ruins, 500 city blocks were leveled and a handful of people had been shot or bayoneted by Funston's inexperienced militia who had poured into the streets to keep order

cent of the state's population (it is now around 3 percent) the effect was cataclysmic. Although the awareness of the mighty San Andreas Fault extended back a dozen years, there had been no prior warning of, or preparations for, this major upheaval. Only an unearthly low rumble preceded fissures opening up and spreading wave-like across the city.

With its alarm system destroyed, the Fire Department lacked coordination. When the brigades did arrive, they found mangled mains lacking any water supply. The situation was worst in the area south of Market Street where expert demolition work might have prevented the fire from spreading. Experts were lacking

and prevent looting. Golden Gate Park became the home of as many as 300,000 people for at least the next few weeks. Cooking inside the tents was banned, sanitation was rudimentary, water was in very short supply and rats (and therefore the threat of the bubonic plague) a dark, lingering menace.

But there was a strong will to recover. A Committee of Forty on the Reconstruction of San Francisco was formed to define the tasks to be undertaken and A.P. Giannini's tiny Bank of Italy, making loans to small businesses intent on rebuilding, was at the forefront of those determined to revive the city's fortunes. The bank was later to become the Bank of America, the country's largest. Aid poured in from all over the world, $8 million worth within the first few weeks. Even the much-reviled Southern Pacific Railroad pitched in generously, freighting in supplies without charge, offering free passage out of the city and putting heavy equipment and cranes to work on the enormous task of clearing the debris.

The photographer Arnold Genthe wrote, "While the ruins were still smoking, on top of a heap of collapsed walls, a sign would announce: 'On this site will be erected a six-storey office building to be ready for occupancy in the fall'." San Francisco's renaissance was inevitable. The Francisco's giddiest times. The 1915 Panama Pacific International Exposition, which occupied 600 acres (243 hectares) of reclaimed land in what is now the marina, is still considered one of the greatest of the world's fairs. Today, only one vestige of the flamboyant celebration remains: the Palace of Fine Arts Theatre, intended by its architect, Bernard Maybeck, to impart a certain "sadness modified by the feeling that beauty has a soothing influence." It was saved from gradual decay by civic benefactors in the 1960s.

The initial unparalled growth of Southern California was due in large part to the Owens

new, improved, taller buildings of Montgomery Street, the Wall Street of the west, were needed to process all the money churned out by the state's industries, farms and banks. The Port of San Francisco was still one of the world's busiest harbors. San Francisco's historic business of making business was unstoppable.

In 1911, San Francisco elected a new mayor, James "Sunny Jim" Rolph, a purveyor of goodwill whose reign encompassed some of San

WEALTH BY STEALTH

An infamous plot hatched in 1904 to steal water from the Owens Valley via a 250-mile (400 km) pipeline over the Tehachapi Mountains to Los Angeles made fortunes for a private syndicate and allowed LA to grow to unprecedented levels. One of the syndicate's members was General Moses H. Sherman, whose advance knowledge of what land was about to be enriched came from serving on Los Angeles' Board of Water Commissioners. This scandal, which left the Owens Valley dry, formed part of the storyline for Roman Polanski's 1974 film *Chinatown*.

LEFT: despite measuring 8.25 on the Richter scale, San Franciscans did not let the 1906 earthquake dampen their appetites or dining habits.
ABOVE: something fishy going on in 1920s Hollywood.

Valley scandal *(see box, previous page)*, and additional water brought in by Los Angeles' Water Bureau Superintendent William Mulholland. Today, these aqueducts supply 525 million gallons (nearly 2 billion liters) of water a day, and all firmly believed this would take care of Southern California's thirst forever. But LA has been adding sources ever since: more water from the Parker Dam on the Arizona border arrived in 1941, but it cost the city a staggering $200 million. Electric power now comes mostly from the Hoover Dam on the Colorado River, about 206 miles (330 km) away.

Even as water problems slowed to a trickle,

the flood of newcomers to Southern California continued at an astonishing rate. "California became that legendary land of perpetual summer, of orange groves in sight of snowy peaks, of oil wells spouting wealth, of real-estate promising fortunes, of cinema stars and bathing beauties. It seemed to promise a new start, a kinder providence, a rebirth of soul and body," enthused a writer in the Federal Writers Project guide to the state in the 1930s, by which time the movie industry was one of the country's top 10 industries.

"Have you no slum districts?" an admiring President Taft had asked during a 1909 visit to Los Angeles, to be answered a year or two later

by a writer in *Sunset* magazine who rhapsodized: "Go north, south, east, west or any point in between on both urban and inter-urban lines and just inside the city limits or outside... you will find climbing the hillsides, slipping along the valleys, stretching across the plain until they join fields still planted in grain, street after street of cozy homes – miles and miles of houses for one man and his family. *These* are the tenements of Los Angeles..."

Six years after the Wright brothers made their pioneering 59-second airflight in North Carolina, Los Angeles hosted America's first international air show, partly financed with a $50,000 contribution from Huntington, the railroad magnate. Among the half a million visitors who thronged the old Dominguez Ranch to watch Glenn Curtis set a speed record of 55 mph (88 kph) was Glenn Martin, who promptly set up a plant that by World War I was turning out a plane a day. One of his employees, Donald Douglas, peeled off to begin his own company. Douglas's DC3, the first commercially successful aircraft, was within a couple of years carrying 95 percent of all US air traffic.

Cecil B. de Mille had an airport at Fairfax and Wilshire across from one operated by Charlie Chaplin's brother, Sydney. Goodyear began a blimp service to Catalina, and Western Air Express was formed to carry mail across the country. In 1920, scheduled flights began from Los Angeles to San Francisco.

Movie madness

It was the film industry that shot Los Angeles to fame and, unwittingly, it was Leland Stanford whose wager about a galloping horse helped launch it *(see page 75)*. With its origins in the nickelodeon, the movie industry began to emerge around the turn of the 20th century and headed west partly to escape the stranglehold patents held by the New York-based Edison company and partly because of California's superb climate, which made outdoor filming cheaper and easier.

Within a dozen years, the streets of Harvey Wilcox's sedate town of Hollywood were filled with intruders bearing cameras and megaphones, roping off streets, crashing cars and staging pretend shoot-outs. Some prolific directors were turning out one-reel Westerns or comedies almost daily. The locals didn't like it at all. "They thought we were tramps," recalled screenwriter Anita Loos. "They saw themselves as being invaded and supplanted as elegant ladies and gentlemen so they ganged up on us."

For years, directors could only shoot outdoors due to a lack of sophisticated photographic equipment. Even indoor scenes were shot outdoors in strong sunlight. From 1926, the Pickford-Fairbanks Studio immortalized such luminaries as actor Charlie Chaplin and directors D.W. Griffith and Cecil B. de Mille. Comedy became king. Mack Sennett's Keystone Kops had the whole nation laughing.

LA TAKES THE LEAD

By 1920, the population of Los Angeles surpassed that of its rival, San Francisco.

than from their original novels. Studios started instant fads, and shaped tastes and ideas the world over. In the summer of 1920, the population of Los Angeles for the first time surpassed that of San Francisco's 508,000, undoubtedly initiating the furious jealousy that still exists between the two cities today. The southern portion of the state was "the world's closest approach to bedlam and babel," sneered George Creel, with columnist Westbrook Pegler urging that the same territory "be declared incompetent and placed in charge of a guardian."

Before long, studios sprang up in Culver City, Universal City as well as Hollywood. The latter name, particularly, had by now become more or less synonymous with the word "movies."

Silent movies accompanied by organ music gave way to the "talkies." Hundreds of movie houses sprang up. If a movie wasn't doing good box-office business, dishes were given away. Instant fortunes came to stars, directors and producers. Novelists earned more from film rights

During the 1930s, troubles broke out in the great central valleys of the state which, with ample supplies of water for irrigation, combined with skillful techniques developed by the new agribusiness barons, were bidding to feed the world. The workers, long exploited by greedy and brutal bosses, staged spontaneous strikes, which were met not with an improvement in their condition but by arrests under the oppressive Criminal Syndicalism Act.

Fortunately, amid all of this strife, the completion in San Francisco of the Bay Bridge and the Golden Gate Bridge gave the whole state a much-needed shot of enthusiasm and an undisputed cause for celebration. ❏

LEFT: oil wells like these at First and Temple streets, Los Angeles, boosted the southern economy.
ABOVE: the construction of the Golden Gate Bridge in the 1930s gave San Franciscans a morale boost.

MODERN TIMES

Beatnik bards and happy hippies flocked to find fulfillment

in the state where experimentation was encouraged

World War II gave a tremendous boost to California's aircraft industry, which increased statewide from fewer than 10,000 employees to more than 300,000. When the war was over, a gradual shift in the industry's workers from mainly blue-collar laborers to scientists and technicians meant, as historian Bruce Henstell wrote, that "aeronautics was replaced by something called aerospace." In 1940, the population of Los Angeles was 1.3 million, of which about 9 percent was Mexican, 3 percent Asian and 3 percent black. By 1950, the City of Angels' 2-million population made it the fourth-largest city in the United States.

War rewards

The war had plunged California into a spasm of activity. Twenty-three million tons of war supplies and 1½ million men and women passed through the Golden Gate during the war's 46 months. The ports of San Francisco, Sausalito, Oakland, Vallejo and Alameda were busy around the clock building and repairing ships, and loading supplies for the war machine.

In the Bay area alone, the federal government spent $3 billion on shipbuilding. A new wave of immigration swept into the region as new factories needed new workers – 100,000 at the Kaiser Yards in Richmond, 90,000 more at Sausalito. Within two years of America's entry into the war, the number of wage-earners in San Francisco almost tripled. The federal government doled out $83 million in contracts to the California Institute of Technology (Cal Tech) alone.

Even though 750,000 Californians left for military service, the state's wage-earners increased by nearly a million in the first half of the 1940s. After the war, the great suburban sprawl got under way as war workers and their families settled down to post-war prosperity.

Eventually, the film industry shook down into

the seven major studios that dominate the industry today: Sony Pictures Studio in Culver City, 20th Century Fox in Century City, Paramount in Hollywood, and four studios in the San Fernando Valley: Studios Warner Brothers and Walt Disney in Burbank and Universal Studios and Dreamworks in nearby Universal City. Also in Burbank is television's NBC. ABC is located on the Disney lot in Burbank; CBS is at Fairfax Avenue and Beverley Boulevard.

The Hollywood area is still host to a few smaller production companies and all kinds of ancillary businesses and services such as recording studios, prop houses and talent agencies, lighting equipment companies and equipment rentals.

Also remaining in Hollywood are Eastman Kodak and Technicolor Creative Services (which has acquired several other post-production facilities in recent years), which process millions of feet of film every day. Technicolor, which in 1931 developed the three-strip color

LEFT: 1967's Summer of Love in San Francisco's Golden Gate Park made international headlines.
RIGHT: America's favorite tough guy, Humphrey Bogart, reached the heights of Hollywood stardom.

process, was for 40 years located in an Art Deco building on Romaine Street.

The entertainment industry is one of the most highly unionized industries in Southern California, with the Screen Actors Guild (of whom Ronald Reagan was once president), and the American Federation of Television and Radio Artists (AFTRA) collectively claiming more than 100,000 members nationwide, with most of them in Los Angeles. The Directors Guild of America and the Writers Guild of America account for most of the rest

CITY OF LOVE

Long-haired youths went to San Francisco to pen odes and wear flowers.

As a new, almost instant society, California has always felt free to experiment. Many of its newcomers, from the "Anglo hordes" of the 1840s to Gold Rush adventurers to present-day arrivals, have come to the state to escape the burdens of conformity elsewhere. The great majority of Californians have always been settled and to one degree or another, God-fearing. But the anti-conformists – the colorful, sometimes crazy minority – have given California its name for verve and drive.

In the 1950s and 1960s, according to author

of the talent, in addition to all the behind-the-camera workers such as grips, gaffers, film editors, carpenters, plasterers, publicists, costumers, art directors, sound people and cinematographers, who are represented by the International Alliance of Theatrical Stage Employers (IATSE) and the American Federation of Musicians (AFM). Studio drivers are in the Teamsters.

It is very difficult for a non-union person to get a job in the movies. In the 1930s and '40s, the IATSE was headed by a Chicago hood named Willie Bioff, who took pay-offs from studio presidents to keep down union demands. He was eventually convicted and ousted.

Mike Davis, Los Angeles became "the capital of youth," but it was in San Francisco that the first stirrings of post-war protest and florid eccentricity were felt. While the American nation was settled into a prosperous torpor, the city's historically Italian North Beach area became the haunt of a loosely defined group of poets, writers, declaimers and pavement philosophers – the beatniks.

In the 1950s, they seemed titillating and somehow significant, a tempting combination for the nation's press who ogled at their rambling poetry readings, sniffed at the light marijuana breezes drifting out of the North Beach coffee houses and wondered if civilization could stand such a limpid assault. The beatniks, it seems, mostly wanted America to go away. But it wouldn't, and before long "beat" had become a fashion and North Beach a tourist attraction.

The beats, however, had struck a nerve of dissatisfaction and alienation in America. Though it was never a coherent movement, it produced juice-stirring literary works like Allen Ginsberg's *Howl* and Jack Kerouac's *On the Road.* That inspired alienation gave rise to two parallel, dissimilar, but oddly congruent movements: the angry politics of the New Left and

CITY OF UNCERTAINTY

"I had already wondered whether God intended for people to live in LA."

Hall were heard around the world. The locus of dissent was the University of California at Berkeley. There the Free Speech Movement kept up a steady assault against racism, materialism and the stifling "multiversity" itself. As the war in Vietnam grew in horror, the New Left spread across America and the world, tilting at governments, bombing, marching, changing the way America looked at itself.

The hippies attacked their target with gentler weapons. While the New Left ranted at the evils of an affluent and smug, hypocritical society,

the woozy love fest of the hippies. The first significant protest of the great, protest-rich 1960s took place in San Francisco in the decade's first year. In mid-May, the House Un-American Activities Committee opened a series of hearings in City Hall. When hundreds of demonstrators met the committee in the rotunda, the police reacted furiously, turning water hoses and billy clubs on the crowds. Dozens of protesters were carted off to jail, but the angry shouts in City

---

FAR LEFT: the beat generation's Jack Kerouac.
LEFT: beatnik bard Allen Ginsberg.
ABOVE: 1992's riots over the acquittal of Rodney King's arresting officers left 51 people dead.

the hippies tried to undermine that society with glimmering love and peace, and wearing far-fetched clothes.

The Summer of Love

In the mid-1960s, San Francisco became the center of the hippie revolution. It was a natural refuge for spacey idealists, having been created by youthful myth-chasers. Former beatniks slid easily into the free-and-easy hippie style centered around the Haight-Ashbury neighborhood, with its funky, cheap Victorian houses and Golden Gate Park handily nearby for roaming. By 1967, the Haight was thronged with long-haired young men and women, the movement reaching its apogee in the massive Be-In assemblage and the celebrated Summer of Love.

At first, San Francisco was amused by the hippies. But as altogether too many sons and daughters of wealthy, respected citizens took to marijuana-induced meandering, and as the LSD hysteria took full flight, public sympathy for the nomads gradually began to evaporate.

Tensions and trial by TV

By the mid-1960s, blacks in LA had multiplied tenfold and were fed up with discriminatory employment and "unwritten" housing restrictions. On one hot summer evening in 1965, the palm-

shaded ghetto of Watts exploded. For six days, the inner city boiled until the National Guard restored order. Almost 30 years later, in April 1992, with conditions in the black and Chicano areas largely unchanged, violence erupted again. The acquittal of four police officers recorded on video beating a black man, Rodney King, sparked the worst racial violence in California's history.

By the time the dawn-to-dusk curfew was lifted, there were over 50 dead and 2,500 injured, and 5,200 fires had occurred. South Central LA was devastated. The Rodney King case provided the spark for already existing tension, setting off the intricately connected time bomb of race, poverty and the state of the inner city. The seem-

ingly never-ending explosion of gang violence in Los Angeles, for example, has focused national attention on the problem of urban poverty.

Barely a year goes by without major California events making headlines the world over. From 1994 to 1997, TV viewers were glued to their screens by the arrest and trials in Los Angeles of former football hero O.J. Simpson. There was the much publicized 2003 recall of Governor Gray Davis and the election of mega movie star Arnold Schwarzenegger in his place. The 2005 Michael Jackson trial and aftermath continues to draw the curious. Not long after the Jackson verdict, Scott Peterson was sentenced to death for killing his beautiful pregnant wife – a trial that held the attention of many Americans for more than a year. The same has been true for the 2005 trial and acquittal of TV star Robert *(Baretta)* Blake, accused of murdering his wife; the drawn-out murder trial of music producer Phil Spector in 2007; and the legal troubles of troubled starlets like Paris Hilton and Britney Spears.

These human acts are conducted alongside all-too-frequent earthquakes, landslides, floods and wildfires. And, sometimes all this hubris has interesting consequences. "I had already begun to wonder whether God intended for people to live in LA. Certainly he never meant for millions of them to live there," noted writer Richard Reeves. "LA," he suggested, "is not at peace with nature – that's why we get these periodic punishments."

Developers still pit their wits and legal expertise against environmentalists who are gaining in number and strength. The Sierra Club is now the caretaker of the wilderness; the Coastal Commission reviews all construction near the coastline; and all plans for major construction require a federal environmental impact report.

Leading the Way

Whether it's the dramatic rise and fall of the dot-com economy, scandals or the thrill of celebrity, California will always be on the radar. Over 35 million people live in the state and speak over 90 different languages. There will always be much excitement in a place with such diverse communities and a high concentration of artists, entrepreneurs, scientists and trendsetters. ❏

LEFT: the arrest and trials of former football hero O.J. Simpson riveted the nation from 1994 to 1997.
RIGHT: carefree scenes like this one on Santa Monica Pier continue to attract residents to sunny California.

CULTURAL DIVERSITY

Newcomers bring new values. California's changing ethnic mix has significant political, social and artistic implications

California, the third-largest state in the Union, ranks highest in number of inhabitants, but perhaps what is less appreciated is that no other part of America can claim such ethnic diversity. The students of the Los Angeles Unified School District (LAUSD), for example, speak more than 90 different languages. From the onset of the industrialized era, the state's population has been melded by boom cycles of immigration: Mexicans, Anglos from the Midwest, the Chinese and Japanese, African Americans from the South, Russians, Armenians, Asian Indians, Koreans, Salvadoreans, Iranians, Filipinos, Samoans, Vietnamese. Almost 60 years ago, the well-known historian Carey McWilliams was already referring to Southern California as an "archipelago of social and ethnic islands, economically interrelated but culturally disparate."

State of being

When California joined the Union in 1850, it was considered to be the final frontier, a land promising spiritual and social riches. Pioneers armed with little more than faith came in search of sunshine, fertile soil and freedom from oppression. Like the grape vines and citrus trees, the people could bloom under the gentle sun. Boosters furiously sold the fable of the Golden State to the rest of the Union, a dream that more than a century later has yet to lose its tenacious hold on the imagination.

The eruption of civil unrest in Los Angeles in 1992 was a reaction to California's apparent failure to achieve the myth, to become an egalitarian plurality that offered up a better life for migrants' children. California's multi-culturism was founded on a dream, but also on the backs of minority labor. The uprising in Los Angeles was a wake-up call to the entire US, an indication that the ethnic stew was boiling over.

PRECEDING PAGES: California Koreans pose for the camera; in Los Angeles, everybody's a star.
LEFT: flashy sax at Fisherman's Wharf.
RIGHT: love in Lincoln Park, San Francisco.

The miscegenation of cultures had an early start over two centuries ago when Spanish Franciscan monks arrived to set up a string of missions throughout the state, spreading a Catholic hand across the souls of the heathen indigenous peoples. In 1834, by now the state having passed from Spanish to Mexican rule, a procla-

mation was issued providing for the secularization of all the missions.

Before the end of the century, the American Indian population had been decimated and their offspring, the Mestizos, found themselves pushed southward by an influx of miners flooding the foothills of the Sierra Nevada mountain range. To this day, the preponderance of the Latino population rests in Southern California where people with at least part African ancestry were also found in large numbers.

When Los Angeles was founded in 1781, more than half of the settlers were Mulattos (those of mixed black, American Indian and Spanish blood). Beverly Hills, once called *Ran-*

cho Rodeo de Las Aguas, was owned by Maria Rita Valdez, the granddaughter of black founding settlers.

The development and growth of California's industries throughout the 19th century brought a tide of immigration. The Chinese initially came as railroad workers on the Central Pacific construction gangs, before branching into agriculture and fishing. African Americans also came as railroad employees, in smaller numbers at first and then, during World War II, to fill manufacturing and service jobs. And towards the turn of the century, Japanese immigrants arrived in search of opportunities

in the emerging produce industry, which they eventually came to dominate, from packing and shipping the fruit to setting up small stands to sell it.

Enter the Okies

Nothing, however, compared to the tidal wave of Anglos who arrived from the Midwest during the 1880s (and then again – fleeing the parched dustbowl farms of the prairies – in the 1920s). Already having established major colonies around the San Francisco and Sacramento areas, they saturated Southern California with visions of manifest destiny.

But destiny's capricious nature has a habit of throwing a dash of irony into the stew. During the 1980s, hundreds of thousands of Mexicans and Central Americans fleeing civil strife and political persecution immigrated, both legally and illegally, to California. By the year 2020 – some people say even sooner – it is estimated the number of Latinos in California will surpass that of Anglos, becoming once again the majority ethnic group.

The mix has understandably had significant political implications. More than any time in the history of the state, multi-culturalism has begun to be reflected in the offices of elected and appointed officials: mayors and congressional representatives, city council members and police chiefs. As a consequence of lawsuits brought by such groups as the Mexican American Legal Defense and Education Fund and the American Civil Liberties Union in the past decade, districts have been reshaped to give African Americans and Latinos a chance to elect representatives of their communities. (Asian-American populations in California – as well as most other ethnic communities – tend to be more geographically spread out, making voting blocs more difficult.)

Although Latinos in California are heavily involved in community activism, they are vastly under-represented politically, one reason being that the number of Latinos who are citizens and therefore capable of voting is much smaller than the actual population. For many years, the only notable leader was the late Cesar Chavez, the widely admired president of the United Farm Workers of America, who gained fame during the early 1970s for his battle to gain decent working conditions for the mostly Mexican farm laborers.

Immigrants from Asia and the Pacific Islands, who are the third-largest ethnic community in California after Anglos and Latinos, in many ways tread the same path as Latinos. To bolster their power they have formed various cross-cultural alliances and coalitions throughout the state. In Sacramento, for example, after friction between newly arrived Vietnamese and other minorities – as well as with the police – some ethnic groups joined members of the Latino community to form an Advisory Coalition on Minority Law Enforcement Issues.

It is African Americans, however, who have probably had the most success with community and political organizations. Groups ranging from the Black Panthers (which originated in Oakland) to Recycling Black Dollars have made great strides in forwarding black causes. But California's African-American population has been declining in the past few years with a consequent stagnation in their political progress. With notable exceptions, most of the influential African-American politicians were elected in the fervor of the civil rights movement of the 1960s and '70s.

Some non-whites have become police chiefs around the state, with a commitment to revamping police departments with long histories of repression of and blatant racism towards

decade that African-Americans who escaped the repression of the Deep South found that they were barred from living in certain neighborhoods by restrictive housing covenants.

As a result, clusters of ethnic communities formed where people could be protected and cultures preserved – San Francisco's famous Chinatown being one such example. Now considered a charming tourist attraction, Chinatown developed out of necessity as a refuge from abuse: until the 1960s, when immigration laws changed, the Chinese had been subjected to severe and continual harassment, and discriminatory legislation had deprived them of

minorities. They are transforming the relationship between law-enforcement departments and the public by installing community-based policing programs – taking cops out of the isolation of police cars and putting them on foot patrol, where they can better interact with the citizens.

How Chinatown was born

Early in World War II, the notorious Executive Order 9066 authorized the internment of all Japanese on the West Coast – most of whom lost everything they owned. It was during that same

eligibility for citizenship, ensuring that they had no legal recourse.

In California's sprawling metropolitan areas, many without any recognizable center, it has often been the churches and temples that have served as the nexus of a community – spiritually, socially and politically. First was the African Methodist Episcopal Church in South-Central Los Angeles, which began in the home of a former slave and became the first African-American church in the city. One of its pastors, Dr Cecil L. Murray, considered one of the community's most vocal and visible leaders, established close ties with former mayor Tom Bradley during the latter's 20-year reign. As a

LEFT: San Francisco sushi bar.
ABOVE: Juanita Juanita restaurant near Sonoma.

result, the media tends to descend upon First AME for statements relating to African-Americans in the city.

It is perhaps the necessity of asserting one's identity in this Babel-like sea of cultures that has made California the state in which more trends and artistic movements take flight. East Coast pundits have long joked about California's lack of culture. To be sure, it is a culture without a face – without *one* face, anyway. It is as much a refined performance of *Swan Lake* at San Francisco's War Memorial

> **2020 VISION**
>
> By the year 2020, it is thought the number of local Latinos will surpass Anglos.

"Tagging" (initialing) property provided inner-city teens – primarily Latino – with a voice that the larger culture refused to hear. Today, rap's impact on the media and advertising has been palpable. And Anglo kids from essentially conservative areas like Orange County, San Diego and Santa Barbara, infatuated with the image of defiance, have been known to don "gangsta wear," the cartoonishly oversized, fall-down clothing favored by gang members, rappers and taggers.

Arching towards the exotic Far East (or West,

Opera House as a barrio mural spray-painted by talented teenaged graffiti artists.

Multi-culturalism in California is a fact, not something to be argued by theorists. Ideas, language, art – these are generated by the streets, by the co-mingling of people's needs and desires. Rap music, for example, has been linked to the malaise that occurred after the Watts rebellion in 1965. Assembled from the shards of the uprising, the Watts art renaissance delivered up a number of visionaries. Theirs was the poetry of frustration, self-assertion and, unlike some contemporary rap, hope. Bold, bright graffiti art also arrived hard on the heels of disenfranchisement.

depending on one's point of view), California inevitably adopted the customs of Asian immigrants. Health-conscious Californians submit to strenuous programs of yoga and meditation, while eating brown rice and soy sauce. Beat Generation writers, who tumbled around San Francisco in the 1950s, derived much of their inspiration from Buddhism, and Japanese and Chinese poetry.

The experience of facing society as "other" in California has produced some of America's finest writers and artists of the past half-century, including playwright William Saroyan, who grew up in an Armenian enclave of grape growers and farmers in Fresno; poet and novelist

Alice Walker, best known for *The Color Purple*; essayist Richard Rodriguez, who writes about gay and Latino assimilation and the politics of multi-culturalism; Filipino-born artist Manuel Ocampo, whose paintings often depict symbols of racism and the brutish imperialism of the colonials; theater artist Anna Deavere Smith, whose performance piece *Twilight: Los Angeles, 1992* concerned the riots that devastated the city, told through the voices of the people who experienced it; and novelist Amy Tan, who found the characters of her widely acclaimed *Joy Luck Club* from the Chinatown (San Francisco) of her childhood.

what being a truly multi-ethnic society can mean. There are some who believe that the obsession with tribalism is a leading factor in causing the sometimes bitter divisiveness throughout the state; viewing others always through the prism of your culture deepens the trenches and hinders society's gains. It's the cult of "other." Critics of this argument say that recognition of California's many ethnic groups is the first step towards peaceful coexistence. Promoting minorities to meaningful positions in public policy – whether it be through affirmative action or some nebulous sense of political correctness – will eventually mitigate the issue.

Mingling of styles

What has become more and more evident, though, is that the people of California have slowly amalgamated each other's habits and styles, tastes and mannerisms. While most California towns and suburbs do tend to stay relatively homogeneous, pockets of cultures border one another, stitched by the colorful religions and customs of their people. California is hip-hop and cha-cha-cha wrapped in a dazzling gold-flecked sari.

California epitomizes the best and worst of

LEFT: California girls taking surf seriously.
ABOVE: California boys getting body conscious.

FESTIVALS

There are celebrations up and down the state honoring California's multi-ethnicity. Chinese New Year in San Francisco is one of the biggest in America; Vietnamese New Year has devotees in San Jose. Oakland has a Greek cultural festival in May; San Diego a Pacific Islander's festival in summer. Cinco de Mayo, the Mexican holiday, is celebrated in all major cities, while Brazilians, Scots, Irish and Germans all have their own street parties. For a list of monthly festivities, consult the "Calendar" section of the *LA Times* or check the *San Francisco Chronicle*.

The recession that hit California in the 1990s knocked the smile from its sunny face. As has occurred throughout the history of the state, tensions between ethnic groups amplify when the job market plummets and the window of opportunity slams shut – and illegal immigrants are always the first to feel the blow. During the depression in the 1930s, the county of LA "repatriated" thousands of Mexicans on relief, loading them like cattle onto trains. When the need for cheap labor beckoned, Mexicans once more became a necessary commodity in the burgeoning economy.

Today, politicians and economists have

latched onto the issue of immigration. Even in liberal San Francisco, where law enforcement is prohibited from reporting illegal aliens, there's been an uproar about the growing number of Central Americans standing on street corners attempting to get hired out for menial work.

In San Diego, suburban residents have taken action against nearby encampments of immigrants, citing to government officials everything from unsanitary conditions to spousal and child abuse. (Border crossings from Mexico into San Diego County are so prevalent that there are signs cautioning drivers to be watchful of immigrants running across the highway.)

It has been suggested by the media that Cali-

fornia is becoming dangerously Balkanized, that the cities especially are starting to resemble such racially- and ethnically-driven areas as the former Yugoslavia. What is evident, however, is not that the hope for multi-culturalism is withering, but that it is being realized.

At the very least from an economical standpoint, many business and political leaders are making a concerted effort to adapt to California's quickly shifting social landscape. Neighborhoods that had previously been abandoned after the flight of the whites are now targeted for revitalization according to the new communities they serve.

Los Angeles' Broadway, once the hub of the white entertainment industry with Sid Grauman's spectacular Million Dollar Theater premiering the films of stars such as Charlie Chaplin and Mary Pickford, is now mostly a Latino commercial district. Broadway is vibrant with the exchanges of everyday life – racks of clothing spilling onto the sidewalk, the smell of espresso wafting over crates of fresh produce, trinkets and gifts, and food and toiletries. Its centerpiece, Grand Central Market, has housed Chinese herbalists, black-owned juice bars and tortilla stands operated by inner-city Latino youths.

The future of democracy

California urban theorists like Mike Davis, author of *City of Quartz: Excavating the Future in Los Angeles*, have proposed the idea of neighborhood planning councils in order to give responsibility to the many ethnic populations that are not adequately represented. Although the current Citywide Alliance of Neighborhood Councils is a start, many would prefer to see a rotating group of representatives elected from each neighborhood that would convene on issues concerning their community – including revitalization, law enforcement and public safety, business development and education.

These representatives would then meet with their city council member or county supervisor. Bringing an additional level of representation to the local citizens might help to render impotent the power-breaking restructuring of districts. Maybe this, at least in California, is the future of democracy.   ❏

LEFT: Yurok tribesman at a festival in Klamath.
RIGHT: wedding couple at the Spanish-Moorish style Santa Barbara courthouse.

CALIFORNIA CUISINE

The menu is as varied as the people. From soya burgers to sushi to
sun-dried tomatoes, the state is a food-lover's fantasy

What are you hungry for? It is often said that California is the land of fantasy, and why should food be any exception? Walk just a few blocks in most sizeable cities and you'll have a choice to whet even the most cosmopolitan of appetites: hamburgers and fries, tacos and burritos, pasta and pizza, noo-

dles and sushi, tandoori and curries, Mongolian barbecue, falafel and bagels, piroshki and baklava, and on through the global menu.

To understand what makes this incredible array possible, it helps to consider California's geographic and cultural orientation: the influence of Mexican neighbors to the south and Asian neighbors to the west; the vast tracts of rich soil that make it one of the most fertile and productive places on earth; a climate friendly to growing just about every kind of crop all year round; local waters that yield a bounty of fish and seafood. Mix all this with liberal dashings of sun and easy living, and there's California's recipe for innovation and culinary awareness.

But more than these factors, local food is defined by the many people who call themselves Californians. The vast majority came from other parts of the world (many recently, others a generation or two ago), bringing native regional foodways with them. This has created a food scene that is much more than just a few ethnic restaurants scattered around. Particularly in California's large cities, sizeable ethnic communities support their own specialty food shops and produce markets, as well as an often remarkable number of restaurants (Los Angeles, for example, claims to have around 500 Korean eateries).

This results in a vitality, availability and diversity within a native cuisine that, for the curious diner, can make for a fascinating food experience. Not, however, that every ethnic restaurant is authentic (or, for that matter, very good) and it isn't always easy to find the best ones. Especially in small cities and towns, the highways are lined with the ubiquitous multitude of fast-food outlets, coffee shops and diners serving "American food" found everywhere around the country. To locate the individually owned gem, you may have to ask the locals. An excellent place to do this is at a farmers' market where you can stop to buy food for yourself.

Links with Europe

Traditional European fare, especially Italian and French, has long been available in California, particularly prominent among the more expensive restaurants. Today, these upscale restaurants have also become highly regionalized, reflecting Californians' passion for European travel and an increased familiarity with specific regional dishes from, for example, Tuscany and Provence. In fact, the chefs at these fine California establishments are likely to have trained at equally good restaurants in Europe. Many European food trends – as in other areas of life – make their US debut in California, where the transference of culinary ideas, techniques and food fashions is picked up, adapted as needed, and passed on eastward across the country.

Perhaps it was inevitable that this state of agricultural abundance, with its myriad intersecting food traditions, would also have a cuisine named in its honor, a cuisine that has swept the world and produced thousands of imitators. But what exactly is it?

There is no strict definition of California Cuisine, and rightly so. Using classic French cooking techniques and what used to be known as "continental cuisine" as its base, the California phenomenon seeks to combine disparate tastes and textures, with an emphasis on the freshest

KOREAN COUNTDOWN

Los Angeles claims to have around 500 restaurants serving Korean food.

tifiably proud. California vintages from the Napa and Sonoma valleys northeast of San Francisco first achieved world-class status in the 1970s, and along the way have been joined by ever better wines from other parts of the state. To augment the vast selection of viticultural selections, the micro-brewery, offering patrons beer brewed on the restaurant premises, is a popular hang-out.

To round out a good meal, you won't have to look far to find a selection of sidewalk cafés and espresso bars in cities and towns throughout the

seasonal ingredients to create imaginative and delicious presentations. In other words, think of tofu loaf made with whole grains and vegetables, covered in sautéed mushrooms and jack cheese. Weird but wonderful.

A thirst for life

No discussion of California eating pleasures would be complete without mentioning its world-famous wines, of which locals are jus-

LEFT: the California emphasis on healthy food using natural ingredients has spawned many imitators.
ABOVE: San Francisco's Chinatown, the biggest in the Western world, offers dining opportunities galore.

state. Imported from Europe, and augmented by the wonderful weather, this habit suits perfectly the California "hangin' out" lifestyle.

It would be remiss not to mention California's magnificent supermarkets. Competing keenly for the allegiance of the state's increasingly discriminating household shopper, these 24-hour super-convenience emporia are definitely worth a visit: a trip down the aisles, perusing special displays and sampling frequently showcased freebies, can be as enlightening as an outing to the local museum. If time permits, seek out the town's weekly outdoor farmers' market, a staple in many communities that allows urbanites to buy produce directly from local growers. ❏

THE FINE WINES OF CALIFORNIA

There are commercial wineries in 44 out of 58 counties, with local wines winning awards and making headlines around the world

In the 18th century when the Franciscan fathers began winemaking, the grapes were dumped into troughs, trampled into pulp and hung in cowskins to ferment before leaking into casks. "In those days the flavor was not described with enthusiasm," wrote the Napa Historical Society's Meredie Porterfield, "but that is what passed for wine in early LA." Today, there are commercial wineries in 44 of California's 58 counties, the state produces 90 percent of total US production and the wines themselves consistently win awards in blind tastings against the world's best.

More than 556,000 acres (225,000 hectares) in California are planted as vineyards and although Napa and Sonoma get the lion's share of publicity, they produce only about 20 percent of the wine, many more millions of gallons emanating from the San Joaquin Valley, the so-called "jug wines" which are mass-produced and low-priced. Other major wine areas are around Paso Robles, Santa Cruz, the Santa Ynez Valley near Santa Barbara and, in the far south, the emerging vineyards of Temecula.

California ships almost 500 million gallons to the US and abroad. Top wine grapes routinely fetch $2,000 per ton. Chardonnay is still the leader, with 60,000 acres (24,280 hectares) devoted to its white grapes, while Zinfandel and Cabernet Sauvignon lead production of reds with about 35,000 acres (14,163 hectares) each.

Despite increasing sophistication in bottling, manufacturing and marketing, basic winemaking has changed very little over the centuries. Wine is just fermented grape juice, not manufactured but generated by living yeast cells that ferment grape sugars into grape alcohol.

For more about wine and the Wine Country, see the chapter on p.177.

△ NAPA WINE TRAIN
Passengers can sample local vintages during a three-hour lunch or dinner on the relaxing 38-mile (61-km) round trip up the valley and back. Tel: 800-427 4124 for information and bookings.

◁ WINE PRESSING
The basic function of the press is to separate the juice from the stems and seeds. This basket press is from the Zaca Mesa Winery.

△ TREFETHEN VINEYARDS
More than a century old and restored in the 1970s, Trefethen typifies the tranquil beauty that visitors associate with the Wine Country.

▽ BARREL ROOM OF MERRYVALE WINERY
The perfect setting for dinner or even the sort of "tasting class" that this and many other wineries offer to educate the public palate.

△ AGING WITH ATTITUDE
For aging wine, barrels have a life of five to ten years and come in many sizes, although 225 liter-barrels are the standard.

▽ VALLEY VISITORS
Napa's five million visitors each year bring about $500 million to the valley.

FOOD, WINE, AND THE ARTS

Before the Culinary Institute of America (CIA) was founded half a century ago in Connecticut, many cooks were so secretive about their recipes that it was hard for a novice to break into the profession. These days, the California branch of the CIA, Greystone Cellars at St Helena (*pictured above*), works hard to ensure that knowledge is shared, embellished and preserved. It is appropriate that the CIA is headquartered in the Wine Country because the "pairing" of food and wine is very much a preoccupation of today's culinary industry. The CIA's restaurant has professional chefs and an open kitchen so diners can watch. Tel: 707-967 1100.

In the same spirit, well-known winemaker Robert Mondavi opened Copia, the American Center for Food, Wine and the Arts, to celebrate and encourage study about his culinary and artistic passions. Completed in 2001, the impressive structure located on the Napa River houses gallery spaces, a theater, a demonstration kitchen and a gourmet dining room. Tel. 707-259 1600.

WELCOME to this world famous wine growing region

NAPA VALLEY

...and the wine is bottled poetry...

THE MOVIEMAKERS OF SUNSET BOULEVARD

From such humble beginnings as filming in directors' living rooms,

the movie industry became both star-maker and style-setter

Although its beginnings were elsewhere, Hollywood is what comes to most people's minds when they think of the film industry. Many also think that the first half of the 20th century was both the most interesting and the most important. That's when things were at their peak, when the studio system was in flower and when the major changes were made, from silence to sound and from black and white to color. On or around Sunset Boulevard – the road leading to the "Sunset Sea," as the Pacific Ocean was then called – was where most of the early studios grew up, and *Sunset Boulevard,* the quintessential movie about the industry, came along at the halfway point of the century. The street and the film together neatly encapsulate the story of the movies.

Eccentric pioneers

The ostensible inventor of the moving picture, an English eccentric named Eadweard Muybridge, set out to prove that a trotting horse had all four hooves off the ground simultaneously to enable Leland Stanford, then governor of California, to win a bet. It took five years' work, but, in 1877, Muybridge eventually filmed a horse galloping at 20 mph (32 kph), using a series of 12 cameras. Printing the individual shots onto a revolving disk enabled Stanford to win his $25,000 bet. Tripling his battery of cameras, Muybridge devised faster film, mounted his photographs on a wheel combined with light and called his process Zoopraxiscope.

The Paris inventor Étienne-Jules Marey improved on this by developing a photographic gun with a long barrel for the lens and a circular photographic plate that rotated 12 times in the chamber during the single second the shot was being taken – the first movie camera.

PRECEDING PAGES: the Babylon set from *Intolerance.*
LEFT: Gloria Swanson in front of the street sign that immortalized them both.
RIGHT: sound arrives with *The Jazz Singer.*

By 1888, George Eastman had produced celluloid film and Thomas Edison, who at first envisioned film as being merely a pictorial addition to his phonograph, added sprockets to synchronize the sound. It was the director of his

project, William Laurie Dickson, who filmed an assistant sneezing, who is on record at the Library of Congress as producer of the earliest movie: *Fred Ott's Sneeze* (1890). Eadweard Muybridge died in 1904, unaware of the industry to which he had given birth, an industry that was about to move west.

The first Hollywood census, in 1907, showed that among its population of 3,500 were 103 immigrants from England, 102 from Germany, 86 from Canada, 20 from France, 28 from Ireland, 24 from Scotland and 158 from New York. There was also one man from Chicago named Francis Boggs, a film director from that city's Selig Polyscope Studios, which had been doing battle with Thomas Edison's movie trust over the important subject of patents.

A year later, when the studio's film of the *Count of Monte Cristo* was enduring a severe winter in Illinois, Boggs recalled the warmth of Hollywood and moved cast and crew to the coast to complete the production near Laguna Beach, thereby earning his place in the reference books as the first director to shoot at least part of a film in California.

In 1911, David Horsley from New Jersey paid $30 a month to lease the dormant Blondeau

WHAT'S IN A NAME?

The movie mogul Samuel Goldwyn changed his name from Samuel Goldfish.

Ranch. Meanwhile, Cecil B. de Mille, Jesse Lasky, Samuel Goldfish and Arthur Friend formed a company under Lasky's name and planned to make *The Squaw Man* starring Dustin Farnum in Arizona, but found the scenery unsuitable. They continued westwards to Hollywood and rented part of a barn one block north of Sunset at Vine and Selma, completing the film there at a total cost of $15,000. It earned $225,000.

The greatest name in early film, David Wark Griffith – "the teacher of us all," said Charlie

Tavern (Hollywood had gone "dry") at Sunset and Gower for his Nestor Film Company and made Hollywood's first studio film, *The Law of the Range*. On a budget of just $1,200 a week, the company churned out a dozen movies each month, shipping the roughly cut negatives back east to be processed, rarely seeing the completed films until they played Hollywood's Idyll Hour theater several months later.

The following year, Carl Laemmle's Universal Film Manufacturing Company began operations at Sunset and Gower and quickly absorbed Nestor, eventually moving through the Cahuenga Pass to found Universal City on 350 acres (142 hectares) of what had been the Taylor

Chaplin – had begun as an actor and playwright, working in bit parts before being offered a job as a director. With the hundreds of stylish two-reelers he directed for Biograph, he brought respectability to the movies, helping them attract middle-class audiences. Wanting to make longer features, he left to strike out on his own.

Other pioneers on the scene were Lubin, Essanay, the Kalem Company, the New York Motion Picture Company and the prolific Vitagraph Company, which eventually became Warner Brothers. It was scarcely a decade since the Los Angeles Chamber of Commerce had launched a publicity campaign boasting the attractions of its climate, scenery and sunshine.

Charlie Chaplin, then 21 years old, was not impressed with LA when he paid his first visit in 1910 while touring with one of Fred Karno's variety troupes. It was, he thought, "an ugly city, hot and oppressive, and the people looked sallow and anemic." London-born Chaplin and his fellow Brit, Stan Laurel, both playing on tour in vaudeville, were invited by Sid Grauman, the owner of San Francisco's Emperor's Theater, to create their own vaudeville team.

In May, 1913, Chaplin received a telegram from director Mack Sennett who remembered having seen him in a variety show. Sennett, an actor-turned-director who had appeared in early Griffith two-reelers, was now producing three silent comedy shorts a week through his own company, Keystone. He offered Chaplin $125 a week, which was double the amount he was then being paid. Chaplin held out for $200 and got it. Subsequently, he built his own mock-Tudor-style studio near Sunset on La Brea Avenue. Today, it houses the Jim Henson Company.

Birth of a notion

In 1915, Griffith joined up with Thomas Ince and Sennett to make films in the old Majestic Reliance Studio (4500 Sunset Boulevard), which was renamed Fine Arts Studio. His first major feature, *The Klansman* (which later became *Birth of a Nation*), was a sensation, introducing new techniques and a grandeur that impresses even today. The controversy over its apparent glorification of the Ku Klux Klan has retained its inflammatory powers.

Griffith followed up with an even more remarkable work, an anti-censorship tract called *Intolerance,* for which he erected an enormous set at the corner of Sunset and Hollywood boulevards, which towered over its neighbors for years afterwards. Griffith is credited with many of the basic stylistic devices that define the modern film, and was one of the first to move dramatic action off the stage.

Louis B. Mayer, a scrap merchant in New York, discovered the movie business when he dropped into a nickelodeon in Boston and was amazed to discover that there were 3,000 of them throughout the US – double the previous

year. It was a cheap entertainment that even non-English-speaking immigrants could enjoy, and more than 20 million Americans were frequenting the 5¢ theaters regularly every week.

It was "the academy of the working man, his pulpit, his newspaper, his club," commented *The World Today* in October 1908. Many of the earliest movies were adapted from newspaper stories. Nickelodeon audiences were mostly working-class, prompting a member of the Canadian parliament to express the view, as late as 1920, that pictures were "an invitation to the people of the poorer classes to revolt. They bring disorder into the country."

Spotting a trade paper ad about a vacant 600-seat theater on the East Coast in Massachusetts, Mayer rented and renovated the place and negotiated with the Jesse Lasky company to distribute their films, first *The Squaw Man* and then *Brewster's Millions.* He eagerly acquired the New England franchise to show Griffith's *Birth of a Nation,* later boasting it had made his company a million dollars (although records show it was nearer to $600,000).

Films were still being shot quite casually around Hollywood, using private homes for domestic dramas, banks during weekends for hold-up scenes and passers-by conscripted on the spot for crowd scenes. But making movies

Left: the first moving picture machine, Eadweard Muybridge's 1877 Zoopraxiscope.
Right: 1921 photograph of the studio Charlie Chaplin built near Sunset on La Brea Boulevard.

had become expensive because they were no longer simple. The easy days when sound pioneer Jack Foley was able to simulate galloping horses with coconut shells in a sandbox were giving way to times when the people required to make a film would include visual effects researchers, recording mixers, wranglers, gaffers, dialect coaches and boom operators, not to mention caterers.

In the early days, Gower Gulch – the corner of Sunset and Gower – had been the rendezvous of dozens of would-be movie cowboys hoping to be called for work in one of the dozens of small companies operating in the adjoining streets. The formation of Central Casting elim-

inated this casual approach (although, in the 1928–29 season, only about 200 of CC's 10,000 extras worked for more than two days per week – earning about $14 when studio bosses were already making $500,000 a year).

A big merger

In 1924, both Metro and Goldwyn – which had moved onto the former lot on which the Pickford-Fairbanks studio had begun in 1922 – were merged. Mayer was hired at $1,500 a week as first vice-president and general manager of Metro-Goldwyn, with Irving Thalberg as second vice-president and production supervisor. Mayer was quoted in *Motion Picture Weekly* as

saying they aimed to produce 52 films per year, which he hoped would fill the 250,000 seats owned by the Loews theater chain.

This era saw the birth of the new system under which directors virtually ceased to be independent agents and became employees of "a massive, assembly-line organization." "So began the great debate about studio versus artist, commercialism versus personal integrity, the desecration of great masterpieces and promising careers through the insensitivity of philistine management," wrote Gary Carey in the Mayer biography *All the Stars in the Heaven*.

By 1927, cinema attendances were slumping. The four Warner Bros – Harry, Albert, Sam and Jack – had added a musical background to their film *Don Juan* (John Barrymore and Mary Astor), which was greeted enthusiastically. They had Al Jolson say a few words in *The Jazz Singer*. Although mostly background music with a few songs, the picture made millions and forced the other studios into sound.

In July 1928, Warner released *The Lights of New York*, another instant hit. One month later, MGM's trademark, Leo the lion, roared from the screen showing a semi-documentary called *White Shadows in the South Seas*. The first MGM sound film was *Broadway Melody*. One scene was reshot and MGM experimented with leaving the music as it was and having the players mime the number for the cameras – the beginning of pre-recording. It cost $280,000, grossed $4 million and won an Oscar for the best picture in the Academy's third year of awards.

From the beginning, there were reformers who wanted to censor the films and keep the industry under some restraints. In 1921 and '22, such scandals as the Fatty Arbuckle rape case, actor Wallace Reid's drug death and the (unsolved) murder of director William Desmond Taylor lent them ammunition at the same time as movies were appealing to wider and more middle-class audiences. Lewis Jacobs (author of *The Rise of the American Film*, 1968) wrote that "as the poor became less important as the mainstay of the movies, the ideals and tribulations of the masses lost some of their importance as subject matter."

Hoping to pre-empt the would-be censors, the movie industry invited Will H. Hays, an Indiana crony of President Warren G. Harding, to be its moral watchdog. Only months after taking office, Hays banned Arbuckle from the screen, although, even when the ban was lifted, the actor was never again a major star.

Hays's authority as head of the otherwise toothless National Association of the Motion Picture Industry was only moral – a smokescreen, charged some critics – although, for a while, most producers obeyed at least the letter of the law. But, late in the decade, such daring productions as Raoul Walsh's *Sadie Thompson*, in which actress Gloria Swanson portrayed the sad prostitute of W. Somerset Maugham's novel *Rain*, and the MGM filming of

PICTURE PALACES

By 1934, there were around 100,000 movie houses – a third of them in Russia.

MGM), Paramount Pictures, 20th Century Fox and RKO – while Universal, Columbia and United Artists (which had been set up by Chaplin, Pickford, Fairbanks and Griffith to distribute the work of themselves and other independents) played a minor role.

Accelerated by the Depression of the 1930s was the development of color on celluloid, which, by 1934, had progressed enough for Walt Disney to produce his first full-length animated feature, *Snow White and the Seven Dwarfs*, an assemblage of 250,000 sepa-

another banned title, Michael Arlen's *The Green Hat* as a vehicle for Greta Garbo, reduced the Hays Office's credibility.

The big five

By the 1930s, the industry – one of America's top 10 – was dominated by the Big Five majors, all with production studios, large theater chains and worldwide distribution – Warner Brothers, Loews Theatres (the theater chain that owned

LEFT: Charlie Chaplin hit the big time in Hollywood, despite being unhappy when he first arrived.

ABOVE: the closing scene from *Sunset Boulevard*, the quintessential movie about the film industry.

rately painted frames. *Ben Hur*, which took around three years in the making, cost about $4 million.

By this date, there were almost 100,000 movie houses in the world – a third of them in Russia; only half that number were in the US. Every country's film industry needed foreign sales in order to be viable, which created a touchy situation for the US with the rise of Nazism because Germany was a major market for US films. MGM was cautious and not until Germany had actually declared war on Poland did it start producing anti-Nazi films.

Gone With the Wind was passed up by Mayer and instead was developed with great difficulty by David Selznick, who had to turn to Mayer for help. In return for the loan of Clark Gable, Selznick was obliged to let Loews distribute the movie. He also had to borrow money from Mayer in return for which 50 percent of the film's profits went to MGM. *Gone With the Wind* turned out to be MGM's top-grossing release of 1939 and 1940.

The US Courts, after a decade of hearings, ruled in 1947 that the film studios' method of production and distribution violated anti-trust laws and that the studios must divest themselves of their theater chains. It took Loews 10 years before finalizing this move.

At the end of the 1940s, the studios also underrated television and concentrated too much on films for younger audiences. Attendances began to drop. In 1947, the House Un-American Activities Committee (HUAC) targeted the industry for promoting communist propaganda, and influential columnists urged a boycott of "red" actors.

The Hollywood Ten were cited for contempt and denied work. Most top stars escaped attention, although actress Katharine Hepburn, who had addressed a large gathering of people supporting Henry Wallace (a presidential candidate who had been labeled a communist by far-rightists), came in for a good deal of criticism.

Boulevard beginnings

When director Billy Wilder and producer Charles Brackett (together with co-writer D.M. Marshman) finished their script for *Sunset Boulevard* in 1949, they were "acutely conscious of the fact that we lived in a town which had been swept by social change so profound as that brought about in the old South by the Civil War. Overnight the coming of sound brushed gods and goddesses into obscurity. At first we saw [the heroine] as a kind of horror woman... an embodiment of vanity and selfishness. But as we went along, our sympathies became deeply involved with the woman who had been given the brush by 30 million fans."

Several former silent stars were approached: Mae West, then 55; Mary Pickford, 57; and Pola Negri, 51. All of them rejected the role as being too close to real life. The final choice, Gloria Swanson, 50, had left Hollywood a decade earlier after a 45-movie career that began in Mack Sennett comedies when she was still a teenager.

Swanson embraced a lifestyle that typified its time – extravagant parties at which hundreds of the movie elite were presented with gold cigarette cases as party favors. "The public wanted us to live like kings and queens," Swanson recalled. "We were making more money than we ever dreamed existed and there was no reason to believe it would ever stop."

The ultimate Hollywood movie

Sunset Boulevard, which portrayed the pathos of a former silent superstar in her declining years in a broken-down Hollywood mansion, struck a chord with critics as the ultimate inside-Hollywood movie. It garnered 11 total Academy Award nominations and won three Oscars (best writing, score, art direction). But not everybody in the city was pleased by the way the industry was depicted. "You bastard," shouted an outraged Louis B. Mayer to Wilder at a preview screening made on the Paramount lot. "You have disgraced the industry that made and fed you. You should be tarred and feathered and run out of Hollywood."

Half a century later, the success of Andrew Lloyd Webber's retelling of the tale in a stage musical demonstrated how timeless the story of *Sunset Boulevard* and the movies really is. ❑

LEFT: Valentino vamps – in French.
RIGHT: West was one of many considered for *Sunset.*

THE GREAT OUTDOORS

Like a surfer waiting for a wave, the outdoors enthusiast in California floats on a sea of possibilities

There are endless ways to enjoy the outdoor landscape of California, and, to experience the state as its natives do, you'll do well to elevate your heartbeat by some activity – walk, roller-skate, ride a bike, paddle a kayak, climb a granite face or "catch a wave." California is rife with outfitters, schools, clubs, rental shops, guides, resorts – and even tour buses – that specialize in outdoor adventure. There is as much choice in things to do as there is in the breathtaking landscape itself.

The far north

The far northern corner of the state, still partly populated by native tribes, is home to the legendary Sasquatch – Bigfoot to modern locals – a huge reclusive ape-like creature whose red fur camouflages him among the towering redwood trees and river canyons. The rivers and streams bear names that join in a confluence of Native American mythology and the whims of 19th-century prospectors: Klamath, Ukunom, Trinity, Salmon, Smith. Fishing and floating on these rivers is by no means limited to natives; the streams are big and cool in hot summers, and rafting and fishing guides take visitors down many of the most inviting canyons.

Prospectors of adrenalin seek out the thundering rapids of Burnt Ranch Falls on the Trinity, the cataracts of Hell's Corner Gorge or the Ikes Falls on the Klamath. The breathtaking forest drops of the California salmon are at once beautiful and thrilling. On the other hand, you can float for many days in inflatable kayaks with nary a ripple on the lower Klamath and parts of the Trinity.

Salmon and steelhead trout still spawn in these rivers and the fall run is unparalleled in the state. The Hoopa and Klamath tribes own ancestral fishing rights and still set their traps and dip their nets at the foot of Ishi Pishi Falls.

PRECEDING PAGES: Yosemite National Park.
LEFT: the Big Sur coast.
RIGHT: Death Valley, the lowest point on the North American continent.

Guides with graceful, swept-ended rowboats, called "MacKenzies," will lead you to the finest holding pools. Stealthy visitors are sometimes rewarded with sightings of eagle, river otter, great blue heron, duck, fox, bobcat and the occasional great bear.

Here, and especially in the old-growth state

parks of these northern coastal mountains, can be found the redwood trees. Some of these majestic giants, 1,000 years old and reaching 300 ft (90 meters) into the sky, are the largest living things on earth.

Sun filtering through the redwood canopy as if through leaded glass, the cool enveloping shade and the imposing sense of age, often draw comparisons to the cathedrals of Europe. Rain in the summer and snow in the winter keep forests lush and rivers flowing. Backpackers can explore a vast wilderness, called the Trinity Alps, a region of high, craggy peaks and sparkling lakes.

The northwest coast is somberly beautiful:

long, empty beaches littered with driftwood, rugged sea cliffs, sawmills and fishing towns, and forests that come to the edge of the cliffs. Swimming is none too inviting here – the sky is usually gray and the water is a constant 50°F (10°C) – but you can enter the surf with a wetsuit. Surfing has a loyal following, particularly at the point breaks of river mouths and harbors.

Because of undertows and riptides, the waves here are powerful and dangerous, and no place for the novice. Cold-water diving gear (a 7-mm wetsuit, hood, booties, fins, mask, snorkel and 20 lbs/9 kg of lead to sink all that neoprene) equips you to hunt for abalone. This giant mol-

Northeast corner

By far California's most remote region, the northeast part of the state was home to its most recent volcanic eruption: Mount Lassen blew its lid in 1914 and, at Lassen Volcanic National Park, you can view the bubbling mud pots of Bumpass Hell or hike to the rim and peer into the crater. Backpackers will find hot springs and geysers throughout the huge park.

Northwest of Lassen, near the town of Weed, an ancient volcano named Mt Shasta (14,162 ft/ 4,317 meters), the southern point of the volcanic Cascade Range that extends all the way to Alaska, stands solitary sentinel at the head of the

lusk is a delicacy, but prying them off the rocks at depth is not for the casual swimmer. Sometimes, at low tides, the intrepid wader will find a legal-sized "ab" in the tide pools.

Fishing abounds on the coast. You can cast from rocks or piers, or embark on a "party boat" to probe the depths for salmon, ling cod, rockfish and other denizens of the deep. Unusual, chilling sport can be had pursuing surf smelt. The fisherman uses a big triangular net on a frame. Plunging the net into oncoming breaking waves, he tends to get soaked completely. The nets are available for rent; the smelt, sometimes caught by the bucketful, are deep fried for dinner and then eaten whole.

Sacramento Valley. The glacier-capped peak is a moderately difficult all-day climb in the summer, with climbers offered a sweeping view of the Central Valley to the south, the Trinities to the southwest and the Sierras to the southeast. In the winter, the mountain is buried in snow, but still open to enthusiastic skiers.

Backpackers and cross-country skiers will revel in the wilderness of Lassen Volcanic National Park and the surrounding National Forest. Many alpine lakes dot the area, and children will spend long days paddling driftwood logs like surfboards and watching the big, wary trout cruise slowly below.

Fishermen, particularly fly fishermen who

enjoy floating tiny nymphs in the surface film of chalk streams, will find abundant game and frequent caddis and mayfly hatches in the McCloud, Pit and Fall rivers, as well as within the winding banks of Hat Creek, Hot Creek, Battle Creek and the many other notorious streams of the area.

Eagle Lake, an anomalous, highly alkaline body of water straddling the Eastern Sierras on one side, sage desert on the other, is home to a splendid species of oversize Eagle Lake rainbow trout, found nowhere else in the state. As the name of the

HARD DAY AT THE LAKE

Children will spend long, lazy days paddling drift-wood logs like surfboards.

much more solitary than their handsome African cousins), black bear and North America's only antelope, the Pronghorn. From the foothills to the high Sierra ridges, this region is more wilderness than otherwise. Bicyclists (of both the road and mountain variety) will find abundant trails and out-of-the-way roads to explore on two wheels, as long as the bikes are sturdy. (Be sure to have them checked out before you undertake a trip like this; garages are few and far between.) Backpackers will find endless untrammeled trails.

lake implies, osprey, golden eagle and bald eagle – the national bird – are often seen skimming this lake for hapless, loafing fish.

Nearby Lake Almanor, a massive man-made reservoir, is a resort area with plentiful opportunities for waterskiing, sailing, lake trolling and sunbathing.

All the mountains of this region are notorious for their massive deer herds, stealthy cougar (aptly called "mountain lions," but smaller and

LEFT: gathering seaweed for personal use has become a popular pastime on the Northern California coast.
ABOVE: Southern California's image of sea and endless sunshine is reinforced by residents of Malibu.

The Central Coast

California's Central Coast is a region about 50 miles (80 km) wide beginning roughly 100 miles (160 km) north of San Francisco and extending all the way to Point Conception, where the coast takes a sharp bend and heads east towards Santa Barbara and then on south to Los Angeles.

Within that span, adventurers will find redwood forests, lakes, rivers, estuaries, San Francisco Bay, which contains many environments unto itself, rolling grass-covered hills and down-sized mountains, hundreds of miles of trails for hiking, horseback riding, cycling and mountain biking. Travelers will find massive herds of marine mammals; kelp beds alive with fish, birds and sea otters; cypress gardens; underwater marine sanctuaries; and fishing fleets for salmon, sturgeon and crab.

Just north of the Golden Gate Bridge, opposite San Francisco, the Marin Headlands and Mount Tamalpais are considered the birthplace of mountain biking. Miles of scenic trails are the perfect routes for this bouncy recreation, bikers sharing the trails with hikers and equestrians.

The valleys of Napa and Sonoma, about 30 miles (48 km) north, are the heart of California's

> ### HIGHWAY 1
>
> The coastline is a rough jumble of broken cliffs and long, misty beaches.

ing is popular here, as is hang gliding and, closer to Santa Cruz, competitive surfing.

On a spring or summer afternoon, you're likely to catch sight of hundreds of windsurfers braving the cracking swells and blowing sands of Gazos Creek, Scott Creek and Waddell Creek, the last considered one of the best windsurfing spots in the country, where experts are often spotted jumping waves and pulling spectacular aerial maneuvers with names like "killer loop" and "cheese roll."

Año Nuevo State Reserve, a mile or two up-

Wine Country. Road cyclists take long Wine-Country tours on the rolling hills that wind through the scores of vineyards. On rainy spring days in the forest slopes above Sonoma, thousands of red-bellied salamanders come literally out of the woodwork, crawling to the stream beds to spawn. Within sight of fertile vineyards and cottage-style wineries, the Russian River and Cache Creek are popular rafting and canoeing streams.

Monterey

Heading south from San Francisco along Highway 1, the coastline is a rough jumble of broken cliffs and long, misty beaches. Surf fish-

wind, is a carefully protected nursery for the giant, billowing elephant seals, most noted for the male's ability to inflate its prodigious fleshy nose, and the fact that the male is often five times the size of the females in its harem. The seals don't trouble boardsailors and surfers, but this is the one area in California that's truly a lunch counter for the great white shark. One attack per year is the norm, although few turn out to be fatal.

Actually, the sharks are under far more predatorial pressure than the surfers and windsurfers are; many biologists fear that the prehistoric fish are being hunted to extinction out of misplaced fear and misunderstanding.

A popular pastime in Monterey is to rent simple open-topped kayaks, called "scuppers," to paddle out to the local kelp beds. The kelp, long and spindly at the base and stretching up to form thick mats at the surface, ranges all along the coast, forming fantastic underwater forests through which divers swim in search of the Garibaldi, lingcod and many types of rockfish. Scuba diving is extremely popular in Monterey and southwards along this particular coast.

Where the divers and kayakers converge at the surface, both are likely to encounter one of California's most delightful wild animals, the winsome and intelligent sea otter, once hunted for its fur but now a favorite of animal-lovers.

by the confluence near sea level of the Sacramento and San Joaquin rivers. As has often happened at many other huge river mouths, the Sacramento Delta has been turned into an agricultural bonanza.

The water of the Sacramento River, by far California's largest, is a hotly contested commodity. A major dam, Shasta, at the northern end of the state, is the first plug in the Sacramento's flow and other dams block the progress of most of its tributaries. The huge river is the source of all kinds of wild scenery. People have been known to canoe it, swim it, drive boats up and down its length and, in summer, spend long

The creatures are often seen floating on their backs with an infant sleeping on their belly, lolling about in the water, fastidiously cleaning their fur or crunching on a just-caught shellfish.

The Sacramento Valley

Heading inland from San Francisco on a freighter toward the source of the muddy water that flows into San Francisco Bay, you will soon enter a wide, twisting delta that has been formed

hours floating in the tube of a truck tire.

The Sierra Nevada range, 400 miles (640 km) long and up to 100 miles (160 km) wide, peaks at the summit of Mt Whitney, which is 14,495 ft (4,420 meters) high. The range is only 50 miles (80 km) as the crow flies from the lowest point in the continental US's 48 states, Death Valley (282 ft/86 meters below sea level). This gives some idea of its severity: an imposing wall facing east. To the west, however, are the long, sloping Sierra foothills, ponderosa, alpine meadows and granite domes. The sky here is clear and brilliant, the rivers steep and serious.

A wilderness trail of several hundred miles bears naturalist John Muir's name, as do a vast

LEFT: Southern California's wonderful weather and laid-back lifestyle lends itself to beachside cafés.
ABOVE: Northern California and the Central Coast are full of safe harbors for sailboats.

wilderness and a University of California college. Any visitor to these mountains will find a deep spiritual connection in Muir's writing *(see next page)*.

Yosemite, now a national park, was his chief inspiration, a wondrous collection of granite domes and towers thousands of feet high, as sheer as if they had been lopped off with a knife. In summer, the high season, avoid the crowds and buses of Yosemite Valley, opting instead for a visit to the more remote locations of the park, perhaps not as spectacular but just as scenic –

PEAKS AND LOWS

Towering Mt Whitney is only 50 miles (80 km) as the crow flies from Death Valley.

Many smaller areas, with names like Kirkwood, Homewood, Sugar Bowl, Northstar and Donner Ridge, are more friendly spots to ski, although the sheer vertical drops are not as great. In summer, adventurers can carry mountain bikes on the lifts of many ski areas to explore the alpine network of trails, some with a bird's-eye view of Lake Tahoe.

On the Sierra's east slope, Mammoth Mountain is Central California's premier ski area. Here, the mountains slope down to the desert plain of the Owens River Valley, not far north

and lacking bumper-to-bumper traffic.

Lying northeast of San Francisco and Sacramento is the sapphire of the Sierra, Lake Tahoe, the largest and most scenic lake in two states (it is split down the middle by the California-Nevada line). Tahoe offers California's best snow sports – skiing and boarding – plus golfing, riding and waterskiing.

Attracting the most skiiers are Squaw Valley on the North Shore, and Heavenly mountain at the South Lake, both huge, full-featured resorts. Squaw has a giant hotel, an Olympic history, an ice-skating rink on top of the mountain, a climbing wall, a spa and several shops. Heavenly is just as good; it's a question of choice.

of the precipitous drop into Death Valley. Near this mountain is Devils Postpile National Monument, the gigantic, geometrically fractured core of an ancient volcano. The streams and lakes of this region are famous for their trout fishing. Hikers marvel at the ruggedness of the high peaks and the tiny sky-colored lakes.

California went from Native American settlement dotted with Spanish missions to a gold-frenzied boomtown nearly overnight. The rush of 1849, which forever changed the wilderness with hydraulic mining, began at a mill in Coloma, on the South Fork of the American River. Although the gold is mostly gone, Coloma still profits from a summer rush of visitors when throngs float the Chili Bar run and Gorge of the South Fork, California's most popular white water.

Close to the masses of Southern California, the Southern Sierra is an anachronism, somehow remaining more isolated and remote than most of the mountains to the north. The most spectacular region – due east of the sprawling valley town of Fresno – comprises the adjoining John Muir Wilderness Area, Kings Canyon National Park and Sequoia National Park, separated only by the ridge lines of spectacular alpine mountains, yet each pristine wilderness area sporting its own distinctive flavor.

lakes that are stocked from the air by the Department of Fish and Game. Kern Canyon is the nearest west-slope river to Los Angeles (about six hours away) and is the entry point to a vast wilderness of high Sierra landscape, as well as to the Kern River itself.

On the end of Point Conception, the jutting corner of the state where the coast turns east, is a rugged spit of sand called Jalama Beach County Park where the fury of the northern Pacific collides with warm serene waters. Wind that whips across the point propels windsurfers up and over the biggest and ugliest of the waves.

Below Jalama, the road meanders towards

Good backpacking

Kings Canyon, less accessible and more rugged than Yosemite National Park, is, like the latter, alternately chiseled and smooth granite. Here is some of the Sierra's best backpacking country, where one can hike for many days without reaching a road. Careful planning and wilderness permits are required.

Smart hikers will carry very light fly or spin fishing gear to try for trout in the hundreds of

LEFT: Cathedral Rocks in Yosemite National Park is a popular site for hikers.
ABOVE: shy and elusive Thule elk can be seen in the San Joaquin Valley.

THE SIERRA FOOTHILLS

"Probably more free sunshine falls on this majestic range than on any other in the world I've ever seen or heard of. It has the brightest weather, brightest glacier-polished rocks, the greatest abundance of irised spray from its glorious waterfalls, the brightest forests of silver firs and silver pines, more starshine, moonshine, and perhaps more crystal shine than any other mountain chain, and its countless mirror lakes, having more light poured into them flow and spangle most" – a poetic description by naturalist John Muir (1838–1914), founder of the Sierra Club.

Morro Bay and San Luis Obispo. The region's long beaches, interspersed with high cliffs, are a haunt of surfers, and diving and fishing are popular among the kelp beds. Just west of Santa Barbara, surfing and ocean sailing predominate at a seaside campus of the University of California, a bonus for any student. Mountaineers will be interested to know that at Ventura the popular supplier Patagonia sells discounted clothing and equipment at Real Cheap Sports.

The 130-mile (210-km) area between LA and San Diego stands out for the sharp blue line of the ocean. The water is warm here, pushed north by the Japan current, and the swells are man-

ageable in most places, even for novice surfers. But be aware that surfing has become a sharply territorial pastime and has gained a somewhat unfriendly reputation. However, if you're will-ing to settle for mushy waves, you can paddle out at almost any non-surfing beach and be as-sured of a good time.

Southern desert

The desert landscape is alternately twisted and folded, then smoothed over. Wide planes of sage and low desert scrub soon give way to high jagged mountains covered in smooth, house-sized boulders.

Climbing out of the desert toward the eastern

ridges of the Sierras will bring hikers to many trailheads that lead into the vast Sierra wilderness areas. Joshua Tree National Park, widely publicized by the album cover of a popular Irish rock band, is a strangely alien place. Huge sandstone boulders the color of sunsets and rust are interspersed with oddly shaped and often very old Joshua and yucca trees.

Back in the desert, the Mojave – named after a Southwestern native tribe and pronounced *mo-hahv-ee* – covering much of the southeast portion of California, floats like a mirage out of Arizona, ending against the precipice of the Sierras at their southern extreme. Death Valley National Park is the lowest point on the North American continent. If the sea were to have access here, Death Valley would drown under some 282 ft (86 meters) of water. Death Valley is the result of a geological phenomenon. At least 5 million years ago, the deep gap between the Panamint and Funeral mountains was formed by earthquakes and the folding of the earth's crust. This created, technically speaking, not a valley, but what geologists tend to call a graben rock.

The name comes from the stupefying summer heat, which sometimes exceeds 130°F (54°C). Shade trees are rare. In the springtime, however, Death Valley suddenly comes to life. Spring rains bring brilliant blooms of cactus and desert wildflowers. Their color is glorious against the spare desert backdrop.

Opening your senses to the nuances of desert life, you may be lucky enough to spot California's horned lizard, a chuckwalla or diamondback rattlesnake, a desert tortoise, a gila monster (North America's only poisonous lizard, which is high on the endangered species list). Pack rats and kangaroo rats, bats, hawks and low-swooping falcons make their home here, too. At night, you'll very probably fall fast asleep to the melancholy yipping and howling of coyotes.

California could be a dozen states, each with its own outdoors personality, its own climate, its own natural wonders, its own rules for being and behaving. For many Californians – and visitors, too – the outdoors is synonymous with activity. It's a big state, the theory goes, and you'll have to keep moving to see it. ❑

LEFT: monument to John Muir
RIGHT: Mono Lake, one of the oldest in the US.

EARTHQUAKES AND OTHER DISASTERS

"Living in paradise" has its downside, although Californians usually regard its crop of natural disasters as a worthwhile price to pay

Living in anticipation of "the Big One" is a fact of life in the state, rarely discussed but an ongoing subtheme for all who live here. It has given rise to a series of myths, the main one focused on "beachfront property in Arizona" (a jocular reference to the state being washed away). "The idea of California falling into the ocean has had an enduring appeal to those envious of life in the Golden State," wrily observes a brochure issued by the Southern California Earthquake Center (SCEC). "Of course, the ocean is not a great big hole into which California can fall but is itself land at a somewhat lower elevation with water above it."

California is big-time earthquake country. According to official records, the southern part of the state alone has experienced more than 200,000 earthquakes in the last few years, even though most of them were too mild to be felt. The cause of earthquakes is fairly well understood as the constant shifting of huge blocks of the earth's crust. The southern portion of the state straddles the boundary between the Pacific plate (extending as far west as Japan) and the North American plate (eastwards to Iceland) with the former moving northwest at a rate of 1¾ inches (45 mm) per year (about as fast as fingernails grow).

Unfortunately, this shift is not steady but one that stores up the energy, releasing it with the enormous burst that we know as an earthquake along one or another of the scores of fault lines. Although there have been recorded earthquakes since 1765, it was not until 1935 that Charles F. Richter devised the scale by which seismographs plot today's temblors. Still, according to SCEC, awe-inpiring holes exist only in movies. "If the fault could open there would be no friction, and without friction there would be no earthquake," they explain.

△ **LOS ANGELES 1994**
The 6.7 quake resulted in over 60 deaths, almost 9,000 injuries and 12,000 buildings damaged or destroyed.

▽ **FLOOD ALERT**
Brush fires destroy trees and hillsides, leaving the country-side vulnerable to flooding.

▽ **WILDFIRES**
Multimillion dollar homes like this one are not spared when brush-filled hillsides catch fire and flames, fanned by erratic Santa Ana winds, sweep across parched crests and canyons.

▷ **SAN ANDREAS FAULT**
An 835-mile (1,344-km) troublemaker stretching from the Mexican border to Cape Mendocino has averaged a major earthquake every 130 years with the last major upheaval, ominously, in 1857.

COPING WITH CALAMITIES

After a series of seemingly never-ending natural disasters that include fires, earthquakes and floods, Californians began to joke that maybe its telephone area code should be changed to 911 (the number for emergencies), and more than one writer has suggested that the southern portion of the state, at least, should never have been developed.

Maybe a stoic but light-hearted approach is the best way to handle the hazards of living in a state with the potential for so many natural calamities. It seems that way: the photo above, of a globe with a bandage around its head, dates from very early last century. More recently, Universal Studios' simulated earthquake was popular from its inception (even though it featured what looked suspiciously like a New York subway train), and Chinatown's souvenir of an earthquake in a can *(see lower left-hand corner)* became an instant hit. "Make the earth move for you" chortled the blurb, as the battery-operated can rocked dizzily out of control.

After spring floods have repeatedly poured down Malibu hillsides and inundated coastal homes, residents are invariably seen on TV sweeping up the mess. "Leave? Why should we leave paradise?" they always say to the camera.

SAN FRANCISCO 1906
sudden right slip movement up to 16 ft (4.9 meters) of e San Andreas Fault caused 8.2 temblor that leveled the ty, killing 315 people and using a fire that took days extinguish.

SAN FRANCISCO 1989
quake measuring 7.1 on the chter scale caused deaths d collapsed the Bay Bridge.

CALIFORNIA'S CAR CULTURE

There's a revered rite of passage in California. You truly regard yourself
as an adult when you can legally get behind the wheel of a car

The coming of age in California is marked by the ability to obtain a car or at least a driver's license, without which one is likely to feel like a second-class citizen. It is not only mobility that is conferred on the driver, but a kind of nobility, too, an exalted state from which he or she can survey the world with bemused tolerance.

Increasingly, though, automobile ownership – or, at any rate, its side-effects – is becoming one of the state's most insoluble problems. In Los Angeles County alone, there are more than 5 million cars registered – some representing two- or even three-car families. And, as the average Californian drives more than 100 miles (160 km) a week, traffic pumps 18,000 *tons* (16,300 tonnes) of carbon monoxide into the air each year.

Car crazy

A poll by the *Los Angeles Times* reported that, although 40 percent of the respondents believed cars had ruined that city, 80 percent of those hadn't ridden a bus in the past year, a not unfamiliar pattern throughout the state. And so, as it's unlikely that drivers are going to abandon their cars to any great extent, the major current campaign is to persuade more of them to share daily rides.

In addition to the sharing of journeys, however, there are other plans under way to thin out the traffic. Six counties in Southern California are currently spending $2.3 billion in state and federal funds on rail projects – including LA's subway system – compared with $1.5 billion on highways. In the Bay area, similar plans are on the books.

Such ideas are long overdue. In 1911, Bion J. Arnold, consulting engineer on the development of New York City's subway and the planner responsible for Chicago's transport system, was brought to LA to anticipate the city's transport needs for the next 10–15 years, during which

the 350,000 population was expected to triple.

He recommended a "one city, one fare" rail-road to add 80 miles (130 km) to LA railways' 320 miles (515 km) of single track, and urged the creation of a Planning Commission "to replace the present haphazard system of growth." But, instead of taking this advice and extending

or even maintaining its extensive network of light rail services, Southern California scrapped it in favor of more highways.

Ecology and the economy caused a major change in attitudes in the 1990s. "I think we're talking about strategies and forces that will lead people to use their autos more wisely," says transportation analyst Steve Heminger of the Bay Area Councils.

An old idea, in fact, is getting a new lease of life. At the turn of the 19th century, more electric cars than gasoline models were being built in the US, with about 6,000 electric cars and trucks being produced annually by 1913. Registered for road use were 34,000 buses, cars and

---

PRECEDING PAGES: fins to the fore in downtown LA; classic cars are seen everywhere in California.
LEFT: a mode of transportation and self-expression.
RIGHT: uptown babe with classy convertible.

The Feeway

For more than half a century, one of California's proudest boasts was that its highway system was extensive but not expensive – roads, in fact, that are literally freeways. But now a new wrinkle has been added: feeways. In different parts of the state, toll roads have appeared. Cal Trans has signed a franchise agreement with the California Private Transportation Company (CPTC) in Irvine, CA, allowing the latter to collect tolls for 35 years, after financing construction costs of $88.3 million.

CPTC expects to turn a healthy profit on the first

private road – a 10-mile (16-km) stretch in Orange County between the Riverside County line and the Riverside Freeway (Route 91) – from electronically-collected tolls. Other fee-paying roads include an 85-mile (137-km) highway between Vacaville and Fremont, a short 1-mile (1.6-km) link from Angel Stadium to Interstate 405 in Orange County, and a stretch in southern San Diego County that extends to the Riverside County line. Several new toll roads are being constructed annually.

The toll roads are one of the ways in which the state's transit officials are trying to solve the problem of increasing congestion, whose undesirable byproducts include pollution, human stress and expense, plus too many fatal accidents.

The top four of America's 10 busiest freeway interchanges, all in LA County, carry an average of 500,000 vehicles each a day. The busiest interchange is the one in East LA connecting Interstates 5 and 10, State Route 60 and US 101. The second busiest is where the Santa Monica and Harbor freeways meet near Downtown.

In the Los Angeles area alone, there are an average of 75 freeway accidents every day – 27,000 a year – of which about one-third cause injuries and 1 percent are fatal. The main reasons for accidents are driver fatigue, alcohol and cars following each other too closely. Highway officers also notice men shaving, reading or using car phones, women putting on make-up, drivers doing crossword puzzles or even engaging in heavy sexual activity.

Attempting to reduce freeway congestion, authorities have been experimenting with coordinating helicopter traffic surveillance with tow-truck routes to get stalled cars out of the way as soon as possible, well aware that every minute a static car is on the freeway causes at least four minutes of stalled congestion.

"There simply (isn't) enough room for more freeways to be built," says Catherine Wasikowski, a transport director of the clumsily titled Air Quality Management District, "so we must maximize our resources." The department heavily promotes a program called Regulation xv, which requires employers to reduce the number of single-occupant drivers commuting to work.

Potential ride-share commuters can call a special number posted along the area's freeways to find willing matchmates. This can cut commuting costs by half, which, say the organizers, can amount to well over $1,000 per year for a commuter traveling 20 round-trip miles (32 km) a day. For some drivers, this arrangement brings a bonus in other ways. Some people are so nervous about driving the freeways that they develop what USC Professor L. Jerome Ozil describes as "an avoidant lifestyle," always making excuses to vacationing visitors as to why it's taking so much longer to get to their destination. In fact, they're taking different, often less direct routes that eliminate the freeways entirely.

Over 1 million drivers in the state have paid for personal license plates, which the issuing department vets with a full-time staff to avoid offensive or illegal suggestions. The most requested plate is for one that says peace. ❏

LEFT: the top four out of America's 10 busiest freeways are all located in LA County; "feeways" are an attempt to reduce congestion.

trucks. But cheap gasoline, the invention of the electric starter, mass production of the Model T and the extended range of the internal combustion engine all combined to virtually eliminate electric car production by 1930.

Now, with state legislation demanding reduced pollution, coupled with the demands of the federal government's Clean Air Act, electric cars are seen as the only likely solution. California originally ordered 10 percent of cars – 200,000 vehicles – to be pollution-free by the year 2003, but, because of stalling by the industry, this goal was not achieved.

Even though recent statistics suggest that the automobile accounts for less pollution in California than previously thought (industry is now seen as the main contributor), electric cars cause 97 percent less pollution than gas-powered automobiles. Highly relevant to the new controls is the fact that America's oil is expected to run out in the year 2020 if not earlier, and the world's supply, together with natural gas reserves, only a couple of decades later.

Gas-guzzlers preferred?

The new requirements are not being universally welcomed by the automobile and oil companies. "It's a mandate to sell, not a mandate to buy," says Ric Geyer, a marketing executive for Ford's electric vehicles, referring to the California legislation. At what price, he asks, can several thousand people be enticed to buy cars that cost more than existing models and need constant recharging?

Even so, General Motors has invested hundreds of thousands, if not millions, in "a bunch of mavericks in the San Fernando Valley who had never made a real car before," vowing to become first in the marketplace. Amy Rader, designer of GM's electric car advertising strategy, says, "GM sees a profit opportunity here and sees that it is probably the only one with all the resources to pull something like this off. For us, it's a moonshot." In 2003, GM announced a plan to offer a variety of energy-efficient hybrid versions of their most popular vehicles by 2007 – a plan, sadly, not yet realized.

Meanwhile, other ideas are constantly emerging: Los Angeles-based Luz International, the world's major supplier of solar energy, has devised a silvery liquid zinc slurry, which can be charged and recharged and thus used to refuel batteries instantly when they run down.

Tops for design

It is not, of course, surprising that America's auto-crazy state should be in the forefront of such developments. Southern California in particular has been the automotive world's key design center since Toyota first established its design studio here in 1973. Today, it is home to over a dozen foreign and domestic automakers.

PETERSEN AUTOMOTIVE MUSEUM

Los Angeles' Petersen Museum is one of the world's largest devoted exclusively to the history and cultural impact of the car. With a board of advisors comprising high-profile enthusiasts like actor Paul Newman and racing ace Parnelli Jones, the four floors of this $40 million building detail everything you ever wanted to know about four wheels. The second floor is the best, housing racing cars, classic cars, hot rods, movie-star cars and vintage motorcycles. Open Tues–Sun 10am–6pm, tel: 323-930-CARS or www.petersen.org. Admission charge.

RIGHT: the Petersen Automotive Museum is a division of the Natural History Museum of Los Angeles County. It is located at the corner of Wilshire Boulevard and Fairfax Avenue, on LA's "Miracle Mile."

Gerald P. Hirshberg, former chief designer for the Buick division of General Motors, who was hired to run Nissan's design company more than a decade ago, is himself car crazy and exclaims: "It's a car-loving culture. It's very exciting. We're working in a place where people enjoy driving, enjoy cars, and don't give a damn where they come from. California has long accepted foreign cars. It's had more than 50 percent foreign cars for 20 years. Living out here is like living in a permanent international automobile show."

AUTOMANIA

Some drivers commute 100 miles (160 km) or more each way in order to go to work.

concluding that what they sought most was "an antidote to stress." John Schinella, former head designer at GM's center in California's Thousand Oaks, says, "This is the place where trends start, and we're here to pick up on them before somebody else does."

Of course, much of this is in the future. Both residents and visitors who try driving here are troubled by a much more mundane problem: the difficulty of finding a parking space. The city of Los Angeles has 40,000-plus parking meters, almost half the total for the whole county, as

Selling cars is big business, of course, with salesmen making anything up to a $500 commission per car, and some salesmen earning as much as $200,000 a year. Mercedes is the car that most people say they would like to own, but Hondas sell the best. The automobile industry had its own prototype of "the Calif Car,"the Mazda Miata convertible.

When the Miata was launched, some customers were willing to pay more than double the $14,000 sticker price to avoid joining the waiting list. Nissan's $38,000 Inifiti was the result of years of study, which included a Japanese re - searcher's lengthy stay in a California house-hold, noting the family's views and habits before

well as 150,000 No PARKING signs, 41,000 No STOPPING signs and 40,000 signs noting a time limit. Sometimes, there is a confusing mix of up to four signs posted on a single pole.

LA has about 600 meter maids (parking enforcement officers), who, in the past few years, have more than tripled their parking ticket issuance to 4 million each year. This means revenue of $100 million a year from meters and fines, a quintuple increase in less than 10 years.

Some avoidance methods: passengers jump out of cars to save spots until the motorist can get to them; motorists feign poverty after they are parked in a pay lot; they place old tickets under their wipers or spray paint curbs a different color.

Officers chalk tires, motorists rub it off. Drivers keep refeeding meters past the posted limit, or pull out of one space when time has run out and park in a new space a few feet away, both illegal practices. If a valet parks your car and it then gets ticketed, you are responsible, because tickets follow the car, not the driver.

Los Angeles locates offenders with the aid of 13 two-man teams from its Habitual Parking Violators division. Its avid members drive randomly around feeding license numbers into mobile computers. A huge,

STOP-START

Los Angeles has 150,000 "No Parking" signs and 41,000 "No Stopping" signs.

Of the 50,000 or so parking tickets that are disputed in the average year, about 20 percent of cases are won by the motorist. If the description of the vehicle on the ticket differs from the actual car, the judge usually dismisses the ticket, as he does if the driver shows up in court and the parking cop doesn't bother.

Photographs are helpful evidence, especially if they show an unreadable sign. Some people even take in video tapes, a receipt from a repair shop or a note from a doctor giving legitimate reasons for being illegally parked.

40-lb (18-kg) orange metal boot is placed on 60 or 70 vehicles a day that have accumulated more than five current parking tickets.

Needless to say, the Boot Officers are even more unpopular than the meter maids, which is partly why they travel in pairs, one distracting the motorist while the other takes less than a minute to install the device. Having it removed costs money, on top of the ticket's cost. If the matter isn't resolved within 72 hours, the car is towed away, with additional penalties. Half the cars that are towed away never get reclaimed.

LEFT: just another car in Bolinas, California.
ABOVE: just another day on Sunset Boulevard.

With the difficulty of parking, valet parking is big business, with women tending to take better care of cars, according to a (somewhat biased) representative of the parking service Valet Girls.

In 1954, Los Angeles mayor Norris Poulson, trying to deal with the growing traffic problems, argued for a ban on curbside parking during rush hours, more one-way streets and the provision of parking lots at bus and street car terminals. Four decades later, the parking problem is universal throughout the state, with LA, the biggest city, having the biggest problem.

"The practice of making love on the highways is becoming alarmingly prevalent," the LA's Board of Supervisors was told by a captain in the LA Motorcycle Squad in the year 1921. The state's once-envied network of freeways has become so congested that traffic has slowed to a crawl at almost any time of the day.

Because of escalating housing costs, some drivers commute 100 miles (160 km) or more each way daily, which employers note is causing increasing stress. Around 1,150 bright yellow call boxes placed along Orange County freeways for stranded motorists can sometimes cause unexpected problems. An enterprising hacker made 11,733 calls, charging them all to a single box on Route 57, after apparently matching the individual electronic serial number for the call box to its telephone number.

Along a stretch of freeway in Oakland, a pair of sea lions emerged from the chilly waters of San Francisco Bay, wandering into traffic and causing three accidents. Scientists explained that, because uncommonly warm ocean currents had reduced the population of fish the sea lions eat, they were beginning to seek food on land.

Extra attractions

One design quirk that appears to be more important in California than elsewhere is the need for car accessories to aid those who guzzle as they drive. Local drivers who invest $40,000 or so on a European car are united in their complaints about the lack of cup-holders. Eating at the wheel is such a common preoccupation of freeway drivers who are always "in a McHurry" that Gerald P. Hirschberg, former vice-president of Nissan Design International, speculates that future innovations might include ashtrays replaced by larger cup-holders, a built-in trash container and an arm-rest made of double-walled plastic to act as a Thermos.

Peter O'Rourke, director of the California Office of Traffic Safety, says he has already encountered such munching-while-motoring aids as refrigerators plugged into cigarette lighters, dashboard hotplates and mini microwave ovens that fit under the seat. Ted Sturges, a California Highway Patrol officer, says that citations written for "unsafe speed at existing conditions" have included not only eating while driving, but also using laptops, talking on cell phones, groping a passenger and passing around sushi. ❑

RIGHT: pretty as a painting: the mural, by T. Bernard, is called Miss Liberty; the decorative car is the owner's pride and joy.

NORTHERN CALIFORNIA

*The following chapters provide a detailed guide to the region,
with main sites cross-referenced by number to the maps*

Almost a century ago, a perceptive author declared: "California, more than any other state in the Union, is a country by itself, and San Francisco a capital." The statement is still absolutely true, although boosters of Los Angeles doubtless crow that it, too, has become a capital since that time. (As it happens, neither of them is the state capital – an honor that goes to Sacramento.)

Southern Californians, it's said, spend much of their time exploiting the attractions of Northern California – its water, its crops, its lumber. Then, as if to add insult to injury, they want to come and visit it as well.

But it's certainly understandable, because so do millions of tourists worldwide. To begin with, San Francisco is most Americans' favorite city. The Golden Gate Bridge and Fisherman's Wharf are the stars of a thousand postcards. But consider, too, the austere glacial cirques around Desolation Valley… the small peaceful tidepools on the Monterey Peninsula… the windswept meadows on the Mendocino coast.

Northern California isn't Paris or the Pyramids, compact and easy to explore. It helps to make a little time, to take a few chances. The upper half of the state of California harbors more places of interest than the Gallo family has grapes.

There is rich bottomland and high desert plains, raging whitewater rivers and sweeping freeways, roller coasters and ski runs, and lava caves and granite cliffs. And, as if that wasn't enough, Northern California is also home to Yosemite, arguably the most beautiful valley to be found anywhere worldwide.

Imagine a line drawn north of San Luis Obispo and south of Paso Robles, over the mountains and through the central valley just south of Fresno, with a dip down to the southern tip of the Sierra then up to the Nevada state line. Within this arbitrary border which we have assigned to Northern California lies more natural and social variety than in any similar-sized territory in the world.

Visitors can follow the crowds, or be utterly alone. They can drink America's best wines, eat the West Coast's best seafood, slither around in the best mud baths. They can try the top golf courses, climb the highest mountain, see the oldest tree, surf the biggest waves. Or, better yet, they can just take a map – and a walk – and discover a few other natural wonders the authors of this book don't even know about.

Certainly, this is a place worth exploring, a place with secrets worth discovering by foot, bicycle, bus, car, train or plane. Where else can you find a state that takes as its official motto the confident name of one of its remotest northern towns? The town is Eureka. And its meaning? "I have found it!" ❏

PRECEDING PAGES: homesteaders at home near Orleans in Northern California; San Francisco's Nob Hill.
LEFT: Fisherman's Wharf, a fisherman, and its attractions.

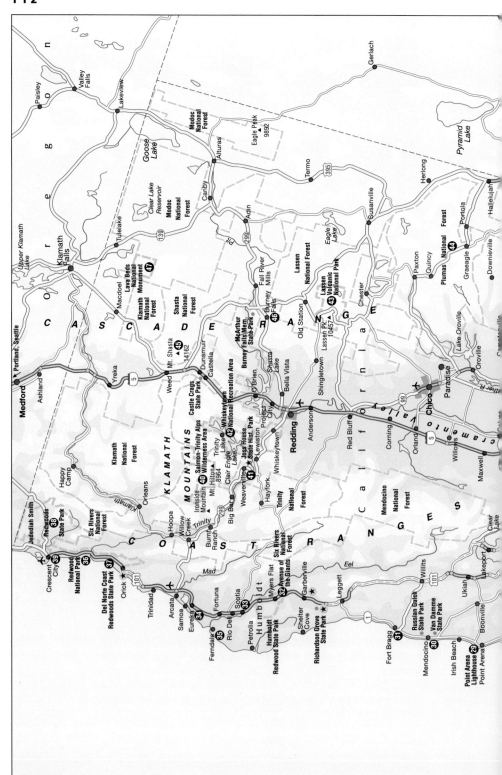

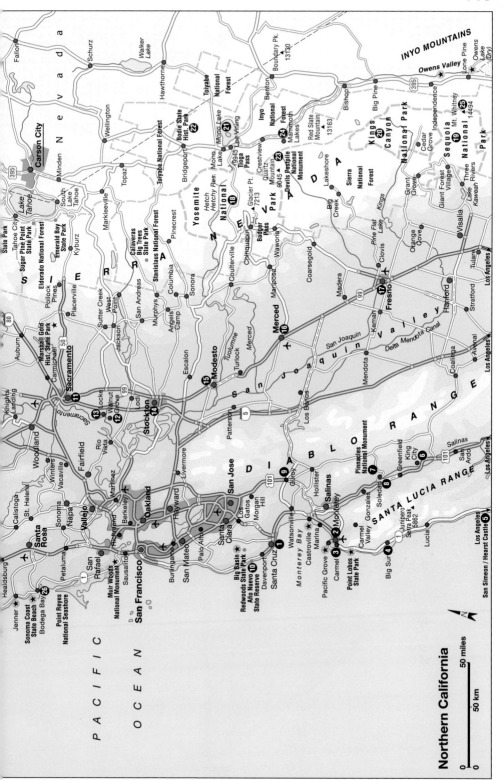

Northern California

SAN FRANCISCO

Map, page 116

Tony Bennett sang it like it is. The City by the Bay, long celebrated in lyrics and postcards, wins visitors' hearts straight away and effortlessly

San Francisco is a pastel city for lovers and pleasure-seekers, soft and feminine and Mediterranean in mood. Foghorns and bridges, cable cars and hills, Alcatraz and Fisherman's Wharf, Chinatown and North Beach – all invite feelings of fascination or enchantment.

The city sits like a thumb at the end of a 32-mile (50-km) peninsular finger, surrounded by water on three sides and blessed by one of the world's great natural harbors. It is joined to the mainland by two of the acknowledged masterpieces of bridge design and construction, which blaze at night like strings of glittering jewels. In the daylight, San Francisco's profile of towers and hills looks promisingly like a foreign land of exotic dimensions. In many ways, it is – elegant and cosmopolitan, San Francisco is a sleek courtesan among the cities of the world; beautiful, narcissistic and proud of it.

Poll after poll acclaims San Francisco as the city Americans most like to visit, while nine out of 10 people who come to the United States on foreign-exchange programs ask to be taken here. As a result, more than three million visitors a year come to the city and leave behind more than $1 billion annually, making tourism San Francisco's most profitable industry.

San Francisco (population 770,000) is a city of at least a dozen neighborhoods, as distinct and original as the people who live in them. Traveling from one to another is like watching a tightly edited color movie. The character of each comes clearly into focus – different, and yet connected to the others by a common history. Only a resident like Dickens could do justice to the vast incongruities of the city. But, unlike so many other places, social and economic diversity is embraced here. The boundaries between social classes are less clearly drawn than elsewhere. The promise of social mobility at least seems more tangible.

Stake in the city

Of course, the vast majority of San Franciscans are middle-class. The people who fall within this broad category range from the ambitious young professionals who have invaded the city's fashionable districts to the immigrant families who run neighborhood businesses. More than other people, all San Franciscans – from the richest to the poorest, from the hushed precincts of Presidio Terrace to the run-down projects of Hunters Point – have a stake in their city. They are all an integral part of San Francisco's heritage.

The residents of this charmed city, the nation's 14th largest, form a demographic bouillabaisse not found elsewhere on the North American continent. Although the descendants of early Italian, German and Irish families are still found in snug neighborhood enclaves, their numbers have been greatly diminished over the past

LEFT: view from Pier 39. **BELOW:** cable-car shopping.

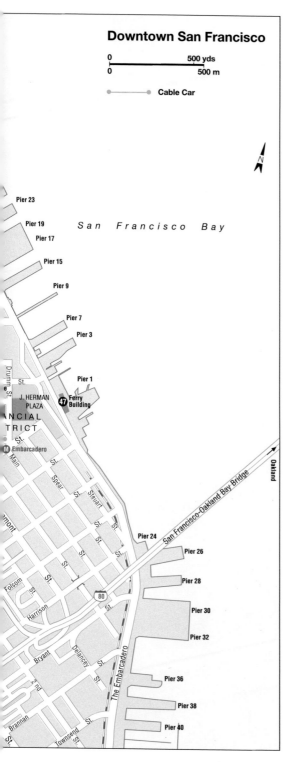

Downtown San Francisco

0   500 yds
0   500 m

Cable Car

San Francisco Bay

Pier 23
Pier 19
Pier 17
Pier 15
Pier 9
Pier 7
Pier 3
Pier 1

Drumm St.
J. HERMAN PLAZA
47 Ferry Building
NCIAL TRICT
St.
M Embarcadero
Main
Spear
Steuart

Pier 24
Pier 26
Pier 28
Pier 30
Pier 32
Pier 36
Pier 38
Pier 40

San Francisco-Oakland Bay Bridge
Oakland
80
Folsom
Harrison
Bryant
Delancey
2nd
Brannan
The Embarcadero
Townsend

couple of decades by the lure of suburbia, with its cheaper and bigger houses. Their place has been filled by an influx of Asian and Latino people.

The city in recent years has become a mecca for Filipinos (the fastest-growing minority); for refugees from Southeast Asia; and has attracted both wealth and people from jittery Hong Kong. One consequence has been that the small 23 square blocks of Chinatown haven't been able to absorb the new arrivals. So they have spread their cultures west into the formerly all-white Richmond and Sunset districts.

San Francisco is to an extraordinary degree a city for young singles. Although the dot-com bust has had a knock-on effect, in just one 10-year period the number of singles aged 25 to 34 jumped an astonishing 40 percent. The traditional family was, meanwhile, decamping; the number of children below 18 in San Francisco dropped by 27 percent.

Many of the new singles who arrived were homosexuals fleeing hometown disapproval for San Francisco's famed easygoing tolerance. Over the past 30 years, San Francisco's gays have emerged from a guilt-ridden existence to play a major role in the city's political, cultural and economic life. They have even been elected presidents of the 11-member board of supervisors, which governs the city along with the mayor. The police department recruits both gay men and women.

Waiting for "the big one"

No one can predict when the next earthquake will come and lay waste to the great beauty of San Francisco as it did in 1906 and, more recently, in October 1989. This last quake caused billions of dollars of damage to the city (although most of Downtown remained intact) and cost many people their lives. Although the 1989 quake was a major one, and there have been smaller "shivers" since, none has proven to be "the big one" Californians talk of someday facing.

Perhaps this underlying tension is what gives the city of San Francisco its special zest. It may also help explain why it abandons itself so freely to self-indulgence. ❏

UNION SQUARE TO NOB HILL

Map, page 116

Some of the most famous attractions in America are contained within these few square miles, from Chinatown and Fisherman's Wharf to the notorious offshore prison of Alcatraz

Every visitor takes a different memory away from San Francisco. There is the street that drops off steeply toward the white-capped bay, where sailboats heel before the wind. There is the fog drifting through the Golden Gate, blurring the bridge's sparkling lights. There are the delicious savory dishes that are expertly blended to make the perfect meal. There is the simple fun of a cable-car ride. San Francisco – the city that may be gone tomorrow – has mastered the art of today.

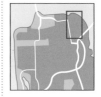

Union Square ❶ is within easy walking distance of most of the city's hotels. It was regarded during pioneer days as San Francisco's geographical center, and was deeded to public use in 1850. The square received its name a decade later from meetings held to demonstrate solidarity for the union of American states, then threatened by southern secession in the impending Civil War.

Apart from the shaft supporting the winged statue commemorating Admiral George Dewey's naval victory over the Spanish in 1898, there is not a great deal to be said about Union Square, which tends to be on the way to interesting places rather than being of interest itself.

Just west of the square is the **Westin St Francis ❷**. The city's second-oldest hotel, it's a majestic reminder of the past; it was renovated in 2002 and much of the grass was covered over with concrete to the dismay of many. On the south of the square, facing Geary Street, are two department stores – one, **Neiman Marcus ❸**, featuring a glorious rotunda saved from its predecessor on the same site. To the north, on Post Street, are the **Grand Hyatt** hotel, with a detailed fountain by sculptress Ruth Osawa; and a couple of other, rather posh, department stores.

LEFT: street classics. **BELOW:** east meets west.

The theater district

A couple of blocks west from Union Square along Geary Street, shopping ends and San Francisco's theater district begins. Geary Street and Sutter Street contain the most theaters. The **Curran Theatre** and the **Geary Theater** stand side by side. The Geary is the home of the **American Conservatory Theater**, one of the nation's best repertory companies and winner of several Tony awards. The Curran offers some of the biggest hits and stars from New York.

There are four theaters on Sutter Street – the **Lorraine Hansberry Theatre**; the nearby **Marines' Memorial**, which specializes in Broadway musicals; the **Plush Room**; and the **Actors' Theater**, which performs classics by luminaries like John Steinbeck.

Follow **Maiden Lane ❹** from Stockton Street on

the east side of Union Square for cafés serving good coffee. It's easy to see how this little pedestrianized street got its name; during the tough Gold Rush era men came here to look for female company. At the junction of Maiden Lane and Grant Avenue, the attractive green roofs of the **Chinatown Gate ❺** appear.

Chinatown

This is the entrance to exotic **Chinatown ❻**, a cramped neighborhood where no sane resident attempts to enter with a car. If Chinatown were the only attraction San Francisco had to offer visitors, it would still be worth it. While this is no secret to tourists, the clacking of mahjong tiles from overly populated apartments and crowds of Chinese residents vying for space on the sidewalk ensure that the area still caters to the local populace.

Buddhist temples occupy the upper floors of buildings on Waverly Place.

Extending for eight blocks, it's the biggest Chinatown outside of Asia, and the steady influx of immigrants keeps it growing. Its streets are narrow, crowded, and alive with color and movement. You feel after a while that you might almost be in Hong Kong or Shanghai. Mysterious alleys abound. Tiny cluttered herb shops offer powders and poultices promising everything from rheumatism relief to the restoration of sexual powers.

In Chinatown's dozens of hole-in-the-wall shops, one can buy anything from cheap trinkets to exquisite screens and massive hand-carved furniture costing thousands of dollars. Silken clothing, hand-painted vases, paper lanterns, rattan furniture, and many other Asian articles are for sale.

BELOW: the city's Chinatown is the biggest to be found outside Asia.

Dozens of Chinese restaurants can be found in this quarter, from the fancy and the famous to any number of obscure eateries and tiny cafés where diners can sit down with the Chinese locals and eat well and very cheaply. Veteran foodies have been known to cry out in ecstasy after a meal of dim sum. These delicious pastries, filled with meat, chicken, shrimp or vegetables, are a favorite Chinatown lunch. Waitresses push them from table to table on carts like peddlers. Diners select the dishes they want; the number of empty dishes on the table at the end of a meal determines the charge.

Intriguing though it is, **Grant Avenue** should not be the sole focus of Chinatown exploration. Grant is the face Chinatown wears for tourists. One block west of here, between Washington and Sacramento streets, is **Waverly Place ❼**, an alley renowned for its colorful Asian architecture. Northeast of Grant on Washington is the **Bank of Canton ❽**.

Its bright, three-tiered edifice is the oldest of its kind in Chinatown. West is **Stockton Street**, where the real business of life is carried on. Tiny Chinese women clutch plastic bags in both hands as they totter along on shopping errands. Old men smoke cigarettes and read Chinese-language newspapers.

South of Grant, between Washington and Clay streets stands **Portsmouth Square ❾**, an urban park where children play and men gather to bet over mahjong and Chinese cards. Across the street inside the Holiday Inn on Kearny Street is the **Chinese Cultural Center ❿**. Well worth a visit, the center offers art shows, entertainment and guided tours.

North Beach

East to the busy thoroughfare of Columbus Avenue, Chinatown ends where North Beach begins. The once tawdry **Broadway** strip has been gentrified quite a bit in the past few years. While a few seedy clubs still beckon with promises of lap dances and naked girls, critically acclaimed restaurants, posh nightclubs and hip, trendy bars entice a different crowd altogether. On Columbus Avenue, you will also find a variety of wonderful coffee shops where midnight snackers can sip espresso or caffe latte, fork down pastry, and eavesdrop on some first-rate conversation at neighboring tables.

This area has always been congenial to writers, artists and deep thinkers. At the same time, it has retained the flavor of an old-fashioned Italian neighborhood, full of little working-men's bars where elderly Italians sip red wine and muse about life. The outside tables at **Enrico's** on Broadway are a good place from which to study the passing scene. Many interesting local characters and home-grown celebrities drop by at night, including entertainers from up and down the street who are taking their breaks between shows.

Woody Allen and Bill Cosby had their taste of the limelight here at the Hungry I. The likes of Lenny Bruce, Jonathan Winters, and the Smothers Brothers plied their trades at the original Purple Onion, which has recently reopened. A favorite venue from the old days is the **Condor**, a historical site that became famous when a waitress named Carol Doda peeled to the waist one night in 1964 and ushered in the topless boom. The venerable Doda used to descend nightly from the ceiling atop a piano. She was clad only in a G-string, showing her debt to silicone technology.

Moose's is a hangout for lawyers, politicians, writers and others who make

Map, page 116

TIP

Parking in North Beach at night can be quite a challenge, and police are very strict on illegally parked vehicles. It's best to walk or take a taxi.

BELOW: North Beach street artists.

Founded in 1953 by Beat poet Lawrence Ferlinghetti, City Lights bookstore is still a favorite haunt of wordsmiths.

BELOW: the ever-popular sea lions of Fisherman's Wharf.

their livings from words. A piano in the middle of the room adds to the ambience. Another favorite haunt of the wordsmiths is the **City Lights ⓬** bookstore on Columbus Avenue (open late), which has been run since 1953 by poet Lawrence Ferlinghetti, one of the literary luminaries of the 1950s Beat era. Across the alley is **Vesuvio**, a wonderfully atmospheric bar where intellectuals in rimless glasses sip aperitifs and think long thoughts. The little alley between City Lights and Vesuvio was renamed **Jack Kerouac** in honor of the area's Beat status. And nearby, on Columbus, is **Tosca Café**, where off-duty cops and society swells listen to opera records that play on the jukebox.

Above North Beach, at the end of Lombard Street, is **Telegraph Hill ⓭**. As well as being one the city's most famous sites, it also offers spectacular views across the bay. The moderne tiara crowning the hill is **Coit Tower ⓮** (tel: 415-362 0808), built in 1934 by Mrs Lillie Coit in memory of San Francisco's heroic corps of firefighters. Its momentous views and WPA frescoes entice thousands to wait bumper-to-bumper for a coveted parking space.

At the intersection of Columbus and Union is **Washington Square ⓯**, a grassy expanse, favored morning tai chi location and perfect picnic spot.

Fisherman's Wharf

Straight up Columbus Avenue is another of the city's premier attractions. Tourism surveys claim **Fisherman's Wharf ⓰** – and, perhaps, its unruly but entertaining gang of resident sea lions – is what 70 percent of all San Francisco visitors have come to see. Although the fishing boats look like parts of a quaint set designed in the Disney studios, they are actual working vessels that put out before dawn to fish the abundant waters outside the

Golden Gate. The catch they bring back often determines the "special of the day" at the numerous restaurants clustered around the wharf. Italians historically skippered and manned the boats and also ran the restaurants. A glance at the names of the restaurants indicates that not all that much has changed, with Italian dishes a not-always-second choice to some of the freshest fish around.

Chances are Fisherman's Wharf will be where visitors have their first encounter with one of the city's proudest legends, its crusty sourdough bread. It is quite unlike anything found elsewhere. Natives swear the secret ingredients roll in with the fog, working a mysterious influence on the bacteria in the sourdough starter. The best way to enjoy this bread is with sweet butter, Dungeness crab and a crisp Chardonnay.

The wharf has catered to generations of tourists and knows how to do it with skill. At sidewalk concessions, strollers can watch crabs being steamed and can buy shrimp or crab cocktails as takeaway treats. A recent attraction is **Forbes Island**, based on a self propelled motor vessel – with palm trees, a sandy beach, waterfall and 40-ft (12-meter) high lighthouse with observation deck.

Ripley's Believe It or Not! Museum assembles under one roof a collection of some 2,000 peculiar things once belonging to the late cartoonist Robert Ripley. **The Guinness Museum of World Records** offers a gallery of biggest, smallest, fastest, slowest and other such pacesetters from the pages of this bestselling book. It is only a short hop, step and jump from here to the other attractions on nearby **Piers 39** and **41**, which also serve as the departure points for boat trips around the harbor; and **Pier 33** for the ferry to Alcatraz island and its extremely moving tour.

Map, page 116

BELOW: peering at the attractions on Pier 39.

Chicago mobster Al Capone (1898–1947) was one of Alcatraz island's better-known residents.

Alcatraz Island

Due to age and vacancy, **Alcatraz** ⑰ (ferries leave from Pier 33, tel: 415-981 7625) is slowly falling apart. Its steel bars are being eaten away by salt air and its pastel buildings are giving way to the ravages of time. In the case of Alcatraz, part of its appeal lies in its location and its notorious past. Just over a mile offshore from San Francisco, it is windswept and scoured by swift tides. When it was first sighted in 1775 by Spanish Lieutenant Juan Manuel de Ayala, the only occupants were pelicans, so Ayala named it Isla de los Alcatraces – the Island of Pelicans. Its strategic location in the bay suited it to military purposes and it was garrisoned with soldiers in the 1850s. Because escape from the island was a remote possibility, renegade servicemen were incarcerated on Alcatraz, to be followed by Apaches, taken prisoner in Arizona during the 1870s Indian wars, and then prisoners from the Spanish-American War.

Alcatraz evolved into a federal prison that housed such case-hardened criminals as Mafia leader Al Capone and the notorious Machine Gun Kelly. Those few desperate inmates who managed to escape their cells in bids for freedom perished in the frigid waters surrounding the island. The prison was finally closed in 1963 when the costs of repairing the constant ravages of wind and weather grew too great.

So the prison buildings crumble away bit by bit as people increasingly think the best thing to do with Alcatraz is just to leave it as it is, a symbol of "man's inhumanity to man." It is now part of the Golden Gate National Recreational Area: park rangers give guided tours of safe parts of the island, including a peek at some of the cell blocks, while the evocative, award-winning taped cassette tour features voices of some of the original prisoners.

BELOW: Alcatraz prison lies a mile offshore.

(Less visited than Alcatraz is the larger **Angel Island** – accessible by ferry from several Bay locations – which has picnic sites, hiking trails, historic buildings and an educational tram tour. Call 415-435 1915 for information.)

Pier 39 is another popular section of Fisherman's Wharf, perhaps due to those previously mentioned sea lions. This 45-acre (18-hectare) collection of shops, arcades, fast-food restaurants and other diversions lure tourists by the thousands to places like the big-screen **San Francisco Carousel**, the **Riptide Arcade** and the **Aquarium of the Bay**. The oldest thing at Pier 39 is the **Eagle Café**, a fixture favored for decades by fishermen and longshoremen before it was moved intact from its original site a couple of blocks away.

Ghirardelli Square

Heading west along the water's edge and back near the main section of Fisherman's Wharf, you'll soon come to the popular **Cannery** ⓲. Built in 1909 to serve as Del Monte's canning plant, it capitalized on the success of nearby tourist sites and now houses dozens of shops and restaurants. A couple of blocks west is the popular and fanciful **Ghirardelli Square** ⓴ (tel: 415-775 5500), another superb example of putting the past to work in the present. Ghirardelli Square was built as a wool mill during the Civil War era and later became a chocolate factory.

When the chocolate business moved elsewhere, it could easily have been torn down to make way for something modern. But William Matson Roth, a financier with a keen aesthetic sense, saw the possibilities for a rebirth of the building. Over a five-year period, starting in 1962, it was transformed into a brilliant showcase for retail shops, restaurants, bookstores and bars. There's

Map, page 116

TIP

When boarding your ferry, regardless of the season, be sure to bring a jacket as warm protection against the wind is essential.

BELOW: Lombard Street, star of movies and car chases.

Map, page 116

usually free entertainment going on somewhere in the square, likely including tomfoolery by theater troupes or mime artistes, who are nearly as common as seagulls.

Only a few steps west of Ghirardelli Square is **Aquatic Park ㉑**, a terraced greensward that leads out to a small beach and curving municipal pier sometimes dotted with fishermen. The park houses the **National Maritime Museum ㉒**, (housed in a 1930s building that resembles a ship) which has all kinds of natural displays and photographs, and is adjacent to the Hyde Street Pier, where the museum's floating displays are docked. These include a sidewheel ferry and three schooners that carried heavy freight in the days of sailing ships.

The tall masts and rigging at the water's edge belong to the graceful Scottish-built clipper **Balclutha**, a 301-ft (81-meter) beauty open to the public. Her maiden voyage was in 1887 and she made many trips around Cape Horn. Two piers away is the **Pampanito**, a World War II submarine whose narrow passageways may awaken claustrophobia. **San Francisco Helicopter Tours** (tel: 800-400 2404) offers spectacular views of the bay. The price for a "flightseeing tour" is steep, but circling around Alcatraz in a pulsating chopper is an unforgettable experience.

Two blocks inland from the Hyde Street Pier is the **cable-car turnaround**, where the Powell-Hyde car begins its ascent into the wealthy neighborhood of **Russian Hill ㉓**. A ride on this route is one of the best ways to see the hill, whose high-rise apartments and mansions have cashed in on the vistas and charming neighborhood appeal. The trundling cable car passes near to that curvy section of **Lombard Street ㉔** made famous in countless movies and TV shows for its twisting, winding lanes and rarely fatal celluloid car chases.

BELOW: Grace Cathedral.
RIGHT: Coit Tower and Telegraph Hill.

The mansions of Nob Hill

The cable-car ride continues up to one of the best-known of the city's hills – just to the west above Chinatown – **Nob Hill ㉕**. An epicenter for the city's elite, the hill is celebrated mostly for the size and elegance of the mansions built there a century ago. Writer Robert Louis Stevenson called Nob Hill the "hill of palaces."

Here, the **Mark Hopkins Hotel ㉖** occupies the site of the former Mark Hopkins mansion where a cocktail at the **Top of the Mark** bar on the 19th floor is on most visitors' must-do lists (tel: 415-392 3434). The lovely **Stanford Court** and **Huntington** hotels were also built on the ashes of mansions, and the **Fairmont Hotel ㉗** retains an aura of (rebuilt) splendor, having been open only two days before being burned down in the fires that raged after the 1906 earthquake. It reopened for business just one year later.

All these lavish structures encircle and provide the perfect setting for the neo-Gothic **Grace Cathedral ㉘**, where acoustics are unparalleled for the house organ and boys' choir. The cathedral is said to have been a copy of Notre Dame in Paris, and is the seat of the bishop of the Episcopal Church. Northeast, at the corner of Washington and Mason streets, is the **Cable Car Museum ㉙**, which exhibits the city's transit history as well as the actively operating machinery and cables that pull the glamorous transportation through the town. ❏

SAN FRANCISCO'S CABLE CARS

They're much more than a means of transport. They've been designated a National Landmark, and in 1962 even featured on a postage stamp

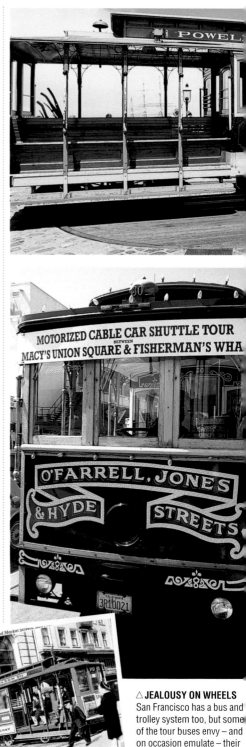

Operating on three routes – the Mason-Taylor, Powell-Hyde and California lines – San Francisco's cable cars are almost the only remaining ones in the United States; at least 100 cities having abandoned this type of transit in favor of buses. Underestimating the universal fame of its famous tourist attraction, San Francisco tried to abandon them back in 1947, but after a vigorous local campaign they were saved by a City Charter perpetuating the system.

Today, the cars service 12 million passengers a year, more than half of them local residents. It is the visitors, of course, who buy the vast numbers of engraved knives, belt buckles, coins, posters and T-shirts, all emblazoned with pictures of the beloved cars. Real aficionados can also find for sale genuine cable car bells and walnut music boxes that play crooner Tony Bennett's sentimental hit song *I Left My Heart in San Francisco*.

On June 3 1984, after a $65 million refurbishment which had deprived San Franciscans of the cable cars for 21 months, a city-wide party celebrated their return. During their absence, the number of visitors to Fisherman's Wharf dropped by 15 percent. "They're Back" read the inscription on thousands of colored balloons, and employees of MUNI, the city-owned transit system that operates above-ground transportation, served free coffee, brownies, donuts and wontons to lines of customers who had waited since dawn to be among the first passengers. Three weeks later, Tony Bennett himself turned up for the official party.

Even from their earliest days, visitors have been impressed. "They turn corners almost at right angles, cross over other lines and for aught I know run up the sides of houses," wrote Rudyard Kipling, who visited in 1889 on his way to India.

▷ **POSTCARD ON POWELL**
This 1848 image of a cable car on the turntable at Powell and Market streets shows how little things have changed.

△ **JEALOUSY ON WHEELS**
San Francisco has a bus and trolley system too, but some of the tour buses envy – and on occasion emulate – their more famous stablemates.

◁ **CABLE CAR TURNAROUND**
The car is pulled by a wire rope running beneath the track's route, passing through the machinery in the Cable Car Barn at Mason and Washington streets, also a working museum, tel: 415-474 1887. The turnaround must be done manually.

▽ **MAKING TRACKS**
At the beginning of the 20th century, 600 cars rolled over 115 miles (185 km) of track. But a fleet of electric trolleys powered by overhead wires hastened their demise. Today, the system has only 30 cable cars and a mere 17 miles (25 km) of track.

ANDREW SMITH HALLIDIE

Andrew Hallidie, a British-born inventor, is usually credited with creating the cable car system in 1876. Seven years before, it's said, he saw a horse slip, causing the chain to break on an overloaded streetcar it was pulling uphill. Hallidie rushed to devise a system to eliminate such accidents.

Although Hallidie and his friends put up the $20,000 to get the cable cars operating, he was anticipated in 1870 by Benjamin Brooks, son of a local lawyer, who had been awarded a franchise to operate a similar system, but had failed to raise the necessary financing. When the Hallidie plan finally came to fruition, skepticism was the order of the day. "I'd like to see it happen," said realtor L.C. Carlson, "but I don't know who is going to want to ride the dang thing."

Criticism of the system is still around today. Some say that the cars, which are of course on a fixed track and thus have no ability to duck potential collisions, are inherently unsafe.

Columnist Dick Nolan called the braking system "unimprovable" or "blacksmith shop crudity at its worst." And one family living at Hyde and Chestnut streets initiated an (unsuccessful) lawsuit against the loud noise, which measures 85 decibels at street level.

GOING FOR A SONG
uring the tourist season,
nes to board a car can be so
ng buskers have taken to
ntertaining the crowds.

▷ **CALIFORNIA STREET**
his old photograph *(below)*
om 1890 shows the
alifornia Street cable car
assing railroad magnate
ark Hopkins' mansion, on

the far right of the picture with the tower. The Hopkins home is now the Mark Hopkins hotel, where a well-dressed doorman *(right)* greets each guest with a smile.

MARKET STREET TO THE FINANCIAL DISTRICT

Map, page 116

Art meets high finance in three distinct neighborhoods: the political culture of the Civic Center, the trendy culture of SoMa, and the money culture of the Financial District

While Union Square acts as the hub of the downtown area's shopping, entertainment and tourism, a few blocks in either direction lead to more locally utilized sections of the city. To the west, the Civic Center area, though a little downtrodden with homeless people and litter, harbors grand civic buildings, such as City Hall and the Opera House. To the northeast, high-rises pronounce the banking capital of the west, the Financial District. Everywhere just south of Market in the downtown area is known as SoMa (South of Market), a vast area crammed with museums, restaurants and nightclubs.

Market Street ㉚, the southern border of Union Square, leads to all these areas and is a thoroughfare of variety. Along the Financial District, it's comfortably interesting. But it turns seedy down toward 5th Street, and stays that way for five or six blocks before beginning to revive. The street finally merges into Portola Drive and Diamond Heights Boulevard southwest of the Castro, one of the busy hubs of gay life. Broad, tree-lined and well-lit at night, it has all the elements needed to become one of the world's great avenues. The city even spent millions of dollars building a tunnel beneath Market Street to eliminate the clutter of streetcars. Yet the street has never achieved its potential.

LEFT AND BELOW: contrasting views of Embarcadero: the soaring center and the farmers' market.

Civic Center

Suffering a tiny bit with the effects of urban living is the still-grand **Civic Center ㉛**, a neighborhood and a huge grassy square where protests and celebrations are often held. Off Market Street a few blocks north on Polk Street, its grand buildings surround the plaza.

The **Asian Art Museum ㉜** moved from Golden Gate Park to occupy the 1917 Beaux-Arts style premises that once housed the old public library (the main branch of the **Public Library** is nearby). The museum (200 Larkin Street, tel: 415-581 3500; Tues–Sun 10am–5pm, until 9pm Thur; admission charge) houses the Avery Brundage Collection and is one of the largest museums of its kind outside Asia, replete with Japanese paintings, ceramics and lacquer; Chinese bronzes and jade; and sculpture from Korea and India. At the south end of the plaza is the **Bill Graham Civic Auditorium ㉝**, built in 1913 and renamed in honor of the city's late, great rock entrepreneur.

The north side has the **State Office Building ㉞**, constructed in 1926. Together, they present an appearance of order and harmony. The brutal federal building standing behind the state building on Golden Gate Avenue is a reminder of how badly the Civic Center could have turned out had it been planned less carefully.

West of the square is **City Hall** ❸, one of the most beautiful public buildings in the United States. It was designed by Arthur Brown, an architect so young and so unknown that he figured he might as well shoot for the moon in the early 20th-century competition to select the building design.

To his surprise, Brown and his partner, John Bakewell, won with a design that called for the lavish use of costly marble, and a dome that was patterned after St Peter's Cathedral in Rome. Built in 1914, City Hall is honeycombed with municipal offices, and both civil and criminal courts. The full effect is best felt from its Polk Street entrance, which faces the plaza. The magnificent stairway inside leads to the second-floor Board of Supervisors' chambers.

This is the building in which Supervisor Dan White shot Mayor George Moscone in 1978 for refusing to reappoint him to the seat White had resigned. White then shot gay supervisor Harvey Milk for smirking at him. After White was convicted of manslaughter and given a remarkably lenient sentence, mobs descended on City Hall. The episode made headlines around the country and became a rallying cry for gay activists. Since then, the building has undergone loving retro-fitting and restoration in order to showcase its architecture.

Opposite City Hall on Van Ness Avenue is a series of distinguished buildings. The **War Memorial Veterans Building** ❸ at the corner of Van Ness and McAllister streets was built in 1932 and houses the **Herbst Theatre**. Next to it is the **Opera House** ❸, one of the country's greatest, and built the same year as the Veterans Building. It has a summer opera festival and a regular season running from September to December.

The opera company, which draws the foremost artists of the day to its stage, shares quarters with the highly regarded San Francisco Ballet. The **Opera Plaza**

The Bay-to-Breakers footrace is one of the best-known sports events in the city. The route takes in many of San Francisco's streets on its 7.6 mile (12 km) run, and is held each May. Expect outlandish antics and costumes.

BELOW:
San Francisco's
grand City Hall.

complex, where apartments go for astronomical sums of money, is a highly desirable address. Across the street from the Opera House is the lavish **Louise M. Davies Symphony Hall ❸**.

Map, page 116

SoMa's attractions

In the years leading up to the millennium, especially during the dot-com boom, "**South of Market**," or **SoMa**, became one of the hottest locations in the city. Centered around **Yerba Buena Gardens ❸**, the area is a focal point for art galleries, cafés, internet businesses and general places to see and be seen. Encapsulating it all is the **Metreon Center**, an entertainment, food and shopping complex with 15 cinemas and an IMAX theater. The Metreon Marketplace is good for original souvenirs of the city.

Nearby is the bold **San Francisco Museum of Modern Art ❹** (151 Third Street, tel: 415-357 4000; www.sfmoma.org; Fri–Tues 11am–5.45pm, Thur 11am–8.45pm; admission charge). Some think the building is better than the art contained inside, but of course it's all a matter of taste. Across the street is Yerba Buena Gardens. What started out as a lovely public park with a waterfall monument honoring Martin Luther King, Jr has now become a mecca for art and entertainment. Buildings around it house, for instance, the **Center for the Arts ❹**, where plays, modern art exhibitions and experimental multi-media performances are staged.

Down the street from the square are the **Cartoon Art Museum ❹**, dedicated to pop cartoon art (and where children will particularly enjoy the comic playroom); the still-to-be-completed state-of-the-art **Mexican Museum** (check www.mexicanmuseum.org for news), where it will move to from its previous

BELOW: Yerba Buena Gardens with the Museum of Modern Art behind.

MUSEUM OF MODERN ART

San Francisco's answer to New York's Museum of Modern Art was completed in 1995, and was, among other things, an attempt to regain cultural supremacy over Los Angeles. The Southern California city had in recent years swiped the cultural mantle, due mainly to the astonishing collection and wealth left to his LA-based trustees by J Paul Getty. SFMoMa was designed by the Swiss architect Mario Botta and cost over $60 million to build.

It is worth stepping inside if only to admire the sunlight effects in the entrance hall beneath the five-story glass-roofed staircase. But many also come here to admire its collection. Works by American and European expressionists, such as Max Ernst, Picasso, Paul Klee and the Californian painter Richard Diebenkorn, are exhibited on the first floor. The second floor consists of the architecture and design sections and also stages special touring exhibitions.

Very interesting displays of experimental 1920s and 1930s photography can be found on the third floor, while the fourth floor is devoted mainly to contemporary works of art. Even if you're seduced by the art and the interior, be sure to leave enough time to visit the museum shop, which sells some of the best souvenirs in the city, and have a cup of coffee in the steel and chrome café.

Map, page 116

premises in Fort Mason; the **Museum of the California Historical Society**; and the new **Contemporary Jewish Museum**  (736 Mission Street, tel: 415-344 8800; www.jmsf.org), housing one of the world's leading collections of art and artifacts of the Jewish experience.

Across 4th Street is the **Moscone Convention Center** ❹, which accommodates more than 30,000 people and is constantly busy due to the conventioneers who pour into the city most weeks. A couple of blocks away on 5th Street is another fine old building (*circa* 1875), San Francisco's **Old US Mint** ❺. Dating from the days when the city was still a Wild West town, it was in this massive building that silver from Nevada was first converted into dollars and then stored in huge safes in the cellar.

Walking around SoMa is a treat, as it is the area where things are changing the fastest. As well as the locale for some of the city's trendiest nightclubs and local theaters, it emerged as the high-tech district with many innovative internet, design and programming firms moving in.

To the east bordering Market Street and New Montgomery Street is the venerable **Palace Hotel** ❻, which hails from the ranks of the city's premier hotels. The Palace, opened in 1875, is San Francisco's oldest luxury hotel. Its 150-ft (46-meter) Palm Garden, with its leaded-glass dome roof bathing diners in light, remains as striking as ever. The Pied Piper bar with its beautiful Maxfield Parrish mural is a fine place to have a drink. Seven American presidents have stayed here, from Ulysses S. Grant to Franklin Roosevelt. One of those presidents, Warren G. Harding, died at the Palace in 1923 while still in office.

Where Market Street ends, the bay begins with the **Ferry Building** ❼, whose design was influenced by the Cathedral Tower in Seville, Spain. It's still the gateway for ferry riders from all over the bay; 2004 saw the Ferry Building reopen as a farmers' market and upscale food esplanade. It's especially convenient for commuters who need only to cross the Embarcadero intersection to reach the **Financial District**.

BELOW: the highly visible Transamerica Pyramid. **RIGHT:** the soaring Garden Court of the Sheraton Palace.

The Financial District

Roughly bounded by Kearny Street on the west; Washington Street, a quaint neighborhood of tasteful antiques shops and interior decorator showrooms, on the north; and Market Street on the southeast, the most immediate attraction in the Financial District is the sprawling $300 million **Embarcadero Center** ❽. In its four-square-block structures connected by bridges this city-within-a-city has numerous shops, restaurants and high-rise apartments, as well as the **Hyatt Regency Hotel**, which boasts a spectacular 20-story atrium lobby and rotating restaurant on top. Noticeable from any part of town is the **Bank of America** ❾ building, which is so tall its roof sometimes disappears in the fog.

Equally distinctive is the **Transamerica Pyramid** ❺⓿ on Montgomery Street; its 48 floors making it the tallest building in the city. When it was completed in 1972, a lot of people were appalled by its pointy, unorthodox appearance, but now almost everyone has come to appreciate its architectural eccentricity. South on Montgomery is the **Wells Fargo History Museum** ❺❶ (420 Montgomery Street, tel: 415-396 2619; Mon–Fri 9am–5pm), which displays Gold Rush relics alongside the history of the Wells Fargo company. ❑

AROUND SAN FRANCISCO

Map, page 140

Latino culture meets gay culture in this trip around the city,
which also takes in Haight-Ashbury, Golden Gate Park
and the most famous bridge in the world

W hile it's easy to get caught up in the excitement of Downtown, the neighborhoods that make up the rest of the city are equally intriguing and wonderfully diverse. Exploring these areas may seem daunting at first, but they're easily navigated and full of what makes San Francisco one of the most beloved towns on the planet. Mission Street heads due south into the heart of the **Mission district**, San Francisco's great melting pot of Latin American cultures. **Mission Dolores ❶** (Dolores Avenue near 16th Street) was founded less than a week before the American Declaration of Independence was signed in 1776, and its thick adobe walls still form what is the oldest building in San Francisco. The graves of many early pioneers, and thousands of native Costonoan Indians can be found in the mission cemetery.

The Mission district oozes Hispanic culture. Nowadays, while Mission still caters to the Latino community, many newcomers are settling in the area because it's more affordable than most. But the expanding community hasn't yet affected the district's night-time reputation: it's still not the safest place to stroll after dark. In a town as condensed as this one, you need only head a few blocks to find yourself in an entirely different community. To the west of Mission, near Dolores, the sunny districts of **Noe Valley** and the **Castro** are comprised of many well-kept Victorian homes and shopping streets.

LEFT: local twins pose for the lens. **BELOW:** ever body-conscious Castro.

Gay abandon

More a neighborhood than a district, the **Castro** is the world's most celebrated gay community. The streets are filled with same-sex couples, rainbow flags, hopping bars, and whimsical novelty shops. A recent addition to the neighborhood is the **San Francisco Lesbian, Gay, Bisexual and Transgender Community Center ❷** (1800 Market Street, tel: 415-865-5555). The Center is home to a dynamic range of organizations and activities that supports the community.

Here, it's possible to attend a Mensa bisexual support group, view a show of Robert Rauschenberg or obtain personalized legal services all in one place. Another testament to the gay community is **Harvey Milk Plaza ❸**, a MUNI bus stop that's been dedicated to celebrated gay resident Supervisor Harvey Milk who was shot and killed in 1978, along with Mayor Moscone, by anti-homosexual Supervisor Dan White.

The westernmost section of the Castro leads into the **Twin Peaks ❹** area, full of elegant homes. The neighborhood is named after the two 900-plus-ft (274-meter) hills that provide stunning views of the entire city, and are well worth the short ascent to the top. Heading north, ie, back towards Downtown via Stanyan Street, leads to lively Haight-Ashbury and tranquil Golden Gate Park. Stanyan Street borders the eastern edge of

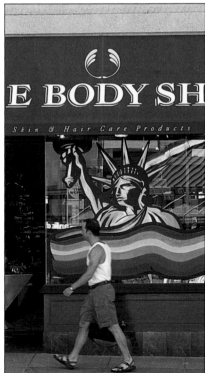

the park and intersects with **Haight Street**, a world-famous thoroughfare in the 1960s, when long hair, tie-dyed fabrics, hallucinogens and a belief in the power of love and peace persuaded a generation that they could create an alternative lifestyle. They were called "hippies." They openly smoked marijuana, took up forms of Eastern mysticism, declined to fight in foreign wars, and otherwise were a thorn in the sides of their elders, who sometimes sent police in riot gear to the middle of the **Haight-Ashbury ❺** district to clean it up. Haight Street was once so gaudy and bizarre that tour buses full of goggle-eyed tourists ran up and down it. Like most such radical departures from the social norm, the hippie experiment fell victim to time and fashion. The neighborhood still retains its anti-establishment roots, but today flower power has been replaced by piercing shops and tattoo parlors. It's still a lively, colorful stretch, however, with great shopping and a wide range of good, inexpensive restaurants and cafés.

Golden Gate Park

The squatters keep mostly to themselves, in fact, and pose no threat to the hordes of tourists and locals who pass through their makeshift bedrooms into one of the greatest – and most famous – urban parks in the world. **Golden Gate Park** (tel: 415-831 2700) is 3 miles long and half a mile wide (5 x 0.8 km), and consists of groves of redwoods, eucalyptus, pine and countless varieties of other trees from all over the world. It is dotted with lakes, grassy meadows and sunlit dells. There can be thousands of people within its borders, but Golden Gate Park is so large that one can easily find solitary tranquillity in a misty forest grove or by a peaceful pond. More than a century ago, the park was painstakingly reclaimed from sand dunes through the Herculean efforts of a Scottish landscape architect named John

ABOVE AND BELOW:
The world-famous hippie haven. Wear flowers in your hair.

Map, page 140

McLaren. Park superintendent for 55 years, McLaren so disliked statuary that he shrouded all human likeness in dense vegetation. Most statues remain "lost" today.

Along John F. Kennedy Drive about seven blocks into the park, it's impossible to miss the **Conservatory of Flowers ❻**. The incredible glass structure was built in 1878, modeled after the Palm House at London's Kew Gardens. But the park has feasts for the mind as well as the eyes. Further along JFK Drive, a road branches off to the left for the **Music Concourse ❼**, an esplanade built in 1894 offering Sunday concerts. The nearby **California Academy of Sciences ❽** is undergoing massive reconstruction and is expected to reopen in October 2008.

The fabulous **de Young Museum ❾** (tel: 415-863 3330; Sun-Sat 9am–5.15pm, admission charge) recently reopened in a new building, after earthquake damage forced the previous one to close. Somewhat controversial in design, the angular copper building houses a varied collection of fine arts, from American paintings to arts from Africa, Oceania, and the Americas, and has a 9-story observation tower, which closes slightly earlier than the rest of the museum.

The beautiful **Japanese Tea Garden ❿**, built in 1894, is a harmonious blend of architecture, landscaping and pools. It is said that fortune cookies were invented here. The custom spread to Chinatown, then traveled throughout the Chinese food industry in the Western world. The garden was disassembled during World War II, then restored when the threat of wartime vandalism had passed. The **Strybing Arboretum ⓫** (weekdays 8am–4.30pm, weekends 10am–5pm; free guided walks daily at 1.30pm) is an urban oasis of extraordinary beauty that delights the senses with some 6,000 plant species on 70 acres (28 hectares). Specialty gardens include the Library Courtyard that's filled with pink flowers of Himalayan luculia, the Rock Garden with circular raised beds of rock- garden plants from all over the world, a

BELOW: the 1878 Conservatory of Flowers was based on the Palm House in London's Kew Gardens.

Succulent Garden in which limestone walls warm giant aloe plants and cactus while woodpeckers nest, and the Moon Viewing Garden where magnolias, Japanese maples and camellias surround a reflecting pond with a platform used to view the autumn moon.

The stretch of neighborhood north of the park is the **Richmond district**, fog-bound much of the summer and renowned for its orderly streets which blend well into the **Sunset district**, equally conservative and flanking the south side of Golden Gate Park. The simple grid of numbered streets is as mundane as the quiet neighborhood itself, so the best thing drivers can do is to follow the signs that guide them along the more fascinating **49-Mile Scenic Drive**.

The drive can be picked up as it snakes past the **Cliff House** ⑫, which overlooks the Pacific Ocean and peers down upon barking seals clinging wetly to the rocks below. The present Cliff House is the fifth to have been built here since 1863; its predecessors have burned down or suffered some other disaster. The food's not great, but for years down the steps from the restaurant there was a fanciful blast to the past at the (free) Musée Mecanique, a penny arcade featuring the largest collection in the world of coin-operated mechanical musical instruments. The museum moved in late 2002 to Pier 45 at the foot of Taylor Street in Fisherman's Wharf, where hopefully it receives more attention.

North of the Cliff House is verdant **Lincoln Park**, whose 270 acres (109 hectares) include an 18-hole municipal golf course and the stunning neoclassical French-style **California Palace of the Legion of Honor** ⑬ (tel: 415-750 3600; Tues–Sun 9.30am–5.15pm; admission charge). Smack dab in some of the hottest real estate in town, the $35 million renovated museum is spectacular: located at the entrance is one of five existing bronze casts of Rodin's *The Thinker*. The cliffs

This drive takes about a day.

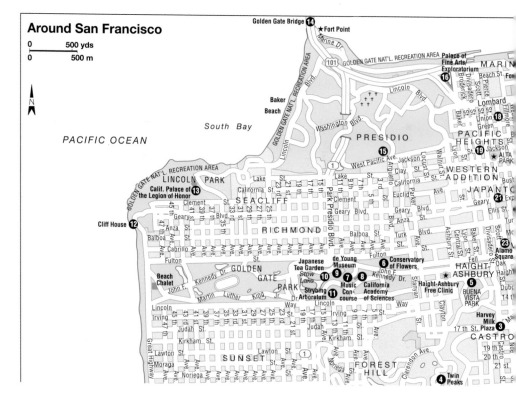

Around San Francisco

wind east along a protected area known as the **Golden Gate National Recreation Area**, (the largest urban park in the world) under the Golden Gate Bridge, past **Fort Point** to **Golden Gate Promenade**. Further down the promenade is the **Marina Green**, beloved by kite flyers and joggers. The yachts in the harbor belong to the members of the **San Francisco Yacht Club**, whose clubhouse looks out on the bay, which is often alive with windsurfers.

Map, page 140

Golden Gate Bridge and the Presidio

Whether sailing under the **Golden Gate Bridge ⑭** or taking in its enormity from the Marina's shore, it is interesting to consider that at one time many reputable engineers argued that it would be impossible to build a span at this point because of the depth of the water and the powerful tidal rush in and out. The city authorized the first studies in 1918, but it was 1937 before the bridge was finished at a cost of $35 million and the lives of 11 construction workers. The full splendor of this vast, reddish-gold structure can be appreciated from a viewpoint near the access road on the south of the bridge. A bronze memorial of Joseph B. Strauss, the man who built the bridge, looks down on the throngs of visitors.

Part of the promenade goes through **Crissy Field**, an airfield-turned-picnic area belonging to the 1,480-acre (599-hectare) **Presidio ⑮**. Established by the Spanish in 1776 and once owned by the US Army, the Presidio is a very unwarlike military installation. Decommissioned in 1992, the National Park Service currently oversees the manicured grounds, which include stands of pine and eucalyptus, and even a lake. After fierce debate concerning its fate, film director George Lucas was allowed to build a $300 million, 900,000-sq-ft (84,000 sq-meter) film studio in the park, headquarters to Industrial Light & Magic, and LucasArts.

The Art Deco towers of the Golden Gate Bridge (see below) reach a height of 746 ft (227 meters). When first built, they were the highest structures in the West. With a span of 3,950 ft (1,204 meters), the Golden Gate, when completed, was also celebrated as the longest suspension bridge in the world.

Map, page 140

One of the most beautiful man-made sites stands a few blocks inland from the promenade. The Plaster Palace, across Marina Boulevard to the south, is the classic rococo rotunda of the **Palace of Fine Arts** ⑯. It stands before a reflecting pond where ducks and swans glide. Designed by Bernard Maybeck, the palace was originally built of plaster of Paris for the Panama Pacific Exposition of 1915. It wasn't meant to last, but somehow it did. Not until 1967 was it strengthened and made permanent. The palace houses the **Exploratorium** (3601 Lyon Street, tel: 415-561 0360; Tues–Sun 10am–5pm; admission charge), an interactive children's museum with more than 600 exhibits to awaken even the most dormant interest in science. This was founded by Frank Oppenheimer, brother of the inventor of the atom bomb. Further east along Marina is **Fort Mason** ⑰, a decommissioned military base whose long huts house art galleries, ethnic museums, workshops and a gourmet vegetarian restaurant called Greens.

Union Street

Turn inland to **Chestnut** and then on to **Union Street** ⑱. By day, Chestnut acts as one big outdoor café where the next generation of yuppies congregate in workout gear, when they're not shopping in the trendy boutiques. After dark, the same crowd meets in the plethora of tasty and inexpensive restaurants, then heads to the post-collegiate-type bars. Union Street is a chic stretch of boutiques, antiques stores, gourmet shops, delicatessens and classy restaurants. At night, the singles bars are the main attraction where the beautiful go in search of each other's images.

South of Union Street, the massive hills of one of the city's wealthiest neighborhoods, **Pacific Heights** ⑲, provide unparalled views of the bay and are home to local luminaries like romance novelist Danielle Steele and prestigious oil family, the Gettys. Stunning mansions line every steep-and-wide street whose integrity is maintained by the upkeep of underground telephone lines. A stellar example of Victorian Queen Anne architecture that is also open to the public is the beautiful **Haas-Lilienthal House** ⑳ (Franklin and Washington streets, tel: 415-441 3004; Wed and Sat noon–3pm, Sun 11am–4pm; one hour guided tours).

Further south, the hill crests at Jackson Street to mark the beginning of **Fillmore Street** ㉑. Further south of Fillmore itself at Post Street is the heart of **Japantown** ㉒. The **Japan Center**, the neighborhood's focal point, is an Asian-oriented shopping center, which stretches three blocks and is filled with affordable Japanese restaurants and little stores featuring everything from kimonos to bonsai trees. It is a concentrated expression of Japanese culture in the middle of San Francisco. The handsome, distinctive five-tiered peace pagoda, designed by the Japanese architect Yoshiro Taniguchi, stands as a monument of goodwill between the Japanese people and those of the United States.

Nine blocks south, at the corner of Fulton and Steiner streets, a very different history is preserved. The "postcard rows" of perfectly maintained Victorian houses surrounding a grassy square with skyscrapers peeping over the top is called **Alamo Square** ㉓ and the location of thousands of photographs of the streets of San Francisco. The graceful beauties, called "Painted Ladies" are characterized by pointed gables and tiny oriel windows. ❑

BELOW: the rococo Palace of Fine Arts.
RIGHT: Alamo Square, star of a thousand photos.

OAKLAND, BERKELEY AND THE PENINSULA

Maps, pages 148 & 152

Jack London's Oakland and the people's Berkeley lead the way to Stanford University and the tech communities of Silicon Valley

D espite all the hard knocks – especially Gertrude Stein's infamous quip that "there is no *there* there" – Oakland ❶ is doing all it can to emerge from the long shadow cast by its older sister to the west. Oakland and the rest of the East Bay – which existed, said the late *San Francisco Chronicle* columnist Herb Caen, only because "the Bay Bridge had to end somewhere" – seems to thrive on such adversity. And diversity. Cheaper rents and a slightly slower urban pace have attracted would-be San Franciscans, much like Brooklyn can draw frustrated Manhattanites in New York City.

At second glance, Oakland seems to offer much of what San Francisco has – even a Chinatown and thriving waterfront – without the fog, the crowds, and stop-and-go traffic. More than half a century after Stein passed through town, visitors might reconsider: there is a there here. It's just a little harder to find.

Jack London's legacy

Oakland's version of Fisherman's Wharf is the restaurant and shopping pedestrian walk, **Jack London Square ❹**. The author of *The Sea Wolf* and *The Call of the Wild*, who died in 1916, might not be impressed to see the overpriced restaurants and T-shirt shops, but he'd be able to munch crab, listen to live music and watch the sailboats pass by without having to elbow his way through crowds to the pier.

The **First and Last Chance Saloon**, which London himself (an Oakland native) used to frequent, is here, as is London's sod-roofed Yukon cabin, which was moved from Alaska to the waterfront as part of a tribute to the city's native son. On Sundays, there's a farmers' market, open until early afternoon.

Oakland's most obvious landmarks are the handsome **Tribune Building ❸**, with its distinctive tower; the post-1989-earthquake renovated **Oakland City Hall ❹**, with its wedding-cake cupola; and, in the hills above, the five-towered, white granite **Mormon Temple ❹**, which is the only Mormon temple in the state. From its lofty heights are wonderful views of the bay.

Visible from the Nimitz Freeway, if you're driving toward the airport, are **McAfee Coliseum**, which is the home to both the Oakland As baseball team and the Oakland Raiders AFC football team; and **ORACLE Arena**, home to the National Basketball Association's Golden State Warriors.

On the eastern edge of town is a natural landmark, **Lake Merritt ❹**. This large salt-water lake and wildlife refuge, rimmed by Victorian houses and a necklace of lights, is home to **Children's Fairyland** (tel: 510-238

PRECEDING PAGES: Pigeon Point lighthouse on Highway 1 west of San Jose. **LEFT:** gondola on Lake Merritt. **BELOW:** Oakland's well-known harbor.

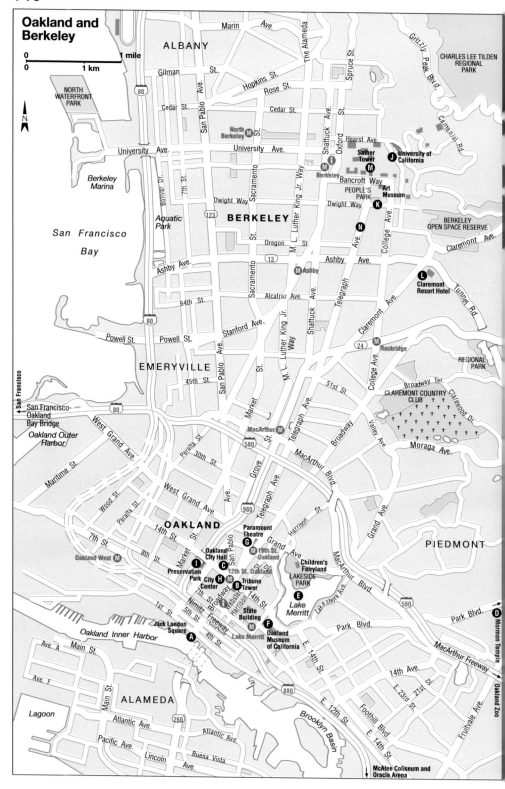

Oakland and Berkeley

0 _____ 1 mile
0 _____ 1 km

N

ALBANY

CHARLES LEE TILDEN
REGIONAL
PARK

NORTH
WATERFRONT
PARK

Marin Ave.

Gilman St.

Hopkins St.

Rose St.

Cedar St.

Cedar St.

The Alameda

Grizzly Peak Blvd.

Spruce St.

Centennial Rd.

North
Berkeley Ⓜ

University Ave.

University Ave.

Hearst Ave.

Sather
Tower Ⓜ

University of
California Ⓙ

Berkeley
Marina

San Francisco

Bay

Aquatic
Park

Ⓘ
Berkeley

Bancroft Way

PEOPLE'S
PARK

Art
Museum Ⓚ

BERKELEY
OPEN SPACE RESERVE

Dwight Way

BERKELEY

Dwight Way

Oregon St.

Ⓝ

Claremont Ave.

Ashby Ave.

Ⓜ Ashby

Claremont
Resort Hotel Ⓛ

Tunnel Rd.

64th St.

Alcatraz Ave.

Powell St.

Powell St.

Stanford Ave.

EMERYVILLE

45th St.

REGIONAL
PARK

San Francisco-
Oakland
Bay Bridge

West Grand Ave.

Oakland Outer
Harbor

Maritime St.

West Grand Ave.

MacArthur Ⓜ

51st St.

Broadway Ter.

CLAREMONT COUNTRY
CLUB

Clarewood Dr.

Rockridge Ⓜ

Moraga Ave.

Wood St.

Peralta St.

30th St.

MacArthur Blvd.

OAKLAND

14th St.

Paramount
Theatre Ⓖ

PIEDMONT

Oakland West Ⓜ

7th St.

8th St.

Oakland
City Hall

19th St.
Oakland Ⓜ

Children's
Fairyland

LAKESIDE
PARK

Ⓘ
Preservation
Park

City
Center Ⓗ

12th St. Oakland Ⓜ

Tribune
Ⓑ Tower

Lake
Merritt

Jack London
Square Ⓐ

State
Building

Ⓕ

Ⓜ
Lake Merritt

Oakland
Museum
of California Ⓔ

Park Blvd.

Ⓓ
Mormon Temple

Oakland Inner Harbor

Ave. A

Main St.

ALAMEDA

Lagoon

Atlantic Ave.

Pacific Ave.

Lincoln Ave.

Buena Vista
Ave.

Brooklyn Basin

E. 12th St.

Foothill Blvd.

E. 14th St.

14th Ave.

21st Ave.

Fruitvale Ave.

Oakland Zoo

McAfee Coliseum and
Oracle Arena

6876), touted as the country's first "3-D" theme park. Visitors can board a pirate ship reminiscent of Peter Pan, or step into the mouth of the whale that "swallowed Pinocchio." The lake is also good for sailing or picnicking all the year round. At the modern **Oakland Zoo** (tel: 510-632 9525; admission charge), visitors can ride in the sky in gondolas overlooking some of the zoo's 300-plus animals.

Within walking distance of the lake are two contrasting architectural delights – the **Oakland Museum of California** ◗ (1000 Oak Street, tel: 510-238 2200; Wed–Sat 10am–5pm, Sun noon–5pm; admission charge; free on second Sunday of every month) and the Art Deco-style **Paramount Theatre** ◗ sited at 2025 Broadway.

The Oakland Museum, wonderfully landscaped with terraces and gardens, occupies three levels, and is considered the finest museum in the state for information on California's art, history and natural science. The Cowell Hall of California History has a huge collection of artifacts, while the Gallery of California Art is known for its oil paintings of Northern California sites. (Tip: before you leave, be sure to take the museum's simulated walk across the state.)

The Paramount is the home of the Oakland Ballet and the Paramount Organ Pops, and shows old movies and newsreels. Among Oakland's newer attractions are the **City Center** ◗, a pedestrian mall with quaint restaurants, jazz concerts and art exhibits; **Preservation Park** ◗, a restored Victorian village complete with 19th-century street lamps and lush gardens; and the **African American Museum and Library** at 659 14th Street. For many black Americans, Oakland has a special significance; it was here in the 1960s that the Black Panther Movement was founded. The politics espoused by the Panthers spread from here to the East Coast and then to college campuses around the country.

Map, page 148

In the books Martin Eden *(1909) and* John Barleycorn *(1913), Jack London wrote about the waterfront home in Oakland in which he grew up.*

BELOW: Jack London Square.

Berkeley

Just north of Oakland is **Berkeley ❷**, another East Bay rival of San Francisco. A city famous for social experimentation and the birth of the Free Speech movement, Berkeley has, in recent times, become slightly less flamboyant, slightly more commercial and the home of Chez Panisse (one of the country's most coveted restaurants, tel: 510-548 5525).

The city grew up around the **University of California ❿** (tel: 510-642 5215), known simply as "Cal," considered one of the country's finest public universities, and outranking all other American universities in the number of Nobel laureates it has educated. Berkeley began as a humble prep school operating out of a former fandango house in Oakland, and eventually grew into the nine-campus University of California system. But it was the Free Speech movement of 1964 that put Berkeley on the map. At issue was a UC Berkeley administration order limiting political activities on campus. This touched off massive student protests and, in turn, similar protests on campuses nationwide. For several years the campus remained a smoldering center of protest and politics.

In 1969, students once more took to the streets to stop the university's expansion in an area they wanted to preserve as **People's Park ⓚ**. They prevailed ultimately, despite the intervention of 2,000 National Guard troops and violence that led to the death of an onlooker. Years later, People's Park began to draw more drug dealers and drifters from the city's homeless than it did students. Today, the student unrest here has turned to rest and recreation: the city has added basketball and volleyball courts to People's Park.

ABOVE: power to the people.
BELOW: Claremont Resort Hotel.

On the approach to Berkeley from Oakland, two buildings catch the eye. On a hillside toward the south is a fairy-tale white palace, otherwise known as the

Claremont Resort & Spa  (tel: 510-843 3000), which, like San Francisco's Palace of Fine Arts, was finished just before the Panama Pacific Exposition of 1915. The other landmark is a tall, pointed structure, the university's bell tower. Its official name is **Sather Tower** , but it's known to everyone simply as the "campanile" because it's modeled after St Mark's campanile in Venice, Italy.

To get the feel of Berkeley at its liveliest, visitors should take a walk down **Telegraph Avenue**  from Dwight Way to the university. Here students, townspeople and "street people" pick their way between rows of shops and street vendors offering jewelry, pottery, plants and tie-dyed everything.

Like Oakland, Berkeley offers respite for those who run screaming from the headaches of San Francisco traffic and weather – it can be freezing and fogbound in the city, but sunny here – but who still yearn for a lively, cosmopolitan community that represents urban life, albeit on a slighter, smaller scale.

The Peninsula

West of the Bay Bridge and south of San Francisco, orchards once graced the fertile landscape south of San Francisco where today industrial parks and seemingly endless commercial and condominium strips now spread inland from the edge of the bay. But this is also the land of high-technology and suburban dreams, a place that sprang up with its own virtually created industry as quickly as the original *Sputnik* satellite came down.

The San Francisco **Peninsula**, roughly a 55-mile (89-km) swath of high hills, tall trees and beautiful estates, is wedged between the Pacific Ocean and San Francisco Bay. To its north is San Francisco. At its southern end lies the sprawl of the **Silicon Valley** – or what used to be known as Santa Clara Valley when

Maps, pages 148 & 152

BELOW: Berkeley was a hotbed of student unrest in the 1960s.

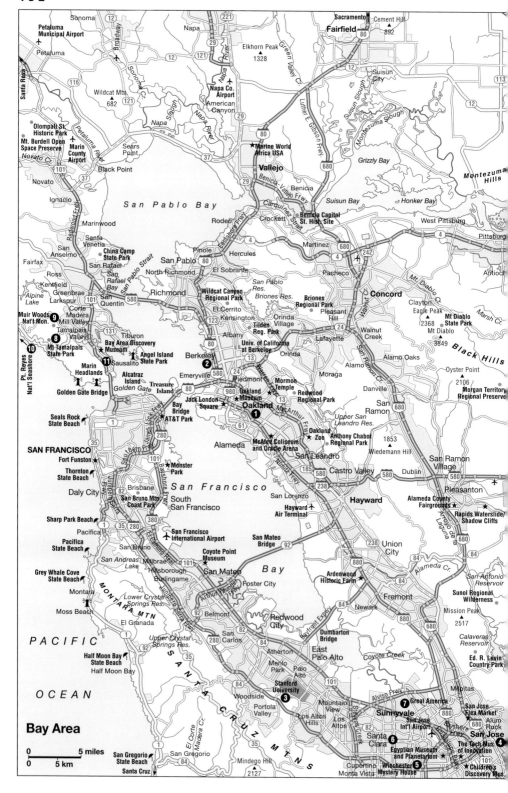

Bay Area

apples and pears, not computers and silicon chips, were harvested here. In the valley, the peninsula's highlands segue into the affluent, high-tech communities of Palo Alto, Los Altos, Sunnyvale, Santa Clara and San Jose. As the drive south on **El Camino Real** – the main thoroughfare that runs through all these cities down to San Jose – will prove, the only true borders between peninsula cities seem to be stoplights. Where the commercial and spartan-finish industrial strips end, the wealthy suburban homes begin, spread like a heat rash across the ample flatlands. In fact, housing in Silicon Valley is now so scarce its impact can be felt in commuter-distance San Francisco, where rents in the Bay City soared during the latter half of the 1990s, and leveled out only recently, after the dot-com bust around the millennium.

The style of the peninsula is sophisticated, shamelessly commercial, and contemporary. Six thousand residents have doctorate degrees, and Stanford University is the hub of academic and cultural activity. Mixed with the high-mindedness, however, is lots of new money (millionaires from scratch as common as tennis courts) and old money (San Mateo is one of the four wealthiest counties in California). Both types shop at the impressive **Stanford Shopping Center**.

Stanford University

A farm – blue-blooded horse ranch – is exactly what the campus of renowned **Stanford University** ❸ (tel: 650-723 2300) was a little over a century ago when Leland Stanford and photographer Muybridge began their experiments with moving images (which were to lead to the creation of motion pictures). Today, it is the academic lifeblood of the peninsula, located in the northwestern corner of **Palo Alto**, a city known for its strict environmental policies and

ABOVE: the republic of California.
BELOW: Memorial Church, Stanford University.

Map, page 152

TIP

While you're in San Jose, take a look at the Tech Museum of Innovation in the city center (Park Avenue and Market Street, tel: 408-795 6100, www.thetech.org). It's a hands-on museum documenting the development of the local industry.

BELOW: oarswoman in Oakland.

praised as one of the best "model little cities of the world." Architecturally, Stanford's handsome, rough-hewn sandstone buildings are Romanesque in style, though the red-tiled roofs, the burnt adobe color of the stone, and the wide arches give the university a Spanish mission look. The exception to the overall prosaic qualities is beautiful **Memorial Church**, which dominates the **Inner Quad** (the quad is also known as the central courtyard). The church is resplendent in stained glass and with a domed ceiling.

South peninsula

San Jose ❹ was the first pueblo to be founded in Northern California by the Spanish, in 1777. Until 1956, the San Jose area was providing America with half its supply of prunes. But the orchards of five decades ago have now sprouted condominiums and industrial parks. Today, San Jose is the third-largest city in California with a population that is booming due to the influx from around the world of high-tech personnel and like-minded groupies.

It is a busy, fast-paced community (population over 900,000), with several major hotels, nightclubs, the **San Jose Museum of Art**, and no fewer than 100 shopping centers that cater to all the techies with money to burn – often, it seems, on their pets. Sightseeing is pretty minimal in metropolitan San Jose, although two major wineries are located within the city limits and offer tours and tastings – the **Mirassou** and **J. Lohr**.

For entertainment of a more eccentric bent there is the red-roofed, sprawling, touristy but nonetheless fascinating **Winchester Mystery House** ❺ (tel: 408-247 2101, near I-280 and Highway 17; daily, but hours vary; admission charge) in downtown San Jose. It was built in convoluted stages by local eccentric Sarah L. Winchester, who inherited the fortune of her father-in-law, the famed gun manufacturer. Sarah was a spiritualist who believed that she would live as long as she kept adding to her house. Sixteen carpenters worked on the mansion for 36 years, adding stairways that lead to nowhere and doors without any rooms.

The spiritual realm is also the basis and reason for the **Rosicrucian Egyptian Museum and Planetarium** (tel: 408-947 3636; closed holidays) in San Jose on the way to **Santa Clara** ❻. A re-created walk-in tomb of 2000 BC and the West Coast's largest collection of Egyptian, Babylonian and Assyrian artifacts are contained within the building. The Ancient Mystical Order Rosae Crucis is an international philosophical order said to have been established nearly 3,500 years ago.

Lighthouse and laser show

Anyone longing for the sound of the sea should nip over to Highway 1 west of San Jose near the little town of **Pescadero** where there is a particularly atmospheric site – **Pigeon Point Lighthouse**, the second-tallest lighthouse in the United States. Youngsters are more likely to long, not for the sea, but for **Great America** ❼ (tel: 408-988 1776; hours vary, open Mar–Oct; admission charge) located off the Bayshore freeway not far from the town of **Sunnyvale**. A theme park drawing on venues of old America and the TV network Nickelodeon, it has an IMAX theater, bungeeing jumping and stage shows. ❏

Silicon Valley

Silicon Valley, which stretches about 20 miles (32 km) from the lower San Francisco peninsula to San Jose, embodies the very definition of modern America, but with a Californian state of consciousness.

Endowed with the enterprising spirit of pioneers, it is a place that nurtured many of the technological advances that catapulted the world into the electronic age, a place where international giants in the electronics and computer industries got their first ideas in suburban garages, and where futuristic dreams have been recognized – then manufactured – into reality.

Formerly known as Santa Clara Valley and settled in the mid-1800s by farmers, it is bounded to the east by the bay and to the west by the mountains. It embraces nearly 15 cities, of which one of the most important is Palo Alto, home to Stanford University, to whose engineering school America's brightest technical minds migrated to study radio, the valley's first high-tech industry.

In 1938, two Stanford students living at 367 Addison Street – David Packard and William Hewlett – founded what would one day become one of the world's corporate giants: Hewlett-Packard. The same house on Addison Street is now a state historical monument, popular with fans and tourists.

In 1956, valley native William Shockley returned home after receiving the Nobel Prize for developing the electronic transistor. He intended to build an empire, but instead found himself alone: all eight young engineers he had hired left to form the Fairchild Semiconductor Company.

Fairchild is where Bob Noyce developed in 1959 the miniature semiconductor set into silicon. Noyce is known to many as the father of Silicon Valley and founded Intel – where the microprocessor was developed – in 1968, foreshadowing the personal computer revolution.

In the last of the great valley garages – at 2066 Crist Drive in the town of Cupertino – Steve Jobs and Steve Wozniak turned out their first micro computer and later formed Apple. Now a huge, sprawling complex, Apple's headquarters are still located in Cupertino, not far from where it all began.

During the 1980s, personal computers replaced arcade games as the entertainment of choice. Researchers worked on a new kind of computer game that seemed to create a new dimension in which humans and computers could coexist. Most know it now as Virtual Reality. Along came e-mail and the Internet, at first seen as little more than electronic notice boards for tech-junkies; later the indispensable commercial tools no one could afford to be without. Stock in tech companies soared to unprecedented levels.

Silicon Valley continues to mutate, but where will it end? There is oft-repeated speculation that the valley's time has come and passed. Certainly, with the dot-com bust early in the new millennium, the region had its first set-back in almost 50 years. At this stage it's impossible to know, but anyone prepared to write off the valley and its entrepreneurs could easily be eating their words, byte by byte. ❑

RIGHT: the high-rise buildings of Silicon Valley's high-tech industries.

MONTEREY BAY TO BIG SUR

Map, page 112

Highway 1, the first scenic highway in the state, hugs the coast from Santa Cruz to Monterey to Carmel, before meandering past Big Sur toward San Simeon

The stretch of Northern California coast from Santa Cruz to San Simeon is one region that does not exist in a state of implicit apology for not being San Francisco. The pace might be slower, but the highly differentiated and individualistic communities which occupy this shore are so busy leading their own lives, the thought of doing otherwise does not occur to them.

At the northern end of Monterey Bay is **Santa Cruz ❶**, a cool, green, redwood-shingled beach town hoisted for the moment on the leftward swing of its own political pendulum. The **University of California** opened its Santa Cruz campus in 1965 and within a few years this influx of academic activity transformed what had previously been a quiet backwater town into an activist community. Santa Cruz was rejuvenated with excellent restaurants, cafés, pastry shops, bookstores and a multitude of shops selling everything from 10-speed bicycles to Japanese kites. Old buildings were refurbished, cement block and aluminum replaced with natural redwood and hanging ferns. Santa Cruz has sparkling clean air in the summer; its only drawback is the torrential winter rain that turns canyons into rivers.

Amusing attractions

The Santa Cruz **municipal pier** features restaurants, fish markets and fishing facilities. Next to it is a wide white sandy beach. On the other side is the **Santa Cruz beach boardwalk**, with its carousel, Ferris wheel, thrilling rollercoaster and old-fashioned arcade containing shooting galleries. Note: Santa Cruz is one of the sunniest spots on this stretch of the coast, usually unaffected by the chilly winds and blinding fog that can blanket Big Sur further south in minutes. Sun-lovers should linger here, and, to enjoy the atmosphere to its fullest, keep your swimming suit handy: not for nothing does the town have one of the few – if not the only – monument to a surfer on the promenade looking out over the water.

Highway 1, probably the most beautiful road in the state, hugs the coast here in a beautiful arc around Monterey Bay. During the spring, the high sand dunes are covered in a colorful carpet of marigolds. The road is fairly built up around the beach town of **Capitola**, but then chills out dramatically toward Big Sur. Peanut stands and agricultural produce stands make brief stops pleasant; they're also good for picking up snacks.

Cannery Row

The city of **Monterey ❷** (population 30,350), at the northern end of Monterey Peninsula, comes as a surprise after this peaceful journey. Thanks to John Steinbeck, the famous attraction in town is the former Ocean

PRECEDING PAGES: Big Sur coastline. **LEFT:** rural living. **BELOW:** chipmunk on Bird Rock, 17-Mile Drive.

View Avenue, now known as **Cannery Row**. During World War II, Monterey was the sardine capital of the Western hemisphere, processing some 200,000 tons a year. As Steinbeck described it then, the street was "a poem, a stink, a grating noise, a quality of light, a tone, a habit, a nostalgia, a dream."

When the fishing boats came in, heavy with their catch, the canneries blew their whistles and the residents of Monterey came streaming down the hill to take their places amid the rumbling, rattling, squealing machinery of the canning plants. When finally the last sardine was cleaned, cut, cooked and canned, the whistle blew again, and the workers trudged back up the hill, dripping wet and smelly. After the war, for reasons variously blamed on overfishing, changing tidal currents and divine retribution, the sardines suddenly disappeared from Monterey Bay and all the canneries went broke.

California-born John Steinbeck (1902–68) is best known for his 1939 novel The Grapes of Wrath. *He won the Nobel Prize in 1962.*

But, as Steinbeck pointed out, it was not a total loss. In those heady early years of the industry, the beaches were so deeply covered with fish guts, scales and flies that a sickening stench covered the whole town. Today, the beaches are bright and clean, and the air is sparkling fresh. Cannery Row, located along the waterfront on the northwest side of town just beyond the Presidio, has become an impressive tourist attraction, its old buildings are filled with lusty bars, gaudy restaurants, a wax museum, dozens of shops, a carousel and food vendors.

A spectacular aquarium

A trip to Cannery Row these days invariably includes visiting one of the world's premier aquariums: the **Monterey Bay Aquarium** (886 Cannery Row, tel: 831-648 4888; daily 10am–6pm; admission charge). The enormous building, with its outdoor pools overlooking the sea, stands on the site of what was Cannery

BELOW: Cannery Row, Monterey.

Row's largest cannery, the Hovden Cannery. More than 100 galleries and exhibits include over 350,000 specimens, from sea otters, leopard sharks, bat rays and giant octopuses, to towering underwater kelp forests. Feeding time is particularly fascinating, when keepers in glass tanks talk to spectators through underwater microphones. Although always crowded, this spectacular sanctuary – the biggest in the US – is worth any amount of waiting time, but be warned: it may spoil visits to lesser aquariums.

In downtown Monterey, the main visitor attraction is **Fisherman's Wharf**. (The real working wharf is two blocks east.) Fisherman's Wharf is lined with restaurants, shops, an organ grinder with a monkey, fish markets and noisy sea lions which swim among the pilings. To see the rest of Monterey, a 3-mile (5-km) walking tour, called **The Path of History**, leads past the more important historical buildings and sites. These include the Customs House, the oldest public building in California, now a museum; Pacific House, a two-story adobe with a Monterey balcony around the second floor; and impressive historical exhibits from the Spanish, Mexican and early American periods.

Other attractions include **Colton Hall**, a two-story building with a classical portico which was the site of the state's first (1849) constitutional convention; Stevenson House, a smaller former hotel where the romantic (and sickly) Robert Louis Stevenson lived for a few months while courting his wife; and the **Royal Presidio Chapel**, in constant use since 1794. (US President Herbert Hoover was married in a courtyard here.)

The **Presidio**, founded in 1770 by Gaspar de Portolá, now serves as the **Defense Language Institute Foreign Language Center**. Other points of interest in Monterey are the **Monterey Peninsula Museum** of regional art, and the

Map, page 112

BELOW: Monterey squid festival.

The Lone Cypress landmark is at the southwestern corner of 17-Mile Drive.

BELOW: the mission in Carmel was once the administrative center of Northern California.

Allen Knight Maritime Museum, featuring relics of the era of sailing ships and whaling. In mid-September each year, the hugely popular **Monterey Jazz Festival** (tel: 925-275 9255) attracts many of the biggest names in music to the Monterey Fairgrounds. It was here that Jimi Hendrix was brought to the attention of the world.

Kayaking on Monterey Bay is growing in popularity, too, offering a delightful opportunity to get out among the otters and sea lions. A local company operates tours out to see the gray whales on their migration past here between Alaska and Baja, California, down Mexico way.

17-Mile Drive

Just north of the foot of Ocean Avenue is the Carmel Gate entrance to the 3-hour-long **17-Mile Drive**, which meanders around the Monterey Peninsula, via the **Del Monte Forest**, to Pacific Grove. Because all the roads in the Del Monte Forest are privately owned, travelers on the 17-Mile Drive must pay a fee to the Pebble Beach Company (note: no motorcycles allowed). Close to the **Ghost Tree** cypress, a big stone mansion looks like something seen in a lightning flash which cleaves the midnight darkness of the Scottish moors.

The attitude of the Pebble Beach Company toward tourists seems more than a little condescending, however. Along its exclusive golf courses are many signs warning visitors that trespassing on the course is a misdemeanor punishable by a fine and imprisonment. At the famous **Lone Cypress**, a single gnarled and windswept tree near the top of a huge wave-battered rock, the sign on the protective fence reads: "No Trespassing Beyond This Point," as if merely being in the forest were a trespass in itself.

Charming Carmel

The southern gateway to the Monterey Peninsula is the town of **Carmel ❸**. A couple of chance factors made Carmel what it is today: starving writers and unwanted painters in flight from the devastation of the 1906 San Francisco earthquake; and canny property developers who, to reduce their taxes, covered the treeless acres with a thick, lush carpet of Monterey pines.

Map, page 112

The result is one of the most endearing seaside towns on the West Coast. When the evening fog rolls in from the bay, the lights inside the cozy houses, combined with the faint whiff of wood smoke from roaring fires, give Carmel the peaceful feeling of an 18th-century European village. Although some 3 or 4 million people visit each year – popularity boosted when actor Clint Eastwood became mayor for a couple of terms – Carmel has resisted any temptation to yield to fast-food franchises and neon signs. The streets, plazas and upscale little shopping malls attract pedestrians to wine shops and antiques stores, art galleries and numerous boutiques. The local market offers good produce, fresh artichokes and racks of wines.

At night, on the side streets, a dozen couples might be dining quietly by candlelight behind dark restaurant windows. In the residential parts of town, the streets meander casually through the forest, sometimes even splitting in two to accommodate an especially praiseworthy specimen of pine. Having said all this, the town is not to everyone's taste. Its sweetness can be cloying, and its plethora of gift shoppes just a little too removed from real life to digest without a healthy touch of irony. Nevertheless, **Carmel Mission** (1770) is definitely worth a visit, and the beach at the bottom of the hill is stunning.

South of Carmel is **Point Lobos State Reserve**, a rocky park overlooking the

BELOW: Carmel is full of antiques shops and quaint bed- and-breakfast inns like this one.

Map,
page 112

sea. Nature trails crisscross the reserve, and big natural rock pools are home to lolling sea lions. Be sure to take water and a picnic: there are no food facilities.

Highway 1 south of Point Lobos begins to swoop and curve in dramatic fashion. The San Lucia Mountains rise steeply to the left; the foamy sea to the right changes shape and color constantly. Only the two-lane road separates the two, which means the curling ribbon of road has its own distinct weather pattern. For this read: fog. Although the sun may be shining brightly on the other side of the mountains, and can often be seen through the trees, Highway 1 can be distinctly chilly (travelers in convertibles or on motorcyles take note), and the fog comes on very quickly, obliterating the world for unexpected moments.

Big Sur

This is a suitably theatrical entrance to **Big Sur ❹**, arguably California's most beautiful stretch of coastline. Its most photogenic site is **Bixby Bridge**, north of Big Sur Village, spanning the steep walls of Bixby Canyon. Until 1945, Big Sur was mainly populated by ranchers, loggers and miners. But soon literary people began turning up, attracted by the idea of living cheaply, growing marijuana in remote canyons and communing with what long-time resident Henry Miller called "the face of the earth as the creator intended it to look." The **Henry Miller Memorial Library** (tel: 831-667 2574), near **Nepenthe** restaurant where everyone goes for sunset, has works by and about this local hero.

BELOW:
rustic retreat.
RIGHT: Bixby Bridge, Big Sur, was called an engineering marvel in 1932.

Big Sur Village is really little more than a huddle of shops and a post office. Places to stay in Big Sur are scarce, and if planning a weekend visit, book early for any of them. There's a couple of campsites, a couple of motels and inns, and a couple of beautiful but pricy hot-tub-and-fireplace country inns, usually described in glossy travel brochures as "hedonistic hideaways" and "sensuous, sumptuous and serene." Notable among them are the **Ventana Inn** (tel: 800-628 6500) and the **Post Ranch Inn** (tel: 831-667 2200), designed by local architect Mickey Muennig. South of Big Sur Village, Highway 1 winds past several state parks, including stunning **Julia Pfeiffer Burns State Park**, with its twisting nature trails and silvery waterfall, and the entrance to 1960s alternative haven the **Esalen Institute**, before ending 16 miles (25 km) north of **Hearst Castle ❺** (*see page 166*).

Beyond Hearst Castle, Highway 1 branches off to hug the coast passing close to **Morro Bay**, dominated by a 576-ft (176-meter) rock just offshore. To take the fast track back to San Francisco, turn at Morro Bay onto State 41, which eventually joins US 101.

Heading north, US 101 passes through the town of **King City ❻**; to **Pinnacles National Monument ❼** with its ruined mission on the fringes not far from **Soledad ❽** and on to **Gilroy ❾**, best known for its Garlic Festival. If Big Sur has made you long for the coast, head for **Año Nuevo State Reserve ❿**, off Highway 1, 20 miles (32 km) north of Santa Cruz near the San Mateo-Santa Cruz county line. Here, whiskered and roly-poly elephant seal pups are born in January, when entire seal families are visible from lookout points along the beachfront. It's a popular sight, however, so book a place in October for this unique natural spectacle. ❑

HEARST CASTLE AT SAN SIMEON

Tycoon William Randolph Hearst was larger than life and so is his mansion. Indeed, it is so lavish that it is often referred to as "Hearst Castle"

After Disneyland, California's most visited site is the baroque home that newspaper and movie tycoon William Randolph Hearst *(left)* had built for himself by his favorite architect, Julia Morgan. Craftsmen labored for 28 years to create *La Cuesta Encantada*, "the Enchanted Hill," with its acres of gardens, terraces, pools and walkways.

It was Hearst's father George, a multimillionaire from his gold, silver and copper mines, who first acquired the 275,000-acre (111,300-hectare) ranch. On his parents' death, the younger Hearst hired Morgan to design the highly ornate twin-towered main house which ended up with 38 bedrooms (some high up in the elegant belltowers), a Gothic dining room, two swimming pools and three sumptuous guest houses.

Next, he stocked the grounds with animals from all over the world, and filled the buildings with carvings, furnishings and works of art from European castles and cathedrals. To hide from view a water tank on the adjoining hill, Hearst had 6,000 pine trees planted.

Hearst, who at his death in 1951 owned the country's largest newspaper chain, and was the subject of Orson Welles's 1941 movie *Citizen Kane*, lived in his 130-room hill-top mansion at San Simeon for 20 years until 1947, when ill health caused him to move to Beverly Hills. Ten years later the Hearst Corporation deeded the San Simeon property to the state of California, where it is an historical monument.

Hearst Castle, 750 Hearst Castle Road, San Simeon, reservations required, tel: 1-800-444 4445, many tours most days; admission charge.s

△ **UNDERWATER ROMANCE**
The indoor Roman swimming pool took over three years to build. Replete with decorative tiles in Venetian glass and hammered gold, the pool room is big enough to house twin tennis courts on its roof.

◁ **WORKS OF ART**
In addition to statues, paintings and tapestries, Hearst's collection included oriental rugs, Navajo blankets, furniture, silver and stained glass.

△ **NEPTUNE POOL**
This enormous outdoor pool was the favorite among the castle's guests. Marble colonnades and white marble statues front an impressive Greco-Roman temple facade

◁ **CASTLE IN THE CLOUDS**
Perched up so high, San Simeon is often wreathed in fog. All supplies were brought up the coast by steamer, then had to be hauled up the hill.

▽ **THE ASSEMBLY ROOM**
This lavish room is 85 ft (26 meters) long and constructed around a 400-year-old carved wooden ceiling from Italy.

HOLLYWOOD HIGHLIFE

Virtually every weekend San Simeon welcomed moviedom's elite. A special train with a jazz band and open bar from Glendale station brought the party guests 210 miles (338 km) from Hollywood to San Luis Obispo, where limousines transported them through the estate's grounds filled with lions, bears, ostriches, elephants, pumas and leopards. On arrival at the floodlit mansion, each was allocated a personal maid or valet and was free to wander – except for a mandatory attendance at the late-night dinner. There were also special occasions: among the hundred guests who attended a covered wagon party were the Warner Brothers, the Gary Coopers and William Powell.

"The society people always wanted to meet the movie stars so I mixed them together," wrote actress Marion Davies *(above)*, Hearst's longtime mistress. "Jean Harlow came up quite frequently. She was very nice and I liked her. She didn't have an awful lot to say… all the men used to flock around her. She was very attractive in an evening dress because she never wore anything under it." Clark Gable was another regular guest. "Women were always running after him but he'd just give them a look as if to say 'how crazy these people are' and he stayed pretty much to himself."

▷ **THE REFECTORY**
Most nights the publisher would preside over dinner at the 16th-century monastery table *(right)* where catsup from bottles and the absence of tablecloths preserved the illusion of "camping out." Liquor was strictly banned (so guests drank in their rooms). After dinner Hearst often showed an as yet unreleased movie; *Gone With the Wind*, for example, was screened six months before its December 1939 premiere.

MARIN COUNTY

Map, page 152

One reason why San Francisco is so popular lies just across the Golden Gate Bridge. Here are pristine forests, pretty beaches and old-fashioned towns that lend themselves to strolling

San Francisco

Los Angeles

For decades San Franciscans have been quietly passing lazy Saturday and Sunday afternoons in the upscale, windswept towns of Marin County, where the trappings of city life seem to fall away as soon as you cross the Golden Gate Bridge. Small wonder: life here seems to fall into a cycle of great repose. In this sparsely populated landscape, you find your way around on two-lane roads, braking sometimes for deer. Dine in old-fashioned, uncrowded restaurants, and sleep in charming bed and breakfasts. Sift for sand dollars on lonely beaches and hike on mossy wilderness paths. Lean into the salt spray and watch the waves pound the rocks. Venture inland into the hillside neighborhoods, and you come across more than a few redwood cottages with stained-glass windows. Is this place for real?

Hot-tub heaven

Encircling San Francisco Bay from the north, and lying at the tip of a metropolitan area of some 5 million inhabitants, Marin County is home to tens of thousands of acres of pristine coastline, unspoiled redwood groves and mountain meadows, untrammeled by development. This luxurious green belt offers seemingly limitless options for hikers and nature-lovers, as well as those following the self-gratifying regimen of hot tubs, relaxing massages and good food that the stereotypically upscale Marin lifestyle affords.

We don't know for sure what the hot-tub-per-capita ratio is currently, but what will remain constant is that the county offers some of the finest scenic and outdoor experiences anywhere around.

In recent years, **Mount Tamalpais ❽** has become a weekend traffic jam of hikers, mountain bikers, and runners. Still, there seems to be enough beauty to go around. Over 30 miles (48 km) of trails wind their way through 6,000 acres (2,430 hectares), as well as many more miles of hiking in the contiguous watershed lands. (Biker-hiker relations have soured in the past few years. If you're walking, watch your step. If you're riding, beware: bike cops now issue speeding tickets even on the mountain.)

On Mount Tam's lower elevations, often shrouded in fog, are stands of virgin redwood. Above, the mountain's chaparral-covered high slopes jut proudly into the sunshine, overlooking San Francisco Bay and the Pacific. It's a fantastic sight.

At the very base of Mount Tamalpais is wonderful, woodsy **Muir Woods National Monument ❾**. At the turn of the 20th century, the Marin Water District planned to condemn a property called Redwood Canyon, cut the timber on it, and with the profits build a dam and reservoir. The scheme so appalled one wealthy

PRECEDING PAGES: a California dreamlife. **LEFT:** sailing past Sausalito. **BELOW:** Muir Woods.

MUIR WOODS NATIONAL MONUMENT
NATIONAL PARK SERVICE DEPARTMENT OF INTERIOR

Elephant statue in Vina Del Mar Park, Sausalito.

Marinite, named William Kent, that he bought the land outright, then cleverly deeded the redwood stand to the government, who turned it into a national monument. Kent modestly declined to have the monument named after him, out of deference to his old friend, naturalist John Muir.

About 1 million tourists a year visit the giant sequoia trees here, which grow to 200 ft (61 meters) in height, 16 ft (5 meters) in diameter, live up to 1,000 years, and are spread out through Muir Woods' 300-plus acres (120 hectares). Energetic walkers might be advised to leave parked cars behind and head up the steep slope of Mount Tam on the **Ben Johnson Trail** through deeply shaded glens rife with ferns and mushrooms, past ever-changing groves of bay, tan oaks, madrona and nutmeg.

Headlands

Beyond Mount Tam, Marin County's green belt extends some 50 miles (80 km) to the distant tip of Point Reyes National Seashore. The coastal country, known as the **Marin Headlands** (easily accessible off Highway 1 just north of the Golden Gate Bridge), has miles of coastal and beach-bound trails. Stellar views can be had by driving up the Fort Baker Road. **Stinson Beach**, at the foot of Mount Tamalpais, is San Francisco's favorite playground, popular among anglers hoping to hook surf perch and rockfish, and among bird watchers who want to spy such out-of-the-way creatures as the sooty shearwater, brown pelican, Western grebe, killdeer and millet. When the fog pulls back, the beach also attract hordes of sunbathers. Stinson gets especially crowded on fine weekends, or when sweltering inland weather drives home-dwellers as near to the sea as it's possible to get.

BELOW: view of San Francisco and the bay from Mount Tamalpais.

Point Reyes

A triangular peninsula, **Point Reyes** is separated from the rest of the world by the main fissure line of the San Andreas Fault, which is nudging Point Reyes northeast at an average rate of 2 inches (5 cm) a year. This 65,000-sq-mile (105-sq.km) seashore park, which draws over 2 million visitors a year, is one of the most frequented of the country's national parks.

Add quaint inns and diners in the little towns of **Inverness** and **Point Reyes Station**, and it seems as close to untouched paradise as you can get. (Word to the wise: avoid the weekend crowds.) The epicenter of the 1906 San Francisco earthquake was a half-mile from where the main park headquarters now stands on Bear Valley Road. On **Earthquake Trail**, visitors can see where the quake moved one old stone fence a distance of at least 15 ft (5 meters).

To get to the park headquarters and most of the trailheads in the National Seashore, drivers must travel up State Highway 1 past the town of **Olema** to Bear Valley Road. The park is open only to those who are willing to walk or ride a horse. The terrain is varied; much of it very steep. Gloomy forests suddenly open on lush, sweeping meadows. The coast is rockbound with occasional pocket beaches. Hikers may see owls, foxes, raccoons, bobcats, deer and almost every kind of bird imaginable, especially herons, egrets and ducks.

A hike up wind-whipped, 1,400-ft (427-meter) **Mount Wittenberg** rewards out-of-breath hikers with a truly breathless view of the California coast: green-black forests and golden meadows that roll down to a coastline the eye tracks for miles without seeing a soul. Below is **Drakes Beach**, where the famous Elizabethan sea captain Sir Francis Drake is said to have set ashore in 1579 for ship repairs.

At the tip of the Point Reyes promontory perches a **lighthouse** which warns ships away from the treacherous coast. One of the foggiest places in Marin County, it usually has no view at all. When the fog lifts and at the right season, however, it is a good place from which to spot migrating whales.

On the northern edge of the seashore, Pierce Point Road meanders around to several beaches – **Abbotts**, **Kehoe**, and the most ruggedly dramatic, **McClures**. These beaches are not recommended for swimming because of the danger of sharks, undertow and rip tides. Better to head for Drakes Beach on the southern side, which is somewhat protected from winds.

Sausalito

With the lighter regimen in mind, the first – or last – stop for most Marin visitors is **Sausalito** ⑪, tucked inside the bay to the east behind the Golden Gate. There is a ferry service to the Sausalito dock from San Francisco. The waterside shops, the warrens of pricey but perfect boutiques, and the houses perched behind them on a steep slope draw inevitable comparisons to Mediterranean *villes* of the Riviera. The Spanish word *saucelito* (meaning "little willow") is said to have been the name's origin. There is, in fact, very little to do in Sausalito except stroll around, have lunch or dinner in one of the restaurants – California Cuisine a specialty – and admire all the boats and pretty people. ❑

Map, page 152

BELOW: the streets of Sausalito.

WINE COUNTRY

Although wine is grown all over the state, it is the Napa
and Sonoma Valleys that personify California
Wine Country for most visitors

Map,
page 178

S tanding on the summit of Mount St Helena, you can see the vast expanse of emerald vineyards of Napa, Sonoma, Mendocino and Lake counties stretching for miles below your feet. From the redwood groves surrounding the Russian River to the burgundy-hued Mendocino ridges, the Northern California vineyards are renowned for producing some of the finest wines in the world. The area owes its premier grapes to the excellent growing conditions found here: temperate climate and rich, drainable soil.

In fact, there is no one California wine county. Wine grapes are grown in most of California's counties, and the northern wineries produce just a fraction of the state's total output. Most of the remaining grapes come from the hot, arid San Joaquin Valley, several hundred miles south, and are often used to make modestly priced "jug" wines.

Some vintners have discovered pockets of land in California that can match the growing conditions of the great north, among them Monterey's Gavilan Mountain foothills, the south-central coast in San Luis Obispo and Santa Barbara counties, and the Temecula Valley outside San Diego. But when most people think of California Wine Country, they think of the areas discussed here: the Napa and Sonoma valleys. *(For more on wine, see pages 70–71.)*

PRECEDING PAGES:
winery wedding.
LEFT: grapepickers.
BELOW: stained
glass in Sonoma.

First vintage

The first wine-makers in California were 18th-century Spanish missionaries who used wine in religious ceremonies. Father Junípero Serra, who founded the state's earliest mission in San Diego in 1769, had no taste for California's indigenous wild grapes and instead imported quality vines from his native Spain. Large-scale vineyards were established around the Los Angeles area in the 1830s by Jean-Louis Vignes, a French vintner. Vignes's wine operation lasted until 1862; after that, California's first commercial vineyards closed and were swallowed by Los Angeles' expanding suburbs.

In the north, it was two men – Father Jose Altimira, founder of the Mission San Francisco de Solano at Sonoma, and General Vallejo, who colonized Sonoma and Napa counties with land grants to his relatives and friends – who first dabbled in California wine-making. But it was Count Agoston Haraszthy who pushed the Sonoma region into wine stardom.

Haraszthy, a flamboyant Hungarian political refugee, began Buena Vista, Northern California's oldest winery, in 1857. He trekked across Europe to cull wine-grape cuttings for California's growers. Ever restless, Haraszthy migrated to Nicaragua, but his career there was unfortunately short-lived; he was killed and eaten by alligators.

He wasn't forgotten, however. One of Haraszthy's

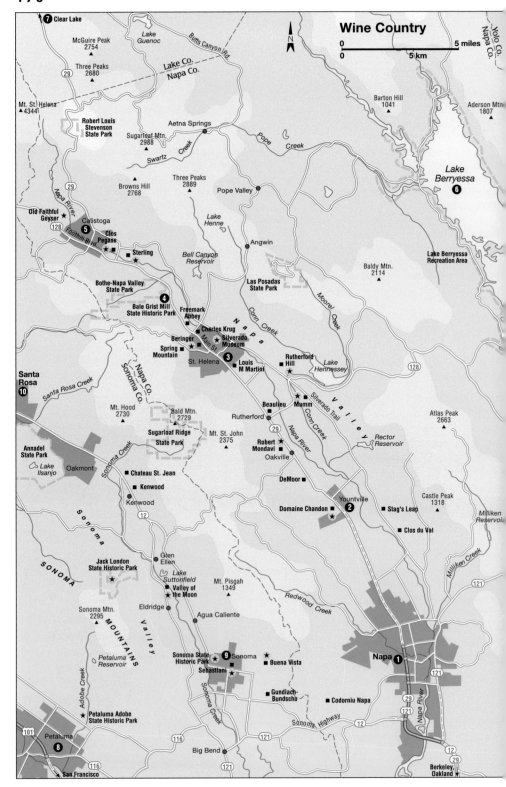

Wine Country

0   5 miles
0   5 km

Yolo Co. / Napa Co.

Clear Lake 7

McGuire Peak 2754
Lake Guenoc
Butts Canyon Rd.

Three Peaks 2680
29

Lake Co. / Napa Co.

Barton Hill 1041

Aderson Mtn 1807

Mt. St. Helena 4344
Robert Louis Stevenson State Park
Aetna Springs
Pope Creek

Sugarloaf Mtn. 2988
Swartz Creek

Lake Berryessa 6

Napa River
29
Browns Hill 2768
Three Peaks 2889
Pope Valley

Old Faithful Geyser
Calistoga 5
128
Foothill Blvd.
Clos Pegase
Sterling

Lake Henne
Angwin

Baldy Mtn. 2114

Lake Berryessa Recreation Area

Bothe-Napa Valley State Park
Bale Grist Mill State Historic Park 4
Freemark Abbey
Charles Krug
Beringer
Spring Mountain
St. Helena 3
Silverado Museum
Louis M Martini
Rutherford Hill
Lake Hennessey

Bell Canyon Reservoir
Las Posadas State Park

Napa Valley

Moorel Creek
Corn Creek

128

Santa Rosa 10
Santa Rosa Creek
Napa Co. / Sonoma Co.

Mt. Hood 2730
Bald Mtn. 2729
Mt. St. John 2375

Beaulieu
Mumm
Rutherford
Silverado Trail

Atlas Peak 2663

Annadel State Park
Lake Ilsanjo
Oakmont
Sonoma Creek
Sugarloaf Ridge State Park

Chateau St. Jean
Kenwood
Kenwood
12

Robert Mondavi
Oakville
29
Napa River
Corn Creek

Rector Reservoir

DeMoor

Yountville 2
Domaine Chandon
Stag's Leap
Clos du Val

Castle Peak 1318
Milliken Reservoir

S o n o m a   M o u n t a i n s
SONOMA

Jack London State Historic Park
Glen Ellen
Lake Suttonfield
Valley of the Moon
Mt. Pisgah 1349
Redwood Creek

Milliken Creek
121

Sonoma Mtn. 2295
Eldridge
Agua Caliente

S o n o m a   V a l l e y

Napa 1
121

Petaluma Reservoir
Adobe Creek

Sonoma State Historic Park 9
Sonoma
Sebastiani
Buena Vista
Gundlach-Bundschu
Codorniu Napa

Napa River
29
121

Sonoma Highway
12

Petaluma Adobe State Historic Park

101
Petaluma 8
116

116
Big Bend
121

San Francisco

Sonoma Creek

12
29
Berkeley/ Oakland

protégés, Charles Krug, a German political exile, opened Napa Valley's first commercial winery in 1861. And by the 1880s, valley wines were winning medals in Europe. The advent of Prohibition nearly decimated this blossoming industry. Following repeal of Prohibition in 1933, Beaulieu Vineyard's Georges de Latour, the Mondavi family and others began resurrecting the wine industry.

Map, page 178

In the 1960s, a wine boom began as large corporations marketed vintage-dated varietal wines at reasonable prices, and small, privately owned wineries produced more expensive, estate-bottled wines at higher costs. Old-time wine-making families were joined by oil barons, engineers, doctors and actors who revitalized old wineries and opened new ones. Many vintners began exploring the regions beyond the Napa-Sonoma valleys and they established premier wineries elsewhere. By 1976, California wines were beating French vintages in European tastings.

Napa County

Wineries, delicatessens, restaurants and country inns lie close together in compact **Napa Valley** and the town of **Napa ❶** (*napa* meaning "plenty" in the local Indian dialect). Although rural, the area's mix of San Francisco socialites, titled Europeans, semi-retired Hollywood directors and producers gives Napa County a genteel, wealthy, if sometimes slick, aura.

A 30-mile (48-km) thrust of flat land between the pine-forested Mayacamas Mountains and the buff-colored Howell Mountains, the Napa Valley is pinched off in the north by **Mount St Helena**. The valley's expanses of vineyards are broken up by farmhouses, stone wineries and a series of towns stretched along State Highway 29, "The Great Wine Way." Strict land-control measures have

ABOVE AND BELOW: grapes: after and before.

A WINE PRIMER

Wines begin at the crusher, where the juice is freed from the grapes. Red wines are created when the grape skin and pulp are put into the fermenting tank, where yeast is added to convert sugar to alcohol and carbon dioxide. Grape skins are pressed to extract more juice, then the reds are aged in stainless steel or wooden tanks. The wine is clarifed, then aged further before bottling.

White wines are made from the fermentation of the juice alone, drawn off from the grapes immediately after crushing. Yeast is added, and fermentation occurs in stainless steel tanks. Leaving the yeast in creates very dry wines; stopping yeast action makes sweeter wines. Champagne, or sparkling wine, begins the same way, then undergoes a second fermentation. The carbon dioxide is trapped within the bottle, hence the heady bubbles.

Most wineries are open 10am–4pm daily; some are by appointment only. It's a good idea to try a tour (usually 1–2 hours) and a tasting at one of the larger wineries, then follow that up with tasting-room stops at a few of the smaller wineries. For more information and a list of local wineries, contact Napa Valley Tourist Information at 1310 Napa Town Center, tel: 707-226 7459 and Sonoma Valley Tourist Information, 453 1st Street E., tel: 707-996 1090.

kept valley development confined to the towns and the freeway south of Yountville, but these have also escalated land prices.

With the exception of the excellent **Copia** *(see page 71)*, the town of Napa is mainly an administrative center, so wine country itself begins in earnest at **Yountville ❷**, where the vineyards abut the village's renovated brick and stone buildings. Yountville's city-park picnic stop is across from George Yount's grave at the pioneer cemetery. One of General Vallejo's beneficiaries, Yount received his huge land grant for roofing Vallejo's Petaluma adobe – surely one of history's most lucrative contracting deals. **Domaine Chandon Winery** (tel: 707-944 2280) just west of town is French throughout; in deference to Gallic law, the champagne is called sparkling wine. The winery, owned by Chandon of Moët and Chandon fame, makes sparkling wine in the *méthode champenoise*; that is, it is fermented in the same bottle from which it is poured. The outdoor restaurant is good, too. Just north of Oakville is the **Robert Mondavi Winery** (tel: 707-968 2000), a sleek operation, as befits such a famous local name. Guided tours only.

St Helena

The undisputed capital of the Napa Valley is **St Helena ❸**, noted for its 40 (or thereabouts) wineries, historic stone buildings, picnic parks, chic shops, pricey hotels and the CIA *(see page 71)*. The **Silverado Museum** is stuffed with Robert Louis Stevenson memorabilia – collectables like first editions of his work and souvenirs of his global jaunts. South of town, the **Louis M. Martini Winery** (tel: 707-963 2736), run by one of the valley's oldest wine-making clans, offers reasonably priced wines in an unpretentious setting. Two historic wineries lie just north of St Helena. Jacob and Frederick started the **Beringer Vineyards**

BELOW: the Rhine House at Beringer Vineyards.

(tel: 707-963 7115) in 1876, modeling the Rhine House (1883) after their ancestral estate in Mainz, Germany. They dug limestone caves for ageing wine. Today's winery, owned by Foster's (yes, the Australian beer people), features Fumé Blanc and Cabernet Sauvignon in the mansion tasting room. Outside, spacious lawns and a regal row of elms fronts the winery. The building of the other founding father, **Charles Krug Winery** (tel: 707-963 5057), dates from 1874. The lavish Greystone building nearby was the world's largest stone winery when it was erected in 1889 by mining magnate William Bourn; today, the mansion is run by the California headquarters of the **Culinary Institute of America**, a brilliant cooking school with a restaurant that is open to visitors (professional chefs). To clear your head and take a break from wine tasting, the **Bale Grist Mill State Historic Park ❹** is 3 miles (5km) north of St Helena.

Map, page 178

Between Bale Grist and the town of Calistoga are two excellent places to stop: **Sterling Vineyards** (tel: 707-942 3344) – part-Spanish mission, part-fantasy – reigns over the upper valley atop a knoll. A tram whisks visitors 300 ft (91 meters) up for a self-guided tour. The tram fee is applicable toward the purchase of Sauvignon Blanc and other wines. Close by is **Clos Pegase** (tel: 707-942 4981), designed in 1986 by architect Michael Graves in sleek, modern style. Clos Pegase is known almost as much for its art collection as for its wines.

Domaine Chandon has landscaped grounds and a museum devoted to champagne.

The one-street town of **Calistoga ❺** is a gem; wooden hangings shading the shopfronts give it a Wild West feel. In fact, Calistoga is a spa town, rich in mineral springs and hot, therapeutic mud. A variety of low-key treatment centers are scattered around town, busy making beautiful Californians even more beautiful. Two miles (3 km) north of town, **Old Faithful Geyser** (tel: 707-942 6463) spouts jets of boiling water high into the sky every so often. Although the tickets are somewhat expensive for what takes place, there are tables inside the little waiting area, so you can have a pleasant picnic while waiting for the water to take off. Just west is the disappointing **Petrified Forest**, where redwoods were turned to stone millions of years ago.

BELOW: lake walk at Chateau Montelena near Calistoga.

Calistoga is surrounded by wineries, far too many to mention. Of note for its historic (1882) lakeside setting with a Chinese feel, however, is **Chateau Montelena** (tel: 707-942 5105), which produces classic Chardonnay and Cabernet Sauvignon. A limited number of reservations are accepted for the picnic sites on Jade Lake in view of the pagoda; if you're an organized kind of wine drinker, booking one of these in advance of a visit would be well worthwhile.

The Silverado Trail

Running alongside State 29 between the towns of Napa and Calistoga, the **Silverado Trail** joins with the highway as the route into Lake County's resort and wine region. Built as the road from Mount St Helena's cinnabar mines to Napa's river docks, it is an elevated, two-lane road above the valley floor offering panoramic views, uncrowded wineries (most with picnic areas) and hidden valleys deep in the Howell Mountains. **Stag's Leap**, a rocky promontory near Yountville where a 16-point Roosevelt elk once plunged to its death, overlooks the award-winning **Stags' Leap Wine Cellars** (tel: 707-944 2020) and **Clos du Val** (tel: 707-259 2200).

Towards St Helena, a popular stop is the **Rutherford Hill Winery** (tel: 707-963 7194), an ark-like structure with picnic grounds and Chardonnay, Cabernet Sauvignon and Zinfandel wines.

St Helena is also the turn-off to a warm-water paradise. The tragedy-ridden Berryessa family lost sons and soil in the Mexican War; today, their Napa land grant is better known as **Lake Berryessa ❻**, reached via State 128 from St Helena or State 121 from Napa. Fishermen pull in trout, bass and catfish, while sailors, waterskiers, campers and swimmers have their choice of several resorts around this lake, which has more shoreline than Lake Tahoe.

Wine-making has attracted a wide variety of people from all over the US.

Back on State 29 and past **Robert Louis Stevenson State Park,** the road heads towards **Lake County** and its bold, friendly, visitor-seeking wineries scattered around **Clear Lake ❼**, California's largest natural lake. (Lake Tahoe lies partly in Nevada.) Besides producing Cabernet Sauvignon, Zinfandel and Sauvignon Blanc grapes, Lake County is famous for Bartlett pears and walnuts. Resorts and campgrounds ring the lake, and there's good walking in **Clear Lake State Park** at the foot of conical **Mount Konocti**, an extinct volcano.

Sonoma County

A patchwork of country roads, towns, orchards, ridges and hills is an apt description of Sonoma, west of Napa and only about one hour's (jam-free) drive from San Francisco. US 101, the wine country's only freeway, traverses the north-south length of **Sonoma County**, entering it near **Petaluma ❽**. The freeway continues on through Santa Rosa, Healdsburg (gateway to the Alexander, Dry Creek and Russian River valleys) and Cloverdale, which is located on the Mendocino County border.

BELOW: olive oil is now the region's second produce.

The **Sonoma Valley** is steeped in wine, wineries (about 35), literary and political history. *Sonoma* is a native Patwin word meaning "Land of Chief Nose," after an Indian leader with a prominent proboscis. Vallejo romanticized it as the "Valley of the Moon," and author Jack London took up the call with a book about frazzled urbanites rejuvenated by clean country living. State 12 runs the length of the valley, passing through the towns of Sonoma and Kenwood.

Father Altimira founded California's last mission, **San Francisco de Solano**, in 1823. Vallejo set up the town in 1835, making **Sonoma ❾** the northernmost outpost of a Catholic, Spanish-speaking realm that, at its peak, extended all the way to the tip of South America. It briefly became a republic after the Bear Flag Revolt in 1846, when Americans stormed Vallejo's home. Haraszthy's winemaking innovations at Buena Vista Winery a decade later forced residents to recognize the region's vinicultural potential. The **Sonoma Plaza**, the largest in California, today dominates this attractive town. Several restored adobes ring the plaza and nearby streets, including the mission, Vallejo's old house **Lachryma Montis** and the **Sonoma Barracks**, all known as the **Sonoma State Historic Park**. The town is a pleasant place, relaxed and well-heeled.

Two blocks from the plaza stand **Sebastiani Vineyards** (tel: 800-888 5532, ext. 3230), some of the land dating from mission days. This winery is one of the largest and most popular in Sonoma and is still in the hands of the Sebastiani family. East of Sonoma, **Buena Vista Winery** (tel: 800-926 1266) has old-style connections with Count Haraszthy. South of town, the Gundlach and Bundschu families were involved in wine-making for more than 125 years. Nearby, the pricey, beautifully decorated **Fairmont Sonoma Mission Inn and Spa** (tel: 707-938 9000) offers health and fitness facilities (with its own source of thermal mineral water), and tasty meals.

St Francis Winery (tel: 800-543 7713) opened an expansive mission-style visitor's center in 2001. Those in the know stop by to purchase a bottle of the Pagani Vineyard Zinfandel Reserve made with grapes from 100 year-old vines. North on State 1 are two fine wineries in Kenwood. **Kenwood Winery** (tel: 707-833 5891) features Zinfandel, Cabernet Sauvignon and Chenin Blanc. Chardonnay lovers head for **Château St Jean** (tel: 707-833 4134), with its medieval-style tower and fine Johannisberg Riesling.

Famed botanist Luther Burbank picked the area around **Santa Rosa ❿** on State 12 as "the chosen spot of all the earth" to conduct his plant experiments. He developed more than 800 new plants, including many fruits, vegetables and flowers, yet relished few of them except asparagus. Visitors can tour the **Luther Burbank Home and Gardens** (home open only certain days April to October, but the gardens are open all year round). Children will want to head for Santa Rosa's **Snoopy's Gallery**, selling the widest range of Snoopy products in the world, thanks to the fame of Santa Rosaite and dog creator Charles Schultz.

The town's trinity of adjoining parks form a 5,000-acre (12,000-hectare) urban oasis with a children's amusement park and lake in **Howarth Park**; camping, picnicking and boating in **Spring Lake Park**; and hiking and equestrian trails in **Annadel State Park**. ❏

Map, page 178

BELOW: Sonoma; the word means Land of Chief Nose.

SACRAMENTO

*California's state capital was an important cutural center
even before the discovery of gold made it a mecca
for miners hell-bent on making fortunes*

Map, page 112

E ven as the state's capital city, Sacramento has always lived in the long shadows of prominence and popularity cast by San Francisco and Los Angeles. Located about two hours north of San Francisco, nestled in the middle of California's 500-mile (805-km) long Central Valley, this once hot and dusty cow town has endured the same dubious distinction that author Gertrude Stein once bestowed on the city of Oakland: there is no *there*, there. At one time, there was at least *gold* to be found here, which was what first put Sacramento on the map. A town called John Sutter's New Helvetia Colony did exist here earlier, but it wasn't until 1848, when James Marshall discovered gold deposits in the nearby Sierra foothills, that it became a substantial draw for gold rush settlers.

The town grew up where the American and Sacramento rivers join, where steamers from San Francisco let off passengers headed for the gold fields. From the ensuing Gold Rush emerged Sacramento, which had been named the state capital in 1845. Sacramento was also the western terminus of the Pony Express, then later of the Transcontinental Railroad.

Today, the area surrounding **Sacramento** ❶ (population 407,000), is home to more than a million people, countless industrial parks, spacious, tree-lined parks, expansive shopping malls, suburban tracts and a tangle of multi-lane highways that joins it all together. But even when the locals speak about going to "the city," they often mean San Francisco. Until comparatively recently, in fact, Sacramento was the ultimate cow town, a nice, big, prosperous, comfortable, tree-shaded cow town.

PRECEDING PAGES: exhibit from the Railroad Museum. **LEFT:** California State Capitol. **BELOW:** Governor's Mansion.

High temperatures

In contrast to its glamorous coastal neighbor, Sacramento is a blazing furnace in midsummer, with temperatures often passing 100°F (38°C) for days at a time. But the weather can still be pleasant, as humidity is low, it seldom rains for long, and the prevailing wind is a marine breeze from San Francisco Bay that cools the nights. In the winter, the city, which lays low in the 150-mile (240-km) long Sacramento Valley, is a resting bed for thick tule fog (a type of ground fog peculiar to the Central Valley), which, like the summer sun, can last for many weeks.

In recent years, Sacramento has joined the ranks of progressive, major-league US cities, becoming a serious player in Pacific Rim trade, as well as the smallest American city to build a light-rail commuter transit line. Sacramento also added a National Basketball Association franchise, the Kings, to its entertainment line-up, and, in 1989, became the first American city to close a nuclear power plant by a vote of the people.

Beneath the imposing facade of Sacramento's mirrored-glass office buildings and slightly away from all the traffic lies a distinct image of the old West. Tucked just

Old Sacramento: both the Pony Express and the Transcontinental Railroad stopped here on the way to San Francisco.

BELOW: reliving the Wild West.

below the fork of the Sacramento and Americans rivers is **Old Sacramento**, where the old Pony Express and Transcontinental Railroad stations have been fully restored. Stop off at the **Visitor's Center** (1608 I Street, tel: 800-292 2334) for a list of the sites, which include the **California State Railroad Museum**, with over 50 restored engines; the **Discovery Museum's Gold Rush History Center**, a reproduction of the 1854 City Hall and Water Works building; and the **Crocker Art Museum**, the oldest art museum west of the Mississippi River, with its constantly changing exhibits and its pleasant, relaxed ambience. The **Golden State Museum** is a fascinating mix of treasures from the California State Archives and cutting-edge multimedia exhibits like the holographic image of naturalist John Muir arguing his environmental stance. In another gallery, earthquake sites and fault lines lit by lasers zigzig ominously across the state when a button is pressed on a 12-ft (4-meter) long topographical map.

Elsewhere in downtown Sacramento you'll find the interesting and nicely restored **California State Capitol**, which is surrounded by the 40-acre (16-hectare) **Capitol Park**. This manicured arboretum has a vast collection of California flora and examples of plants from many different climates and continents. A 400-seat IMAX theater, next to the **Convention Center**, is a popular attraction. Daily tours of the Capitol building are offered on the hour. Also, while Downtown, don't miss the handsome, old **Governor's Mansion**, an 1877 Victorian building where 13 California governors lived between 1903 and 1967.

Now almost overtaken by suburbs, **Sutter's Fort** (2701 L Street, tel: 916-445 4422; admission charge) was once one of the most important in the West. It was an employee of John Sutter's who discovered gold in 1848, but 11 years earlier Sutter had already established the fort as a rest stop and refueling station for

immigrants crossing the frontier from the east. The present site, which includes a prison and a bakery, has been reconstructed to give one of the most authentic pictures of pioneer life in the state.

Seasonal events in Sacramento have also lent it big-city prominence. The **Dixieland Jazz Jubilee**, held each May in Old Sacramento, is the world's largest celebration of dixieland jazz, featuring more than 120 bands from around the world. The highlight of the summer is the **California State Fair**, a colorful occasion which attracts thousands of people from all over the county. It runs for around 18 days before Labor Day at California State Exposition, the city's outdoor exposition facility.

River recreations

When the temperature gets too hot to handle, take the cue of thousands of houseboaters, waterskiiers, anglers and sailors, and head south on Highway 5 or 99 toward the **Sacramento River Delta**, where hundreds of miles of interconnected river channels percolate slowly toward San Francisco Bay and the Pacific Ocean. The *Delta King* is a moored 1920s paddle steamer operating as a hotel and restaurant.

This river country contains hundreds of islands; much of the area is accessible only by water. Still, even land-locked car passengers can choose from a variety of charming olde-worlde towns such as **Walnut Grove** ⓬ and Locke.

Locke ⓭, created by Chinese laborers then building the railroads, has a porticoed street with wooden sidewalks that is right out of the Old West. The deepwater port of **Stockton** ⓮, the "Gateway to the Delta," has 1860s homes, the **Haggin Museum**, which is full of local history, and several wineries. ❏

Map, page 112

BELOW: Sutter's Fort was an important cultural center prior to the Gold Rush.

SAN JOAQUIN VALLEY

*The valley is the lifeline of California, while Fresno is the
only community in the United States to be
within an hour's drive of three national parks*

Map,
page 112

San Francisco

Los
Angeles

Stuck between the magnificent California coast and the awe-inspiring
Sierras, the San Joaquin Valley suffers the kind of image problem more
associated with the Midwest than the Golden State.

That's because, in many ways, it *is* the Midwest. Perhaps as many as 500,000
so-called "Okies" – the Dust Bowl victims of the Great Depression that gave
life to John Steinbeck's *The Grapes of Wrath* – migrated here. Like ants on a
honey trail, they piled into overloaded flivvers and streamed west on old Route
66, through the chalk-dry Mojave Desert, past "bum barricades," and the abuse
heaped on them by native Californians.

What became of them? One-eighth of the current California population – or
nearly 3.75 million residents – claim Okie ancestry, and the core of that gritty,
family-based community is still here in the heart of the San Joaquin. Stop by
any town in San Joaquin Valley and, as one Dust Bowl survivor said himself,
"You might as well be in Tulsa or Little Rock or Amarillo… Same music, same
values, same churches, same politics."

LEFT:
working ranch.
BELOW: time
for lunch at the
Fresno County Fair.

The valley

Though its name is often mistakenly applied to California's entire Central Valley,
the San Joaquin comprises just the southern two-thirds
of that 450-mile (720-km) long, 50-mile (80-km) wide
basin. It follows the course of the **San Joaquin River**,
flowing south to north, to the Sacramento-San Joaquin
Delta, where both rivers empty into San Francisco Bay.

Mostly treeless, the valley doesn't at first appear to
offer much to an outsider. Interstate 5, running the
length of it, is the main link between Los Angeles and
the Bay Area, and the east-west routes to Lake Tahoe
and the Sierras all cross the valley. So it can only sell
itself by virtue of being in the middle of it all. Fresno,
for instance, boasts of being the only community in the
United States within little more than an hour's drive of
three national parks.

The San Joaquin *is* known for some unpleasant natural phenomena. Valley fever – a little-known respira-
tory illness – is spread when strong winds stir up the
spores of a fungus indigenous to the arid soil in parts of
the valley. And in December and January, dense "tule"
fog blankets the area for days at a time, making driving
around hazardous.

But its second-class status bothers San Joaquin
Valley residents very little. The business of the valley
is farming, and it succeeds at that like few other spots
on earth. More than half of California's $25 billion a
year in farm goods is produced in the San Joaquin.
Fresno County alone accounts for a significant portion
of that, making it the number-one farming county in

America. The valley's soil, covering more than a million irrigated acres (405,000 hectares), supports some of the most productive farming in the world.

Recently, with substantial growth in population, the area's cities have experienced a boom as commercial and manufacturing centers. But employment in the valley is most closely tied to farming and rainfall, and it is the abundance of that most precious of the state's resources – water – that makes the San Joaquin Valley a recreational as well as an agricultural heartland. Aside from the Sacramento River Delta and the mammoth irrigation projects it supports, several great rivers flow through the area – the San Joaquin, the **Stanislaus**, the **Tuolumne**, the **Merced**, the **Kings** and, farther south, the **Kern**. Most are renowned for outstanding – and occasionally terrifying – stretches of whitewater rafting. This sport is for serious enthusiasts only, but there are gentler stretches of water where the faint-hearted will also feel at home.

It doesn't take long to see that the valley is the lifeline of California. An hour out of San Francisco going eastward, I-580 crosses **Altamont Pass**, one of the windiest spots on the coast. It is marked by an exquisitely rural sight – a wind farm, overhead power lines and dairy cows peacefully coexisting. The wind may be only 16 mph (26 kph) but the turbines are driven at ten times that speed, effortlessly creating electricity. As the descent begins, the highway crosses a branch of the **California Aqueduct**. Almost immediately the freeway is full of trucks hauling bottled tomato catsup, ripe golden melons or crates of canned peaches.

Like much of California, **Modesto ⑮** is the creation of Leland Stanford's Central Pacific Railroad. The Tuolumne River runs almost unnoticed through the southern fringes of town. An early 20th century steel arch along the main thoroughfare promotes the town's virtues: "Water, Wealth, Contentment,

CARDIFF and PEACOCK
Airlines Ltd.

SERVING THE
SAN JOAQUIN
VALLEY

ABOVE:
aviation sticker.
BELOW:
harvesting corn.

Health." As in most of the valley, food is king – not food eating but food producing. A "Gourmet Taste Tour" includes stops at an almond exchange, a mushroom farm, a cheese processor, a Hershey chocolate plant and local wineries.

Halfway between Modesto and Fresno, **Merced ⓰** is a major access point to Yosemite. The biggest attraction Merced can call its own may be **Castle Air Force Base**, where lumbering B-52s provide a somewhat chilling background to the **Castle Air Museum's** collection of vintage fighters.

Map, page 112

Fresno

The sleeping giant of central California is **Fresno ⓱** (population 428,000). From a train station by the edge of a wheat field, it has become a city with 11 freeway exits and rows of high-rises. The financial and cultural, as well as the service and commercial center of the San Joaquin Valley, it is also as ethnically diverse, with large Mexican, Asian, Armenian and Basque communities. Cultural institutions include the **Metropolitan Museum of Art and Science**, the **Community Theater** and the **Fresno Philharmonic Orchestra**.

For people with children **Roeding Park**, right off State 99 in west Fresno, features a number of family amusements – a zoo, a Playland with rides, and Storyland, a quaint walk-through village where plaster fairy-tale figures tell their story. **Woodward Park** in central Fresno has a Japanese Garden and a bird sanctuary. But the most bizarre attraction is **Forestiere Underground Gardens** (reservations required; tel: 559-271 0734). The gardens were once the beloved domicile of sculptor-horticulturist Baldasare Forestiere, a Sicilian immigrant, who single-handedly carved out the maze of 100 rooms, passageways and courtyards over a period of 40 years.   ❑

BELOW: melon farmer displays his produce.

YOSEMITE AND THE HIGH SIERRA

Map, page 112

It's one of America's most visited national parks, which means massive congestion in summer. But, out of season, Yosemite is magnificent and magical

San Francisco

Los Angeles

The idea of getting away from it all can seem like a cruel joke as you stand in yet another line in the crowded valley, the heart of Yosemite. Is this any way to celebrate the park's beauty, jostled and jammed together in a supposed wilderness setting?

Unfortunately, if you're one of the 3½ million annual visitors to its 761,170,917 acres (308,000 hectares) of parkland – most of whom end up in the 7-sq.-mile (11-sq.-km) Yosemite Valley – **Yosemite National Park** ⓲ can certainly feel like any other urban vacation, complete with scarce accommodations, overflowing parking lots, elbow-to-elbow shuttle buses and packed grocery stores. But 94 percent of its area is designated wilderness and, to experience it properly, you have to get out on a trail, preferably one unpaved. Alternatively, visit one of the following parks in those overheated summer months, and visit Yosemite earlier or later in the year. If you do decide to visit during a busy period, book your lodgings six months to one year in advance.

PRECEDING PAGES: sunset over Half Dome, Yosemite. **LEFT:** backpacker in Kings Canyon. **BELOW:** General Sherman Tree, Kings Canyon.

Sequoia and Kings Canyon

It is tempting to dismiss **Sequoia National Park** ⓳ and **Kings Canyon National Park** ⓴ as Yosemite but without Yosemite Valley. Judging from the statistics, many California travelers do just that. In any given year, over 4 million visitors converge on Yosemite; the comparable figure for Sequoia/Kings Canyon is 1.5 million for both parks combined. (Although Sequoia and Kings Canyon were established separately, their areas are administered as one unit, and thought of together.)

Even though 7,000-ft (2,130-meter) deep Kings Canyon exceeds Yosemite Valley in sheer vertical relief, and the sequoia forests of the southern park are larger and more numerous than Yosemite's groves, the absence of waterfalls and striking rock formations make them pale alongside their more celebrated northern cousin. The result is a national park bereft of the most common national park headaches and reason enough for those seeking solitude to beat a hasty path to the entry station.

Much more so than Yosemite, Sequoia/Kings Canyon is a wilderness park, with only two developed areas near its western boundaries. The back-country extends east across the west slopes of the Sierras as far as the crest of the range, encompassing the headwaters of the Kern and San Joaquin rivers and the highest Sierra summits, including Mount Whitney.

Ironically, a majority of the park's mountain trails are most easily reached from trailheads out of Lone Pine,

In 1864, pressure on the legislature resulted in the Yosemite Grant, the first attempt in the nation's history to preserve an area of scenic beauty from exploitation.

Big Pine and Bishop on the Sierra's east side, a 250-mile (400-km) drive from park headquarters near **Three Rivers**. As in Yosemite park, permits are required for overnight back-country camping. The most scenic approach to the Kings Canyon section of the park, State 180, begins in the sprawling agricultural city of Fresno *(see page 193)*. A 52-mile (84-km) drive from there through the Sierra foothills leads to the **General Grant Grove**, a stand of massive 3,000-year-old sequoia trees notable for the wide-open parkland that surrounds their bases.

Thirty-eight miles (61 km) past the Grant Grove (where campground sites are available by advance reservation), State 180 drops into Kings Canyon at **Cedar Grove**. In contrast to Yosemite Valley, this gaping chasm is V- rather than U-shaped; the smaller flow of the **Kings River** has yet to deposit enough alluvium to level out the canyon's floor. Two trailheads lead north and east toward the High Sierra, but the 6,500-ft (1,980-meter) climbs on south-facing (and sun-broiled) slopes are only for the fit and experienced.

After backtracking to Grant Grove, visitors can proceed into the Sequoia section by following State 198 south for 28 miles (45 km) to **Giant Forest**. A short nature trail leads to the **General Sherman Tree**, a redwood much loved by photographers, who like to pose very small persons next to the very tall tree for contrast. The tree is believed to be the earth's largest living thing. In recent years the park has removed many facilities in an attempt to restore the forest floor to its original ecosystem. Giant Forest is the closest thing to an urban center in the area, highlighted by the **Giant Forest Museum**, built to showcase the huge sequoias and the diverse flora and fauna. State 198 continues southward past good camping and boating at **Lake Kaweah**, and drops back into the San Joaquin Valley at **Visalia**, 50 miles (80 km) from the park boundary.

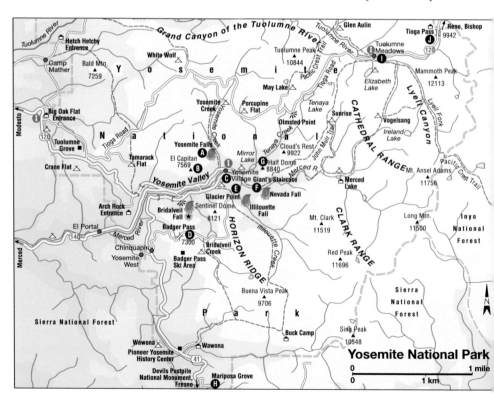

Yosemite National Park

Yosemite: a holy place

A holy place is exactly what Yosemite *(yo-SEH-mih-tee)* Valley was to its origi-nal inhabitants, the indigenous Ahwahneechee. Because of its isolation, the tribe managed to keep its mountain paradise a secret from whites until 1851, a full year after California attained statehood, when the US Cavalry arrived and herd-ed the natives across the Sierras to a barren reservation near Mono Lake. As with much of the American West, subjugation of the Indians paved the way for settlement. During the decade following its "discovery", Yosemite Valley was fenced, farmed and logged by homesteaders.

Later on, with thousands of hotel rooms and campsites, plus supermarkets and even a jail, Yosemite Valley was in danger of becoming a textbook example of overdeveloped parkland. But now stringent measures are being taken to con-trol the crowds, often by eliminating accommodation and parking spaces, and making better use of shuttle buses.

But there's a reason why the crowds come in such numbers. Nowhere else in the world are there so many big waterfalls in such a small area, including 2,425-ft (739-meter) **Yosemite Falls Ⓐ**, the highest in North America. When Ice Age glaciers scoured out 8-mile (13-km) long, mile-wide Yosemite Valley, they left behind several smaller hanging valleys on either side of the main feature, high but not dry conduits for free-leaping torrents whose very names suggest their infinite variety: **Ribbon**, **Bridalveil**, **Silver Strand**, **Staircase**, **Sentinel**, **Lehamite**, **Vernal**, **Nevada**, **Illilouette**.

In early June, one of the rarest of Yosemite sights – the "moonbow" at the foot of lower Yosemite Falls – sometimes appears. It shows up only in the spring, when the falls are running full, and only in the days around the full moon, when

Map, page 198

BELOW: Yosemite Falls; view of Yosemite when first entering the park.

the moonlight shines on the spray from the falls, producing a ghostly rainbow. Visitors should note, however, that the falls is often dry out of season.

"Great is granite," wrote New England clergyman Thomas Starr King in 1878, "and Yosemite is its prophet." As the prehistoric ice floes melted and retreated, they exposed the colossal building blocks of the Sierra Nevada, shaped and polished into scenery on a grand scale – **El Capitan ❸**, **Cathedral Rock**, **Three Brothers**, **Royal Arches**, **Clouds Rest**. In the daredevil world of technical rock climbing, this is the one true mecca.

Getting around

Many feel cars ought to be banned altogether, but in the meantime roads in the east end of the valley near **Mirror Lake** have been restricted to shuttle buses, bicycles and pedestrians. A convoluted one-way traffic pattern almost everywhere else makes driving a masochistic experience, especially in summer. You can arrange to take a guided horseback trip at the valley stables near **Yosemite Village ❻** (the first large developed area on the Yosemite loop road). Bicycles may be rented at the village and at **Yosemite Lodge** (tel: 559-253 5635), and several bikeway trails make two-wheeled travel the most efficient choice of locomotion. Lodging runs the gamut from inexpensive cabins at the village to the palatial suite atop the **Ahwahnee Hotel** (telephone number as above), with Yosemite Lodge somewhere in the middle.

In summer, Yosemite Valley's singular concentration of natural beauty has its far less felicitous human analogue, complete with overcrowded campgrounds, traffic jams and hour-long waits in cafeteria lines. Although the valley comprises only 8 sq. miles (21 sq. km) of the park's 1,189-sq.-mile (3,080-sq.-km)

BELOW: rafting in the park, Yosemite.

area, it plays host to more than 90 percent of all Yosemite's overnight visitors. The best way of seeing Half Dome *(see below)* is during the off-season, September to May. Autumn brings a rich gold to the leaves of the oak trees, and the sun's lowering angle etches the granite domes and spires into sharper relief. Nights are cool, mornings are apple-crisp. Autumn also brings herds of wild deer, migrating to winter forage in the Sierra foothills.

Yosemite Valley is emptiest in winter, when the action shifts to the ski resort of **Badger Pass Ⓓ**, 21 miles (34 km) away and 3,000 ft (900 meters) higher. Badger's gentle, pine-fringed slopes offer few challenges for accomplished skiers, but prove ideal for family groups and novice-to-intermediate skiers who don't mind the 45-minute commute by car or bus from the valley. But spring is the favorite season of many. Wild flowers carpet the meadows, and the roar of wild water resounds throughout the valley.

Glacier Point

To the south, State Highway 41 climbs 9 miles (15 km) to **Chinquapin** junction, where a 15-mile (25-km) paved road departs for **Glacier Point Ⓔ**. From this famed viewpoint, 3,200 ft (975 meters) above the floor of Yosemite Valley, the entire park comes into unforgettable, stomach-clutching focus. No less compelling is the 80-mile (129-km) vista to the east and south, a panorama of lakes, canyons, waterfalls and the rugged peaks of Yosemite's High Sierra. Close at hand are the granite steps of the **Giant's Staircase Ⓕ**, where Vernal and Nevada falls drop the raging waters of the **Merced River** 320 and 594 ft (98 and 181 meters) respectively.

From Glacier Point, **Half Dome Ⓖ** is the most prominent landmark, a great solitary stone thumb thrusting skyward. What became of Half Dome's other half? In fact, the dome never had another half of solid rock, only slabs of granite on the sheer north face that were peeled away like onion skin by advancing Ice Age glaciers.

At the height of glaciation, 250,000 years ago, Glacier Point itself lay under 700 ft (213 meters) of ice, and interpretive markers explain how the 2,000-ft (610-meter) thick Merced and Tenaya glaciers ground down from the high country to merge near Half Dome and hollow out vast Yosemite Valley. The mighty glacier filled the valley to its brim, and extended all the way down the Merced canyon to **El Portal**, 15 miles (24 km) to the west.

Five miles (8 km) south of **Wawona**, just inside the park's southern boundary, a short side road leads to the **Mariposa Grove Ⓗ** of giant sequoias, a preserve containing more than 500 mammoth redwood trees. It was here that John Muir slept under the stars alongside President Theodore Roosevelt, and persuaded the chief executive that the forest should be added to the infant Yosemite National Park. The grove's largest tree, the **Grizzly Giant**, is at least 3,800 years old, 200 ft (60 meters) high and with a girth of 94 ft (29 meters). The best way to experience the trees is on foot, wandering among living things that were already giants when Christ walked the Holy Land.

If Wawona and the Mariposa Grove are Yosemite's

Map, page 198

TIP

Wilderness permits, available free of charge at park ranger stations and visitor centers, are required for *all* overnight trips in the Yosemite backcountry.

BELOW: horseriding is often the best way to get around.

Unlike the camp-grounds on the west side of the Sierra, many on the east do not accept advance reservations. All ask that you respect Smokey the Bear, however, and put out your campfires.

Black Forest, **Tuolumne Meadows ❶** is its Switzerland. Reached by an hour's drive north from Yosemite Valley on the scenic **Tioga Pass ❶**, and situated at 8,600 ft (2,620 meters) above sea level, Tuolumne is the gateway to an alpine wilderness. The only way to see the more remote areas of the back-country is to pick up your feet and hike, with the minimum of creature comforts carried in a backpack that may tip the scales at 50 lbs (23 kg) or more. A less arduous alternative – at least on some of the smoother trails – is to arrange a horse-packing trip, details of which can be discovered locally or by calling Yosemite Park information services on 209-372 8344.

Tuolumne is also the site of **Tuolumne Meadows Lodge**, central star in the summer constellation of high Sierra camps. Arranged roughly in a circle, about 9 miles (14 km) apart, these six permanent tent camps provide lodging, meals and hot showers to hikers and horse-packers on the popular High Sierra Loop trail. Elevations of the camps vary from 7,150 ft (2,180 meters) to 10,300 ft (3,140 meters), and a night of acclimatization in Tuolumne is recommended before departure. In a typical year, camps are open from June 14 through September 1, with advance booking essential.

The Eastern Sierra

Approached from the west, through the foothills of the Gold Country and on into Yosemite or Sequoia and Kings Canyon, the Sierra Nevada begins gently. Low, rolling hills studded with oak trees give way to pine-blanketed higher hills, which in turn give way to an accelerating crescendo of granite domes, spires and ridges. These culminate in the 13,000- and 14,000-ft (4,000- 4,267 meter) peaks of the crest. But there is nothing gradual about the Sierra when approached

BELOW: Lambert Dome and the Tuolumne River, Tioga Road.

from the east, up US 395 from Southern California. On the east side, the mountains of the crest drop precipitously nearly 10,000 vertical ft (3,000 meters) in the space of a few miles, a single great front nearly 200 miles (320 km) long. From **Walker Pass** at the southern end of the range to Tioga Pass on the eastern Yosemite boundary, not a single highway cleaves the scarp, the longest contiguous roadless area in the United States outside Alaska.

Maps, pages 198 & 112

Skiers and devils

At **Deadman Summit**, north of June Mountain, US 395 begins a long descent into Mono Basin, once the site of an inland sea. **Mono Lake ㉑**, the last remnant of that sea, is the oldest continuously existing body of water in North America, and islands near the lake's northern shore are breeding grounds for 90 percent of the world's California seagulls. Eerie calcified rock formations on the shoreline are called tufa and some of the best examples are strikingly preserved at **Mono Lake State Tufa Reserve**.

From May until November, or until the first winter snow falls, the town of **Lee Vining** on Mono Lake's western shore is the east entry to Yosemite National Park, via 9,990-ft (3,045-meter) Tioga Pass. From Lee Vining, Tuolumne Meadows is a 45-minute drive away; it takes at least two hours to reach Yosemite Valley. Campgrounds are spaced every 15 miles (24 km) or so, and, unlike the rest of the park's sites, are *not* reservable in advance; just show up and see if space is available.

North of Mono Lake, the Sierra crest begins to lower, although "lower" in this case still means snowy summits 11,000 ft (3,350 meters) high. Just under 12 miles (18 km) north of Lee Vining, a graded side road leads 13 miles (21 km)

BELOW: calcified rocks rise from Mono Lake, the oldest body of water in North America.

Map, page 112

to **Bodie State Historic Park ㉒**, which offers both an excellent panorama of the northern Sierras and a reasonably authentic glimpse into the life of a '49ers boomtown. Once the wildest camp in the West, Bodie was home to a ragtag collection of miners and confidence men who made silver fortunes by day and squandered them by night in opium dens, saloons and bawdy-houses. Both professional and amateur photographers love Bodie Park, whose eerie, abandoned buildings perfectly evoke an era long past.

Heading south past Tioga Pass is **Devils Postpile National Monument ㉓**, just west of Mammoth Lakes. Its abrupt geometric pickets (80 ft/24 meters high, 350 yards/320 meters long) testify to the power of the twin forces that shaped the Sierras – fire and ice. There's some camping in summer at **Agnew Meadows** (just before the monument boundary on State 203) and **Red's Meadows** (just after the boundary).

Winter sun fanatics head for **Mammoth Lakes ㉔**, one of the largest downhill ski resorts in America. In the snowy season, Mammoth is where Los Angeles goes skiing, and it is not uncommon to share lift lines with 20,000 other powder hounds. On the plus side, Mammoth offers gourmet dining at several eating establishments, plus wine and cheese shops.

Owens Valley

Heading south further still, dramatic scenery begins on the shores of **Owens Dry Lake**, near the hamlet of **Olancha**. To the left, the tawny, unforested peaks of the southern Sierras rise abruptly, cresting in granite pinnacles 12,000 ft (3,650 meters) high. To the right, across the wide, shimmering lake bed, the softer, more rounded contours of the somewhat lower **Inyo Range** dissolve into

black and purple foothills. These are the portals of **Owens Valley**, deepest in America, and "The Land of Little Rain". The vegetation here is hardy desert flora – scrub oak, mesquite and sagebrush. Owens Valley and the Inyos receive less than 10 inches (25cm) of rain every year.

Just past the northern end of the lake bed, 21 miles (34 km) north of Olancha, State 136 departs east for Death Valley. Located at this junction is the **Visitor Center** which dispenses maps, information and wilderness permits for the extensive public lands under federal jurisdiction. In wintertime, the visitor center is a mandatory stop for the latest word on campground closures, road and weather conditions. In the busy summer season, rangers will direct travelers to campgrounds with vacant spaces.

On a patio outside the Visitor Center, telescopes are trained on the summit of **Mount Whitney ㉕** *(also see page 347)*, at 14,495 ft (4,418 meters) the highest mountain in the United States outside Alaska. A trail leads to the very top of Whitney where portable latrines have been set up to cope with the tide of visitors. It's a strenuous three-day hike (two up, one down), but no technical skills are required, and thousands make the trip every summer. The hardest part can prove to be acquiring a reservation: many Mount Whitney trail permits are reserved up to a year in advance. For details or more information, telephone 760-876 6200. ❑

GOLD COUNTRY

Map, page 210

Many of the towns that straddle the Mother Lode, California's richest mineral vein, have been expensively restored to their pioneer glory

The Gold Rush may have ended, but it wasn't because they ran out of gold. They just ran out of the gold lying near the top of the ground. As the holes got deeper and more dangerous, the work got harder, slower and more expensive, until finally it was no longer cost-efficient to dig.

Geologists say there is at least as much gold in the Mother Lode today as was taken out in the past 100-odd years. Latter-day gold miners say the 7 million lbs (3.2 million kg) extracted by the old-timers was only 10 percent of the wealth that nature had deposited there. Either way, there is a good deal left – and quite a few people are looking for it. Modern mining operations dig deeper and deeper into the Sierra with automated machinery, but there are still the rough-hewn old-timers who crouch by mountain streams, squinting for the glimmer of gold flakes in shallow tin pans.

There's another rush going in the gold country foothills from Mariposa to Nevada City, but it's real estate, not just valuable minerals, that is at stake. Travelers on State Highway 49, Gold Country's main highway, are likely to see more real-estate signs than ghost towns. The modern miner now competes with housing developers – not claim jumpers – for land.

Them thar hills

The placid Gold Country landscape hides its treasures well. In the lowest of the Gold Country foothills, spring begins as early as March. The roadsides from the Central Valley towns of Sacramento, Stockton and Fresno are crowded with wild mustard, an edible plant that adds piquancy to a salad and covers the beef-cattle grazing land with yellow blossoms. In spring, a succession of wild flowers moves up the hills and turns entire mountainsides blue and purple with lupine and brodiaea. There are larkspur and popcorn flowers, purple vetch and baby blue eyes, and the maroon of the red bud, a local flowering bush.

Sonora ❶, named for the Mexican state from which many of its first '49ers came, is a city again, one that may be losing a struggle with the real-estate hustlers. But the houses and shopping centers have sprung up because Sonora is as beautiful as it was during the Gold Rush – and its quaint Downtown has remained true to the miners' spirit.

In the 1870s, there was a pocket mine at the north end of Sonora where the operators found a vein of nearly pure gold and recovered, they say, $160,000 worth of gold in one day. It was part of *La Veta Madre*, otherwise known as **"the Mother Lode,"** from which the legends sprang. It is the kind of story that still keeps miners at work today, toiling in the dark tunnels.

But, for the most part, it is tourism, not treasure, that

PRECEDING PAGES: Fiddletown, in the Mother Lode. **LEFT AND BELOW:** the sparkle in his eye says "Gold!"

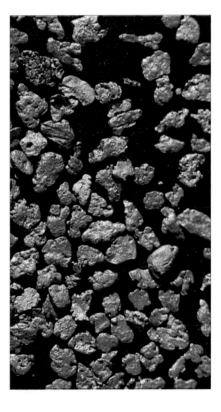

This early satirical portrait of a laden-down, roaming gold-seeker says: A Gold Hunter on his way to California, via St Louis.

plays a key role in the area's resources. A real gem of Tuolumne County these days is the town of **Columbia ❷**. Just a few minutes north of Sonora and just off State 49, this old town has been restored as the **Columbia State Historic Park** (tel: 209-588 9128). For those who have traveled in the eastern United States, Columbia can be compared to Williamsburg, Virginia, another restored historical town. Columbia once had a population of 15,000, 50 saloons, competing daily newspapers and at least one church. Nearly $90 million in gold was mined there over a 20-year period. Much of restored Columbia is closed to cars, but the easy layout of the town makes it well worthwhile parking and walking around. The best sites are the Wells Fargo Express Office; the old schoolhouse, used until 1937; and the old city hotel.

Around Columbia, as in many of the Gold Country towns, there are several rock or gold shops whose proprietors may be willing to show visitors where to look for gold and perhaps even teach them how to mine. There are even tour companies that will set up trips to local mines.

Mark Twain lived here

Back on State 49, still headed north, a sign indicates the way to the summit of **Jackass Hill**. It is named for the animals so central to gold prospecting, and it is the place where Mark Twain lived in 1864. The Twain cabin has been reconstructed around the original hearth. During the time Twain lived in the cabin, he wrote one of his most famous yarns, *The Celebrated Jumping Frog of Calaveras County*. The actual jumping frogs were supposed to have been a bit north in **Angels Camp ❸** – and that's where they can still be found.

Angels Camp still harbors the **Angels Hotel**, where Twain is said to have

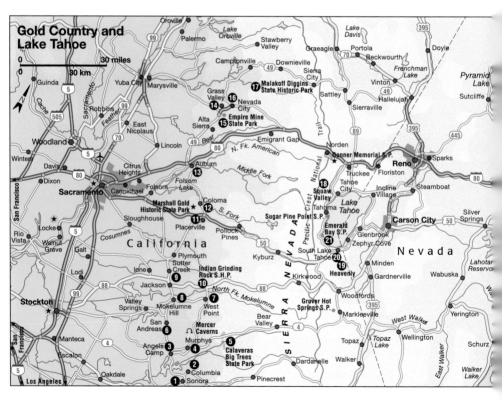

Map, page 210

heard the frog story. Better yet, each May the community holds a frog-jumping contest that attracts thousands of people to the area – so many, in fact, that the only way actually to see a jumping frog is to enter your own in the contest. Any frog more than 4 inches (10 cm) in length is eligible. The wiser course may be to avoid Angels Camp during the week of the frogs. Mark Twain would certainly have done so. From the Angels Camp area, a detour leads up into the mountains to the town of **Murphys ❹**, a Gold Rush period settlement far enough off the track to be a natural museum. The excellent **Mercer Caverns**, well worth a visit, are in this area. Farther up State 4 is **Calaveras Big Trees State Park ❺**, with magnificent sequoia trees.

San Andreas ❻ is another town whose present is a triumph of development interests, but whose past is alive with romantic echoes. Black Bart, a real stage-coach bandit, was tried here in 1883 for some of the 28 robberies he allegedly committed. Bart, a San Franciscan with expensive tastes and little income, embarked on a series of polite, bloodless robberies of the gold-laden stages. His shotgun was always unloaded and no one was ever hurt, but he served six years in San Quentin's rough prison. Then he disappeared.

In good weather, the drive from San Andreas to **West Point ❼** on the Mountain Ranch and Railroad Flat roads is beautiful. There have been recent attempts to reopen some of the 500 local mine shafts. A few shafts now crush ore and even welcome visitors. If you stand in the mouth of a mine shaft, even in midsummer, you can see your breath condensing in the cold air seeping up from thousands of feet beneath the ground. Modern techniques of deep-rock mining differ little from those used by the '49ers. The gold pan and sluice boxes used by weekend miners are essentially the same tools that were used 100 years ago.

BELOW: Columbia once had a population of 15,000, plus 50 saloons.

TIP

For those who don't
want to spend all their
time meditating on
history, Coloma is a
pleasant place for a
raft trip. A number of
companies offer one-
day and longer trips
rafting down the
American River.

From West Point, travelers can loop back west to **Mokelumne Hill** , a town once so rich in gold that its claims were limited to 16 sq. ft (about 1.5 sq. meters). According to legend, the lust for wealth ran so high that there was a murder a week here for more than four months. On a more benign note, Mokelumne Hill is the site of the founding of the **E. Clampus Vitus Society**, a group devoted to good deeds and good times. The society is still around and active, and generally has an entry in any local parade or fair.

From **Sutter Creek** ❾ to Grass Valley, about 75 miles (120 km), the countryside surrounding State 49 is mostly a commuter suburb of Sacramento. For a more authentic look at the old west, drive east to **Chaw'se Indian Grinding Rock State Historic Park** ❿ near the town of Jackson, one of the largest Native American sites in the United States. The park and its museum are a celebration of the contributions made by the Miwok tribe.

Placerville gold

At the junction of highways 49 and 50 is **Placerville** ⓫, once called Hangtown because of its chosen method of execution. Placerville was the nexus of wagon, mail, Pony Express and telegraph routes, and consequently a busy and exciting place. Now it may be the only town in America with its own gold mine. The **Gold Bug Mine**, north of town, is located in a public park where there are several other mines, and is open to visitors for inspection.

North of Placerville on State 49 is **Coloma** ⓬, the birthplace of the Gold Rush. There is a state historic park now at the spot where, in 1848, James Marshall was building a waterway for John Sutter's lumber mill and was distracted by something glittering in the water. The state has reconstructed the mill, though not exactly at the same place, since the **American River** has changed its course in the past century.

Auburn ⓭, at the junction of State 49 and busy Interstate 80, is very much a part of the Sacramento economy. The **Placer County Museum** in Auburn is counted as one of the best in the mountains, with its collections of Indian materials as well as gold-mining paraphernalia. Nearby is the unusual **Firehouse**.

Auburn is a good place to jump off for a visit to Lake Tahoe (up Interstate 80; *see pages 217-9*) with a return via State 20 near **Emigrant Gap**. State 20, the old Tahoe-Pacific Highway, is one of California's great drives. It rejoins State 49 in the Nevada City-Grass Valley area.

Grass Valley ⓮ was the center of the deep mines, and there are several splendid places to get a sense of what they were like. Some of them, including the **North Star**, have shafts that go hundreds of feet below sea level. These shafts are now closed and flooded. The **Nevada County Museum** in the town of Grass Valley is good for local history. **Empire Mine State Park** ⓯, east of town, is the site of the oldest and richest mine in California that once produced no less than $100 million worth of gold before it was closed down in the mid-20th century.

Grass Valley is now a center of high-technology industry, most notably the manufacture of equipment for television broadcasting, and is once again a name recognized around the world.

BELOW: the City Hotel in Columbia.

Antique city

Nevada City ⑯ is as old-fashioned as Grass Valley is up-to-date. It is the kind of place that attracted city people early. They busily converted the old factories and miners' stores into restaurants, museums, antiques stores and theaters, many of which have been restored. There are a couple of pleasant bars and the **National Hotel** (tel: 530-265 4551) still puts up overnight visitors in rooms tastefully furnished with antiques.

Map, page 210

Ten miles (16 km) north of Nevada City is a large state park at the old **Malakoff Diggins** ⑰, a place that generated one of the very earliest pieces of environmental legislation. Visitors to the Malakoff mine can see the effects of hydraulic mining, a method of gold extraction in which high-powered streams of water were directed from cannons at the side of the mountain. This method was highly effective, but it devastated the mountain, and waterways were clogged with mud as far away as San Francisco Bay. The technique was banned in 1884 but the scars, which have been only slightly healed by time, are still grimly awesome.

It's an hour's drive from Nevada City to **Downieville**, a fitting end to a tour of the Gold Country. The country here is higher, cooler and much less crowded than further south. From **Camptonville**, midway along the route from Nevada City, the pretty **Henness Pass Road** veers off into the mountains. In good weather, it is a lovely side trip. There are a number of campgrounds a few miles toward the pass. Downieville itself is almost as perfect as a picture. It is a remote place hemmed in by steep hillsides, with a population of under a thousand people. Despite its seclusion, however, there are a few places for visitors to have a meal or relax for the night, taking in the sweet mountain air. ❑

BELOW: the isolation of the Wild West can still be found.

LAKE TAHOE

*It's the gambling that makes the headlines, but there's
also a huge variety of top skiing in the Lake Tahoe area
in winter, and great hiking and biking in summer*

O f Lake Tahoe, the Sierra explorer and America's most famed naturalist John Muir wrote: "A fine place this to forget weariness and wrongs and bad business." Mark Twain was no less impressed. "The lake burst upon us," he wrote in *Roughing It*, describing the moment he reached the summit overlooking Tahoe, a "noble sheet of blue water lifted 6,300 feet (1,920 meters) above the level of the sea, and walled in by a rim of snow-clad mountain peaks… I thought it must surely be the fairest picture the whole earth affords."

Twain might eat his words today. Several communities – and countless casinos, fast-food joints, strip malls, and water- and snow-sports outfitters – now dot the 71-mile (114-km) shoreline of this crystal-blue lake, which straddles Nevada and California, and stands at 6,229 ft (1,898 meters) in the Sierra Nevada, about 50 miles (80 km) southwest of Reno. But in many ways, especially during winter, Tahoe does still possess a unique allure.

When Twain and Muir discovered Tahoe, the lake was as pure and sparkling as the silver being dug out of the nearby Comstock Lode. These days, its blue waters are sometimes green with algae, and its blue skies dimmed somewhat by smog. The indoor attractions (roulette wheels and craps tables) rival the outdoor ones (sun, water and winter snow) for the attention of the travelers, while a seemingly endless array of restaurants, motels, condominiums, boutique stores, miniature golf courses and McDonald's – cater to their every need.

**PRECEDING PAGES,
LEFT AND BELOW:**
winter, summer and
night-time activities
in Lake Tahoe.

Outdoor attractions

But only a few miles from the furious bustle of the Nevada casinos are wilderness, hiking trails, hidden lakeshore caves, snow-covered backroads ideal for cross-country skiing and quiet beaches that look much the same as when Twain dug a toe into them.

Recreation is the lake area's lifeblood, and in winter that means downhill and cross-country skiing, and lots of snowboarding. On Friday nights, the weekend exodus from San Francisco's Bay Area begins. Tens of thousands of cars, skis strapped on their roofs like sections of picket fences, stream up Interstate 80 or US 50 toward the lake.

The largest ski areas are **Squaw Valley** ⓲ (tel: 800-403 0206) at the northwest side of the lake, and popular **Heavenly** ⓳ (tel: 775-586 7000) on the south side. Heavenly, which stretches across two states, has a total of 29 lifts including five high-speed detachable quads plus a snowboard park, and a half-pipe.

Another local favorite, the family-run Sierra-at-Tahoe, 12 miles (19 km) west of South Lake Tahoe on Highway 50, has three high-speed detachable quads and is popular with snowboarders.

Heavenly is the favorite ski area for those who like

TIP

Another way to see the area is from above. HeliTahoe tours (tel: 530-544 2211) take off from the Lake Tahoe airport in South Lake Tahoe. The Heavenly Gondola (tel: 775-586 7000) goes 2.4 miles (4 km) up the mountain for views and trails departing from an observation deck. The Squaw Valley Cable Car (tel: 530-583 6985) also offers great panoramas year-round.

BELOW: sloping off.

to duck into the casinos at night, as it is located at **South Lake Tahoe** ⓴, the busiest part of the lake and just a stone's throw from Nevada. For all their commotion, the casinos can actually come in handy for skiers in the evening – most offer inexpensive all-you-can-eat buffet dinners to lure customers to the gambling dens. Gambling is, of course, the area's biggest and most lucrative business. There's no law, however, that says a person can't just visit the dining room, eat a filling meal after a tough day of skiing, and depart with dollar bills still snugly in a pocket.

Most skiers, however, prefer the northern half of the lakeshore on the California side, particularly the area around **Tahoe City**. It's quieter, cleaner and the selection of ski areas is better. In addition to Squaw Valley, skiers can choose **Alpine Meadows**, **Sugar Bowl**, **Boreal** and **Northstar**. The latter caters particularly for families – its gentler slopes keep most of the show-offs away. Boreal, perched on the edge of four-lane Interstate 80, is the easiest to reach. Sugar Bowl is the oldest. Alpine Meadows is preferred by experienced skiers, as runs rated "expert" make up 40 percent of the terrain.

Even if you don't care for skiing, the outdoors is the central focus. To get off the beaten track, **Lake Tahoe Adventures** (tel: 503-577 2940) leads snowmobile tours through a series of meadows, lakes and mountain forest. Wilderness dinners, weddings and overnights in igloos can be arranged. At **Northstar Stables**, off Highway 267 between the towns of Kings Beach and Truckee, visitors can explore the snowy terrain by horse – and sleigh. To take the wintry chill off, try a hot soak at **Walley's Hot Springs Resort**, located 12 miles (19 km) east of South Lake Tahoe on Foothill Road in Genoa.

Cross-country and telemark skiing, which is more like a hike in the woods than a flight down a mountainside, is attracting more people each year. The skis are longer and narrower, the uphill stretches can make the legs ache, but the silence and solitude are blessed.

Summertime exploits

Even if there's still snow on the mountaintops, it will likely be hard to choose between outdoor sporting options when the summer sun comes out. Rent in-line skates or a bicycle to explore the local roads, or a mountainbike to blaze down the bare ski runs at Squaw Valley. Several parks and reserves have well-marked hiking trails. The lake offers great fishing, as well as jet-skiing, waterskiing and kayaking. There is usually good river rafting on the **Truckee River**. The local tourist office has information on operators and rental shops to help you get going on these activities.

A great way to see Lake Tahoe is to take a ride on one of the large vessels that cruise around the lake all year round. The *Tahoe Queen* (tel: 800-238 2463) is an authentic steam-paddle boat which departs from the Ski Run Marina on the south shore; another paddle wheeler is the *Tahoe Gal* (tel: 800-218 2464), which departs from the North Shore Marina. The *MS Dixie* (tel: 800-238 2463) leaves from Zephyr Cove Marina on the Nevada side of the lake. All offer lunch, dinner and dancing cruises, as well as sightseeing trips along the shoreline and through spectacular Emerald Bay, an iso-

Map, page 210

lated, tree-lined wilderness tucked into the southwest corner of the lake. Hikers and backpackers usually head for **Desolation Wilderness**, a lake-studded area located west of Emerald Bay. A wilderness permit must be obtained for back-packing in Desolation Wilderness – it's a popular place that often fills to capac-ity in summer. The 165-mile (265-km) **Tahoe Rim Trail** offers magnificent views and can be accessed from several points around the lake. The **Granite Peak** area is also good for backpacking, and the extremely pretty **Emerald Bay State Park ㉑**, as well as **DL Bliss** and **Sugar Pine Point** state parks, are excel-lent for short walks and picnics.

On any summer weekend, joggers and bicyclists take to the roads ringing the lake. The 75-mile (121-km) circle makes a strenuous one-day bike ride or a leisurely two-day trip.

Getting there

Getting to Lake Tahoe is easy and, thanks to the many casinos seeking to lure fresh blood from the Bay Area or even Los Angeles, relatively inexpensive. Package tours (which include accommodation, food and cocktail vouchers, and, sometimes, even some time at the tables) are easy to purchase in the large cities. The drive from San Francisco, where most out-of-towners seem to come from, takes four to five hours in good weather and light traffic.

Traveling to Tahoe in the wintertime is a different story: chains should always be carried in case of ice and snow, and drivers should be prepared either to lie on their backs in roadside slush to put them on, or to pay one of the "chain mon-keys," young people who cluster on the side of the road hoping to earn money by carrying out the task. ❑

BELOW: boating on Emerald Bay.

THE NORTH COAST

*California's huge stands of protected redwood trees
mean that urban civilization has been kept
at bay on this wild coastline*

Map,
page 112

San Francisco

Los Angeles

F ew places in America are as wild as California's North Coast. Developers may have tried to replicate Southern California's coastline, but in the upper reaches of the north the elements still rule and the eye can scan miles of majestic coastline and inland hills without spotting a living soul – except perhaps the legendary Sasquatch, the ape-like beast who supposedly roams the redwood forests. Although most towns along Highway 1 are small, visitors are welcome and accommodations plentiful.

The absence of development is partly due to the California Coastal Commission, formed in the 1970s when the state seemed fated to become a 400-mile (644-km) ribbon of private marinas and ocean-view condominiums. The only unchecked development is the Sea Ranch, a chic subdivision north of Marin County designed to blend into the environment. Residents are not allowed to paint their homes or go beyond minimal landscaping.

PRECEDING PAGES:
flying north by northwest.
LEFT: Crescent City fishing fleet.
BELOW: one type of coastal cuisine.

A comfortable coast

North of **Bodega Bay** ㉖, most of the Sonoma County coast is a state beach, with comfortable access, plenty of parking, thrilling views, no camping, and appropriate beach names like **Mussel Point**, **Salmon Creek**, **Hog Back**, **Shell Beach** and **Goat Rock**. As you travel north on Highway 1 from Bodega Bay, the prevailing scenery is fog, cypress trees, pines, old barns, and grazing sheep and cows. As real estate, this grazing land is so valuable that local ranchers are termed "boutique farmers," because they don't really have to farm. They could sell the land for easily more money than they'd make in a lifetime of farming.

"I'd rather look at my cows than count money in a bank," says one North Coast dairyman. "If my cows are happy, I'm happy." The cows, at least, have a million-dollar view. This same man once owned a chunk of Marin County pastureland that was sold years back for unknown millions of dollars to film-maker George Lucas for his Skywalker Ranch.

Tourism – as with most of California – is now the growth industry, having overtaken logging and fishing. Although demand for trees and fish is on the increase, the supply is diminishing, as are the people prepared to do the work.

The boats in the Bodega Bay salmon fishery, declared an "economic disaster" in the early 1980s, remain berthed during the salmon season because it is too expensive to cruise for a product that may not be there. As a result, salmon fishermen sell extremely tasty, freshly caught albacore (a long-fin tunny) directly from their boats in order to recoup any losses. The winner in this market may be the camping traveler. Fresh barbe-

cued albacore is far better than the deep-fried frozen fish served with professional indifference in tourist cafés along State 1.

North of **Jenner**, State 1 weaves through daily fog, rolling pastures and sudden canyons that drop 1,000 ft (over 300 meters) into the blue and foamy Pacific. The road passes historic **Fort Ross** ㉗, a careful reconstruction of the original fort built by Russian traders in the early 19th century. There are tours, but the best way to see the fort is to stroll through and around on your own. The small Russian Orthodox chapel is worth a special stop.

One compelling way to pass an afternoon in north Sonoma County is to visit the coastal tidepools. At **Stewart's Point State Park** ㉘, a popular place for abalone divers, the pools are accessible at most tides, and there's little risk (present at some North Coast beaches) that the explorer will be swept away by what the California State's warning signs call "sleeper" waves.

Travelers enter Mendocino County just north of Sea Ranch at **Gualala**, notable for its fine old hotel in the center of town. Fifteen miles (24 km) north, a coastal access path leads to **Point Arena**, a tiny bayside beach that comprises several dozen weathered mobile homes, two disintegrating and dangerous piers, and a few shops selling bait and fishing tackle. However, bed and breakfast inns are springing up all along the coast as city dwellers buy up Victorian homes, preserve them, fill them with antiques and surrender with relief to a lifestyle change in the countryside.

The Coast Guard's **Point Arena Lighthouse** ㉙ occupies the point of the US mainland closest to Hawaii. Many ships have crashed near Point Arena. Lots of free literature is available to tell visitors which ships, and where, and what was lost as a result.

B&Bs (bed and breakfast inns) have proliferated so fast in Mendocino, 32 miles (51 km) north of Point Arena, that the city has passed laws prohibiting any new ones from opening.

BELOW: barbershop in Mendocino.

Map, page 112

Preserving its heritage

In a sense, **Mendocino** ⑳ is a victim of its own beauty: it's just too lovely to be ignored. A century-old former logging village, it's set on a long bluff above a small bay and is full of picturesque Victorian structures. The town is now treading the narrow line between "quaint" and "cute."

For a small town with a population of approximately 1,100, Mendocino is hectic. Once visitors find (with difficulty) a place to park, they are confronted with restaurants bearing names like **Whale Watch**, and menus listing such delicacies as "Sempervirens Steak" – a "highly seasoned tofu loaf made with whole grains and vegetables and covered with sautéed mushrooms, onions and jack cheese." Nevertheless, if comfort and good cuisine in the countryside is something you've always wanted to aspire to, Mendocino is difficult to beat. Travelers who want to escape from all this leisure chic can go to two nearby state parks, **Van Damme** and **Russian Gulch**, which offer camping, hiking, bird-watching, fishing, beach-combing and other quiet pleasures.

To the north, the city of **Fort Bragg** ㉛ is the frumpy flipside of Mendocino. It is an unpretentious, working-class, beer-bellied hick town that greets the wayfarer, not with an historical bed and breakfast inn, but with roadside cafés and restaurants with names like Cap'n Flint's. Fort Bragg's love affair with the architectural present (Safeway supermarkets, Walgreens and Payless drugstores) can be a shock, like a breath of unexpected air freshener. Some of the best of its unpretentiousness can be found in **Noyo Harbor**, a sunny inlet lined by docks, characterful boats and seafood restaurants. These are likely to be simple cafés with plastic tablecloths, paper-napkin dispensers and bottles of McIlhenny's tabasco sauce on the tables. The fish will be fresh, but be warned: as tourism creeps closer even this atmosphere won't last forever.

The cloud of steam over Fort Bragg is produced by the Georgia-Pacific Corporation's lumber mill. The largest coastal settlement between San Francisco and Eureka, Fort Bragg is still an active logging town.

Redwoods and marijuana

Much of the North Coast's mystique is in the tall redwood trees, which have survived attempts to transform them into everything from lumber and ashtrays to mulch for suburban rose gardens. Most of California's remaining old-growth redwoods are now protected in parks, where tourists are invited to admire them, to drive through holes burnt or cut through the larger ones, and to buy objects made of their wood.

Notices tacked to buildings and utility poles offer "Sinsemilla Tips." Says another bulletin: "Don't get caught with your plants down." The plant in question is marijuana, a multimillion-dollar black market commodity. Until 1981, it was listed in Mendocino County's agricultural report as the largest local cash crop; since then, officials have chosen not to include the estimated marijuana gross.

The **Kinetic Grand Championship**, an annual Humboldt County event in which participants race humanpowered contraptions across rough terrain from Eureka to Ferndale, imparts the wacky spirit of the place.

North of Garberville a 33-mile (53-km) scenic drive called the **Avenue of the Giants** ㉜ follows the South

BELOW: Yurok Indian, a fisherman on the Klamath River.

Fork of the Eel River through **Humboldt Redwoods State Park**. The giants –
redwood trees, otherwise known as *Sequoia sempervirens* – are tall and sometimes surprisingly wide. Their size can be marketed: "Drive through a living
tree" is the come-on from the **Drive-Thru Tree** in the town of **Myers Flat**.

Those seeking to avoid this kind of commercialism can take the difficult road
west from Garberville over the **King Mountains** to **Shelter Cove**. North of this
isolated outpost is **Petrolia**, site of California's first oil well.

An honest glimpse into the spirit of the early Anglo life along the North Coast
is aptly afforded by **Scotia ❸❸**, a crisp little company town built entirely of redwood – the wooden visitors' center is in the style of a classic Greek temple –
and dominated by the **Pacific Lumber Company mill**, the world's largest redwood mill. The company owns the town and keeps it tidy.

Eureka's attractions

From the moment you arrive, it is obvious that **Eureka ❸❹** is a good place to
buy such commodities as sewer pipe, lumber, a slab of redwood burl, a life-sized
statue of a lumberjack carved from a redwood log, or a fresh fish dinner. Often
shrouded in fog, it's the largest Pacific Coast enclave in North America north
of San Francisco. It is a sprawling, busy, industrial place, still with a large fishing industry. Eureka is also the location of the North Coast's only institution of
higher learning, called, appropriately enough, **Humboldt State University**.

Eureka's ubiquitous and impressive Victorian architecture in **Old Town** is
highlighted by the **Carson House** at the end of 2nd Street. Visitors can't go
inside this much-photographed house because it is now a private men's club –
which makes it seem all the more Victorian. Anyone interested in this type of

BELOW: Eureka's
Carson House.

architecture will want to head to the little town of **Ferndale** ③,10 miles (16 km) southwest of Eureka, which has a very good sampling of well-maintained Victorian buildings.

Orick is the entrance to **Redwood National Park** ③, established in 1968 to consolidate 40 miles (64 km) of majestic forested coastline under federal jurisdiction. A visitors' center in Orick gives out directions and shuttle-bus information for excursions up **Redwood Creek** where, southeast of Orick, three of the six tallest trees ever identified, including the record holder – 368 ft (112 meters) in height – are located. They are clustered in the unimaginatively named **Tall Trees Grove**. It is difficult to recommend much of the scenery north of the **Klamath River** bridge, however, because you probably won't see much of it. The stands of redwood in **Del Norte Coast Redwoods State Park** ③ and **Jedediah Smith Redwoods State Park** ③, both extensions of Redwood National Park, are noteworthy. But the foremost fact is fog, which can come in thick and fast and without warning. Be sure to take a sweater, just in case.

Crescent City ③ – a grim, gray gathering of plain houses and vacant lots around a semi-circular harbor – has never fully recovered from a 1962 typhoon which devastated the town and the traveler's best bet is to head inland to higher and hotter ground. Fifteen minutes east of Crescent City, on US Highway 199 toward Grants Pass, Oregon, the last undammed river in California flows gin-clear through the 90°F (32°C) summer twilight. Although the **Smith River** is wild, its accommodations are civilized. There's a lodge on **Patrick Creek** with a restaurant and bar. There are clean campgrounds, public and private, under the peeling red madronas. The attractions here are simple: boulder-lined banks, clear pools, good fishing – and no redwood souvenirs. ❑

Map, page 112

Paul Bunyan statue and the Trees of Mystery near the town of Klamath.

BELOW: a homesteader at home.

THE HIGH NORTH

The key to unlocking the secrets of the north is State Highway 299. This two-lane blacktop cuts across some of the state's least-populated wilderness

Map, page 112

San Francisco

Los Angeles

Mountainous State 299 should be savored like a fine wine; at least five days should be allowed. On its winding trek, it cuts across a remote domain of mountains, valleys, volcanoes, rivers, canyons, basins and, at the end, barren desert. The time to visit is mid-April to mid-November, but even under the best of weather conditions, rock slides and heart-stopping curves make driving no experience for the timid, the inebriated or the impatient.

Coming from the Pacific Coast, State 299 branches off US Highway 101 at Arcata, north of Eureka, and crosses the low **Coast Range** to the wilderness realm of the **Klamath** and **Trinity** rivers. These two principal rivers drain the Coast Range and **Klamath Mountains**.The Klamaths comprise a series of smaller ranges – the **Siskiyou**, the **Trinity**, the **Trinity Alps**, the **Marble**, the **Scott Bar**, the **South Fork** and the **Salmon** mountains. They cover about 12,000 sq. miles (about 31,000 sq. km) of Northern California and southern Oregon. **Mount Hilton** is the highest peak in the region.

Bigfoot

The Klamaths are famous as the home of **Bigfoot**, also known as Sasquatch, the giant humanoid who – according to legend – stalks these mountains. There *is* something wild about the Klamaths: with more than 70 inches (1,780 mm) of annual rainfall in some parts, they sustain a lush forest of ferns, hemlocks, pines and spruce. And some native tribes still inhabit the area. Except for the highest of the Trinity Alps, glaciers are rare, so most peaks retain a raw, jagged quality. River canyons lack the graceful horseshoe shape of their glaciated Sierra Nevada counterparts.

Three national forests contain most of California's Klamaths – Klamath, Shasta and Trinity. Within these forests are more strictly protected wilderness areas. The best-known and most popular is the **Salmon-Trinity Alps Wilderness Area** ❹, laced with hundreds of miles of trails for hiking and camping. Ranger stations along State 299 at **Burnt Ranch**, **Big Bar** and Weaverville, and on State 3 at **Trinity Center**, will issue free permits, answer flora and fauna questions, and provide up-to-date information on weather and trail conditions.

About 10 miles (16 km) east of the Trinity River bridge marking the Humboldt-Trinity county line, near the community of Burnt Ranch, State 299 passes just south of **Ironside Mountain** (5,255 ft/1,602 meters). Ironside's sheer, scenic face is the eroded, exposed tip of a much larger piece of granite – the Ironside Mountain Batholith. About 165 million years old, this batholith is typical of other such intrusions in the Sierra Nevada and Klamaths. Batholiths distinguish the Klamaths from the neighboring Coast Range. Under a recent federal law,

PRECEDING PAGES: redwoods are synonymous with Northern California. **LEFT:** Mount Shasta and a Shasta City farm in its shadow. **BELOW:** cowpersons posing.

PONY ROOM
NO PERSON UNDER 21 ALLOWED PLEASE

local power companies must purchase any electricity generated by small entrepreneurs. With this in mind, some mountain residents have developed small hydroelectric plants – like the one run by Mom & Pop Power Company in Trinity's **Minersville**. Only a few such plants now operate, but others are planned.

For residents of Trinity County a "night on the town" usually means a trip to **Weaverville** ❹, the county seat with a population of around 3,500. It saw its glory days during the mid-19th century, when it was a supply post for Klamath region gold prospectors. Gold hunters still haunt the creeks of Trinity County, but lumbering sustains the economy.

Old-timers and newcomers

Although lumber ranks first, marijuana ranks second in Trinity County's cash crops. This juxtaposition of enterprises – one traditional, one contraband – is typical of Trinity, and personified in the names given to bars on Main Street – The New York Hotel, or The Diggin's. Trinity County's population breaks into two groups – true locals, and those who have come here since the end of the 1960s. Generally, old-timers tend to be conservative, the newcomers less so – but both groups share an individualism and a jealous regard for the natural environment. While Trinity often votes Republican, it also displays an abiding sensitivity to ecological issues. This is less ideology than simple self-interest.

Many residents hunt for their own food and draw water directly from springs, rivers and creeks. (The bedrock of granite and serpentine is too impermeable for aquifers.) So when the county's residents recently tried to stop the federal government from spraying Trinity's woodlands with an herbicide many feared would end up in water supplies, no politicians – Democrat or Republican –

High priestess of the High North.

BELOW: Chinese joss house in the town of Weaverville.

Map, page 112

penly opposed the grass-roots effort. This closeness to one another and to the and breeds a native suspicion of outsiders.

Visiting motorists should know that Trinity County, like most of California's orth, has "open range." Cattle have never been a major part of the economy ere, and open range is mostly a symbolic vestige of the region's frontier heritage. Open range means that cattle wander beyond their owner's unfenced angelands. It also means that any driver whose vehicle strikes a cow has just urchased damaged livestock. Hikers must be careful to stay away from creek ottoms on which gold prospectors have staked claims. Likewise, those who ome across a patch of marijuana should leave quickly before either (a) they are hot at by its grower, or (b) they are arrested on suspicion of being its growers.

Weaverville is the site of the **Joss House State Historic Park**, a tribute to hinese history in California, particularly of the Gold Rush days. Here, the oldst Chinese temple still in use in the state is open daily; guided tours are available. Nearby is the eclectic **JJ "Jake" Jackson Museum**.

Weaverville is also the gateway to **Trinity** and **Lewiston lakes**, part of the xpansive **Whiskeytown National Recreation Area** ㊷. A short drive north of own, these lakes were created in the 1960s with the damming of the upper Trinty River. They offer outdoor recreation opportunities in the form of fishing, iking, boating and camping.

The **Cascades** run almost due north from California to Canada's British olumbia. In California, the range runs 40 to 50 miles (70 to 80 km) across. arther north, glaciers dominate the range. Here in California, only the highest eaks bear these Ice Age relics. The dominant snow-capped Cascade peaks are oung volcanoes. Some, like Washington's Mount St Helens, are still active.

BELOW: logging operation, Trinity National Forest.

Map, page 112

Unlike the Klamaths, the higher Cascade peaks present a sharply vertical profile of high conical peaks surrounded by lower mountains of the 4,500 to 5,000-ft (1,370 to 1,520-meter) range.

There are few better places to study volcanology than **Lassen Volcanic National Park** ㊸. The park is reached via State Highway 36 stretching east from **Red Bluff**, State 44 east from Redding, or from State 89 south from State 299 beyond Burney. Lassen Peak (elevation 10,457 ft/3,187 meters) marks the southern terminus of the Cascade Range, and is one of only two Cascade volcanoes to have erupted in the 20th century.

Much of 108,000-acre (43,700-hectare) Lassen Park lies within a caldera, the giant crater left by the collapse of an ancient volcano. Out of this caldera, Lassen Peak later rose to dominate this expanse of wilderness, but there are small volcanoes in the park as well. There is also **Bumpass Hell**, a steaming valley of active geothermal pools and vents. And there are lakes, rivers, meadows, pine forests and fine trails for hiking and camping.

Most of the California Cascades fall within two national forests, **Lassen** and **Shasta**. At Shasta's southern boundary lies another prime wilderness, **Plumas National Forest** ㊹. These upland woods cover the northern end of the Sierra Nevada and cradle the **Feather River**, one of the state's best-known wild streams.

BELOW: whitewater rafts on the mighty Trinity River.
RIGHT: Helen Lake, Lassen Volcanic National Park.

Between Redding and Burney, a distance of 53 miles (85 km), State 299 climbs into a gently undulating country of ranches and volcanic debris. The red rocks that litter the landscape and pastures to the south of the road were deposited by hot mud flows from the eruption of Mount Maidu 7 million years ago. This posthumously named volcano collapsed to form the caldera within Lassen Park. Just beyond the lumber and livestock marketing center of **Burney** (population 3,200) is the State 89 intersection. South is Lassen Park; north is **Mount Shasta** ㊺,14,162 ft (4,000 meters) high and usually covered with snow. Mount Shasta is the second-highest elevation in the Cascades; the other is Mount Rainier in Washington State.

Falls and forests

About 6 miles (10 km) north of Burney is pretty, moss-covered 129-ft (39-meter) **Burney Falls** ㊻. East of Burney is **Fall River Mills**, and from here to the Nevada border, State Highway 299 runs across the basins and fault-block mountains of the **Modoc Plateau**, a lava plain similar to the Columbia Plateau to the north. For a large section of its route, the highway follows the deep canyon of the Pitt River, the plateau's main drainage. The plateau extends over some 13,000 sq. miles (33,500 sq. km), taking in the whole of Modoc County and parts of Lassen, Shasta and Siskiyou counties. Vestiges of volcanism make up much of the **Modoc National Forest**, a wonderful green expanse covering 1.97 million acres (800,000 hectares). A pristine example of this volcanic past is **Glass Mountain**, a huge flow of obsidian lava on the forest's western edge.

But the main focus of any geological tour of this region has to be **Lava Beds National Monument** ㊼. A more impressive example of basalt flows cannot be found than this moonlike landscape of lava flows, columns and deep, dark caves. ❑

SOUTHERN CALIFORNIA

The following chapters provide a detailed guide to the region,
with main sites cross-referenced by number to the maps

California is the only state in America that describes itself as having two distinct regions. There's a good reason for that description – Northern and Southern California *are* different. Viewed simplistically, one has water and the other has weather, if we take the latter to mean a supply of almost constant sunshine. (It does rain in Southern California, although seldom in the months between April and November.)

But obviously both sections have very much more to offer. In the south's case, these attractions include three of the country's biggest theme parks (Disneyland, Knott's Berry Farm, Magic Mountain), year-round beaches, zany architecture, easy access to Mexico and – who could forget? – Hollywood. It seems almost superfluous to mention that it also has sprawling, smoggy Los Angeles, which, in the past decade, has become one of America's most varied and interesting places. And San Diego, which, to many people's surprise, is the state's second-largest city.

There's a tendency for almost anybody in the southern part of the state to claim they're "from LA," even when they actually live somewhere down (or up) the coast as much as 100 miles (160 km) away. The Big Orange does tend to sprawl over a great region and certainly gets the lion's share of attention.

But Californians in general, whether from LA or not, all like to think of themselves in trendy terms as taste-makers, arbiters of the future. "All the domestic automobile companies and almost all the Japanese feel they need to keep tabs on the pulse of what is happening in Southern California," says auto market analyst John Rettie. Designer Mark Jordan adds: "People here demand to make individual statements." The Mazda Miata, designed by Pasadena's Bob Hall, was an auto toy created especially for Southern Californians. "You can put the top down year-around and there are a lot of windy roads to drive it on."

Los Angeles novelist Carolyn See says visitors often don't understand the local style because "California culture doesn't pop up on a computer screen. It's like the wind. So outsiders say there's nothing here." Her literary agent, Mort Janklow, says California is "like a teenager growing up." Very nicely, too, most people would say. ❏

PRECEDING PAGES: lounging in LA; up against the wall.
LEFT: triplets on the bed they all shared in Los Angeles.

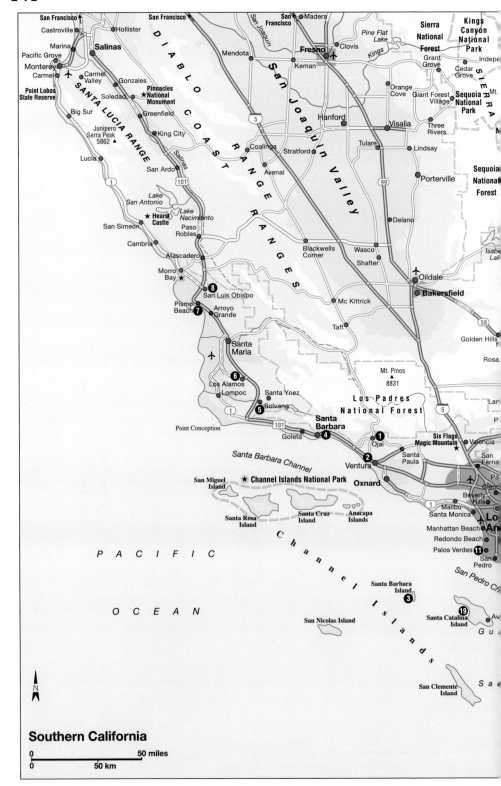

Southern California

0   50 miles

0   50 km

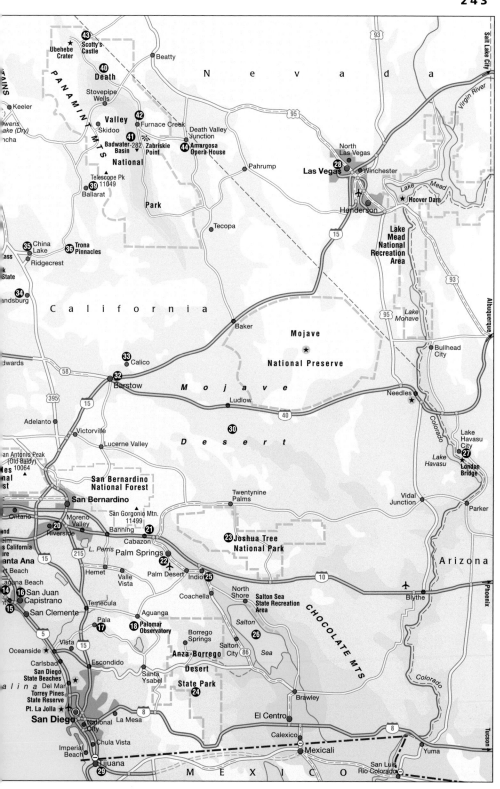

43 Scotty's Castle
Ubehebe Crater

Beatty

N e v a d a

Salt Lake City

93

40 Death

Stovepipe Wells

Keeler

Owens Lake (Dry)

ncha

Valley

Skidoo

42 Furnace Creek

41 Badwater -282 Basin

Zabriskie Point

Death Valley Junction

44 Amargosa Opera House

Pahrump

National

Telescope Pk **39** 11049

Ballarat

Park

Tecopa

95

Virgin River

North Las Vegas

Las Vegas 28 Winchester

Lake Mead

Henderson

★ Hoover Dam

Lake Mead National Recreation Area

Tecopa

15

35 China Lake

36 Trona Pinnacles

Ridgecrest

ass

k State

34

andsburg

C a l i f o r n i a

Baker

Mojave

★

National Preserve

93

95

Lake Mohave

Bullhead City

dwards

58

33 Calico

32 Barstow

M o j a v e

Ludlow

40

Needles

Colorado

Albuquerque

395

15

Adelanto

Victorville

Lucerne Valley

D e s e r t

30

Lake Havasu City

27

Lake Havasu

London Bridge

San Antonio Peak (Old Baldy) 10064

es nal st

San Bernardino National Forest

San Bernardino

Ontario

Moreno Valley

San Gorgonio Mtn. 11499

Banning **21**

Twentynine Palms

23 Joshua Tree National Park

Vidal Junction

Parker

A r i z o n a

20
Riverside

im s California re

Santa Ana

Cabazon

L. Perris **Palm Springs**

215

22

Palm Desert

Indio **25**

North Shore

Salton Sea State Recreation Area

10

Blythe

Phoenix

t Beach

aɔuna Beach

14

16 San Juan Capistrano

15

San Clemente

Hemet

Valle Vista

Temecula

Pala

17

18 Palomar Observatory

Aguanga

Coachella

Salton

26

Salton City

86 **Sea**

C H O C O L A T E   M T S

Colorado

Tucson

5

Vista

15

Oceanside ★

Carlsbad

San Diego State Beaches

alina Del Mar

Torrey Pines State Reserve

Pt. La Jolla ★

San Diego

Escondido

Santa Ysabel

Borrego Springs

Anza-Borrego

Desert

State Park

24

Brawley

El Centro

8

National City

La Mesa

Chula Vista

Imperial Beach

29 Tijuana

Calexico

Mexicali

8

San Luis Rio Colorado

Yuma

M E X I C O

LOS ANGELES

*It attracts myths like a magnet. But then, right from its
beginnings, Los Angeles was an unlikely place,
emerging "out of nowhere without much of a past"*

Map,
page 248

San Francisco

Los
Angeles

Because Los Angeles is such a huge, sprawling city, few of its residents
know it well, or even choose to explore many neighborhoods beyond their
own, most of which are composed of different ethnic populations. The
greater metropolitan area is one of the most crowded in America (12.9 million
versus New York City's 22 million), although in size its city boundary is fourth,
behind Oklahoma City, Houston and Phoenix. Los Angeles is one of North
America's most Hispanic and most Asian cities.

Los Angeles is sixth in the divorce table but on average has the largest families. Los Angeles has the most Rolls-Royce dealers, it also has the most congested traffic (and comes second in the number of cars stolen). It has the least
wind, the most sun, the most smog and – according to a recent Gallup Poll – has
"the most attractive" men and women (as well as the largest number of cosmetic surgeons).

The structure of the big city looked like it might become unglued in 2002
when a long-simmering secession movement erupted into a series of rallies and
publicity. Some residents of both Hollywood and the San Fernando Valley
wanted to detach themselves from Los Angeles and become independent cities
in their own right. Despite all the attention the issue got, however, on the day
of the ballot, voters pledged to remain part of the larger
city, perhaps because there's just no other place like it.

LEFT: Chaplin
in front of the
Chinese Theatre.
BELOW: city of
angels and mice.

Where dreams come true

Where else could you rent a superstar clone such as
John Wayne, Dolly Parton or Elizabeth Taylor – all of
whom were once on hire from a dating service called
Celebrity Dream Date – to accompany you to dinner?
Or have your apartment, or hotel room, tidied up by the
topless girls from Bust Dusters, a cleaning service that
once charged over a dollar a minute (watch, but don't
touch) for providing high-heeled maids wearing fish-
net stockings, G-strings and tiny aprons?

Right from its beginning, LA was an unlikely place,
emerging "out of nowhere without much of a past," in
the words of writer Carey McWilliams who loathed it
when he first arrived in the 1920s. "It lacked form and
identity; there was no center… never-ending spread and
sprawl… a city of strangers, of milling marauders all
staring at one another without a glint of recognition."
Some of those marauders, he felt, were a little *strange*.
In his book, *Southern California: an island on the land*,
he quoted the words of contemporary writer Hoffman
Birney: "Every religion, freakish or orthodox, that the
world ever knew is flourishing today in LA."

In the first 40 years of the last century, the city's population increased 15-fold, making virtually everybody
an alien, as well as the notion of a community itself.

And the fact that this spectacular growth "exactly coincided with the automotive age," wrote Dominick Dunne, weakened even further the idea of community. It was, he pointed out, "the first city on wheels... the first city in the country to be entirely lit by electricity... scarcely older than a century (with) a bumptiousness that was as appealing to some as it was aggravating to others."

Since at least the 1950s, Los Angeles has been a mecca for the young – "the capital of youth," according to author Mike Davis (*City of Quartz,* a history of LA) – and it is still a magnet for the adventurous, for those seeking to begin a new life. During the last decade, more than 750,000 new residents moved into the state, 10 percent from Asia. In the years between 1850 and 1950, almost a score of major utopian colonies were set up compared with no more than three in any other state, and this search for the bizarre hardly seems to have abated.

The listings in a 100-page *Spiritually LA* directory, originally published by a local weekly paper, included six pages of specialist bookstores, hundreds of religious denominations ranging from Ukrainian Orthodox to Eckankar and ads from practitioners of Pragmatic Buddhism, body harmony, extraterrestrial communications and karma-clearing – to name but a few.

The lure of Hollywood

From all accounts, though, it is not spirituality that most of LA's visitors come to seek. Sunshine and sea, shopping and sex symbols – all have their attractions, but, in their secret hearts, what most people hope to see is a star. Or a place where stars spend their time. Or even a place where stars are buried. (The crypts of Rudolph Valentino and Marilyn Monroe – respectively in Hollywood and Brentwood – still draw sightseers in numbers that smalltown hucksters would die for.)

BELOW AND RIGHT:
Venice Beach.

This, remember, is a company town, or at least a town where it sometimes seems that everybody's major preoccupation is with "the industry" and where the appearance of even a minor celebrity can cause outbreaks of hysteria. Not that this is anything to be ashamed of, after all. Unlike super-cool New York, everyone is star-struck here; it goes with the territory.

Maybe some of this devotion to the here and now derives from the very transience of the place. It's easy to imagine that, if everybody left tomorrow, within a year or two, most of Los Angeles would be reclaimed by the desert that nibbles at its borders. Water must be pumped in from hundreds of miles away to keep it alive. Windswept fires race across arid hillsides devouring entire estates in a matter of hours. Spring rainfalls slipslide celebrity-owned, million-dollar mansions down precarious slopes. Storm tides topple beach homes and century-old piers.

Every year, there are earthquakes – on a minor scale in recent years, but everybody knows the Big One is long overdue. Los Angeles, says Richard Reeves, is "not at peace with nature – that's why we get these periodic punishments. It's a man-made city, a tribute to rapacity and tenacity." But with all the hazards, Los Angelenos remain fairly sunny and optimistic in their outlook. Perhaps local publisher Jeremy Tarcher sums it up the best. "We are still the city of the future," he says, "even if nobody knows what the future is." ❑

Los Angeles: West Side

0   2 miles
0   2 km

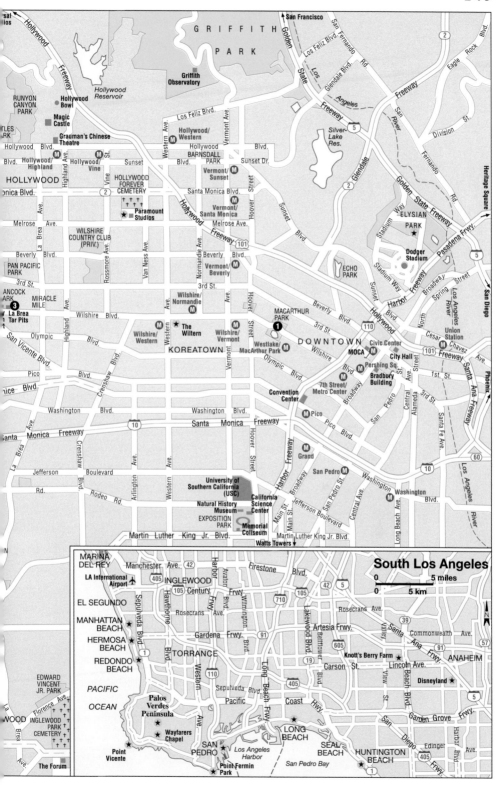

DOWNTOWN LA

*The downtown district of Los Angeles, with its
skyscrapers and ornate movie palaces, represents
both the old and the new faces of the city*

Map,
page 252

I t's fashionable among those living in Hollywood or Beverly Hills to pretend that downtown Los Angeles barely exists – just as many Manhattanites claim they never go south of 34th Street (or north of 14th Street). But downtown LA, in fact, represents both the oldest and newest faces of this multi-faceted city. Millions of dollars have been spent in recent years to transform it into a business and cultural showcase second to none, and, if the results are debatable, they are certainly interesting to see.

Forget about driving; parking Downtown is difficult unless you choose to leave your car on the edge of the area, in a lot opposite The Original Pantry (it never closes), for example, at 9th and Figueroa streets. Only a few blocks east of here is the busy **Flower Market** (7th and Wall) where the main event is over by 8am.

7th + Fig

For those on foot, the bus along 7th operates every few minutes in the downtown area from 6.30am on weekdays, from 10am on weekends. Pick up a schedule before leaving the bus.

Further down Figueroa are several interesting sites if time allows: the**Convention Center**; the state-of-the-art **Staples Center**; the future site of the **LA LIVE** entertainment complex (including a new **Grammy Museum**); the **University of Southern California** (USC), and attractive **Exposition Park**. But before all those, head up towards **7th + Fig Ⓐ**, a stylish mall where the sunken plaza, with its open-air food court, sits among three-story palm trees shading stores. Scattered around are several art works, including a stooping bronze businessman on the north side of Ernst & Young Plaza.

Cross the street and walk half a block to the **Fine Arts Building** at 811 West 7th, artists' studios converted to offices. It has a medieval-style lobby with 15 chandeliers and a tiled fountain, and hosts exhibitions.

Admire the gilded facade of the **Figueroa Tower**, built in 1989, as you head back up Figueroa. The stepped, white form of the **777 Tower** ("subtle profiles and strong silhouettes," says one critic) was created by Argentine-born Cesar Pelli, also responsible for the distinctive Pacific Design Center (known locally as "the Blue Whale") in West Hollywood. A subtle fountain by Eric Orr stands outside the **Figueroa at Wilshire** building while inside one of the 80-ft (24-meter) high Art Deco lobbies, among acres of brown marble, sit two of the largest plants ever seen in captivity. A remarkable late-1980s addition to LA's soaring skyline is the **US Bank Tower Ⓑ**, one of the tallest buildings in the West.

From **City National Plaza** across the street, an escalator leads into the **Westin Bonaventure Hotel Ⓒ** with its multi-level lounges and engaging perspectives,

LEFT: in at the deep end in the corporate swim.
BELOW: interior of the Westin Bonaventure Hotel.

The Angels Flight funicular, billed as the "shortest railway in the world," was built in 1901. It was dismantled in 1969, but opened again in 1996. It is currently closed. City Hall is in the background.

including a panoramic view of the city, courtesy of the hotel's revolving cocktail lounge called BonaVista.

Between Grand, Hill, 3rd and 4th streets, the **Angels Flight ⊙** (tel: 213-626 1901) funicular made its 70-second ride up **Bunker Hill** after a 27-year absence, but is currently closed. A right turn from Hope up Grand leads to the **Wells Fargo History Museum ⊜** (tel: 213-253 7166; closed weekends), where the exhibits recall Gold Rush days and the stagecoaches that tamed the West. The Bonaventure's gleaming cylinders look terrific from the bridge over 3rd Street across from which is the **Museum of Contemporary Art ⊝** (MOCA; 250 South Grand Avenue, tel: 213-626 6222; Mon and Fri 11am–5pm, Thur 11am–8pm, Sat–Sun 11am–6pm; admission charge), an architectural gem harboring notable art created exclusively since the 1930s, in a building outside of which is another eye-catching fountain. Speaking of water, even more spectacular is the waterfall in **California Plaza**. There are numerous tables and chairs in the plaza, which has take-away food counters. This is one of the best spots for a quick lunch.

Asian aura

One of the bus stops is right beside MOCA: a route that goes past the enormous, unmissable **Cathedral of Our Lady of the Angels** and then "touristy" Olvera Street to the far edge of **Chinatown ⊙** at Bernard. Just around the corner on **Broadway**, the gaudy Asian stereotypes of Gin Ling Way surround a stage-sized plaza. Three long blocks south (on the bus route) is **Olvera Street ⊙** with its working craftsmen, Mexican stalls and strolling mariachi who serenade diners as they sip frozen margaritas and eat lunch under the sidewalk awning of **La Golondrina**, the city's first brick building (*circa* 1855). This was home to the

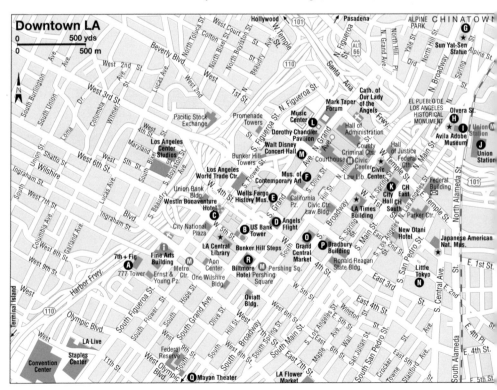

Pelanconi family whose piano, a neighborly gift, sits across the street in the older **Avila Adobe ①**. The Avila Adobe, the home of a prosperous rancher who died in 1832, was deserted for years and condemned by the city as unsafe. It was saved from demolition by a civic-minded group and acquired by the state in 1953. Since then, it has been restored pretty much as it was left by his widow when she died, using some of the original furnishings.

Here, on what began as Wine Street, is where El Pueblo de Nuestra Señora a la Reina de Los Angeles began in 1780 when Felipe de Neve, California's first governor, laid out what was to become California's biggest city.

Notable in the area are the (now empty) **Pico House**, the city's first three-story building and once its finest hotel with 82 bedrooms, 21 parlors, two interior courtyards and a French restaurant; the **Garnier Building** (1890); and the **Hellman Quon** building, which was originally a Chinese store, but is now managed by the Parks Department who offer morning tours of this neighborhood. In the firehouse is a picture of Blackie, the city's last fire horse.

Between the **Plaza Church** (1818) – which is also known as Mission Church – scene of an annual Easter ceremony when children bring their pets to be blessed, and Union Station is a lovely statue of Father Junípero Serra (*see Missions on page 26*).

Majestic **Union Station ①** opened in 1939, and with its leather seats and stratospheric ceiling, it has been seen in scores of old newsreels. It is nicely maintained by Amtrak, which operates about 20 trains a day up the coast, down to the Mexican border and into the desert. You can also get a train from here to Anaheim and Disneyland. LA's subway system, the **Metro Red Line**, begins at Union Station, intersecting with the Blue Line (south to Long Beach) at 7th

BELOW:
the Walt Disney Concert Hall was designed by architect Frank Gehry.

Street. The Red Line runs to Hollywood, North Hollywood and out to Universal City. Behind Union Station sits the glass-roofed **Gateway Transit Center**, the mural- and fountain-filled transportation hub of the region.The bus runs from Olvera Street to LA's restored **City Hall Ⓚ** (whose tower was part of the *Daily Planet* building in TV's *Superman* series). You can take a fascinating walking tour of this landmark and its magnificent rotunda, through the Los Angeles Conservancy (tel: 213-623 2489). In keeping with its public-spirit function, the mortar with which City Hall was built contained sand from every California county and water from every mission.

On a hill a few blocks northwest is the **Music Center Ⓛ**, which includes the **Dorothy Chandler Pavilion**; the **Ahmanson Theatre**, staging plays transferred from New York; and the **Mark Taper Forum**, winner of many awards. Five blocks west of City Hall, the **Walt Disney Concert Hall Ⓜ** opened in 2003 after years of delays. The hall, designed by noted local architect Frank Gehry, was created specifically for orchestral music and is the home of the LA Philharmonic and the Los Angeles Master Chorale. The space also includes an arts theater, two outdoor amphitheaters, a garden, an art gallery and a restaurant.

Little Tokyo

Take the trolley south or walk down Alameda to **Little Tokyo Ⓝ**, where the interesting shops in **Little Tokyo Square** include the Mitsuwa Marketplace. Here, you'll also encounter lush Japanese gardens, Buddist temples, the **Japanese American National Museum** and the **Geffen Contemporary**.

Downtown street life is at its most active on Broadway, where silent screen comic Harold Lloyd once swung from a long-gone clockface in the film *Safety*

ABOVE AND BELOW: dreaming of a life in a new land.

Last. Broadway's attractions include the lively **Grand Central Market ⓞ**, which adjoins one of the city's earliest movie palaces, the **Million Dollar Movie Theater** at 307 South Broadway. Founded by showman Sid Grauman, it had a gala opening in 1918 with Charlie Chaplin, Mary Pickford and Lillian Gish in attendance. Eventually the proprietors were forced to rent its premises to an evangelical preacher, and sadly today, it is abandoned.

Map, page 252

The last of the grand movie palaces, S. Charles Lee's **Los Angeles Theatre**, which opened with the premiere of Charlie Chaplin's *City Lights* (in 1931), is still operating down the street. Opposite the market is the ornate, 1893-built **Bradbury Building ⓟ**, whose winding iron staircases, open elevators and rich woodwork have long endeared it to moviemakers.

The Bradbury Building featured in Ridley Scott's cult movie *Blade Runner* and also passed for private eye Philip Marlowe's down-at-the-heels office in the 1969 adaptation of Raymond Chandler's *The Little Sister*. Chandler, the revered documenter of Los Angeles of the 1940s, felt it was a city "rich and vigorous and full of pride… a city lost and beaten and full of emptiness."

Three other notable buildings are the **Mayan Theater ⓠ** (Hill and 11th streets), now a nightspot, where Norma Jean Baker is said to have appeared as a stripper long before she became Marilyn Monroe; the 1928 **Oviatt Building** (South Olive and 6th streets) whose lobby has more than a ton of Lalique glass; and the awe-inspiring **Biltmore Hotel ⓡ** (now the Millennium Biltmore), with its ornate lobby and photograph of attendees at the 1937 Academy Awards. It was here that MGM's art director is said to have used a napkin to sketch a design for a still-unnamed Oscar statue. At 5th and Grand streets is the **Central Library**, housing around 2 million books and putting to rest the lie that Los Angelenos don't read.   ❏

BELOW: Simon Rodia's astonishing Watts Towers.

WATTS TOWERS

In the Downtown suburb of Watts, in Los Angeles' South Central area, is one of the city's most astonishing sculptures: the Watts Towers. Created between 1921 and 1954 by Simon Rodia, a penniless Italian tilesetter, the trio of lacy columns was intended as an affectionate tribute to his adopted land. Composed of broken bottles, pottery shards, tiles, pebbles and steel rods all stuccoed together and covered with 70,000 seashells, the towers are a set of sculptures so far ahead of their time that they were unappreciated for years: vandals tried to destroy them and the city planned to pull them down.

The towers, the highest of which reaches 100 ft (30 meters), were reprieved after attempts to dismantle them using steel cables pulled by a tractor in full view of TV cameras were unsuccessful. In time, the towers started to accumulate the adulation they had long deserved, but Rodia died in poverty in 1965 at the age of 86, having left town and deeded the site to a friend. The towers can be seen behind the fence even when the adjoining Watts Towers Arts Center, which displays works by African Americans, is closed.

Watts hit the headlines in 1965 when 34 people died in widespread rioting. Take extra care when viewing.

Watts Towers, 1727 E. 107th Street, tel: 213-847 4646.

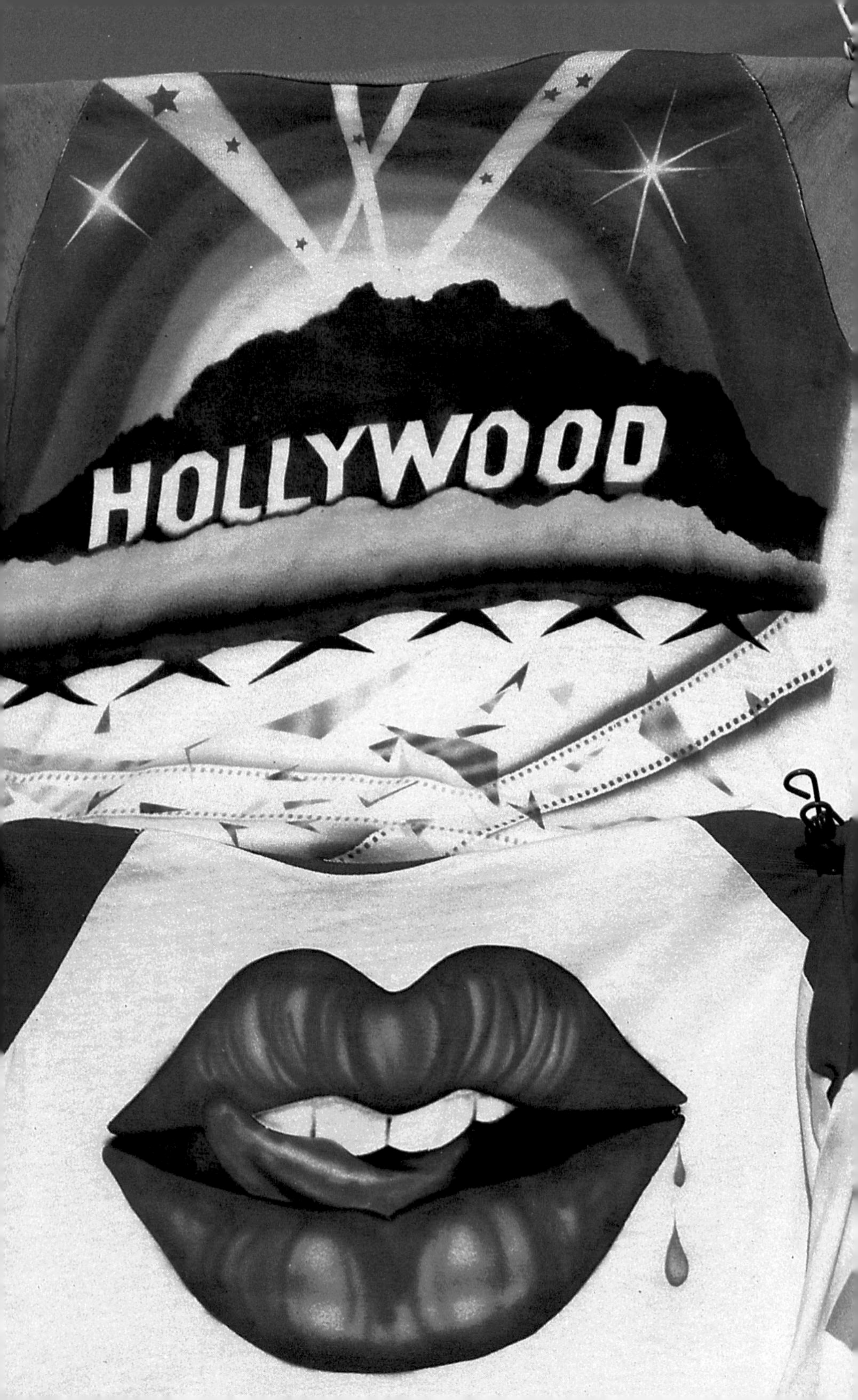
HOLLYWOOD

HOLLYWOOD AND THE WEST SIDE

From Paramount Studios to Grauman's Chinese Theatre, from Beverly Hills to Rodeo Drive – when most people talk about Los Angeles, this is what they mean

Map, page 248

Almost everything west of Downtown is the West Side, or so its inhabitants like to think. In reality, the bottom end of Sunset Boulevard, the section around **Echo Park Lake**, where evangelist Aimee Semple McPherson ("joy! vitality! love!") used to preach at the still-active **Angelus Temple** (a Foursquare Gospel church), and the stylish Victorian houses of **Carroll Avenue** don't have too much in common with the mansions of "industry" millionaires at Sunset's coastal end. Norma Desmond's mansion in *Sunset Boulevard* was actually on **Wilshire Boulevard**. In fact, it is Wilshire, running more or less parallel with Sunset Boulevard, 3 miles (5 km) to the south, that became the major road out to the coast when Sunset was little more than a dusty track leading out of the original Mexican plaza. And the automobile made it so.

Wilshire Boulevard

Nowadays, Wilshire is showing its age, although the Metro Line subway has brought life to otherwise seedy **MacArthur Park ❶** and the ex-Bullock's department store now houses a law library, which has refurbished this Art Deco landmark. Destined for conversion into a school is the site of the Ambassador Hotel, once fabled for the show-biz types who attended (and performed in) its Cocoanut Grove and later, in the 1960s, infamous as the site of Robert Kennedy's assassination. Since closing as a hotel, it was used as a site for moviemaking – until the school district demolished it in 2006.

Miracle Mile's Museum Row, on Wilshire near Fairfax, has Old Masters and other fine paintings, which hang in the **LA County Museum of Art ❷** (LACMA; tel: 323-857 6000; Thur–Tues noon–8pm; admission charge). **La Brea Tar Pits ❸** at the Page Museum (tel: 323-934 7243; daily 10am–5pm; admission charge) is a major tourist attraction. In the 1860s, Rancho La Brea had been bought for $2.50 an acre by Major Henry Hancock, who quarried asphalt and shipped tar to San Francisco to pave streets. The oil company geologists who, in 1989, started uncovering fossils here identified some of the bones as belonging to extinct sabre-toothed tigers, dire wolves and giant sloths.

After a decade of oil drilling, Henry's son, George, allowed LA County to examine the site, deeding the 23-acre (9-hectare) ranch to the county in 1913. The skeleton of a woman from 9,000 years ago was found, but no other humans among what were literally millions of bones. The museum opened in 1972; excavations for the building uncovered skeletons of complete animals, which had been trapped in the tar as they came to drink.

LEFT: Hollywood hype captured on cotton T-shirts.
BELOW: the exotic La Brea Tar Pits.

There's alfresco eating just a few blocks north at the **Farmers Market ④**, where, from 1934, farmers parked their trucks and sold produce from the back. A huge open-air shopping mall, **The Grove**, opened next door in 2002, and the mall and the market are connected with a free trolley service.

Paramount Studios

Two-hour tours of Paramount Studios give the lowdown on both old and new Hollywood. Call 323-956 1777 for more information.

Most of the movie studios that earned Hollywood its reputation have gone, but the famous gate seen in *Sunset Boulevard* still guards the entrance to **Paramount Studios ④**, 5555 Melrose at Van Ness Avenue (tel: 323-956 5000), where *The Ten Commandments* and all the *Godfather* movies were also made. Fans who were not even born when silent star Rudolph Valentino died in 1926 seek out his grave (and those of Douglas Fairbanks, Cecil B. de Mille, Eleanor Powell and Marion Davies) in the adjoining **Hollywood Forever Cemetery,** formerly the Hollywood Memorial Park Cemetery.

Memories of all the low-budget Westerns churned out in moviedom's early days are evoked by the aptly named **Gower Gulch ③**, a frontier-style shopping center opposite **Sunset Gower Studios** on the corner at Sunset and Gower. Across the street, at Columbia Square, is where Hollywood's first film studio, the Nestor Film Company, paid just $40 to rent a defunct tavern in 1911.

Four blocks east, the KTLA TV station replaced the old Warner Brothers studios, where, in 1927, Al Jolson emoted in *The Jazz Singer*. Just north of Sunset on nearby Vine Street, Cecil B. de Mille and Jesse Lasky in 1913 filmed *The Squaw Man*, Hollywood's first full-length feature. Paying appropriate homage to its location, the McDonald's fast-food joint here on Vine Street is decked out in the style of the movie *Casablanca*.

BELOW: three cheers for Hollywood!

A bust of Rudolph Valentino stands in the minuscule **De Longpre Park** ◉ (below Sunset at Cherokee), named after the turn-of-the-20th-century flower painter whose gorgeous house and gardens near Wilcox Street and Hollywood Boulevard was Hollywood's first tourist attraction. Kansas-born Harvey Wilcox and his wife, Daeida, were the founders late in the 19th century of a temperance community they called "Hollywood" that encircled their orchards.

It is this area today that most visitors think of as the heart of Hollywood: the celebrated stars along the **Walk of Fame** ◉ run along Hollywood Boulevard westwards from Vine Street, with Marilyn Monroe's star positioned outside the McDonald's restaurant. The walk was part of a major restoration of the street back in 1958 when the first batch of stars to be cemented into the sidewalk included Burt Lancaster, Ronald Colman and Joanne Woodward. Only one star, it's said – Barbra Streisand – failed to make the obligatory appearance at a dedication ceremony, although it's presumed that she or her agent paid the usual fee of around $15,000 to be listed. The old Max Factor building on Highland just south of Hollywood is now the **Hollywood Museum** (tel: 323-464 7776; Wed–Sun 10am–5pm; admission charge) with hundreds of costumes, film posters and artifacts.

After years of neglect, Hollywood Boulevard is making a comeback: witness the **Egyptian Theatre** in the 6700 block. The theater is a 1,700-seat replica of a palace in Thebes; in its heyday, the theater had a man on the roof in white robes announcing the times of the movie screenings. Now the property of the American Cinematheque, this restored theater presents a movie about Hollywood history on weekends; classics and previews of independent films are also screened, tel: 323-461 2020 for information. Public tours of the theater are conducted every month, for a small fee.

**Maps,
page 248
& 258**

The El Capitan at 6838 Hollywood Boulevard was built in 1926 and bought by Disney in 1989 for public screenings.

BELOW: Sir Elton's star on Hollywood's Walk of Fame.

In the vicinity are two family-friendly establishments: the **Guinness World Record Museum** and **Ripley's Believe It or Not!**.

The Oscar ceremony returned to Hollywood after a long rest and is now staged at the **Kodak Theatre**, part of the **Hollywood & Highland Center ❺**, with shops and eating places. Tours of the venue can be taken where guides provide the low-down on the gossip and glitz of the event, as well as allowing access to VIP areas. Tours are daily from 10.30am to 2.30pm and last 30 minutes. For information, tel: 323-308 6363.

Adjoining is **Grauman's Chinese Theatre ❻**, the famous landmark most notable for its forecourt of famous footprints. Nearby are the **Hollywood First National Bank Building** (a neo-Gothic structure created by the same architects, Meyer and Holler), at the corner of Highland Avenue, and, east of La Brea, the glamorous **Hollywood Roosevelt Hotel ❼**, site of the first public Oscars ceremony in 1929. The hotel once contained a treasure trove of memorabilia, including the first Technicolor camera, used in Disney's *Silly Symphonies* cartoons. Now, such artifacts reside in the Hollywood Entertainment Museum, currently seeking a new home after a decade on the boulevard.

Other nearby landmarks include **Musso & Frank's**, the rendezvous built in 1919 and frequented by writers Nathanael West, William Faulkner and Raymond Chandler; the fabulous Art Deco **Pantages**, that now stages shows from Broadway; the **Hollywood Wax Museum ❽** (on the site of the old Montmartre Café where Joan Crawford flirted); and **Larry Edmunds Bookshop**, a peerless source of Hollywoodiana, the best place for movie souvenirs in town. Not far from **Frederick's of Hollywood ❾** (6751 Hollywood Boulevard, tel: 323-957 5953), with its infamous bras and lingerie, steep Whitley Terrace heads up to **Whitley Heights**, a com-

ABOVE: star stamps.
BELOW: Fredericks of Hollywood is the place for lingerie.

munity of elegant mansions much favored by movie stars of the Gloria Swanson era, preceding the rise of Beverly Hills. Access is easier, however, off Highland Avenue, just before the big yellow barn (moved here long ago) that served as the original de Mille and Lasky studio, now the **Hollywood Heritage Museum** (tel: 323-874 2276; open weekends; admission charge). Across the street is the approach to the **Hollywood Bowl** ❶, an 18,000-seat amphitheater staging "Symphonies Under the Stars" concerts all summer, not to mention jazz, world music and major rock performances.

A movieplex and mall stands on the site of the former Schwabs Drugstore at 8024 Sunset, where F. Scott Fitzgerald once suffered a heart attack in the store while buying cigarettes, and composer Harold Arlen said the light coming from the windows as he walked past one day inspired him to write *Over the Rainbow*. Hollywood Boulevard peters out into hillside suburbia beyond La Brea, but, if you're driving, it's worth going a few blocks along Franklin to take a look at the **Yamashiro** restaurant, a re-created Japanese palace, and its Victorian neighbor, the **Magic Castle**.

West Hollywood

Tourists often assume that the "**Sunset Strip**" refers to the entire length of Sunset Boulevard. In reality, it begins and ends at West Hollywood's city limits, the hippest and most happening of LA's neighborhoods. Little more than two decades old, "WeHo" has a large gay community and a stylish outlook. By day, strollers mean- der (on foot!) from elegant art gallery to bohemian clothing shop to intimate café; by night they glide beween classy bistro, slick hotel lounge and pulsating music club. Some of them are celebrities; some merely gorgeous enough to be.

Maps, page 248 & 258

BELOW: stars in the sky and on the stage at the outdoor Hollywood Bowl.

The castle-like **Chateau Marmont ❺**, on Sunset near Laurel Canyon (tel: 323-656 1010) is almost an historic monument, in part because of guests such as Greta Garbo and Howard Hughes, and its notoriety as the death site of John Belushi; in part because of its current laid-back but starry ambience. The hotel is, loosely, the eastern edge of the Strip. From here, temples of cool march down the boulevard on ever-higher heels, its role call including the **Standard** and **Mondrian hotels**, the **House of Blues**, the **Comedy Store**, the **Whiskey a Go-Go** and **the Roxy**.

Some delightful Spanish-style architecture can be found in the West Hollywood blocks lying between Sunset Boulevard and Fountain Avenue, west of Crescent Heights. The **Villa Primavera** (1300 North Harper), as well as the **Patio del Moro** (8229 Fountain) and the **Villa Andalusia** (1473 North Havenhurst) were the work of the husband-and-wife architectural team of Arthur and Nina Zwebell; others, including **Villa D'Este** (1355 North Laurel) were done by the Davis brothers, Pierpont and Walter. All date to the 1920s, as does the apartment house located at 1305 North Harper where Marlene Dietrich is said to have stayed when she first arrived in 1930.

Mi Casa (1406 North Havenhurst) is the genuine foreign article: an irresistible row of balconied apartments around twin patios brought bodily from Ronda, Spain, in 1926, and since designated as a national historic place. The city's denizens have always had an ambivalent attitude about the local architecture and what survives seems to be largely a matter of chance.

Dominating the hill above Sunset is **Greystone Mansion ❻**. The 18-acre (7-hectare) garden is a popular spot for visitors, although the house (905 Loma Vista Drive) itself usually remains closed. It is, however, often rented out to movie companies for location filming. Built at a cost of $6 million in 1926 by the city's first oil

BELOW:
West Hollywood.

millionaire, Charles Doheny, the 50-room mansion is now owned by the city of Beverly Hills. Down La Cienega at Beverly Boulevard is the **Beverly Center**. For 30 years, until 1974, an amusement park and oil wells stood on the site of what is now an eight-level mall with 140 shops and restaurants and 13 movie theaters.

Map, page 248

Beverly Hills

Drilling for oil on what was once the Rancho Rodeo de las Aguas is what led to the birth of **Beverly Hills**, the unsuccessful oil prospectors subsequently deciding to develop the land. One-acre lots were offered for under $1,000 along the length of Sunset Boulevard. In 1912, Burton Green built the **Beverly Hills Hotel ❼** to be the focal point of the new community *(see page 264)*. One of Beverly Hills' earliest homes is the **Virginia Robinson house and gardens ❽** (tel: 310-276 5367), built in 1911 for the son and daughter-in-law of the owner of the Robinson department store chain. Lushly landscaped gardens include a mini-forest of palm trees and flower-filled terraces. Tours of the home and gardens can be arranged by appointment.

Filmdom's elite built ever-bigger homes in this elegant area, fanning out into the hills and canyons, and around Mulholland Drive, the spectacular highway that runs for 50 miles (80 km) along the crest of the Santa Monica Mountains all the way down to the coast just north of Malibu.

Greta Garbo and John Gilbert shared idyllic poolside afternoons together in a mansion at Seabright and Tower Grove Drive; Rudolph Valentino luxuriated in Falcon's Lair at 1436 Bella Drive; not too far away, the home of Roman Polanski and Sharon Tate at 10050 Cicelo Drive was the scene of the 1969 murders by members of the infamous Charles Manson family.

BELOW: a typical night out.

Beverly Hills Hotel

When the Beverly Hills Hotel closed for two years for a $100 million facelift, the doomsayers forecast that it would never regain its old cachet. But, when it reopened, it found that people were still ready and willing to pay at least $150 per day to rent a poolside cabana (on top of the astronomical price for a room).

For the truth is that the famous pink palace is much more than a hotel, it's a legend – the place where Elizabeth Taylor honeymooned in a bungalow that now costs $2,750 a day and where reclusive resident Howard Hughes ordered pineapple upside-down cake from room service almost every night. Hughes also rented four bungalows at the hotel: one for himself, another for his wife Jean Peters, a third for the blueprints of the *Spruce Goose*, the others for bodyguards and guests. One of his eccentricities was to order roast beef sandwiches delivered to a certain tree.

For a long time, Katharine Hepburn took

lessons from the hotel's tennis pro and one day, after six sets, dived in the pool fully clothed. She was also known to curl up outside Spencer Tracy's locked door, waiting for him to let her in after a drinking bout. Greta Garbo chose the hotel as a hideaway in 1932 and Clark Gable checked in to dodge the press after separating from his wife, Rita.

When the world's then richest man, Hassanal Bolkish, Sultan of Brunei, bought the hotel for $185 million in 1987, it was rumored he would turn it into a private residence for himself, but instead he ordered extensive renovations. Every room in the hotel has three phone lines, a fax machine, climate control, a safe and a butler-service button. The number of rooms was cut from 253 to 194 and gilded ceilings were added to the lobby. New additions included a kosher kitchen. Finally, 1,600 gallons (6,100 liters) of Beverly Hills Pink were computer-matched to old paint samples, so the new extensions matched the old.

Some things, of course, stayed the same, especially the Fountain Coffee Shop with its original iron stools still bolted to the floor and the familiar old banana leaf patterned wallpaper. It was in the coffee shop in 1959 that Marilyn Monroe and Yves Montand romanced over afternoon tea. The menu of the Polo Lounge, where big movie deals are still cut, still features the Neil McCarthy salad, named for the polo-playing millionaire who died in 1972. At first, the bar was called the El Jardin but was rechristened when socialite and polo player Charles Wrightsman turned up with his team's silver trophy bowl. After that, drinkers W.C. Fields and John Barrymore were joined by Will Rogers and Darryl Zanuck who dropped in after their matches.

In a town notorious for its casual attire, decorum still prevails at the Beverly Hills. Mia Farrow was once turned away from the Polo Lounge for wearing pants, and rock manager Arnold Stiefel, who chose the place to sign up Guns N' Roses, recalls that the waitresses "were in shock at all those people with things in their nose. I think it took the coffee shop at least six months to recover." ❑

LEFT: "No one is allowed to fail within a 2-mile radius of the Beverly Hills Hotel," observed writer Gore Vidal after visiting the Pink Palace.

At the canyon's lower end, along immaculate North Roxbury Drive, lived Marlene Dietrich (No. 822), Jimmy Stewart (918), Lucille Ball (1000) and Jack Benny (1002). Greta Garbo's home was nearby at 1027 Chevy Chase Drive and William Randolph Hearst's mistress, Marion Davies, had a home at 1700 Lexington Road. At the time of his death in 1951, Hearst was living with Ms. Davies in a house on Beverly Drive, noted for the huge palms that line the street. With a population of 30,000 trees, Beverly Hills has almost one per resident.

Map, page 248

Rodeo Drive

Land was cheaper down around Santa Monica Boulevard when the community first began, but these days you'd hardly know it considering the prices along famous **Rodeo Drive ❾**, especially between Santa Monica and Wilshire where stores with foreign names like Gucci, Hermès, Chanel, Fendi and Cartier have branches – "the most staggering display of luxury in the western world," says novelist Judith Krantz. **Two Rodeo Drive**, with its cobbled street and bow windows, is a replica of what only Hollywood could believe to be an olde-worlde European backwater; across the street, Fred Hayman's red and yellow showplace has a working fireplace surrounded by photos of celebrity customers who can belly up to the bar while waiting for their partners to drop a few thou.

Even **City Hall**, with its handsome tiled dome, is a splendid sight, part of the Spanish Renaissance-style **Beverly Hills Civic Center ❿**. More interesting architecturally, however, is the intriguingly bizarre **Witch's House ⓫**, at 516 Walden Drive, which began life as a 1921 movie set designed to look like the home of the fairy tale witch in *Hansel and Gretel*. It was later moved to this site. Conscious of its worldwide fame, Beverly Hills maintains an informed, active **Visitors Bureau**

ABOVE AND BELOW: pit stop on the road that has "the most staggering display of luxury in the western world."

Map,
page 248

at 239 S. Beverly Drive (tel: 310-248 1015; Mon–Fri 8.30am–5pm). If you happen to be in LA on a rare rainy day, head for the **Paley Center for Media ⑫** (465 N. Beverly Drive, tel: 310-786 1000; Wed–Sun noon–5pm; free admission), where visitors can listen to news and watch old TV shows. About a mile (1.5 km) to the south is the **Museum of Tolerance ⑬** (9786 W. Pico Boulevard, tel: 310-553 8403; closed Sat, hours longer in summer; admission charge), a sobering look at the history of racism in the US and the Holocaust experience in Germany.

Santa Monica and Wilshire boulevards intersect at the far side of Beverly Hills, beside the **Electric Fountain** that caused sightseeing traffic jams when it was first built in the 1930s. Santa Monica Boulevard heads west past the skyscrapers (filled mostly with corporate law offices and the like) of **Century City**, centered around the luxurious Century Plaza Hotel and another upscale shopping center, before terminating at Santa Monica. Century City's 180-acre (73-hectare) site was once part of the studio back lot of 20th Century Fox.

Westwood Village

Wilshire Boulevard swerves slightly to the northwest out of Beverly Hills along the southern flank of the shopping complex **Westwood Village**, once the headquarters of William Fox's newsreel operations and now home to the interesting **Hammer Museum** (10899 Wilshire Boulevard, Westwood Village, tel: 310-443 7000; closed Mon; admission charge), which exhibits European paintings, da Vinci drawings and traveling art shows. The movie theaters at Westwood are often the places for sneak previews and low-key movie premieres; it's also one of the places where off-duty movie stars take their kids on Saturday afternoons.

BELOW: LA's famous Chinese Theatre.
RIGHT: 77th Annual Academy Awards at the Kodak Theatre.

Westwood also adjoins the tree-shaded **University of California ⑭** (UCLA) campus. UCLA's 130 buildings include Schoenberg Hall (named after the composer who taught here), Bunche Hall Library and the New Wight Gallery, all open to the public. The college's main entrance is on Hilgard Avenue, south of Sunset. A first stop should include one of 11 information and parking booths around the campus.

The gated community of ultra-chic Bel Air is north of Sunset, the road up through Stone Canyon passing what some think of as LA's most beautiful hideaway hotel, the **Hotel Bel Air ⑮**. Grace Kelly lived here for much of her movie career.

Back on Sunset, the boulevard begins a series of dizzying loops and curves passing through **Brentwood**, site of the impressive **Getty Center ⑯** *(see pages 268–9)*. One of Raymond Chandler's many homes was at 12216 Shetland Place and Marilyn Monroe died in a bungalow at 12305 Fifth Helena Drive. Sunset continues through **Pacific Palisades** before sweeping down to the Pacific Coast Highway.

Just before the coast, on the left, is a sharp turn-off to the lakeside shrine of the **Self-Realization Fellowship**, but, a mile or two before that, it's worth turning off to the right for the challenging, uphill drive to the **Will Rogers State Historic Park ⑰**. The cowboy philosopher, who had been America's top box-office star, died in a plane crash in 1935. Ten years later, the ranch was turned over to the state, which has maintained it as a museum pretty much as it was when Rogers lived. ❏

J. PAUL GETTY MUSEUM AND THE GETTY CENTER

More than a dozen years in the making, the billion-dollar Getty Center has been likened to a Tuscan hilltown by its architect Richard Meier

The white city on the hill high above the intersection of the Santa Monica and San Diego freeways has – like most examples of modern architecture – provoked both praise and criticism. Detractors have claimed it resembles an oversize refrigerator or a strip mall while one admirer claims it is "too good for Los Angeles." Richard Meier, winner of architecture's highest honor, the Pritzker Prize, was chosen for the commission after a worldwide search. He described the site as the most beautiful he had ever been invited to build upon, one whose light, landscape and topography provided the cues for his design. The center, he says, "is both in the city and removed from it… evok[ing] a sense of both urbanity and contemplation."

The collections are displayed in a series of five interconnecting buildings – the J. Paul Getty Museum – but the Getty Center site also houses six other buildings, including a research institute, a library, an auditorium and a restaurant, most offering breathtaking views of the city, the sea and the mountains. Between the museum and the research institute is a central garden, designed by artist Robert Irwin, that changes with the seasons.

The Getty Center, tel: 310-440 7300; www.getty.edu. Closed Monday. Free, but fee for parking.

▷ **LANSDOWNE HERAKLES**
This statue discovered in 1790 at Emperor Hadrian's villa near Tivoli is the inspiration behind Getty's decision to build his own Malibu villa and museum.

△ **THE CRUCIFIXION**
This exhibit is from the *Stammheim Missal*, a German manuscript created in Hildesheim *circa* 1160.

▷ **BUILDING BOOM**
In addition to the five buildings housing the works of art, there are six others on-site.

△ **THE HOLY FAMILY**
Buonarroti's drawing, *circa* 1530, was reworked many times in different mediums.

▽ **BERLIN FREE ZONE**
This architectural drawing by Lebbeus Woods of a building facade was one of the inaugural installations.

DAVID HOCKNEY MOSAIC
␣e British-born artist created ␣arlblossom Hwy 11 – 18th ␣ril 1986 # 2 over nine days the Antelope Valley outside ␣s Angeles. Ten feet in width ␣ 6 ft, it is a mounted mosaic ␣700 photographs ␣picting the vast desert ␣dscape) and is the first ␣ajor work by Hockney to ␣ter the museum's ␣ntemporary collection.

◁ **THE GETTY VILLA**
This mansion in Malibu, a re-created Pompeian villa, reopened in 2006 after a nine-year, $275 million restoration. It is America's only museum devoted to Greek, Roman and Etruscan antiquities. In a series of sunlit galleries, 1,200 of Getty's 44,000 ancient artifacts are displayed at any one time. Entry is via timed tickets, limiting the crowds.

THE LA SEASHORE

From the exclusive Malibu Colony to the roller-blading boardwalk of Venice, Los Angeles wouldn't be Los Angeles without its photogenic beach

Map, page 248

O nce, it took a full day's stagecoach ride to get to Santa Monica from Downtown, but, when the freeway opened in 1966, the trip was cut to half an hour: Los Angelenos had discovered the beach. Whereas previously the city's seashores had been the preserve of fishermen and those wealthy enough to build bungalows by the sea, suddenly everyone was sporting a tan and hanging ten.

Where Sunset hits the Pacific Coast Highway (PCH) is 1 mile southeast of the **Getty Villa** ⑱ *(www.getty.edu; Thur–Mon 10am–5pm; admission free, but fee for parking; timed ticket required.).* The villa, one of America's most beautiful museums, has reopened as an evocative and highly suitable permanent home to the Greek and Roman exhibits. These treasures were formerly displayed in highly cramped quarters or more often, packed away in storage. But when the Getty Center opened and many items moved to the clifftop museum, the Getty Villa came into its own *(see page 269).* Up the highway from the villa is **Topanga County beach** with a full range of public facilities, but somewhat territorially minded surfers.

Malibu

A couple of miles farther west on PCH is the community of **Malibu** ⑲ with its free state beach and pier. Southwest of the pier is the historic **Adamson House** (tel: 310-456 8432; Wed–Sat 11am–3pm). There is a small admission charge for guided tours and parking. The Adamson House was built in 1929 by Rhoda Adamson, daughter of Frederick Rindge, Malibu's founder and major landholder. (Frederick Rindge bought hundreds of acres of surrounding land for as little as $10 an acre back in 1892.) The house is as attractive outside as it is inside, and even when it is closed you can drive or walk up the lane (or even come in from off the beach) and admire the tiled terrace, the lovely fountains, bottle-glass windows and well-kept gardens.

A display in the museum, which features old photographs, explains that the real Malibu Gold is real estate: Bing Crosby's house cost him $8,700 in 1931 and was bought for almost $2 million by Robert Redford half a century later. Harold Lloyd's 1928 house cost him $6,400, but singer Linda Ronstadt paid $1.3 million in 1985. Now they sell for tens of millions.

Just northeast of the lagoon (a preserved wetland in which you can sometimes spot ducks, herons and pelicans) is **Malibu Pier**, built by Rindge just before he died in 1905. The pier is open to the public and is a fun place to while away an amusing hour or two.

Dozens of stars live hidden away here, some of them along the well-guarded beachfront **Malibu Colony** at the junction of PCH and Webb Way, but the only place they're likely to be seen in public is the Colony shopping center about a mile to the west of the pier.

LEFT: sand volleyball, always big in California, is now an Olympic sport. **BELOW:** would-be sailors in the sand.

Broad Beach, like so much of the Malibu coastline, is private but only down to the mean high-tide line. Which means that, as long as you stay on wet sand, you have every right to be there. Maybe you'll spot a superstar jogging. Easily missed access to the beach is in the 3100 and 3200 block of Broad Beach Road. **Zuma** beach and **Pt Dume** state beach are public, and therefore understandably become pretty crowded. Up in Malibu's Santa Monica Mountains, the environmentally friendly **Ramirez Canyon Park** (tel: 310-589 2850) occupies the 22.5-acre (9-hectare) site of what was formerly one of Barbra Streisand's estates, donated by the singer in 1993. Walking paths shaded by sycamore, walnut and pine trees wind along Ramirez Creek. The park, used mainly for conferences and classes, is accessible by appointment only.

Santa Monica

At the northern end of Santa Monica, the enormous mansions along the beach were mostly built by moviedom's elite. The grandest, at 415 Pacific Coast Highway, was the 118-room compound designed by William Randolph Hearst's favorite architect, Julia Morgan, for the newspaper tycoon and his paramour, Marion Davies. In 1945, the house was sold for $600,000 to Joseph Drown, owner of the Hotel Bel Air, who turned it into a beach hotel and club. Today, it is being replaced by a public beach club, set to open in 2009.

In those days, before the breakwater extended the beach, the sea came to within 50 ft (15 meters) of most of these homes. It was another famous architect, Richard Neutra, who created Mae West's home at number 514, while Wallace Neff, who designed Pickfair, was responsible for the home of Louis B. Mayer's son-in-law, producer William Goetz, at number 522.

BELOW: the Place for shopping: Santa Monica Place.

Map, page 248

The "Bay City" setting of so many of Raymond Chandler's detective novels is where Wilshire and Sunset boulevards meet the ocean, albeit a couple of miles apart. Discussing the locale of Chandler's novels, his biographer Frank MacShane said he felt the detective story was an entirely appropriate form for LA because such stories "could involve an extraordinary range of humanity from the very rich to the very poor and can encompass a great many different places." And as to involving an extraordinary range of humanity, **Santa Monica** ⑳ certainly qualifies, if only for being the largest coastal town in the 100-mile (160-km) stretch between Oxnard and Long Beach.

Santa Monica is something of an anomaly, being an upper-middle class town with a few places still under rent control; a recently discovered, affordable office space for Hollywood production companies; and a seaside resort in which the sea often seems barely relevant. Except, of course, for the **Santa Monica Pier** (now sparkling after a 10-year, $45-million renovation) with its famous carousel that appeared in *The Sting*. The century-old pier has numerous amusement arcades, eating places and fishing stands, where visitors can gaze at miles of beaches curving gently around the bay, but, unfortunately, all too often the ocean is too polluted for safe swimming. Nearby are lots of restaurants catering to all tastes and budgets with the same drop-dead-gorgeous view of the Pacific sunsets.

Affluent "industry" people stop by Santa Monica from Malibu or their offices nearby to shop or use the excellent library, and people from all over the area frequent the spacious pedestrian mall, the **Third Street Promenade**. The promenade leads to attractive **Santa Monica Place**, an upscale mall designed by acclaimed local architect Frank Gehry, replete with major department stores, scores of eating places and several cinemas nearby.

Raymond Chandler (1888–1959) set many of his books in Santa Monica.

BELOW: the Getty Villa.

Eucalyptus-fringed **Palisades Park** ㉑, overlooking the pier, was given to the city in 1892 for use "forever" by Santa Monica's founders, Col. Robert Baker and his partner, silver tycoon John P. Jones. Jones's house at the corner of Wilshire was where the **Fairmont Miramar Hotel** now sits; the enormous fig tree outside the lobby was planted by a member of the family more than a century ago. Greta Garbo spent her first three years living at the Miramar when she first came to the US in 1924. The pool was seen in the "Bermuda" sequence of *That Touch of Mink* with Cary Grant and Doris Day.

This deceptively casual town embraces both a metropolitan sophistication and a beach-town atmosphere. Many people in the media, arts and design choose to live here, and almost every visitor to Los Angeles under the age of 35 chooses to at least visit, or more often, stay here. It's a great place to walk around and, so unusual for LA, no car is necessary. The **Visitor Information kiosk** at 1400 Ocean Avenue (open daily 10–5pm in summer, 10am–4pm winter) is a great place to start. To the south is a **Camera Obscura** ㉒ for which the (free) admission is via the Senior Recreation Center.

South of the pier, a walkway and bicycle path adjoins the beach all the way down to Venice. Buses run up and down Ocean Avenue, close to **Main Street** with its terrific shops, cafés and **California Heritage Museum** (tel: 310-392 8537; Wed–Sun 11am–4pm; admission charge). On Main Street is Santa Monica's primary **Visitor Information Center** (tel: 310-393 7593; open daily 9am–6pm). Straddling the border with Venice is the **Rose Cafe**, Rose Avenue at Main Street, where locally created artworks are sold in a small shop that's part of this lively setup. Sip espresso and nibble sinfully rich pastries while sitting on stools at high tables or on the outside patio.

BELOW: mood over Malibu.

Speaking of artwork, some of the city's most interesting murals can be seen around Venice – Christina Schlesinger's *Marc Chagall Comes to Venice Beach* at 201 Ocean Front Walk and Emily Winters' *Endangered Species* six blocks down are notable – not far from the headquarters of SPARC, an organization which sponsors such public art. Its greatest triumph is the *Great Wall of Los Angeles*, covering half a mile beside the Los Angeles River in Van Nuys.

Venice

The closer you get to **Venice ㉓**, the odder the ambiance. An early favorite of such silent moviemakers as Charlie Chaplin and Carole Lombard, **Venice Boardwalk** is today jammed almost around the clock with characters who appear to be auditioning for some unannounced contemporary epic. Sights and sounds are likely to include guitar-bearing rollerbladers in robes and turbans, bikini-clad beach bunnies, rainbow-haired punks, lunatic dreamers, outrageous con men, barely dressed cyclists, psychics, chain-saw jugglers and the bicep-bound boasters of **Muscle Beach** (tel: 310-458 8301). There are sidewalk cafés at which it's a relief to rest and watch all this activity.

But there is another less-explored Venice a few blocks to the east. After you have noted the building on **Windward Avenue**, whose colonnaded arches are meant to evoke visions of San Marco Square in Venice's Italian namesake, walk east to the post office, which, earlier in the 20th century, was where most of the canals met. Many are now paved over, but a walk of a few blocks to the southeast will bring you to what remains of the watery network, a charmingly tranquil area of shallowly filled canals lined with houses in myriad styles, mostly with gardens full of flowers that only grow in the hot sunshine. Ducks and geese line the walkways. If you are

ABOVE: Venice.
BELOW: Santa Monica's Ocean Avenue at dusk.

Map, page 248

driving, the route is down Dell Avenue across the humpback bridges. When tobacco magnate Abbott Kinney invested millions in creating his Venice from what was 160 acres (65 hectares) of worthless marshland in the early 1900s, he lined the canals with Japanese lanterns, imported gondolas, encircled the project with a miniature railroad and sold scores of housing lots. Visitors who paid 25¢ to take the new railroad from Downtown ended a busy day on the (now-abandoned) pier watching an armored trumpeter serenade the sunset from a replica of Juan Cabrillo's medieval flagship before retiring for the night in the St Mark's Hotel, modeled after the Doge's Palace in you-know-where.

Despite Kinney's ambitious plans, which included hiring Sarah Bernhardt and the Chicago Symphony Orchestra for his 3,500-seat auditorium before scaling down the attractions for more plebeian audiences, the project gradually deteriorated. And its collapse was speeded by the discovery of oil (there were 163 wells in the area by 1931) and by the shortage of fresh water. Like so many neighboring communities, Venice was obliged to come under the aegis of Los Angeles if it wanted to ensure a regular water supply. With incorporation came less tolerance for canals when paved roads could occupy the space.

The circulation system for what was originally 16 miles (26 km) of canals envisaged seawater pulsing through 30-inch (76-cm) pipes from every fresh tide, but it proved unworkable and the canals themselves became sand-clogged and stagnant. In 1993, an extensive renovation began with plans to dredge the canals, refill them with water, repair the paths alongside and rebuild some of the bridges. Kinney's name has been memorialized in **Abbott Kinney Boulevard** – connecting Main Street with **Marina del Rey ㉔** – along which can be found interesting little cafés, restaurants and lots of shops.

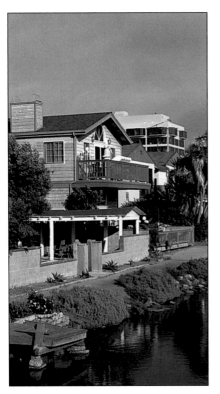

BELOW: watery Marina del Rey. **RIGHT:** a smooch by the seaside.

Marina del Rey

On busy weekends, Marina del Rey's Villa Marina Marketplace may be the nearest place to park, but you can take the bus back to Venice. This seaside place is really near the **Los Angeles international airport** (LAX), and is a good place for a stop over. The marina's tourist attraction is the charming but phony **Fisherman's Village** (the "lighthouse" is a fast-food stand) with a multitude of restaurants for lunch. These range from reasonably priced Mexican fare to Shanghai Red's, which has all the appealing ambiance of a century-old inn but has actually been there for only 40 years or so, since the marina began.

At the end of Basin D is a shallow-water family beach known as "**Mother's Beach.**" All the restaurants overlook the harbor – the world's largest artificial harbor for small crafts – with its berths for 6,000 boats. From Beverly Hills, the bus runs down Robertson Boulevard all the way to Marina del Rey, which is also accessible by Santa Monica's Big Blue Bus.

Back on Ocean Avenue, take the Big Blue Bus up a few blocks to Ocean View Park and transfer to the bus that runs along the north side of **Santa Monica Airport**. From Clover Park, walk a couple of blocks down to the former site of the Museum of Flying. It was here, in 1977, that the DC3 was born and built, and it is here in this unusual setting that you can dine in one of two Asian restaurants with views of the runway. ❑

CANYONS AND VALLEYS

*The best-known spots are the San Fernando Valley
and the town of Pasadena, but the fringes of Los Angeles
offer historic houses and gardens galore*

Map, page 282

Los Angeles

San Diego

Far from the typical glitzy tourist attraction, the San Fernando Valley has a low profile. Tinseltown and the beaches get plenty of television exposure, but, aside from Northridge's 15 minutes of fame after the 1994 earthquake, the rest of Los Angeles isn't seen too much. In fact, even many of LA's longtime residents know almost nothing of the valley – although this situation changed somewhat in the years after the millennium, during which a vociferous group began promoting the valley's secession from Los Angeles.

All of the vague and amorphous references to the valleys and canyons of Los Angeles merit some clarification. Of the three main valleys, the smallest is the **Santa Clarita**, known for its abundance of produce stands and the looming presence of the Six Flags Magic Mountain amusement park; next is the **San Gabriel**, which stretches through Pasadena and Monterey Park toward Riverside and San Bernardino. But the star of the three is the sprawling **San Fernando Valley**, and it is this one to which local people are usually referring when they simply say "the valley."

Various passes and canyons are byways to and from the valley: **Sepulveda Pass** connects it to West LA via the San Diego Freeway; the **Cahuenga Pass** takes it to Hollywood. **Laurel Canyon** connects Studio City and West Hollywood, and **Coldwater Canyon** connects Sherman Oaks to Beverly Hills. The last of the large canyons, **Topanga** and **Malibu**, offer dramatic routes from the landlocked valley to the ocean.

Flatlands of LA

In contrast to neighboring areas, the valley is a staggeringly flat expanse of land bounded by the Ventura county line on the west, the San Gabriel mountains to the north, the Verdugo range on the east and the Santa Monica Mountains and Hollywood Hills on the south. San Fernando Valley is about 24 miles (39 km) wide and 12 miles (19 km) north to south. The west and south sides are the more affluent – cities like **Encino**, **Tarzana**, **Woodland Hills** and **West Hills** display few signs of opulence, but a quiet wealth predominates. Heavy industry is almost all concentrated in the northern area, around Pacoima, Sylmar and San Fernando.

Were it a city unto itself, the valley would be the fifth largest in the country, topped only by New York, Chicago, Houston and, of course, Los Angeles. Despite sporadic efforts to secede, the valley is not its own city, however – with the exception of holdouts Burbank and Glendale. All the differently designated areas are merely neighborhoods in the City of Los Angeles, and compose nearly one-third of LA's population.

The valley more or less begins with **Griffith Park ❶** (tel: 323-913 4688), the immense preserve that begins at Los Feliz Boulevard and extends all the way to the Ven-

PRECEDING PAGES:
Malibu Mountains rancher.
LEFT: someone to watch over you.
BELOW: welcome to the valley.

tura freeway. It has a **zoo**, a wonderful **observatory**, an **open-air theater**, a **train museum**, numerous recreation areas and the excellent **Museum of the American West** (admission charge), but is otherwise more for motorists than for strollers. Not too far away is one of the country's best collections of Native American art, on display at the **Southwest Museum ❷** (234 Museum Drive, tel: 323-221 2164), currently undergoing restoration.

Universal Studios

West of the park, in the Cahuenga Pass that joins Hollywood to the valley, is **Universal Studios ❸** (tel: 800-864 8377 at Hollywood 101; daily 10am–6pm; admission charge), whose daily tours offer glimpses of the studio in what is in effect an amusement park. A 45-minute tram ride visits King Kong and the giant shark from *Jaws,* and negotiates the perils of a collapsing bridge, an avalanche, an earthquake and the parting of the Red Sea. Other additions include *Jurassic Park* – The Ride, the fiery *Backdraft*, the comical *Shrek 4-D*, the unpredictable *Fear Factor Live* and *Terminator 2: 3D*. You can see numerous outdoor sets, including the Bates mansion from *Psycho* and the facades from *Back to the Future*.

Universal Studios is the world's largest working entertainment studio. It can also be a fun day out.

Universal CityWalk (tel: 818-622 4455) is a glittery mall with one-of-a-kind shops, a contemporary art gallery and a 19-screen cinema. Admission is free but there is a parking fee; budget-conscious visitors can take the Metro Red Line from Downtown or Hollywood to the Universal City station.

To the west, in **Studio City**, is CBS **Studio Center ❹** (tel: 818-655 5000) where many sit-coms have been made, including the still syndicated *Seinfeld*. Other tours can be enjoyed at two studios in "beautiful Downtown Burbank" (as the longtime host of *The Tonight Show* dubbed it): the NBC **Television Studios ❺** (tel: 818-840 3537; admission charge) and **Warner Brothers Studios ❻** (tel: 818-972 8687; admission charge), which offers a serious VIP tour of its grounds – watch them make whatever program is on the day's shooting agenda. Also in Burbank, but not open to the public, is the unbelievably successful **Walt Disney Studios**.

Forest Lawn Memorial Park ❼ has two peaceful locations flanking Griffith Park (at 4,000 acres/1,620 hectares, the nation's largest): **Glendale**, and the **Hollywood Hills** (tel: 800-204 3131). The Glendale location, the inspiration for Evelyn Waugh's *The Loved One*, is a must-see. All the park literature studiously avoids

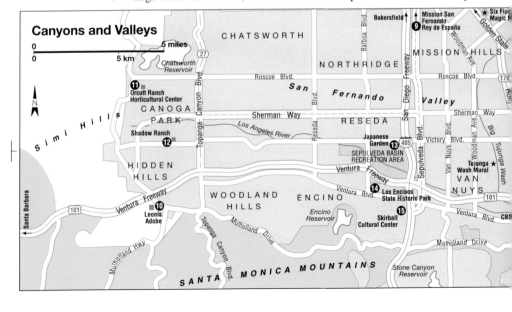

Canyons and Valleys

the word "cemetery," instead describing founder Huber Eaton's vision of "the greenest, most enchanting park that you ever saw…"

Map, page 282

Ultimately a final resting place (for many Hollywood stars, including Clark Gable, Carole Lombard, Nat King Cole and Jean Harlow), Forest Lawn also has reproductions of famous churches from around the world, a stained-glass interpretation of da Vinci's *The Last Supper* and the world's largest religious painting, *The Crucifixion* by Jan Stykam, measuring 195 by 45 ft (59 by 14 meters). The Hollywood Hills branch is dedicated to early American history, and features bronze and marble statuary, including a replica of the Liberty Bell in Philadelphia. Residents include Buster Keaton, Stan Laurel and Liberace.

Northeast a few miles, in the town of **Glendale ❽**, the **Brand Library and Art Center** (1601 W. Mountain Street at Grandview Avenue, tel: 818-548 2051; Tues noon–9pm, Wed 10am–6pm, Thur noon–9pm and Fri–Sat 10am–5pm) houses the art and music section of the city's public library in a Moorish-style mansion. Inspired by the East Indian Pavilion at the 1893 Chicago World's Fair, it was built in 1904 by Leslie C. Brand, and the peaceful, landscaped grounds are perfect for picnicking.

The *Great Wall of Los Angeles* **mural** (west wall of the concrete flood control channel on Coldwater Canyon Boulevard between Burbank Boulevard and Oxnard Street, North Hollywood) claims to be the world's longest mural. It recounts the history of California from dinosaurs to the present, and doesn't leave out the nasty bits. So it's quite a learning experience for participants and visitors alike.

Universal Studios' scary, theme-based action ride: you'll wish it was just a movie, they say.

Fascinating missions

Near the junction of I-5 and I-405 in Mission Hills is the historic and interesting **Mission San Fernando Rey de España ❾** (tel: 818-361 0186; daily 9am–4.30pm; admission charge), California's 17th mission, founded in 1797. Its history has been marked by destruction in two earthquakes (1806 and 1971) and reconstruction. The tour of the working, sleeping and recreation areas, and an extensive collection of artifacts re-create a sense of daily early mission life.

Nearby, the **Andres Pico Adobe**, the oldest home in San Fernando and second oldest in the Greater LA area, was built by Mission San Fernando Indians in 1834. After years of disuse, it was purchased and restored in 1930 by the curator of the

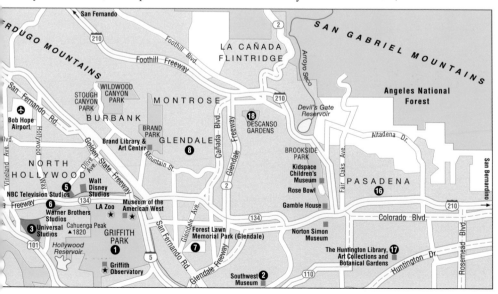

A stunning scenic
route is Mulholland
Drive, which goes
across the local Santa
Monica Mountains
from the Hollywood
Hills and almost to the
ocean. The drive offers
– among other plea-
sures – a 360-degree
view of Los Angeles.

Southwest Museum, housing the **San Fernando Valley Historical Society**. Just to the northeast are the very different **Nethercutt Museum** and **Nethercutt Collection** (15151 and 15200 Bledsoe Street, Sylmar, tel: 818-367 2251), two private facilities owned and operated by the Merle Norman Cosmetic Co. They offer the visitor a world-class collection of antiques, vintage automobiles, rare musical instruments and music boxes. Tours of the collection require reservations, so call ahead, and don't forget that there is a dress code; children under 12 are not allowed.

I-5 continues northwest to **Valencia**, site of the **Six Flags Magic Mountain** amusement park and **Hurricane Harbor** waterpark (tel: 661-255 4100), which have dozens of rides and other attractions.

At the valley's western end, near Mulholland Drive, is the **Leonis Adobe ⑩** (23537 Calabasas Road at Mulholland Drive, tel: 818-222 6511; Wed–Fri and Sun 1–4pm, Sat 10am–4pm; donation suggested), a two-story 1844 Monterey-style ranch house transformed by "King of Calabasas" ("pumpkin" in Spanish) Miguel Leonis into this charming home, fully restored and furnished with livestock and artifacts. Located on the same property is the **Plummer House** (serving as the **park visitor center**), a pretty Victorian cottage, which was transported from a site in Hollywood to avoid demolition.

Orcutt Ranch Horticultural Center ⑪ (23600 Roscoe Boulevard, Canoga Park, tel: 818-883 6641) perfectly recalls a vanished moment in California history – citrus groves bounded by majestic and stately oaks, ancient on their native soil. When the Orcutts purchased the 200-acre (80-hectare) estate in 1917, they named it Rancho Sombra del Roble, "ranch in the shadow of the oak," which is quite literally the case. There is one magnificent valley oak 33 ft (10 meters) in circumference that is estimated to be at least 700 years old. The gardens enclose other areas,

BELOW:
Universal CityWalk.

decorated by statuary and sundials, that are now variously favored for picnics and weddings. The orange groves are open to the public on one weekend announced in July, and the proceeds augment the garden's city-allotted budget.

Shadow Ranch ⑫ (22633 Vanowen Street, Canoga Park, tel: 818-883 3637; Mon–Fri 9am–10pm, Sat–Sun 9am–5pm) is a restored 1870 ranch house built by LA pioneer Albert Workman and located on the remaining 9 acres (4 hectares) of a 60,000-acre (24,280-hectare) wheat ranch. It reopened in 2001, seven years after being damaged in the Northridge earthquake. The stands of eucalyptus are purported to be parents of the towering trees that now blanket the state, and the ranch is currently used as a community center.

The **Japanese Garden ⑬** (6100 Woodley Avenue, Van Nuys), a 6-acre (2-hectare) botanical delight, is little-known despite having been created over two decades ago on the Donald C. Tillman Water Reclamation Plant. Morning tours visit three gardens in distinctly different styles. In summer, there are "sunset" tours on weekdays – so popular that reservations are a must.

Los Encinos State Historic Park ⑭ (16756 Moorpark Street, Encino, tel: 818-784 4849), originally the site of a Native American village, later became a ranch belonging to the de la Ossa family, who planted vineyards and orchards, and raised cattle. Amid the 5 acres (2 hectares) of manicured lawns, duck ponds and eucalyptus and citrus groves is the de la Ossa Adobe, built in 1849 and restored with period furnishings. Also damaged by the major quake, it has since reopened after repairs. A stone blacksmith shop and a two-story French provincial home, built by the ranch's second owners, are also located here.

Some of LA's major restaurants have branched out into the valley, bringing what's been called "310 food" to the 818 area code. More than anything, though,

Map, page 282

BELOW: blazing a trail through the canyons.

this is shopping mall country. "You eat, you shop. It's the valley," as one Sherman Oaks resident put it. Shopping in the valley is easy. Parking is abundant compared with the rest of Los Angeles, although the burgeoning population, combined with the lack of public transportation, has slowed traffic.

There are mega-malls like the **Sherman Oaks Galleria**, which is in mid-valley about halfway between **Westfield Topanga** to the west and **Glendale Galleria** nearer to LA; also at the western end are **Westfield Promenade** in Woodland Hills, and **Town and Country Shopping Center** and **Plaza de Oro** in the town of **Encino**. There's also 21-mile (34-km) long Ventura Boulevard, the valley's upscale artery of restaurants and pricey shops.

South of Encino, west of the 405, lies the **Skirball Cultural Center** ⓖ (2701 North Sepulveda Boulevard, tel: 310-440 4500; Tues–Fri noon–5pm, Sat–Sun 10am–5pm; admission charge). Visitors are treated to Jewish historical exhibits, comedic performances, classic films and world music concerts.

Pasadena

To the east of the San Fernando Valley and bordering almost on the San Gabriel Mountains, **Pasadena** ⓰ comes fully alive once a year during the Rose Bowl football game and the famous Tournament of Roses Parade. A couple of famous houses are well worth inspecting, but note that they close early.

Near the freeway is the 18-room **Fenyes Mansion** (1905), home of the **Pasadena Museum of History**, where D.W. Griffith shot one of his first films (tel: 626-577 1660; Wed–Sun noon–5pm). Half a block away is the impressive **Gamble House**, built for David Gamble (of Procter & Gamble, America's biggest soap company) in 1908. Technically a California-style "bungalow," the terraced, wood-tiled house

BELOW:
Descanso Gardens.

is a product of the turn of the 20th century Arts and Crafts Movement of which the Greene brothers, Charles Sumner and Henry Mather were noted members. Impressive from the outside (and therefore worth seeing even when the house is closed), its interior is a knockout, but to see this you must arrive early (tel: 626-793 3334; Thur–Sun noon–3pm; admission charge).

Just south of the freeway is the **Norton Simon Museum** (411 W. Colorado at Orange Grove, tel: 626-449 6840; Wed–Mon noon–6pm; admission charge), with its major collection of Asian art.

Pasadena's main attraction, however, is the **Huntington Library, Art Collections and Botanical Gardens** ⓱ (1151 Oxford Road, San Marino, tel: 626-405 2100; Tues–Fri noon–4.30pm, Sat–Sun 10.30am–4.30pm; admission charge). Situated just past the California Institute of Technology on California Boulevard at Allen Avenue, walk down to Orlando to enter the former gardens and library of multi-millionare railroad magnate Henry Edwards Huntington. With his wife Arabella, Huntington assembled one of the most important collections of art and rare books in the country.

The main gallery has several world-famous paintings: Thomas Gainsborough's *Blue Boy* (*circa* 1770); Thomas Lawrence's *Pinkie* (1794); Sir Joshua Reynolds' *Sarah Siddons* (1784) and John Constable's *View on the Stour* (1822). But be sure to save time for the library, which has an astonishing five million items. Among those on dis-

Map, page 282

play are a 1410 edition of Chaucer's *Canterbury Tales*, a Gutenberg Bible, Audubon prints and an early Shakespeare folio.

Because the gardens occupy more than 100 acres (40 hectares), it's not difficult to find yourself in some tranquil spot with nothing but the sound of birds for company. Beyond the lily pond are the colorful Subtropical Garden, the Australian Garden and the Japanese and Zen gardens flanking a delightful 19th-century Japanese house. After crossing the little red bridge over the carp-filled lake and climbing the steps, you might find yourself just in time for tea at the charming **Rose Garden Tea Room** (reservations required). Admission to the Huntington isn't free, despite the terms of the railroad magnate's will, but parking is complimentary. The main building has an excellent bookshop with interesting toys.

North of Pasadena, off the Angeles Crest Highway exit on Interstate 210 is fragrant **Descanso Gardens** ⑱ (1418 Descanso Drive, La Cañada Flintridge, tel: 818-949 4200; daily 9am–4.30pm; admission charge), which cover what remains of a 30,000-acre (12,140-hectare) ranch. The 165-acre (67-hectare) gardens take a good couple of hours to explore. The oak and camellia woodlands, with more than 600 varieties, constitute one of the largest camellia collections in the world. The woodlands began as carefully planned landscaping along the private drive leading to a magnificent 22-room house built in 1938 by the energetic *Daily News* publisher E. Manchester Boddy.

This collection is augmented by winding trails, a lilac garden, the International Rosarium (a timeline of roses from Cleopatra's day to the present) and the Japanese Garden and Teahouse, which serves refreshments (admission charge). Something is always in bloom whenever you arrive: daffodils, tulips and lilacs in the spring, chrysanthemums in the fall. ❑

ABOVE: Pasadena is a city of gardens.
BELOW: Pasadena Museum of History.

THE CENTRAL COAST

Map, page 242

Even a century ago, the Santa Barbara area was lauded for "the beauty of its surroundings, the excellence of its bathing beach and its pleasant society." Not much has changed

Calif ornia's coast northwest of Los Angeles, between Ojai and San Luis Obispo, is a pleasant, easy drive. On the way, consider a side trip off the Pacific Coast Highway along State Route 150 to **Ojai ❶**, hidden away on the edge of the Los Padres National Forest. It's one of those sleepy artists- and writers' colonies that's somehow remained unspoiled. The 1926 movie *Lost Horizon* was filmed in the valley east of town, and Shangri-la is the way some residents think of it. The town itself is centered around its main street on which a graceful tower offsets a row of shops behind a covered arcade. The predominantly Spanish-style architecture owes its origins to a glass tycoon, Edward Drummond Libby, who in 1917 built the elegant **Oaks Hotel** opposite the library.

Artifacts in the **Ojai Valley Museum** (130 W. Ojai Avenue, tel: 805-640 1390; Thur–Sun 1–4pm), also doubling as the **Ojai Visitor Center**, include those from Chumash Indian times through to the present. Located in the newly renovated St Thomas Aquinas Chapel (*circa* 1918), permanent and changing exhibits focus on the environmental, cultural and historical factors that shaped the Ojai valley.

The Oaks at Ojai (tel: 805-646 5573), a 46-room spa hotel, is owned by Sheila Cluff, a fitness buff who has written a syndicated column, and where brisk, pre-breakfast walks are the norm. Nearby is what is probably the friendliest bookstore in California, **Bart's Books**. There are over 100,000 volumes, and a 420-year-old oak tree grows through the patio.

Ojai stages a tennis tournament every spring, a film festival in October, an arts festival in May, and a classical music festival in June. Its residents are very happy to live there. West of town, State 150 winds along some 60 miles (97 km) of the shoreline of **Lake Casitas**, but the scenery is even better along the coast.

Ventura and the Channel Islands

The town of **Ventura ❷** is dominated by an ostentatious city hall perched on the hillside, but this is much outshone in style and grace by the over 225-year-old **Mission San Buenaventura** with its pretty garden, founded by the redoubtable Father Junípero Serra *(see page 26)*. It sits on the edge of a restored **"Olde Towne"** area in which antiques shops predominate.

Trips are made from near Ventura to beautiful, desolate **Santa Barbara Island ❸**, whose 640 acres (259 hectares) are a haven for birds, sea lions and 10,000 breeding seals. None of the nearby islands, part of isolated **Channel Islands National Park**, is inhabited, but most of them can be visited on tours conducted by park rangers (for information, tel: 805-658 5730). There are flights to **Santa Rosa Island** from Camarillo Airport (tel: 805-987 1301).

PRECEDING PAGES AND LEFT: Mission Santa Barbara. **BELOW:** the long arm of the law.

Near Ventura, you can catch a boat or an airplane to visit one of the five Channel Islands, or go direct from Santa Barbara. Tel: 805-658 5700 for details on camping and guided tours.

Just on the southern outskirts of Santa Barbara, the charming **Montecito Inn** (tel: 805-969 7854) was popular with refugees from Hollywood in the 1920s when one of its original owners was Charlie Chaplin. Montecito's other legendary hotel is **San Ysidro Ranch** (tel: 805-565 1700), where John F. Kennedy honeymooned with his wife, Jackie; where Lauren Bacall says she fell in love with Humphrey Bogart; and the site of a midnight wedding in 1940 between Laurence Olivier and Vivien Leigh.

The area around Santa Barbara is the jumping-off point for the emerging and increasingly well-regarded **Santa Ynez Valley wineries**, most of which welcome visitors. Included among the 100-plus wineries are the interesting and high-profile **Firestone Vineyard** (tel: 805-688 3940) and also the **Fess Parker Winery** (tel: 805-688 1545), run by the cowboy ex-actor. For an up-to-date list of wineries, a brief summary of their attractions and the times of tours, contact the Santa Barbara County Vintners' Association, P.O. Box 1558, Santa Ynez, CA 93460-1558, tel: 805-688 0881.

Santa Barbara

Santa Barbara ❹ (population 91,600), which got its start as a health resort after glowing articles by New York journalist Charles Nordhoff touted its mineral springs, is an attractive place whose architecture is almost entirely in idealized colonial Spanish style. Following a disastrous earthquake in 1925, a mandatory building code prohibited anything unharmonious in the flood of designs for replacement buildings. Before the earthquake, one author observed, it was "a wasteland of western junk that had spread over the original Spanish architecture like a smothering fungus."

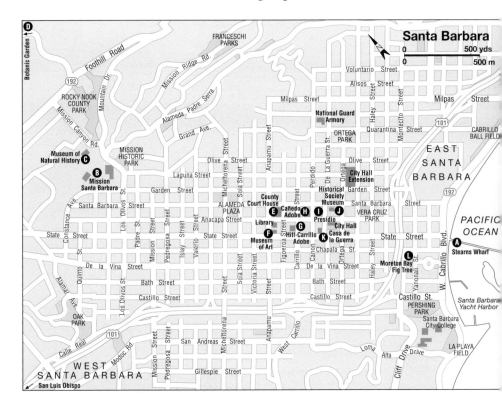

The city has long been admired, and, for many years, it was favored by wealthy retired couples. Today, its palm-lined beaches stretch for 5 miles (8 km), and its movie star residents have included Steve Martin and Cher. Michael Douglas and Catherine Zeta-Jones live nearby, and not far away is **Neverland**, the home of Michael Jackson, even though he doesn't visit now.

Most of Santa Barbara's activities can be found along its main thoroughfare, **State Street**, particularly where it terminates at century-old **Stearns Wharf Ⓐ**, the oldest on the West Coast. This pier offers everything – seafood stands, restaurants, wine tasting, a marine museum and aquarium, fishing – and is the starting point for whale-watching boat trips, which set off most days (February to September) to catch glimpses of the heavyweight mammals returning north with their offspring after a trip to the Baja coast. As well as a maritime museum, Santa Barbara Harbor offers direct service to the Channel Islands *(see page 291)*, details of which can be found at the outdoor Visitor Center on Harbor Way.

A waterfront shuttle tram operates between the wharf, Downtown and the zoo, connecting the beaches that line the shore on both sides of the pier with the volleyball courts and the more expensive hotels at the eastern end. A multi-colored 21-ft (6-meter) high **Chromatic Gate** stands on the waterfront near here. It was the work of Herbert Bayer, last survivor of the seminal Bauhaus school who spent the years before his death in the town.

After having fun on the pier, head north up State Street and turn right for three or four blocks to the **Mission Santa Barbara Ⓑ** (Laguna and Los Olivos streets, tel: 805-682 4149; daily 9am–5pm; admission charge), which, with its twin bell towers, is generally regarded as the most beautiful of the remaining missions. Founded in 1786, it was damaged in both of the area's major earthquakes (1812,

Maps, page 242 & 292

BELOW:
rebuilt in 1925,
Santa Barbara's
architecture is an
idealized colonial
Spanish style.

1925) but lovingly restored and is still in use as a parish church *(see page 26)*. The museum displays relics from the days when Chumash Indians lived at the mission while being "trained" to undertake useful tasks by their Spanish overlords. More about Native American life preceding the occupation can be studied two blocks to the north in the **Museum of Natural History** ● (daily 10am–5pm; admission charge), with its array of inanimate animals, birds, reptiles and fish. There's another attraction in this area, although it's more than a mile to the north up Mission Canyon Road: the **Botanic Garden** ● (tel: 805-682 4726), with trails through 78 acres (32 hectares) of native flowers, shrubs and cacti.

Two blocks from the Greyhound bus station in the center of Santa Barbara is the handsome 1929 Spanish-Moorish **Court House** ● (1100 Anacapa Street, tel: 805-962 6464; Mon–Fri 8am–5pm, Sat–Sun 10am–4.30pm). Its lobby is lined with mosaics and murals and there's a lovely view from the tower of gently sloping roofs and the multi-level lawn below.

Walk past the library to State Street, passing (or inspecting) the **Museum of Art** ● and turning left along Carrillo to visit the **Hill-Carrillo Adobe** ●, built by Daniel Hill in 1826 for his Spanish bride for whom he constructed the city's first home with a wooden floor. Continue down Anacapa Street to Canon Perdido Street. The block to the left, bordered by the **Canedo Adobe** ● (1782), is where the city began, centered around the **Presidio** ● with its chapel and parade grounds, more restored adobes and the **Historical Society Museum** ●.

Head back toward State Street to stop and admire the **Casa de la Guerra** ● (1827), the original home of the Presidio's commander and his family. The plaza here is where the city council first met in 1850, an event still celebrated every August with a fiesta. Here also is the enticing cobbled area, **El Paseo** (or "the street in Spain" as tourist officials call it).

BELOW: El Paseo, a Santa Barbara shopping area.

El Paseo is by far the most attractive place in town to shop and sip a coffee at one of the outdoor cafés around the fountain. Over half a century ago, the El Paseo Theater used to feature on its stage a group of Spanish dancers, which included Rita Cansino, better known as Rita Hayworth.

Heading back down State Street to the pier, you might want to make a short diversion to Chapala and Montecito streets to admire what's said to be the largest tree of its kind in America. It's a **Moreton Bay fig tree** ●, native to Australia and planted here in 1914. Since then, its branches have grown to cover an area of 160 ft (49 meters) and often shade the city's dramatically down-and-out homeless community.

North of Santa Barbara

Leaving Santa Barbara and still traveling north on US 101, the highway passes through **Goleta**, home of a branch of the University of California, and skirts the shore past some gorgeous beaches before offering another side trip at **Solvang** ● (tel: 800-468 6765), a campily amusing replica of a Scandinavian town with horse-drawn streetcars, windmills and Danish bakeries. On nearby **Cachuma Lake**, there are guided cruises in winter to view a rare flock of migrating bald eagles.

Make a point, if time permits, of leaving US 101 at the **Los Alamos** ● turn-off to view this virtually one-block town with its antiques stores, frontier-style buildings and, especially, the **1880 Union Hotel**, which has a wonderful saloon and pool room as well as bedrooms and a restaurant furnished completely in the style of a century ago. The first thought that comes to mind is how much honeymoon couples must love it; indeed, the area seems to be romantically attuned to that notion with similarly exotic theme rooms offered by the famously pink **Madonna Inn** (tel: 805-543 3000), which can be admired from Highway 101 just before San Luis Obispo, and old-fashioned wedding ceremonies being promoted at the nearby town of **Nipomo** in its 19th-century Kaleidoscope Inn's beautiful garden gazebo (tel: 805-929 5444).

Farther north up 101 is **Pismo Beach ❼**, the only shore community actually on that road between Santa Barbara and San Francisco. There's a wide range of places to stay and the usual attractions of a seaside community. The famous Pismo clam, which grows almost to the size of a dinner plate, has almost disappeared, but there's an annual clam festival held in October. Almost as many come from late November through February to see the hordes of colorful Monarch butterflies, which winter in a grove of eucalyptus and Monterey pines.

San Luis Obispo ❽, roughly halfway between Los Angeles and San Francisco, owes its beginnings to the 1772 mission, now a parish church. Its development was due to the arrival of the Southern Pacific Railroad in 1894. It's a pleasant town, which offers attractive historic strolls from the restored adobe on **Monterey Street**. The Victorian homes in the **Old Town** neighborhood around Buchon and Broad streets are worth exploring, and there's a regular Thursday night farmers' market Downtown that turns into a street festival with entertainment and some great barbecues. ❑

Maps, page 242 & 292

ABOVE: fountain in Santa Barbara.
BELOW: San Luis Obispo's famously tacky Madonna Inn.

ANAHEIM

Despite the great popularity of newer theme parks,
there's nothing quite like the original Disneyland,
or the other family attractions around Anaheim

Map,
page 242

Anaheim is best known for its amusement parks and similar attractions, of which Disneyland is by far the most famous. MTA bus 460 travels all the way to Disneyland from Los Angeles, as does a train from Union Station, but, if you have a car (and very limited time), you could just squeeze Disneyland and a visit to the architecturally fascinating **Crystal Cathedral** (12141 Lewis Street, Garden Grove, tel: 714-971 4000; Mon–Sat 9am–3.30pm, Sun 9am–9pm) of evangelist Robert Schuller into the same day, and still have dinner while watching the jousting at Medieval Times.

Another alternative is to stay in the **Anaheim** area overnight. Pushing itself heavily as a convention destination, there's not a lot to see, but it will save traveling. Disneyland itself has pricey but amusing hotels located on its grounds, but there are cheaper motels on surrounding roads; most branches of major hotel chains operate free shuttle buses to the park. Needless to say, you're going to do a lot of walking even if you get there by car.

The Magic Kingdom

Disneyland ❾ (1313 Harbor Boulevard, tel: 714-781 4000; hours vary; admission charge) first opened with the tagline "Magic Kingdom" in 1955. Walt Disney once said that Disneyland grew out of his search for a clean, safe, friendly park where he could take his own daughters.

One of Disney's early designers, John Hench, referred to Walt's knack for putting "little touches of humanity" in everything he did. Hench said that Mickey Mouse's appeal has something to do with his body shape – all circles, all round, harmless and non-threatening. In fact, because of a height restriction – you can't have Mickey towering too much over his fans – most of the besuited Mouse persons in Disneyland are actually girls.

There's still no successful way to avoid the crowds and the lengthy line-ups, however, especially in summertime. Obviously, it helps to get there as soon as the gates open and head straight for the most popular rides. If you want to be truly organized, contact them and order a map so you can plot your Disney strategy months in advance, but do note: Disneyland is almost always undergoing major expansions, and so a map might not be all that useful.

To avoid backtracking, it's probably wise to cover the park logically, one "land" at a time. A more recent attraction is the wild Indiana Jones ride, which, as expected, is pulling in the same huge numbers of people as the ever-pleasing and hugely ambitious worlds of **Fantasyland**, **Adventureland**, **Frontierland**, **Critter Country** and jazzy **New Orleans Square**. **Tomorrowland**, always popular but a slave to the advances of technology, has

PRECEDING PAGES: dressed to thrill. **LEFT:** introducing Mr Michael Mouse. **BELOW:** just kidding around.

undergone a major renovation. Pointing the way to the "land" is **Astro Orbitor**, which has colorful rockets circling a series of moving planets. People pilot their own spaceships as they soar through an animated "astronomical model" of constellations. Favorite thrill rides **Space Mountain** and **Star Tours** are still here, but with updated effects and new technology. As the most popular things to do always seem to be located in Tomorrowland, it makes sense to position yourself at the top of Main Street to maximize your time.

Main Street is the place to get information and maps (City Hall), exchange foreign currency and get money from an ATM, rent a camera or camcorder (Kodak), hire a stroller or wheelchair (just inside the main entrance), stash your surplus items in a locker (adjoining Disney Clothiers) and attend to your infant (Baby Center, near the Magic Castle).

Fantasyland will probably be the kids' favorite, but some of the rides there, such as Peter Pan's Flight, Mr Toad's Wild Ride, Alice in Wonderland and Snow White's Scary Adventures, seem to be aimed as much at adults. The first two are especially interesting, demonstrating how much illusion owes to darkness and luminous paint. From the **Sleeping Beauty Castle** and the steam train to the **Mark Twain Riverboat** (⅝th scale), most structures in Disneyland are scaled down from full size. Movie-set designers are experts at using tricks of scale to make buildings seem taller or further away. The first floors of the buildings on Main Street, for example, are 90 percent of full size, the second floor 80 percent and so on.

Another interesting point concerns the 147-ft (45-meter) **Matterhorn**. After its 500-ton (454-tonne) steel framework was in place, the mountain – ¹⁄₁₀₀th the size of the real thing – was built from the top down. This was to stop the sub-

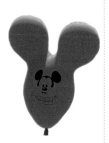

ABOVE:
'ere's Mickey.
BELOW: waiting for
the Fantasmic!

sequent cement droppings spoiling the appearance of the slopes below. A ride called Flying Saucers, based on air-cushion technology developed by the space program, had a short, five-year life, being abandoned in 1966 after continuing maintenance problems. But another aspect of the space program resulted in the triumph of audio-animatronics, of which the moving, speaking figure of Abraham Lincoln is the earliest example of this technology.

This process culminated in the 225 talking, moving birds, flowers and figures of the **Enchanted Tiki Room**. The room was first visualized as a restaurant, but grew into a major attraction. Lincoln had been planned as but one element in a grand Hall of Presidents stretching along Liberty Street, but this scheme never came to fruition.

How much time you have available will pretty much decide your itinerary. The amusingly hokey **Big Thunder Mountain Railroad**, **Jungle Cruise** and the aforementioned Enchanted Tiki Room and Mark Twain Riverboat are all good fun, and the seasonal night-time spectacular **Fantasmic!** is such a sensation that crowds start jostling for good viewpoints two hours' ahead.

But try not to miss **New Orleans Square**, with its **Haunted Mansion** and nearby **Pirates of the Caribbean**. Talking about his cast of 64 humans and 55 animals in Pirates, sculptor Blaine Gibson explained: "In a ride system you have only a few seconds to say something about a figure through your art. So we exaggerate their features, especially their facial features, so they can be quickly and easily understood from a distance… we have to instantly communicate 'good guy' or 'bad guy.' We try to provide the illusion of life."

The same might be said of the guy who started it all. "The way I see it, Disney - land will never be finished," reflected Walt a long time ago. "I've always wanted

Map, page 242

TIP

Disneyland's free FASTPASS service saves your place in line for Space Mountain, Big Thunder Mountain Railroad and other popular attractions, while you explore the rest of the park.

BELOW: Disney's nitetime Fantasmic!

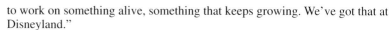

Map, page 242

to work on something alive, something that keeps growing. We've got that at Disneyland."

True to form, Disney's team have now expanded with the most ambitious program since the original began. The culmination of a $1.4 billion scheme is the **Disneyland Resort**, which includes not only improvements to the Magic Kingdom and the existing hotels but **Disney's California Adventure ⑩**, a 55-acre (22-hectare) theme park with a 750-room luxury hotel and a huge shopping, dining and entertainment center, aptly named the **Downtown Disney District**.

Anaheim's other attractions

A few miles north of Disneyland is **Knott's Berry Farm** (8039 Beach Boulevard, Buena Park, tel: 714-220 5200; hours vary; admission charge), a re-created 19th-century gold town, which grew out of a roadside snack bar operated by farmer Walter Knott and his wife, Cordelia, whose reputation spread far and wide for tasty chicken dinners and slabs of boysenberry pie (served on the couple's wedding china). The place actually predates its bigger rival by a few years and is just as interesting, but a little funkier.

The characters are more primitive than high-tech and the staff charm tourists with individual attention. The **Ghost Town** offers panning for gold, a stagecoach ride, a watery log ride and stunt and vaudeville shows. In the contemporary side of the park, the various other theme areas include stomach-dropping rides such as the 20-story-freefall Supreme Scream.

Recent additions are also for thrill-seekers, like the tributes to Southern California's beach culture: the 13-acre (5-hectare) water park, **Soak City**, and the surf-inspired dual roller coaster, Rip Tide. Kids love the cartoon-themed **Camp Snoopy** with its miniature train and other rides. As a tribute to Spanish California, Knott's **Fiesta Village** entices visitors with mariachi bands, ferocious rides like Jaguar! and **Montezooma's Revenge**, as well as scrumptious and reasonably priced tacos, fajitas and burritos.

BELOW:
a thirsty business.
RIGHT: Knott's
Berry Farm.

For over 35 years, Knott's has presented the world's largest (and most famous) theme park Halloween event: the annual Halloween Haunt. From late September to Halloween night, Knott's Berry Farm becomes Knott's Scary Farm, treating fear-lovers to several spooky mazes, where you'll encounter murderous mutants, deadly arachnids, lurking vampires, cursed pirates and the infamous Grendel.

In addition, you'll see irreverent comedy routines, magic shows and "psychobilly" concerts. Some might find the experience corny, but it's definitely worth a look. Be aware that Halloween Haunt is a special ticket event (not covered by regular theme park admission and not recommended for young children).

And speaking of corny, what could be sillier than paying to eat a so-so meal without plates with your bare hands in a fake castle, bowing to a fake king and queen and egging on some pretend-knights in a battle whose outcome is already fixed? Well, hundreds of enthusiastic customers do it at **Medieval Times** (tel: 888-935 6878) every night and enjoy themselves enormously. What the heck, you have to eat dinner somewhere. ❏

SOUTH BAY AND ORANGE COUNTY

Beaches, coves, ecological preserves and a surfer's Walk of Fame are just a few of the coastal attractions south of Los Angeles

Map, page 242

I t takes a little longer to drive down the coast from Los Angeles towards San Diego than whizzing down the freeway, but the route is much more interesting because it passes through the various seaside resorts of the **South Bay**. All this area is still in Los Angeles County; the Orange County border begins after you pass through Long Beach.

If you have time after exploring the South Bay communities, you could make a short diversion around the **Palos Verdes** ⑪ peninsula to see the magnificent seaside homes (buses from the LAX City Bus Center cover most of this route, connecting with another bus going into Long Beach). **Abalone Cove** beach, west of Narcissa Drive, is an ecological preserve at the end of a steep path and is perfect for divers and lovers of tidepools.

Just past the Golden Cove shopping center is a lighthouse beside which, at the **Point Vicente Interpretive Center** (31501 Palos Verdes Drive West, tel: 310-377 5370; daily 10am–5pm; donation requested), are telescopes to look for passing whales (December to spring). The newly expanded center reopened in July 2006 with exhibits that focus on the peninsula's natural and cultural history, including an informative whale-watching video, as well as earphones to hear the mournful voices of these lovable mammals and a relief map of the peninsula showing how mountainous is the terrain. There are nice grassy grounds suitable for picnicking (bring your own food and drink) and leaflets identifying the various plants to be found on the (free) Botanic Trail.

About 2 miles (3 km) further on is the wood and glass **Wayfarers Chapel** (tel: 310-377 1650; daily 10am–5pm), designed by Frank Lloyd Wright's son, Lloyd, whose inspiration is said to have been Northern California's majestic redwood trees. It was built in 1951 as a memorial to the 18th-century Swedish theologian Emanuel Swedenborg. Walking around the peaceful gardens to the sound of songbirds, a fountain and the gurgling stream is a very tranquilizing experience. There are services in the chapel every Sunday.

San Pedro

Eastwards along the coast is **San Pedro**, headquarters of Southern California's fishing fleet, which once distinguished this town as a genuine fishing port. All the genuine old parts of what aeons ago was a little fishing town are gone, of course, replaced by a pseudo construction, called **Ports O'Call Village**. It is surprisingly imaginative: several blocks of saltbox-type New England, apparently weathered shops – all in appealing, matching styles that, alas, are often deserted. Harbor

PRECEDING PAGES:
Long Beach and the
Queen Mary.
LEFT: sun & shades.
BELOW: child's play.

The Queen Mary *was built in 1936. One of the most stylish ships to sail the seas, royals and celebrities were regularly among her passengers. During World War II, and painted gray, she transported 800,000 soldiers in a series of daring cloak-and-dagger missions.*

BELOW: Naples.

tours and fishing trips can be taken from here, as well as a classic sailing ship and the *Catalina Express* (tel: 1-800-833 6685), which sails to Santa Catalina Island *(see page 313)*. There's free parking space beside which a heroic fisherman statue proclaims, "Lo, the fisherman, for his harpoon, hook and net have long harvested the endless sea…" etc, etc.

A few miles south is San Pedro's **Cabrillo Beach**, which has earned a reputation as one of the best places in the area to windsurf. Beginners especially favor the sheltered waters inside the harbor breakwater. Some visitors also relish the nearby aquarium (tel: 310-548 7562) and elevated coastal trail. Palos Verdes Drive segues into 25th Street, from which a left turn on Gaffey (State Highway 110) and up to Highway 47 over the **Vincent Thomas Bridge** takes you straight ahead through Long Beach on Ocean Boulevard.

Out in the bay take a close look at the palm-fringed island with the tall towers: it's actually one of four man-made islands created by a consortium of oil companies to hold (and conceal) all the working oil derricks that, for over 40 years, have been tapping one of the richest offshore fields in the United States. The towers are illuminated at night.

The most famous attraction in the town of **Long Beach ⑫** is the wonderful, historic *Queen Mary* ocean vessel (tel: 562-435 3511; admission charge), whose Art Deco halls, restaurants and lounges have been beautifully restored. Tours are available, as is dinner or hotel rooms on the ship itself.

The local **Museum of Art** is an active one, and Long Beach is well known in particular for its video art and **street murals**. The **Aquarium of the Pacific** (tel: 562-590 3100; daily 9am–6pm; admission charge) is said to be one of the top three in the United States. One of the most attractive suburbs of Long Beach is **Naples**, with its winding streets, waterside houses and one-hour **gondola tours** on boats that cruise elegantly along a series of canals. The tours are very popular, however, so call ahead at 562-433 9595 to book.

The Orange Coast

The Pacific Coast Highway bypasses the sleepy town of Seal Beach and runs beside the ecological wetlands preserve just before Bolsa Chica state beach. At busy **Huntington Beach**, slow down to avoid the surfers carrying their boards across the road. Many of the communities around here are in dispute about which most deserves the title "Surf City," but Huntington Beach claims to have the best case. In fact, a **Surfing Walk of Fame** commemorates legendary surfers on Main Street at the Pacific Coast Highway.

At **Newport Beach ⑬**, the Balboa peninsula with its 6 miles (10 km) of sandy shore encloses a harbor popular with yacht owners. On Main Street, it's hard to miss the **Balboa Pavilion**, built in 1906 as a railroad terminal, with its distinctive but totally unnecessary steeple. Behind it, you'll find fishing boats unloading their catch if you get here early enough.

Almost as old is the ferry that makes the 3-minute trip from Palm Street to **Balboa Island** with its million-dollar homes. On your way back, you can see the former homes of John Wayne and cowboy star Roy Rogers on nearby islands. From **Balboa Pier**, you can admire the kite-flyers, frisbee-throwers, body-surfers and just plain sunbathers. Check out the diner at the end of the pier before finishing up at the Balboa Fun Zone, with its rides and video arcades, and the **Newport Harbor Nautical Museum** (tel: 949-675 8915). Almost a dozen luxury beachfront hotels have been built or are under construction along the coast between here and San Diego.

Map, page 242

Pelicans can sometimes be spotted at El Moro beach. Not far away in **Laguna Beach ⓮**, the annual **Pageant of the Masters** (tel: 949-497 6582) presents tableaux of famous paintings with costumed participants. In the past several years, **Hermosa Beach** (nearer to LA) has become the local nightlife capital with a string of clubs around the pier. Before turning inland, the harbor at **Dana Point ⓯** is worth a stop to browse in the shops and have a drink in the upstairs bar of the Jolly Roger. Then it's off on Del Obispo Street to Camino Capistrano on which sits the **San Juan Capistrano Mission ⓰** (26801 Ortega Highway, tel: 949-234 1300; daily 8.30am–5pm; admission charge), seventh in the chain of 21 missions established by Franciscan padres in the 18th and 19th centuries (*see page 26*).

Oldest church

Father Junípero Serra founded several of the missions, this one included, and his statue stands beside the Great Stone Church to the right as you enter. Behind the church the **Serra Chapel**, which is currently being restored, is the oldest still-in-use church in California. Pick up a free map, which identifies and dates everything, including the bells to the left of the church. The map also tells where the swallows' nests can be found during their residence.

At the mission's far-left corner, where the tanning vats, metal furnaces and tallow ovens can still be inspected, is the archeological field office, which still

BELOW: surf's up in Newport.

Map,
page 242

uncovers old relics from time to time. The lovely gardens were added during the last century, but the main courtyard itself was always the central focus of the mission. It was also the site of rodeos in the old days, with eager spectators watching from the surrounding roofs, including that of the west wing, which now houses the **Mission Museum**.

Just north of the controversial San Onofre Nuclear Generating Station is the town of **San Clemente**. Located northwest in Yorba Linda, the **Nixon Presidential Library and Museum** (18001 Yorba Linda Boulevard, tel: 714-993 5075; Mon––Sat 10am–5pm, Sun 11am–5pm; admission charge) chronicles the life and times of the former US president, who operated his Western White House from San Clemente. San Clemente and Doheny state beaches allow camping for a small fee. Doheny, Dana Point, Laguna Niguel, Irvine Coast and Newport Beach all have **marine life preserves**, which are open to the public.

From Dana Point and Newport Beach, boats run across to Santa Catalina Island, but an interesting drive inland is along Route 76 (near Oceanside) to the village of **Pala ⑰**. The village is notable for the Mission San Antonio de Pala, an *asistancia* (extension mission) built in 1816. Located on the Pala Indian Reservation, it is the only California mission still serving Indians and has cele-brated its Corpus Christi Festival, with an open-air mass, dances and games, on the first Sunday of every June since 1816.

The road continues southeast to **Rincon Springs**, a community to the north of Escondido on Road S6, and the gateway to **Palomar Mountain**. Rising 5,500 ft (1,676 meters) above sea level and stretching for some 20 miles (32 km), Palo-mar is the home of the Hale Telescope and the Oschin Telescope, contained inside **Palomar Observatory ⑱** (Palomar Mountain, which is at the end of S6 Road, tel: 760-742 2119; daily 9am–4pm), which is now owned and operated by the **California Institute of Technology**. Public tours (admission charge), which cover the history and scientific research of the observa-tory, are offered on Saturdays, from April to October.

Off Route 76, you can catch I-15 south towards the town of San Diego and pass right by the **San Diego Zoo's Wild Animal Park** (15500 San Pasqual Valley Road, Escondido, tel: 619-234 6541; daily 9am–4pm, grounds close at 5pm, admission charge), a huge park with multi-species exhibits, including giraffes, rhinos, antelopes, oryx, zebras, primates, lions and tigers. Guests travel around the animal exhibits via monorail. There's also a popular photo safari and an observation station to watch the lion camp. Don't worry, the lions are separated from visitors by laminated glass.

Host for horse lovers

Del Mar, a beautiful spot with a sweeping hillside view of the Pacific, is the site of the San Diego County Fair in June and July, and the Del Mar National Horse Show in the spring, at the **Del Mar Fairgrounds**. This was res-cued from collapse in the 1930s by actor Pat O'Brien and singer Bing Crosby, both racing fans, who pumped a huge amount of money into the facility, turning it into one of America's most popular circuit venues. The sea-son begins in July, a week after the big fair ends, and continues to run until well into September. ❑

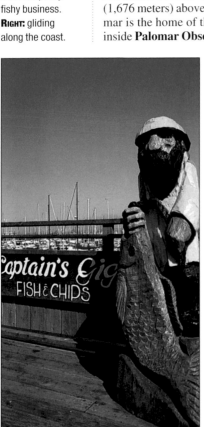

BELOW: a pretty fishy business. **RIGHT:** gliding along the coast.

SANTA CATALINA ISLAND

With two-thirds of its scenic interior protected by an island conservancy council, Santa Catalina is calm, quiet and relatively car-free

Map, page 242

This temperate outcrop 26 miles (42 km) off the coast makes for a lovely weekend excursion, but, with a bit of a rush, it can also all be squeezed into one day. With its steep and rugged canyons, 54 miles (87 km) of coastline and charming capital of Avalon, **Santa Catalina Island ⓳** (for information, tel: 310-510 1520) seduces even the most jaded traveler who has come to regard Southern California as the capital of Automania. Here, there are no rental cars and the environmentally oriented island authority has guaranteed that almost two-thirds of the island will always remain in its natural state. The first steamship service began in 1888, at a time when pigeons were still being used to carry messages to and from the mainland.

Begin early in the day by taking the ***Catalina Express*** (tel: 800-833 6685) in Long Beach, zipping across to **Avalon** in one hour and, with extreme luck, spotting a whale en route. Ferries also run from San Pedro, Newport Beach and Dana Point. The 5-minute walk into town passes a couple of places that rent bicycles or the ubiquitous golf carts, which are the main personal transportation: residents here wait 10 years before being allowed to own a car. Stop at one of the four companies on the pier to book for an island tour before thinking of anything else.

The next thing to do is to take the 45-minute inspection of the **Casino** at the far end of the harbor. It achieved national fame more than half a century ago with broadcasts of such famous bands as Count Basie or Kay Kyser playing in the Art Deco ballroom for as many as 6,000 dancers at a time. Built in 1929 at a cost of $2 million, the casino's ground-floor theater with a full-size organ was the first in America to be built especially for the new talking pictures.

LEFT: sailing towards Avalon Bay.
BELOW: Catalina's famous casino was built in 1929.

Dancing to hidden music

Walking back into town past the Victorian hotels, you'll see, among the varied shops of **El Encanto Market Place**, across from the Via Casino archway, a souvenir shop displaying products from the long-defunct Catalina Pottery and other memorabilia.

A 45-minute trip in a glass-bottomed boat from the **Pleasure Pier** traverses shallow waters filled with multi-colored fish (mostly olive or blue with the occasional orange garibaldi) darting in and out of a seaweed "garden." The fronds of kelp, swaying to the motion of the glass-bottomed boat, seem to be dancing to a hidden music with the little fish acting as random soloists. At night, says the guide, nocturnal creatures take over, including "wimpy" lobsters, which lack the formidable (but so-edible) claws of their Maine cousins.

To really appreciate Catalina and all its attractions, plan to devote the afternoon to the 4-hour **inland motor tour** (tel: 1-800-626 7489), which heads up through the mountains to the island's airport. The tour makes a stop at **El Rancho Escondido**, the Wrigley-owned ranch where Arabian horses are reared. Immaculately trained horses are put through their paces to demonstrate skill and intelligence. The tour continues onwards along the old stagecoach route across the island to various ancient Indian sites or secluded bays. The best parts of Catalina are these wilderness areas, popular with campers and hikers, some of whom find accommodation at the mountainous **Blackjack Campground**.

Early developers

This mural in Catalina's casino shows how elegant a building it is; Count Basie and his orchestra played for up to 6,000 people in the Art Deco ballroom.

Descendants of General Phineas Banning, who operated the earliest legendary stagecoach routes across the West, once owned most of Catalina Island and began the process of turning it into the tourist resort it eventually became, building the luxury Hotel St Catherine at **Descanso Beach** west of town.

William Wrigley, the chewing-gum tycoon, continued this development when he acquired the island after the great fire of 1915. He built the **Hotel Atwater** (tel: 1-800 626 1496), an aviary, the fabulous Casino and a mansion on **Mount Ada** (now a B&B, the **Inn on Mount Ada**, tel: 310-510 2030). He also started the Catalina Pottery to provide tiles for other projects. The Wrigley family still owns about 11 percent of the island, donating the remainder to the non-profit Island Conservancy, which takes its responsibilities very seriously.

BELOW: bison graze in Catalina's rural interior.

Although "discovered" by the Portuguese navigator Don Juan Rodríguez Cabrillo in 1542, and claimed for Spain as a safe anchorage for its Europe-bound galleons 60 years later, Catalina had actually been inhabited by Native Ameri-

Map,
page 242

cans for thousands of years. Two centuries after the Spaniards arrived, they were pretty much eliminated by Russian hunters in their search for sea-otter pelts.

In the 1860s, there were almost 30,000 grazing animals, mostly goats or sheep, which between them de-vegetated most of the terrain. Later visitors, mostly American, included traders, pirates, smugglers and even miners who mistakenly believed the area to be rich in gold and other minerals. All contributed to the devastation of the island by chopping down trees indiscriminately.

Since the Conservancy took over, much of this damage has been repaired. Fauna, such as the bald eagle, fox and wild boar, have been protected and their numbers expanded. Passengers on the bus tour invariably spot a couple of bison – descendants of a herd brought here when the movie of Zane Grey's book *The Vanishing American* was shot on the island in 1925, and never taken away again. The Catalina gray fox is local only to the island. The house that Grey once owned ("Avalon… is the most delightful and comfortable place I ever visited") is now the **Zane Grey Pueblo Hotel** (tel: 310-510 0966). Like the 40 or so other hotels on the island, it tends to be booked up early in summer.

At the airport, 1,620 ft (494 meters) above sea level, a small display includes historical pictures and a diorama featuring local animals; the Buffalo Spring Station sells buffalo burgers. Apart from some flights to San Diego – which offer probably the most spectacular views of the island – there is no longer a scheduled service from the airport, which is now used mostly by a freight company and a few private plane owners. There is a bus connecting with Avalon five times daily, an alternative way to get into the mountains from town.

The island's highest point is **Mount Orizaba** (2,069 ft/631 meters); the second is **Black Jack Mountain** at just over 2,000 ft/610 meters. ❏

Songs about the island include: "I Found my Love in Avalon," "26 Miles Across the Sea" and the sing-along melody "Catalina Aloha-Oe."

BELOW: Little Harbor is on Catalina's windward side.

PALM SPRINGS AND THE DESERT

Map, page 242

Upscale resorts, natural history museums and Joshua Tree National Park are just some of the sites in the desert

The San Bernardino freeway, then Interstate 10, will bring you to Palm Springs (population 50,400) in just under three hours, but you might like to take an alternative route, the Pomona Freeway (continuation of the Santa Monica Freeway) to pass through **Riverside ⓴** with its famous **Mission Inn**. Architect Charles Moore observed that, if you could see only one building in Southern California, this ought to be it. Built by a local eccentric in 1902, the block-long hotel (tel: 951-784 0300), complete with gargoyles, flying buttresses and spiral staircases, was reopened in 1992 after a seven-year renovation that preserved its Tiffany stained-glass windows, the gold-leaf altar from a 17th-century Mexican church, a 120-year-old Steinway piano and the special chair built to accommodate one overweight visitor, President William Howard Taft. Other celebrated visitors have been Richard and Pat Nixon, who held their wedding party in the hotel, and Ronald and Nancy Reagan, who chose it for their honeymoon. Riverside's tourism, however, has declined precipitously since the local movie theater hosted the West Coast premiere of *Gone With the Wind* in 1939.

A half-hour southeast of Riverside, between I-15 and I-215, the **Perris Valley Airport** is a lift-off point for hot-air balloonists, and, at **Perris Valley Skydiving**, would-be parachutists can take a training course that concludes with an actual jump.

PRECEDING PAGES: Joshua Tree National Park. **LEFT:** Palm Canyon. **BELOW:** pleasure among the palms.

Giant dinosaurs

Highway 60 joins I-10 a few miles east of Riverside. Just beyond that, your attention will be caught while passing the truckstop at **Cabazon ㉑**. Many travelers stop off at the **Wheel Inn** (on the left of the freeway) to get a closer look at the giant model dinosaurs towering 30 ft (9 meters) above the highway. From this point, the hillsides are covered with row after row of steel wind turbines generating electric power.

This country was originally the world's biggest producer of windpower but now aims at supplying 20 percent of California's energy by 2010. Though suspended due to renovation, guided tours will resume (tel: 877-449 WIND). These state-of-the-art machines average about 16 mph (26 kph).

Turn right onto State 111 to drive straight into the town of **Palm Springs ㉒**. Once there, turn down along **Palm Canyon Drive**, one of the two parallel main streets around which the town is structured. This palm-lined thoroughfare is as upscale as it looks, and, after a few blocks of enjoyable cruising (traffic permitting), you'll come to the charming **Village Green Heritage Center** (tel: 760-323 8297), which consists of a restored adobe, a handful of 1800s buildings and a re-created general store from

Palm Springs' Moorten Botanical Garden is a "living museum" of cacti, flowers and trees.

the 1930s. In this wealthy, ultra-chic, ultra-modern town, this is more interesting to the casual tourist than almost anything else except perhaps the **Palm Springs Art Museum** (101 Museum Drive, tel: 760-325 7186; Tues–Wed and Fri–Sun 10am–5pm, Thur noon–8pm; admission charge), with its contemporary paintings and sculpture, Mesoamerican art, miniatures and celebrity photographs.

The city now goes beyond its earlier image as a college mecca during spring break by sponsoring events aimed at the more mature visitor. Having achieved a "cool" following the popular remake of the Frank Sinatra movie *Ocean's 11*, it is also a popular spot for a weekend's pampering by stressed out Los Angelenos. Street fairs are also held on weekend mornings.

At the lower end of South Palm Canyon Drive is **Moorten Botanical Garden**, an attractive "living museum" with giant cacti, desert plants, flowers and trees lining shaded nature trails. It is open daily until the afternoon, with a small admission charge. The younger crowd flock to **Knott's Soak City** (1500 Gene Autry Trail, tel: 760-327 0499), into whose well-watered acres are packed a health club, a big swimming pool, volleyball courts and 13 water slides.

Joshua Tree National Park

BELOW: the Joshua tree in this national park was named by Mormons in 1851.

Indian Canyon Drive is the other main street of Palm Springs. It heads north, the route (as Indian Avenue) to **Desert Hot Springs** and, eventually, if you drive for 45 minutes, to **Joshua Tree National Park** ㉓ (tel: 760-367 5500; admission charge). Joshua Tree is a vast parkland established in 1936 filled with strange rocks, fascinating flora and fauna, and the tall, fibrous plants after which it is named (Mormon explorers named the plant in 1851). It's unlikely you'll see any of the mostly nocturnal animals – kangaroo rats, rattlesnakes – other than the occasional coyote

and lizard, unless you stay overnight in one of the camping grounds. It was near here that an earthquake measuring 7.0 on the Richter scale struck in October 1999. Although a train was knocked off its rails, no one was killed.

The easiest way to visit this area, the similarly unspoiled Santa Rosa Mountains and the Indian Canyons with their cool palm oases, is with one of the local adventure tour companies. Among the places they visit, **Indian Canyons** (tel: 760-325 3400; admission charge) are rich in flora and fauna. Hawks and bald eagles circle overhead; tiny kangaroo rats and fleet-footed bighorn sheep can occasionally be seen on the slopes. **Palm** and **Andreas canyons** have the largest stands of palm trees in the world. "Leave nothing but your footprints, take nothing but photographs," reads a sign in this highly protected area.

If you don't have time to explore all or even some of the wilderness, be sure to visit **The Living Desert** (47-900 Portola Avenue, Palm Desert, tel: 760-346 5694; last admission 4pm, 1pm mid-June–August; admission charge), a nature park 15 miles (24 km) southeast of Palm Springs, filled with eagles, irresistible animals such as zebras and gazelles (don't overlook the lovable meerkats), and desert shrubs, flowers and cacti.

Just north of town is the **Aerial Tramway** (One Tramway Road, tel: 888-515 TRAM; Mon–Fri 10am–8pm, Sat–Sun 8am–8pm; admission charge), which, during an awesome 15-minute ride, climbs to an 8,516-ft (2,596-meter) peak of the **San Jacinto Mountains**. From the top, there's a magnificent view. (Take a jacket, especially if you want to explore the trails.)

The 200-sq.-mile (518-sq.-km) valley is huge enough to enclose completely 10 cities and a wildlife preserve. The preserve's star is a rare lizard whose "fringe toes" allow it to swim through the sand as readily as a fish in water.

Map, page 242

Native Americans have moved into the gaming business with enthusiasm. Tribes formed partnerships with MGM Mirage and Donald Trump that created lavish casinos in downtown Palm Springs and elsewhere, to rival those in Las Vegas.

BELOW: trekking in the desert.

Medicine Men

The richest Native Americans in the country hit the headlines when they wanted to open and operate a large gambling casino on their tribal land, several hundred acres of which happened to be in downtown Palm Springs. It took the tireless efforts of dozens of legal friends before the Agua Caliente band of the Cahuilla Indians were able to break a legal deadlock, allowing them to use their land at all. The canny exploitation of their terrain over the past three decades has put them on a par with – or probably better than – most other American landowners.

Although the acquisition of a minor fortune is applauded, it has also resulted in the dilution of centuries-old wisdom and skills that enabled the earliest Native Americans to survive in totally inhospitable desert.

According to Temalpakh ("from the earth"), a seminal documentation about Indian knowledge and usage of plants, many of the Cahuilla themselves regret the loss of a more

traditional way of life whose well-balanced diet produced longevity, mental alertness and good eyesight. "They believe that adopted foods have brought about a general physical weakness, shortened lifespan, a tendency to obesity and proneness to such diseases as diabetes," write the authors, anthropologist Lowell John Bean and tribal authority Katherine Siva Sobel. "When Cahuilla speak of their grievances against the white man, they frequently mention the loss of traditional foods."

The Cahuilla survived in the hostile desert region, not only because of their knowledge of desert plants and animals, but also because of the curing techniques of their shamans (witch doctors), who used natural substances that have enriched medicine ever since. Bean and Sobel say the shamans, because they employed both plant remedies and sacred power, occupied a more prominent place in the community than doctors.

"It is interesting to note that most of the prescribed drugs in use today trace their roots back to medicine plants known for centuries by indigenous culture and their shamans," writes author Lynn V. Andrews. In her book *Jaguar Woman*, she says that the one rift between shamanism and modern medicine that she would like to see bridged "is the one caused by modern medicine's elitism and refusal to communicate."

Among the Cahuilla, as with other Native Americans, shamans – "technicians of the sacred" because they mediate between the world of mortals and the world of spirits, according to ethnologist Mircea Eliade – were believed to possess supernatural powers. They gave advice on political decisions, cured diseases and searched nature for signs from the spirit world. The origin and meaning of the word Cahuilla is unknown: "master" (in both mental and physical strength) has been suggested. Territory ranges from valleys as high as 5,000 ft (1,524 meters) in the Santa Rosa Mountains, to the desert around the Salton Sea, 200 ft (60 meters) below sea level.

South of Palm Springs, the tribe still owns the five Indian Canyons in which their villages used to sit. There are still some traces of house foundations, ditches and dams. ❑

LEFT: portrait of a brave drawn by George Catlin, one of the first artist/explorers of the 1830s.

As might be imagined, the area abounds in luxury resorts, many of whose guest registers are a litany of famous names. The **La Quinta Resort and Club** (tel: 800-598 3828), for example, is where Frank Capra checked in to polish the movie script of *Lost Horizon* and Irving Berlin composed *White Christmas*, a song all the more poignant perhaps due to the hot sunshine outside. Renovations uncovered sketches by artist Diego Rivera on the high ceilings of the lobby. Other resorts include the **Parker Palm Spings** (tel: 760-770 5000).

Map,
page 242

A couple of miles from the Salton Sea, whose salt waters provide a habitat for game, fish and a state recreation area with campsites, is the state's largest park, the 600,000-acre (243,000-hectare) **Anza-Borrego Desert State Park ㉔** (tel: 760-767 5311), its numerous canyons and gullies easily accessible by car. Camping is permitted in the park, which is populated by jackrabbits, coyotes, kangaroo rats and lizards, as well as more than 150 different species of birds. The vegetation is equally varied, ranging from junipers and pines growing at the 5,000-ft (1,500-meter) level to palm trees at sea level. A 3-mile (5-km) hike from Campfire Center to Palm Grove reveals plants used by the Cahuilla Indians for medicines, dyes and food.

Frank Sinatra lived a few miles down State Highway 111 in **Rancho Mirage**, an outlying community of country clubs, golf courses and tennis courts. Former US President Gerald Ford and Mrs Leonard Firestone, the widow of the industrialist and former ambassador to Belgium, once resided there, side by side on a fairway at Thunderbird Country Club.

The town of **Indio ㉕** (population 76,900), on I-10 about 10 miles (16 km) east, has been popular with tourists since 1921 when it began staging its annual National Date Festival (tel: 760-863 8247). The week-long celebration in Feb-

ABOVE: this is not a mirage.
BELOW: looking out over Anza-Borrego Desert State Park.

Map, page 242

ruary includes an Arabian Nights pageant, and ostrich and camel racing. South of Indio and north of the Salton Sea is **Lake Cahuilla** (tel: 800-234 PARK; admission charge). The lake is stocked with rainbow trout, striped bass and catfish. For non-anglers, there are hiking and equestrian trails, shady picnic spots, campsites and a children's play area on the sandy beach – away from fishermen.

The **Salton Sea ㉖**, 35 miles (56 km) long and 9 to 15 miles (14 to 24 km) wide, is flanked by State 111 on the east and State 86 on the west. It was, in fact, all a big mistake. When engineers attempted, in 1905, to divert some of the Colorado River to the Imperial Valley, the river changed course and reflooded the ancient Salton Basin, 235 ft (72 meters) below sea level. This formed a sea of 360 sq. miles (932 sq. km) with royal blue water filling the area where the Coachella and Imperial valleys merge. The sea's saltiness creates a buoyancy popular with water skiers and swimmers. It also provides a habitat for salt-water game-fish. Adjoining marshlands are a refuge for bird-watchers.

The **Salton Sea State Recreation Area** is an 18,000-acre (about 7,300-hectare) park with both developed and primitive campsites. There is a Bird Watch and Nature Trail (tel: 760-393 3059) and, 26 miles (42 km) away on SR-86, a boat basin at **Varner Harbor** where, though currently closed, geology buffs often had a field day with ancient shorelines and layers of marine fossils visible along the base of the Santa Rosa Mountains.

BELOW: Palm Springs Aerial Tramway. **RIGHT:** sunset in the sands.

Into Arizona

About 58 miles (93 km) due east of El Centro is **Yuma**, Arizona, a desert town built on the banks of the Colorado River where it enters Mexican territory. The Colorado forms the entire eastern border of Southern California from Mexico to Nevada. Several dams built across it have created reservoirs while also providing hydroelectric power for the metropolises of Los Angeles and San Diego.

Lake Havasu ㉗ (tel: 928-855 4115), 46 miles (74 km) long, and no more than 3 miles (5 km) wide, is the reservoir trapped behind the dam. Those who don't want to drink the water enjoy playing in it. Along Arizona State Highway 95 between Parker and Lake Havasu City are recreational-vehicle parks, marinas and campgrounds with room for tens of thousands of visitors. Everyone, from water sportsmen and outboard boaters to yachtsmen, water skiers and sail-boarders, love the lake. There's fishing for bass, bluegills and crappies. Small game populates the rugged southeastern (Arizona) shore of the lake that constitutes Lake Havasu State Park. Birds are everywhere, as the entire body of water is contained within the **Havasu National Wildlife Refuge** (tel: 760-326 3853).

Lake Havasu City, nonexistent as recently as the late 1960s, has exploded into a resort center of over 56,000 residents, and has become a popular vacation spot for collegiate types at spring break. Developed by the late millionaire Robert P. McCulloch Sr, its most famous landmark is the original **London Bridge**. (A popular story is that McCulloch thought he was buying the more decorative Tower Bridge.) The bridge was shipped in pieces to the US, then trucked to the "British town" the tycoon created at its feet. ❑

San Francisco
Las Vegas
Los Angeles

LAS VEGAS

Created as a playground strictly for grown-ups,
Las Vegas has transformed itself into a fantasy world
for the whole family. It's a big gamble

ABOVE: Sin
City hype
for hopefuls.
BELOW: Fremont
Street's glitter.

There is only one surefire way to win in "Sin City" and that rule is simple – don't gamble. And although that may seem like a negation of what the place is all about, it makes sense when you realize that what's on offer is virtually everything available elsewhere – only for less money. **Las Vegas** ㉘ is a phenomenon, changing and evolving so continuously that it seems there's a grand new theme hotel every year: New York, Egypt, Monte Carlo, ancient Rome, the Wild West and, more recently, Venice and Paris.

Imaginative architecture and neon lights have been the making of Vegas, but this recent transformation came about in the 1990s. Gambling began here in the 1940s, but it took another quarter of a century before the town fully embraced the showbiz element at which it now excels. The policy is "anything goes," with exploding volcanoes, mock sea battles on Main Street, trapeze acts high above the slot machines, a giant sphinx with laser-beam eyes, even legal prostitution not far out of town. In an *LA Times Magazine* story titled "Future World," writer Aaron Betsky said he was convinced that Las Vegas's "mammoth apparitions" were offering a new kind of urban center, "transforming a real city into a realm of fantasy and conversely building a set of fantasies into a real city.... collectively creating a metropolis whose huge scale is bound by lights and set design rather than by walls and streets."

The Strip

Such as it is, Las Vegas's geography is a simple one. The best-known hotels and casinos are located on the bullet-straight **Las Vegas Boulevard**, otherwise known as **The Strip**. These fantasy palaces include **New York, New York**, the **Excalibur**, the **Tropicana** and the MGM **Grand** – all at one busy intersection called the "Crossroads of the World." Heading north along The Strip towards Downtown, where the other casinos are congregated, are **Bellagio**, the **Venetian**, **Paris**, **Caesar's Palace** and **Wynn Las Vegas**, among others.

The Strip is crammed with family-type attractions, a popular one being the museum-quality **Imperial Palace Auto Collections** at 3535 Las Vegas Boulevard. Its classic cars have included those previously owned by Marilyn Monroe, Hitler and Elvis.

About a mile before arriving Downtown, you cannot help but notice the **Stratosphere Tower**, at 1,825 ft (560 meters) one of the tallest buildings in the West. Topped by a revolving restaurant and observation decks, the view from this structure is the best one in town and worth the admission fee.

Downtown's casinos include the **Golden Nugget** and **Golden Gate**, among many others. Staying Downtown is less glitzy than being on The Strip but does put you in place for the single best free show in America. This is

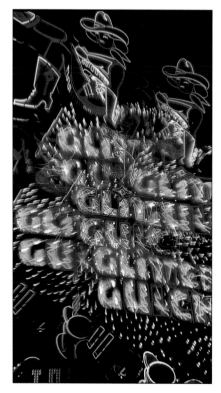

the **Fremont Street Experience** (on the hour, 7pm–midnight each night), which gathers wildly enthusiastic audiences to watch a six-minute show 100 ft (30 meters) above their heads. Five entire blocks have been covered with a metallic mesh screen across which race herds of giant buffalo, Country and Western dancers, screaming jet-fighter planes trailing smoke and teams of undulating maidens. Downtown merchants heavily subsidized this $70 million project to entice visitors back to an area that was becoming moribund. For a time, it worked but now doubts are being raised as to whether it is worth the cost.

Map, page 242

For more information

Write to the **Las Vegas Convention and Visitors Authority** (3150 Paradise Road, Las Vegas, NV 89109, tel: 702-892 7575) before your trip and request a copy of its comprehensive guide, which lists just about everything you need to know. The travel pages of the Sunday edition of the *Los Angeles Times* are also full of Las Vegas offers. Unless you're a high roller, you're not going to find tremendous bargains at the famous hotels (although rates will likely be about half what you'd pay for digs elsewhere), but some Strip hotels such as **Circus Circus** are aggressively marketed with rates often surprisingly low.

Getting around town can be pricey because taxi rides aren't cheap and you'll need to take a lot of them if you plan to see everything. Besides using the new monorail along The Strip, one suggestion is to rent a car at the airport (car rentals are a bargain) and drive along **Tropicana Avenue** to The Strip where, if you turn left (south), you'll find several budget motels. There are other inexpensive motels Downtown on **Ogden Avenue** and around Fremont and **Main Street**.

Of course, you *are* going to gamble, aren't you? Stick to the nickel slots. ❑

TIP

For hotel addresses, see the Travel Tips section at the back of the book.

BELOW: Las Vegas's neon Strip of dreams.

SAN DIEGO AREA

San Diego is California's second-largest city. It is also the oldest, near to pine-tree reserves, glorious beaches and a famous movie-star hotel

Map, page 332

San Francisco

Los Angeles

San Diego

California began at San Diego's Presidio Hill on July 16, 1769, when Father Junípero Serra conducted a mass dedicating first the Mission San Diego de Alcalá and then the military settlement that surrounded and protected it. The mission was moved from the hill to its present site in Mission Valley only a few years later. Because of these events, the busy, elegant harbor town claims as one of its many attributes a history unsurpassed in the state.

If you're heading down Interstate 5 from Los Angeles, you might want to break up your journey to San Diego by stopping off first for a walk through the groves of strangely twisted trees at **Torrey Pines State Reserve ❶** and watch daredevil hang-gliders soar off the 300-ft (90-meter) cliffs. If that seems a little strenuous, try stopping for lunch in the charming town of **La Jolla**, the home of the San Diego campus of the University of California; the highly regarded **Salk Institute**; and the cliff-top **Birch Aquarium at Scripps**. Snorkelers should head for the **La Jolla Caves ❷** after lunch.

Then it's onward toward **San Diego** itself (population 1,257,000). Flanked by Interstates 5 and 8 to the west and north, **Presidio Hill** with its sprawling park is an oasis in a sea of traffic. If you take the curving road east of the Old Town, you'll see, on the hillside, the elegant **Serra Museum ❸** (tel: 619-297 3258; open daily; admission charge), which looks like a mission but was actually built in 1929. There are documents of early California life and a seven-minute historical video, but the original records in Father Serra's own handwriting are displayed in the **Mission San Diego de Alcalá** (10818 San Diego Mission Road, tel: 619-281 8449; daily; donations accepted), which, since 1774, has stood on a site now to the east of I-15.

PRECEDING PAGES:
Horton Plaza.
LEFT: San Diego Bay.
BELOW: Mission San Diego de Alcalá.

Old Town

In the six-block area known as **Old Town ❹** at the bottom of Presidio Hill – now San Diego's most popular nightlife section – are old adobes and restored Victorian homes, shops, museums and charming patio restaurants. Mariachi groups entertain in the **Bazaar del Mundo**, a Spanish-style plaza flanked by craft shops and Mexican restaurants. The **Whaley House**, probably Southern California's first two-story brick home and supposedly one of America's most haunted houses, and the **Wells Fargo History Museum** (free) are of special interest. The visitor center has guide maps.

Across the freeway is the 4,600-acre (1,860-hectare) **Mission Bay** area, combining parkland, beaches and inner lagoons with extensive outdoor leisure activities. Located here is **SeaWorld ❺** (500 SeaWorld Drive, tel: 619-226 3901; daily, hours vary by season; admission charge), a 190-acre (77-hectare) marine zoological park whose "killer" whales are as famous as some movie

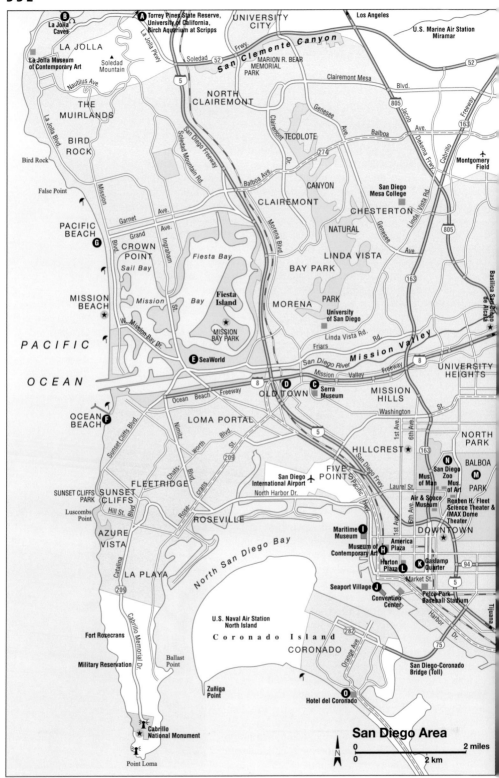

San Diego Area

0 _____ 2 miles
0 _____ 2 km

stars and whose appearances can pack a 5,000-seat stadium. Seals, dolphins, otters and 300 penguins also draw admiring crowds.

South of the channel leading into Mission Bay is **Ocean Beach ❶**; to the north of Mission Beach is **Pacific Beach ❶**, where activities center around Crystal Pier and in the area along Mission Boulevard and up Garnet Avenue. This is where most of the locals shop and dine. The beaches are a great draw most of the year, but there are wonderful beaches along most of this coast – 25 miles (40 km) of them in an unbroken line between Del Mar and Oceanside.

Map, page 332

Downtown San Diego

Towards the top end of the vast bay discovered by Cabrillo is downtown San Diego. A complex adjoining what was formerly the Santa Fe railroad station now consists of the 34-story **One America Plaza** tower, a hotel and a sleek satellite branch of La Jolla's **Museum of Contemporary Art ❶** (1001 Kettner Boulevard, tel: 619-234 1001; Tues–Sat 10am–5pm, Sun noon–5pm; admission charge). Along the Embarcadero just north of the station is the large **Maritime Museum ❶** (tel: 619-234 9153), which encompasses six ships built prior to 1914, among them the 1863 *Star of India*, which is one of the last steel-hulled merchant sailing ships still afloat. The *USS Midway* moored at Navy Pier in 2003 now serves as the *USS Midway* **Museum** (tel: 619-544 9600; daily 10am–5pm; admission charge). San Diego has always been a big naval town and taking a **harbor cruise** will confirm that there is still plenty of activity on the water. In winter, whale-watching tours start from here.

Much of the harbor is centered around attractive **Seaport Village ❶**, with its cafés and live entertainment. Adjoining this carefully landscaped "village" is

ABOVE: taking the plunge.
BELOW: Balboa Park Botanical Building.

Map,
page 332

the spiffy-looking **Convention Center** right opposite **Gaslamp Quarter Ⓚ**, a several-block area of brick-paved sidewalks flanked by restored Victorian buildings now occupied by galleries, trendy boutiques and cafés. This refurbished section, with a demonstrable appeal to artists and young entrepreneurs, has also become the breeding ground of a flourishing theater movement. Almost next door is **Horton Plaza Ⓛ**, a multi-level collection of stores, eateries, cinemas and a theater. Named after a visionary local developer called Alonso Horton, the plaza has a stylish design, layout and omnipresent street performers.

At the northeast edge of town, 1,400-acre (566-hectare) **Balboa Park Ⓜ** contains many of the city's museums in Moorish- and Spanish-style buildings, many of which date back to international expositions held here in 1915 and 1935. A passport available at the park's centrally located **Visitors Center** (tel: 619-239 0512; daily 9.30am–4.30pm) allows admission to up to 13 of the museums. Your choices include the **Air & Space Museum** with a replica of *The Spirit of St Louis* in which Charles Lindbergh crossed the Atlantic; the **Hall of Champions Sports Museum**; the **Model Railroad Museum**; the **San Diego Museum of Art**; the **Museum of Man**; the **Natural History Museum**; and the **Mingei International Museum**. Many people take pleasure in just strolling or picnicking in the park, but Balboa Park is really an activity "city" all on its own, attractions including a science center, an arts center and a couple of theaters.

Occupying the western side of the park is the **San Diego Zoo Ⓝ** (tel: 619-234 3153; daily 9am–5pm; admission charge), one of the largest in America with over 800 different animal species. The zoo has a policy of eschewing cages in favor of moats wherever possible, in an attempt to re-create natural conditions. Admission to the zoo includes a ride on Skyfari, an aerial tramway from which you can admire all the uncaged elephants, lions, tigers, giraffes and bears in their canyon habitats. North of the city is the interesting **Wild Animal Park** (tel: 760-747 8702).

BELOW: SeaWorld.
RIGHT: the fabulous Hotel del Coronado: Thomas Edison installed the lights.

Coronado

A string of communities surround the lower end of San Diego Bay. **Coronado**, with stately Victorian homes among the cottages and condos, is the most popular and weathiest. Access is either off I-5 on the mainland to the east or by the 2-mile (3.2-km) **San Diego-Coronado Bridge**. (There are also buses from Downtown.)

The community is best known for the superlative **Hotel del Coronado Ⓞ** (tel: 619-435 6611), a perfect example of Victorian architecture (1888). A dozen presidents have stayed here since Thomas Edison personally installed the electric lighting: Britain's future Edward VIII met his future wife here, the notorious Mrs Simpson, who lived in a bungalow on the grounds (the bungalow is still there); Charles Lindbergh dropped by for dinner before and after making the first trans-Atlantic flight; and author L. Frank Baum is said to have used it as an inspiration for *The Wizard of Oz*.

Such milestones are memorialized in the **Museum of History and Art**. So eye-catching is the Del that it almost upstaged Tony Curtis and Marilyn Monroe in *Some Like It Hot*. A ferry leaves from San Diego at Harbor Drive and Broadway on the hour; from Ferry Landing Marketplace every hour on the half-hour. ❑

TIJUANA AND NORTHERN BAJA

Map, page 242

Just a few miles to the south of San Diego is another world and another country – Mexico – where the living is easy and the crossing even easier

Baja, California, the slender, arid peninsula that stretches for about 1,075 miles (1,730 km) south of the California border, comprises two states of the Republic of Mexico – the northern state, Baja California, and the southern state, Baja California Sur. Both were largely unexplored land until the completion of the Transpeninsular highway (Mexico Highway 1) in 1973.

Now, there are airstrips here and there, plus big towns largely dependent on tourism, as well as sizable trailer colonies of retired North Americans living inexpensively beside the beaches. But its mountain ranges and deserts have enabled Baja to retain much of its unspoiled character. It is also highly accessible. The major part of both coastlines can be reached not only by car, but via daily buses that operate all the way to Cabo San Lucas at the southern tip. Crossing from San Diego is relatively easy, but be sure that you have proper health coverage and Mexican auto insurance. While non-US citizens have long needed to travel with valid passports, Americans have only recently been required to do so, courtesy of the Department of Homeland Security.

Just under a mile from the border crossing is the tourist zone of **Tijuana ㉙**, which stretches for seven blocks along Avenida Revolución. There are tourist information offices at the border but the main Tourist Assistance Office is in the **Viva Tijuana Shopping Center**, located on Calle Vía de la Juventud. Tijuana is fun, but do be careful when walking around after dark.

LEFT: critter on a cactus.
BELOW: browsing for bargains in Tijuana.

Downtown Tijuana

As you drive into Tijuana or cross the footbridge, you immediately enter the bustling Downtown area. Once named Rancho Tía Juana (Aunt Jane's Ranch), the city became an international border town in the 1840s, following the Mexican–American War. By the early 1900s, Tijuana was enticing countless North Americans with its diverse marketplaces, live bullfights, horse races, thermal baths and other unique attractions. Since then, the city has been growing exponentially. Today, visitors come as much for the duty-free bargains on jewelry, pottery, perfume and fine art as they do for historic sites.

If you begin your day in Tijuana in a shopping mood, you'll find the arts and crafts market nearby, but a greater variety of shops along the city's main drag, **Avenida Revolución**, just to the west. It has lost some of its former tawdry flavor, but is still by far the liveliest street, lined with bars, nightclubs, crafts stores, and clothing and jewelry shops mixed up along with the ponchos and leather sandals.

Behind the Plaza Revolución is the **Wax Museum**

whose eclectic subjects range from Madonna, Gandhi, Marilyn Monroe and the Pope to Cortéz and an Aztec priest holding the bloody heart of a prostrate victim. Mexican Revolutionary heroes are cheek by jowl with Ayatollah Khomeini, Laurel and Hardy, JFK and Fidel Castro. Mexico is also represented by various ranchera entertainers, the 17th-century explorer Juan Cabrillo and a gray-haired lady known as Tía Juana ("Aunt Jane"), the legendary cantina owner around whom the city was founded.

History and culture

A few blocks down Revolución, past the former **Jai Alai Fronton**, turn left on 10th Street to head towards the river. The main street continues south, seguing onto the Boulevard Agua Caliente and running past the city's old bullring, most of its best hotels, Hipódromo Caliente Racetrack and the Sports Arena where concerts and most big events take place. But that's for another time. Head eastwards along 10th Street, watch for the giant globe (indicating a "world of culture") housing the concert hall and the 85-ft (26-meter) high **Omnitheater** in which is shown daily on a gigantic screen the English-language version of a film about Mexico's history and culture.

Adjoining is the ultra-modern **Tijuana Cultural Center**, whose historical survey embraces Olmec stone heads, Aztec charts showing the god of the hour, a meticulous model of the 16th-century Aztec capital, Tenochtitlan, plus skillfully embroidered Indian costumes.

Here also by the river is the **Plaza Río Tijuana** shopping mall (open till 9pm) with over 100 stores. It is the largest shopping center in northwestern Mexico, and Baja California being a free port, most goods cost less than in San Diego.

ABOVE: USA today.
BELOW: leather to go.

Shoppers should remember, however, that US Customs demands receipts to be produced for any daily purchases exceeding $100 per person.

What the *Los Angeles Times* recently described as "a world class" dining area has developed in the **Zona Río** with such fine restaurants as Cien Años and La Diferencia, whose chef Martin San Román aims to become Mexico's first celebrity chef.

The distinctive red **Tijuana Trolley** runs continuously between the city's main sightseeing attractions, but it's a pleasant stroll back northwards along **Via Poniente**, which adjoins the river. It will bring you to an older, funkier shopping center, **Puebla Amigo**, which comes alive at night. There are restaurants, a disco, a theater/concert hall and an ingenious mural.

The famous old **Hipódromo Caliente Racetrack** still has its marble floors, ornate decoration, mirrored elevators and lobby filled with sculptured cowboys, caged birds and an incongruous pair of playful anteaters, but retains little of the glamour that once caused it to be regarded as the American Monte Carlo. In the days when the track's regular clientele included Charlie Chaplin, Jean Harlow and heavyweight champion Jack Dempsey, fortunes were won and lost at dice, blackjack and roulette. Its decline began with the repeal of Prohibition in 1933 and the outlawing of gambling two years later. The tracks still host greyhound racing some nights.

The highway west of Tijuana leads to the **Monumental Bullring**, 6 miles (10 km) away beside the sea. Bullfights take place on various Sundays from May to September. The season is split between the oceanside bullring and the older one Downtown on the Boulevard Agua Caliente. Tickets are on sale at the bullrings and at tourist agencies. There are motels along the seashore road and stalls selling coconut drinks and seafood. The Cuota toll road, on the way to Baja's Ensenada, has some fine ocean scenery. It is recommended over the Libre free road, which parallels the Cuota as far as Rosarito, then dips inland.

About 17 miles (27 km) south of the border is **Rosarito**, a commercialized beach town, which gained popularity in 1927 when the **Rosarito Beach Hotel** began to attract the movie crowd as well as other celebrities, including heads of state. The hotel features glorious indoor murals by Matias Santoyo, a large swimming pool and bar area above the gray, sandy beach, and a spa. Lobster is a favorite in the town's numerous restaurants and there is a so-called "Lobster Village" – **Puerto Nuevo**, 6 miles (10 km) to the south, where the **New Port Beach Hotel** promises an ocean view from each room. South of town is **Xploration** (tel: 661-612 4294, Wed–Sun 10am–4.30pm) where the public can go behind the scenes of a real working movie studio, **Baja Studios**, and view props, sets and costumes from the popular film *Titanic*.

At **El Sauzal**, just before Ensenada, Highway 3 heads across to the east coast, its northbound section bound for the beer-making town of **Tecate**, close to the border. On the way, it passes through vineyards on the boulder-strewn hills bordering the **Guadalupe Valley**, which is the center of Mexico's fast-growing wine business. The most interesting town is **Francisco Zara**, with its cemetery and museum both devoted to the history of the Russian immigrants who colonized the area at the turn of the 20th century. About 19 miles (31 km) south of the border, another free road curves inland off the toll road to head up through the tiny village of **La Misión** where there are crumbling ruins of the San Miguel mission. A cross marks the spot once established as the boundary line between the Dominican missions of Baja and the Franciscan missions in Upper California.

Ensenada

Entering the big city of **Ensenada** (population 370,000) almost 70 miles (113 km) south of the border, it is a good idea to turn right off Highway 1 and drive up Avenida Aleman into the Chapultepec hills, a high-rent district, which offers a magnificent view of the city. A busy port, Ensenada is a regular stop for cruise ships and the furthest south that the majority of casual tourists penetrate. Popular with fishermen, it tags itself "the yellowtail capital of the world" with surf fishing along the rocky shoreline and organized trips from the sportfishing piers off Boulevard Lazaro Cardenas. There are winery tours every day at the Bodegas de Santo Tomás and occasional bullfights.

The main tourist shopping zone is along **Avenida Lopez Mateos**, a few blocks from the bay, but prices are lower in the "non-tourist" part of town off Avenida Ruiz. Along here also, just east of Avenida Mateos, is the popular Hussong's, a wooden-frame cantina, which has been in business for over a century. There are many other restaurants, some with outdoor patios. ❑

Map, page 242

BELOW: painting pottery, Tijuana.

DEATH VALLEY AND THE MOJAVE

Map, page 242

The name says it all. Most people who travel to the desert do so in order to experience some of the most desolate, challenging landscapes in the Americas

The Mojave Desert (named after a Southwestern native tribe, pronounced "mo-hahv-ee") lies between US Highway 395 and Interstate 40, adjoining the Nevada state border. It has come to mean different things to different people: a battleground of conflicting interests between backpackers, miners, ranchers, scientists, environmentalists and off-road vehicle groups. The first settlers who had the misfortune to wander into Death Valley in 1849 on their way to the Gold Rush found the name to be unfortunately true, but travel these days is infinitely easier and safer, with well-supervised roads and accommodations, which, in Death Valley, include two inns and a luxury resort. The climate between November and April is ideal for outdoor travel, while May through October burn with heat like the North African Sahara.

The *WPA Guide*, published in 1939, reported that August travelers found "intense heat" even while still 1,500 ft (457 meters) above the valley. Apparently, experienced travelers could estimate the temperature by putting their hand outside the car and checking how long it took the sunlight "to cause a sharp pain at the base of the nails."

From Los Angeles through the Mojave to Death Valley and back makes for a fascinating two- or three-day trip. Perhaps the best route is to set out from the San Fernando Valley on State Highway 14 through Lancaster to Olancha or Lone Pine and crossing the mountains into Death Valley via State Route 190.

PRECEDING PAGES: the Devil's Golf Course. **LEFT:** Calico Ghost Town. **BELOW:** documenting the dunes.

Borax to B-bombers

At the junction of State Highways 14 and 58 is the small town of Mojave, gateway to the **Mojave Desert ③⓪**. From borax to the B-1 bomber, it has seen more history than places many times its size. Near Edwards Air Force Base, Mojave was part of the Antelope Valley aerospace boom, serving as a temporary community for the aerospace workers, as well as those employed in agriculture and railroads. The winter season is its busiest time, when weekend skiers, heading to and from Sierra slopes, pack the motels and roadside cafés.

About 25 miles (40 km) north of Mojave along State 14 is **Red Rock Canyon State Park ③①** (tel: 661-942 0662), an unusual camping and picnic spot, which, despite its geological importance, has remained relatively little-explored. Great, brightly colored columns of sandstone rise off the desert floor on either side of the highway, sculpted towers in the foothills of the eastern Sierras. About the middle of the 19th century, traffic picked up considerably when desert prospectors began discovering gold nuggets on the surface of dry stream beds. A mini-boom followed, and subsequently about $16 million worth of ore was removed, including one 5-lb (2.27-kg) nugget. On weekends, state rangers give guided nature walks. Picnic tables and about 50 primitive campsites are provided for tents and recreational vehicles. Visitors must bring their own food and water, however, as there are no concessions at the park.

An interesting detour for amateur archeologists lies down Highway 58, east of Mojave and near the town of **Barstow ②**. Paleontologists are still carrying on the work of the late Dr Louis Leakey, the leader of a team of eminent scientists who believed they had found a prehistoric "tool factory" estimated to be some 200,000 years old. The so-called **Calico Early Man Site** is open for public viewing, with guided tours some days of the week. Arrangements can be made with the Federal Bureau of Land Management office in Barstow, a bustling desert town, which is largely the suburb of a military community. Situated at the junction of Interstates 15 and 40, it has a 5-mile (8-km) stretch of motels, gas stations and grocery stores that makes it a very good base for stocking up.

Calico Ghost Town was restored by LA's Walter Knott of Knott's Berry Farm fame. Part authentic mining town, part theme park, it's fun to discover which is real and which is whimsy.

Ghost towns

Calico ③ itself was established by silver miners in the 1880s, its boomtown restored as the **Calico Ghost Town** (tel: 760-254 2122). Half history and half Hollywood, Calico is an amusement park where visitors can explore mining tunnels, ride the ore train and browse in old-fashioned dry-goods shops.

Back then, towards **Randsburg ④**, a 19th-century ghost town that is actually still a thriving hilltop mining community, which is about 20 miles (32 km) east of Red Rock Canyon on US 395. Named after one of the gold towns of South Africa, Randsburg struck it rich three times between 1895 and 1947, first

BELOW: descent from the peaks.

SURVIVAL IN THE DESERT

The Mojave Desert covers an enormous amount of land – roughly that of the states of Massachusetts, Rhode Island and Connecticut combined. It's easy to get lost and, with conventional vehicles, even to get stranded off the main roads. Water can usually be found if you are equipped to dig deep enough, as the native Shoshone tribe knew very well, but few visitors know anything about survival techniques in such a primitive land.

It is quite literally life-theatening to remain under the desert sun for too long a time. Take adequate provisions, and adequate precautions. Have your car checked out thoroughly before setting off, paying particular attention to the tires and any problems concerning overheating. Pack food, water and sunscreen, for use even while in the car (do not make the journey in a convertible).

Once there, don't panic if trouble arises. If you have car trouble, rangers suggest you wait where you are: do not wander off to look for help. Fever from excessive heat can cause delirium and loss of thirst, and people have been known to die with a full canteen of water beside them. Centuries ago, explorer Juan Bautista de Anza experienced the Mojave's natural furnace and referred to the region as Tierra del Muertos, literally "Land of the Dead." Be warned.

with gold, then with silver and finally with tungsten. After its discovery late in the 19th century, its Yellow Aster mine yielded $20 million in gold before it was exhausted. Turn-of-the-20th century Randsburg was as wild and wooly as any Western boomtown, with saloons and dance halls, scoundrels and rogues.

Among the ramshackle remains of the original wood-and-corrugated iron buildings on Randsburg's main street today is the **Desert Museum** (open weekends only), with its collection of mining and geological artifacts. Also open are the town saloon, dance hall and barber shop, which have been quaintly converted into shops offering rocks, bottles and mining curios. At the **Randsburg General Store**, wayfarers can sip a chocolate soda at the same swivel-chaired soda fountain that was hauled into town by mules over a century ago.

China Lake ⑤ is a dry basin near Ridgecrest off US 395. It is best known as the focus of the important China Lake Naval Air Warfare Center. Near the main gate of the naval station is the small **Maturango Museum** (tel: 760-375 6900; daily 10am–5pm; admission charge). The museum occasionally conducts field trips to study aboriginal rock inscriptions found nearby, possibly the best such collection in the state. As a result of the discoveries made at China Lake, some scientists are tempted to say that humans migrated from Asia at least 40,000 years ago, perhaps even 100,000 years ago.

Not far from China Lake, near the banks of the equally dry Searles Lake, are the **Trona Pinnacles** ㊱. This great pincushion of ancient limestone columns in the middle of the Mojave Desert is both rare and bizarre. The spooky stone spires are "national natural landmarks," probably the most outstanding examples of tufa formations in North America, and a challenging moonscape to explore for hikers and rock climbers. The Trona Pinnacles are situated on the west side of

Map, page 242

BELOW: Lone Pine Peak.

Alternate Energy

California, as well known for its climate as for its automobile culture, is at the forefront in researching alternate forms of energy. Three of the state's utilities – Southern California Edison, the Los Angeles Department of Water & Power and the Sacramento Municipal Utility District – joined forces with financial help from the US Energy Department to construct a $39 million plant in the Mojave Desert that they hoped would provide a feasible alternative to fossil fuels.

The initial 10-megawatt plant produced 10 percent or less of the current output of fuel-driven plants, but, if it had been successful, facilities would have been built that were 10 or 20 times the size of the proposed plant.

Known as Solar Two, the plant, which closed in the late 1990s, used hundreds of giant mirrors to concentrate the sun's rays on a 300-ft (90-meter) tower, heating to a temperature of 1,050°F (566°C) molten nitrate salt stored in an insulated tank. When needed, the molten

salt – a yellowish syrup that retains heat better than water or oil – will convert water into the steam required to power a turbine generator.

Earlier experimentation with solar energy has proved economically impractical partly because of the need for a lot of land and a consistently warm and sunny climate. The largest such plant was one of nine owned by Luz International, which used the sun's rays to heat water rather than salt.

Although these generated enough light for 350,000 households in Southern California, Luz filed for bankruptcy due, the company claimed, to confused Federal policies and "hidden subsidies" to utilities, which use regular fossil fuels.

Similar problems have been faced by the pioneers of windpower. The country was originally the world's biggest producer of windpower – producing about 75 percent of the world's supply – but it has substantially downsized. Now it aims at supplying 20 percent of California's energy by 2010, an enormous step down. Which is a shame: nine-tenths of the US's windpower potential is located in the dozen Western states, where ranching and grain production are major industries and where ranchers have warmly welcomed the royalties that are paid for use of their land for such projects.

US Windpower Co. of Livermore, California, once the nation's largest builder and operator of these machines, reported that its 3,700 turbines in the northern part of the state accumulated 40 million operating hours in winds averaging 16 miles (26 km) an hour, driving the blades at almost ten times that speed. Unfortunately, the development of new turbines, 75 ft (23 meters) high with 54-ft (16-meter) blades, could not sustain the industry's growth and potential.

Government investment could make a huge difference, resulting in energy cheap enough to compete successfully with "dirty" (and diminishing) fossil fuels, so that windpower would become more significant than nuclear power within the next 25 years. According to one expert in the field, it could provide up to 20 percent of the country's electricity needs, compared with what it presently supplies. ❏

LEFT: alternate energy from the desert is one hope for California's future fuel consumption.

bleakly awesome **Searles Lake**, access to which is via State 178 north from **Johannesburg**. Camping is permitted at the Pinnacles. Ninety-four miles (151 km) north of Johannesburg on US 395 is **Lone Pine** ㉗, a picturesque village that has been a popular location for Hollywood Westerns.

Map, page 242

Mount Whitney

From here, **Mount Whitney** ㉘ – at 14,494 ft (4,418 meters) the highest peak in the continental United States – is accessible, although it's an 11-mile (18-km) challenge from the end of Whitney Portal Road to reach the summit *(also see page 204)*. After the climb, a good place for a break is **Keeler**, a ghost town about 10 miles (16 km) from Lone Pine. About 50 miles (80 km) to the east, beyond Towne Pass, State Route 190 runs into the Panamint Mountains, some of whose rugged canyons bustled with people and activity in 1873. The town of **Panamint**, now abandoned, came into being when the robbers of a Wells Fargo express discovered silver while hiding out in **Surprise Canyon**.

Persuading two state senators to make a deal with the express company in return for part ownership of the lode, they presided over an instant boomtown with stores, saloons, boarding houses and banks – all along a main street that occupied the entire width of the narrow canyon. Within a year, the boom was over, but the canny miners cast their silver in the form of 700-lb (318-kg) cannon balls, a burden too heavy for robbers to carry away.

Indian Ranch Road, an unpaved track off the Trona-Wildrose road and which forks off up Surprise Canyon, continues down to **Ballarat** ㉙. Only crumbling adobe walls and ruined shacks remain here of what was once an important supply town for the miners, to which the stagecoach used to run all the way from Johannesburg.

Another deserted mining town, off Emigrant Canyon Road, is **Skidoo**. Its name was derived from the phrase "23 Skidoo," it having been 23 miles (37 km) from Telescope Peak. Skidoo is famous for its "million-dollar slope," from which $1 million in gold ore was taken early in the 20th century – "it could be scraped out in wheelbarrows," boasted its former owner.

But Skidoo has gone down in legend more than this as "the town that hanged its killer twice," after an incident in which a drunken saloon keeper killed a popular town banker. Skidoo's citizens were wary of what kind of justice might be administered from the nearest lawmen at Lone Pine, so they took it upon themselves to promptly hang the killer. The next day, when a reporter from the big-city *Los Angeles Herald* arrived, they dug up the body and hanged it again so the newsman could get a picture.

Lowest spot on earth

State Route 190 is the main artery through **Death Valley National Park** ㊵, first established as a national monument in 1933. Its fearsome reputation seems to attract as many as it intimidates. Winter or summer sightseers, hikers and amateur naturalists come to scramble up the sand dunes near **Stovepipe Wells**. They also want to marvel at the view from Zabriskie Point, gasp at ancient Ubehebe Crater, study old mines and abandoned char-

ABOVE: land sailors.
BELOW: abandoned mine shaft at Twenty Mule Team Canyon.

coal kilns, explore old ghost towns and snap scores of both color and black-and-white pictures at humble **Badwater** ❹, 282 ft (86 meters) below sea level, the lowest spot in North America. Death Valley's summer temperatures are exceeded only in the Libyan Sahara. Autumn through spring, the climate is ideal for exploring Death Valley, with daytime temperatures in the 60s and 70s Fahrenheit (about 16–26°C), although it is chillier at night. Skies are usually bright.

Summers are another story. The average daily high in July for the past half-century has been 116°F (47°C). It commonly soars past 120°F (49°C), and once hit a national high of 134°F (57°C). In short, May to October is one continuous heatwave.

Desert facts

This 120-mile long (193-km) valley is the result of a geological phenomenon. At least 5 million years ago, the deep gap between the Panamint and Funeral mountains was formed by earthquakes and the folding of the earth's crust. This created, technically, not a valley, but what geologists tend to call a graben rock.

Despite the harshness of Death Valley's environment, about 900 different species of plant grow in the national park. In many ways, Death Valley's human population of 200 or so seems just as indomitable, enduring terrific heat and isolation. However, the growth of Las Vegas, Nevada, 140 miles (225 km) away, inspired the development of the town of Pahrump. It's now only a 60-mile (97-km) drive to the nearest big grocery store.

Years ago, it was traditional for all concessions to close down in the summer, but the tourists kept on coming. Nowadays, in the town of **Furnace Creek** ❷, the **Furnace Creek Ranch** and the nearby **Stovepipe Wells Village** complex

ABOVE: only 6 miles (10 km) to a bathtub.
BELOW:
Furnace Creek.

stay open throughout the year, and neither is ever empty. Tour groups also arrive in the white-hot summer months from Las Vegas, albeit sheltered from the worst elements by desert-tough, air-conditioned vehicles.

Furnace Creek is a good focal point for a visit to Death Valley. Located not far from Badwater, its **Visitor Center** (tel: 760-786 2331; admission charge) is open daily all year round. Although Furnace Creek Ranch's 18-hole golf course is said to be the lowest course on earth, nobody would hire a caddy for the valley's other links, the so-called **Devil's Golf Course**, an otherworldly expanse of rugged salt crystals that point to the sky in jagged little edges. It lies between the former sites of the Eagle Borax mill, southwest of Badwater, and the Harmony Borax Works, just north of Furnace Creek, which was developed into a resort from the former workers' quarters. At the **Harmony Borax Works**, an old cleanser-processing plant has been stabilized to show interested visitors the now-very-primitive 19th-century manufacturing methods.

Beginning in 1873, borax – a white, crystalline substance used as a flux, cleansing agent and antiseptic – was a major product of the valley, transported by wagons hauled by 20-mule teams 165 miles (265 km) to the town of Mojave. The company set up resting stations with water tanks and feedboxes every 16 miles (26 km). Eventually, the price of borax was undercut by producers in Italy, and the Death Valley companies suspended operations entirely.

Overlooking Badwater to the east is **Dante's View** (5,475 ft/1,669 meters) and, in the west, **Telescope Peak**, the highest point in the Panamint Range (11,049 ft/3,368 meters).

Among Death Valley's other natural beauty spots are **Zabriskie Point**, made famous by a 1960s movie and located southeast of Furnace Creek in the Black

Map, page 242

BELOW:
Scotty's Castle.

Mountains near interesting **Twenty Mule Team Canyon**; **Artists Drive** and the **Golden Canyon**, with its vivid displays of color among old outcroppings; and empty **Ubehebe Crater**, an extinct volcano nearly 2,000 years old at the north end of the national park.

Death's big attraction

Near Ubehebe Crater is the 25-room **Scotty's Castle** ㊾ (tel: 760-786 2392; open daily; admission charge), a $2 million Spanish palace that is Death Valley's biggest visitor attraction. It is operated by the National Park Service, which runs hourly tours. Work on the castle began in 1926, at the foot of a natural spring-fed canyon at an elevation of 3,000 ft (about 900 meters). About 2,000 hard-working men assembled the castle, completing it in 1931, all at the expense and enthusiasm of a young Chicago millionaire by the name of Albert Johnson.

Earlier, he had been charmed into investing thousands of dollars in a fruitless search for gold by an affable roustabout named Walter Scott, popularly known as "Death Valley Scotty." After years of waiting for Scott to strike his fortune, Johnson's patience ran out – but not before he had grown so fond of Death Valley that he decided to build a summer retreat there.

A facsimile of a Spanish-Mediterranean villa, Scotty's Castle contains beautiful continental furnishings and objets d'art. The Chicago financier and his wife lived on and off at the castle for many years until his death in 1948. "Death Valley Scotty," the good-natured rogue, also lived nearby. He died in 1954, and his grave lies along a trail just behind the castle.

State Route 190 exits Death Valley near the Nevada border and joins State 127 at **Death Valley Junction**. It is here that one of the most extraordinary sights of the desert is located – **Amargosa Opera House** ㊿. Performances are held weekly from November through May, and tend to be sell-outs, so be sure to book ahead (tel: 760-852 4441). ❏

RIGHT: the endless, sandy dunes of Stovepipe Wells, Death Valley.

INSIGHT GUIDES

TRAVEL TIPS

CALIFORNIA

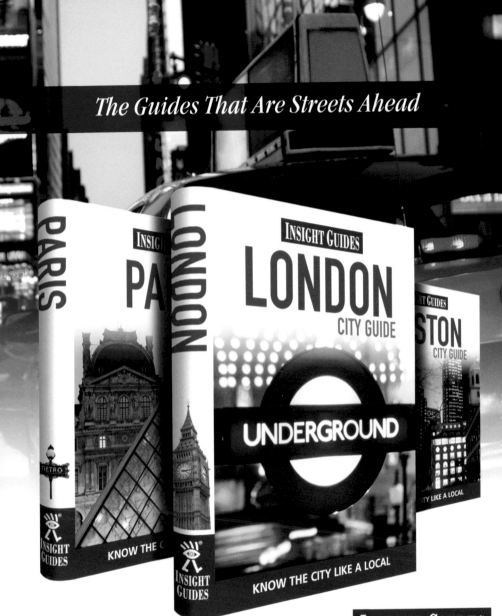

TRAVEL TIPS

TRANSPORTATION

GETTING THERE AND GETTING AROUND

GETTING THERE

By Air

San Francisco International Airport:
Known as SFO, the airport is 14 miles (23 km) south of downtown San Francisco near the town of San Mateo. For public transportation to and from the city, call the Airport Transportation Information line, tel: 650-817 1717. Several private shuttles go to most of the Bay Area. Call SuperShuttle (www.supershuttle.com or 1-800 258 3826) or look around the pedestrian island outside the baggage claim areas for departing vans. Bay Area Rapid Transit (BART) provides a Metro rail service within the Bay Area and has a station at SFO. For airport information, tel: 650-876 7809, www.flysfo.com.

Oakland International Airport:
Much smaller and less crowded than SFO, Oakland Airport is well-served by public transportation and much

Airlines

Airlines that fly regularly into California include:
Alaska Airlines,
www.alaskaair.com;
*American Airlines,
www.aa.com;
Continental Airlines,
www.continental.com;
Delta Airlines,
www.delta.com;
Northwest,
www.nwa.com;
Southwest,
www.southwest.com;
US Airways,
www.usairways.com.

closer to East Bay destinations. Shuttles link the airport with the BART subway system and SFO. General airport information, tel: 510-563 3300; www.flyoakland.com.

Los Angeles International Airport:
LAX is one of the world's busiest airports, handling the majority of the state's international, domestic and regional air traffic. There are information booths just outside the terminal for MTA (Metropolitan Transportation Authority) buses, tel: 213-626 4455. For general airport information, tel: 310-646 5252, www.lawa.org.

San Diego International Airport:
Known as Lindbergh Field, flights arrive from most major American cities. Transportation information, tel: 619-233 3004. General airport information, tel: 619-231 2100, www.san.org.
In addition to the international airports listed above, there are smaller, regional airports in several locations throughout California, including Palmdale, Palm Springs, Ontario, *Burbank, Fresno, Sacramento, San José, Van Nuys and Orange County. Shuttle flights are usually available at all of the larger air terminals.

By Rail

Amtrak (tel: 1-800 872 7245, www.amtrak.com) is the major rail passenger carrier in the US. Though the system is little used and little appreciated by Californians, it can be a pleasant way to get around the state, provided you are not in too much of a hurry. The California Zephyr is the main rail line into Northern California, stopping at Sacramento, Colfax, Davis, Martinez and Truckee before reaching the

Emeryville Station, where there is a free bus service to San Francisco.
Caltrain runs passengers between San Francisco and San Jose, with several stops along the peninsula. This rail service operates from the terminal located at Fourth and King streets in San Francisco, www.caltrain.com.
Amtrak offers several major rail lines in Southern California. The Sunset Limited from New Orleans stops at North Palm Springs, Ontario and Pomona before it reaches Los Angeles. The Pacific SurfLiner links San Diego to Los Angeles and on to Santa Barbara and San Luis Obispo. The San Joaquins runs between Sacramento and Bakersfield, with stops at Stockton, Modesto, Merced and Fresno.
The state is tied together by the Coast Starlight, which travels north from Los Angeles all the way to Seattle, stopping at Van Nuys, Simi Valley, Oxnard, Santa Barbara, San Luis Obispo, Paso Robles, San Jose,

BELOW: San Diego train station.

ABOVE: San Francisco's cable cars are a fun way to get around the city.

Oakland (from here, there's a bus transfer to San Francisco before the route continues), Emeryville, Martinez, Davis, Sacramento, Chico, Redding and across the Oregon border. Amtrak offers some local services also. Contact Amtrak directly for details, tel: 1-800 872 7245.

By Bus

The national bus line, Greyhound Lines (tel: 1-800 231 2222; www.greyhound.com), as well as a number of smaller charter companies provide an impressive network of ground travel throughout California, offering daily service to major towns and cities. Routes and schedules are subject to change; it is a good idea to check all arrangements with local stations, in advance. San Francisco, Oakland, Los Angeles, San Diego and other large towns also have municipal bus systems.

Bus service numbers within major cities include: San Francisco, tel: MUNI at 415-673 6864, www.sfmuni.com; East Bay Transit at 510-839 2882, www.actransit.org; Los Angeles County Metropolitan Transportation Authority at 213-626 4455, www.mta.net; San Diego Metropolitan Transit System at 619-233 3004, www.sdmts.com

By Road

The principal **north-south** byways in California are listed below:

Interstate 5 (the Golden State and Santa Ana freeways), which covers the distance from Canada to Mexico via Seattle, Sacramento, Los Angeles and San Diego.
Interstate 15, which transits San Bernardino and San Diego after a long passage from Montana's Canadian border, via Salt Lake City and Las Vegas.
US Highway 101 (the Ventura and Hollywood freeways), which proceeds south down the Pacific coast from Washington state, crosses San Francisco's Golden Gate Bridge and ends in downtown Los Angeles.
State Highway 1 (the Pacific Coast Highway), which hugs the coast from San Diego to San Francisco and further north.
The principal **east-west** byways in California are:
Interstate 8, which departs from Interstate 10 at Casa Grande, Arizona, and ends in San Diego.
Interstate 10 (the San Bernardino and Santa Monica freeways), which begins on the east coast in Jacksonville, Florida, and continues through New Orleans, Houston, El

Speed Limits

The national speed limit on all interstate highways is 65–75 miles (105–121 km) per hour, and 55 miles (88 km) per hour on most other local highways. California law requires that every passenger wear a seat belt, that small children and babies be secured in youth or infant seats, and that drivers carry a valid license at all times. There is also a state law that requires all motorcycle riders to wear helmets.

Paso, Tucson and Phoenix before cutting through Los Angeles, then ending at the coast in Santa Monica.
Interstate 40, which connects Knoxville, Tennessee, with Barstow, California, via Memphis, Oklahoma City and Albuquerque.

GETTING AROUND

Public Transportation

San Francisco: San Francisco is served by an excellent public transportation system. The city's MUNI (tel: 415-673 6864; open 6am–late, with some night service; www.sfmuni.com) network of buses, street cars and historic cable cars makes getting around a snap. The "owl" late-night service runs every 30 minutes from 1–5am. In addition, the Bay Area Rapid Transit (known locally as BART) subway system (tel: 415-989 2278; open 4am–midnight; www.bart.gov) connects San Francisco with the East Bay via a tunnel that goes under the bay.

BART is one of the most efficient and modern rail lines in the United States. Often compared to the super-subways of Europe and the Far East, BART serves 43 stations in three counties, from San Francisco to Millbrae and throughout the East Bay. Hours are: Monday–Friday 4am–midnight; Saturday 6am–midnight and Sunday 8am–midnight.
Los Angeles: The main public transportation is the Los Angeles County Metropolitan Transportation Authority bus company, which everyone

TRANSPORTATION

ACCOMMODATIONS

EATING OUT

ACTIVITIES

A – Z

calls the Metro. The MTA oversees the city's surprisingly comprehensive bus system, as well as the newer Metro and light rail system.

Southern California is still implementing its most ambitious public transit plans for over half a century, which, when completed, will link areas as far apart as Long Beach and Palmdale, 50 miles (80 km) north of LA. The 400-mile (640-km) system of light rail, subway and other transportation facilities will not be fully in place until 2010, although a few lines in central LA have opened.

The popular Red Line operates between Downtown, North Hollywood and Universal City. The Blue Line operates between Downtown and Long Beach. The Green Line runs all the way to Redondo Beach, crossing the Blue Line just north of Compton. The newest route, the Gold Line, travels between Downtown and Pasadena.

Visitors can buy an MTA pass which is good for seven days on Metro bus and rail lines (call 1-800-COMMUTE to find out the nearest location to buy). There is also a discount of about 10 percent if you buy booklets of 10 tickets or more. For more information and schedules, tel: 213-626 4455; www.mta.net.
San Diego: The state's second largest city has its own widespread public transportation service, the San Diego Metropolitan Transit System (tel: 619-233 3004; www.sdmts.com), which offers bus and trolley routes through the San Diego area – from Old Town to Mission Beach to Mission Valley. The system also provides access to other towns in and around San Diego County. Some of these include Coronado, Del Mar, Escondido, Oceanside, Borrego Springs and Tecate. For tickets, monthly passes, general and route information, contact the Transit store, tel: 619-234 1060.

Private Transportation

Driving is by far the most convenient way to travel in California. Roads are well-maintained throughout the state, and gasoline, although pricier than in other US states, is still a bargain by European standards.

Motoring Advisories

If you plan on driving any distance, it's a good idea to join the American Automobile Association or one of its affiliate offices throughout California (the Automobile Club of Southern California at 4512 Sepulveda Boulevard, Culver City, CA 90230-4833, tel: 310-390 9866, www.aaa-calif.com, is not far from Los Angeles International Airport; in San Francisco, contact AAA, 150 Van Ness Avenue, tel: 415-565 2012; www.csaa.com). In addition to emergency road service, AAA offers maps, guidebooks and insurance.

Car Rental

National car-rental companies are located at all airports and large towns. The best rates are usually available by booking in advance. In most cases, you must be at least 21 years old to rent a car (often 25), and you must have a valid driver's license and at least one major credit card. Foreign travelers may need to produce an international driver's license or a license from their home country. Be sure to take out collision and liability insurance, which may not always be included in the base price of the rental. It is also a good idea to inquire about an unlimited mileage package, especially on a long trip. If not, you may be charged per mile in

There are reciprocal arrangements with many international AAA organizations, such as those in Great Britain, Germany and Australia.

Tips for the Road

Interstate highways are planned to bypass most towns, and they do get you to your destination fast (note in California, even "fast" can mean 4 to 10 hours). Along the interstates there are restrooms and roadside picnic areas, as well as food and gasoline.

The Highway Patrol cruises the state's highways, not just monitoring speed limits but also looking for drivers in trouble. If you have any emergency that won't allow you to continue the trip, signal your distress by raising the hood. Be sure to keep a current driver's license and a certificate proving you have liability insurance with you at all times because you will be required to show them to the law enforcement officer who stops your car for any reason. It is illegal to drive without these items. Motorists are often warned that they are safer staying in the car with the doors locked until a patrol car stops to help, rather than leaving it and trying to hitchhike.

Rules of the Road

Speed limits for roads and highways are posted on white signs to the right, as are all other **road signs**. Some roads are for one-way traffic only and are identified by a black and white sign with an arrow pointing in the permitted direction of travel. At an intersection where each corner has a red stop sign with a smaller sign below it which says "4-Way" or "All-Way," motorists must completely

addition to your rental fee, and considering the vast area of California, those vacation miles can add up quickly.

Alamo	1-800 462 5266
	www.alamo.com
Avis	1-800 230 4898
	www.avis.com
Budget	1-800 527 0700
	www.budget.com
Dollar	1-800 800 4000
	www.dollar.com
Enterprise	1-800 261 7331
	www.enterprise.com
Hertz	1-800 654 3131
	www.hertz.com
National	1-800 227 7368
	www.nationalcar.com
Thrifty	1-800 367 2277
	www.thrifty.com

Car Tours

Seagull signs in blue and white mark San Francisco's 49-Mile Scenic Drive, a name which says it all. A free map from the San Francisco Visitor Center at Powell and Market streets details the route. Drivers who seek to explore old Route 66 in the south of the state can get a free map from the LA Visitors Center, 685 South Figueroa St, tel: 213-689 8822, which charts 29 points of interest along 62 miles (100 km) of the historic road.

stop and then proceed across the intersection following the order in which they arrived at the stop.

In California, it is legal to make a **right turn** on a red light after making a full stop, unless signs indicate otherwise.

Although everyone will pass you, resist the temptation to exceed the **speed limit**. If caught in a "speed trap" by the Highway Patrol, whose black-and-white cruisers have radar, you will get a speeding ticket that has to be paid in a nearby (or sometimes not so near) town before continuing your trip.

The same advice should be followed when driving through towns and cities. Be sure to notice the white signs warning that, upon entering the town, you will be in a different "Speed Zone Ahead." Be prepared to slow to the lower speed you will soon see posted on upcoming white signs. Some very small towns are notorious for catching and fining drivers who have not slowed down quickly enough from the highway speed to the(much lower) in-town speed limit.

Desert & Mountain Travel

A word of caution for desert travelers: the single most important precaution you can take is to tell someone your destination, route and expected time of arrival. Then, be sure to check tires carefully before setting out. Heat builds pressure, so have tires at slightly below normal air pressure. The desert's arid climate makes carrying extra water – both for passengers and vehicles – essential. Carry at least one gallon (4 liters) per person. Keep an eye on the gas gauge; it's a good idea to have more than you think you need. Remember, if you should have car trouble or become lost, do not strike out on foot. A car, visible from the air and presumably on a road, is easier to spot than a person on their own, and it affords shelter from the weather.

Just be patient and wait to be found.

Mountain drivers are advised to be equally vigilant. Winter storms in the Sierras occasionally close major roads, and at times chains are required for tires. Phone ahead for road conditions before you depart.

For 24-hour information on road conditions throughout the state, telephone 916-445 1534.

Traveling to Tijuana/Baja

In 2007, the Department of Homeland Security issued a ruling that requires each US citizen to produce a passport if traveling to Mexico. Anyone staying in Mexico for more than 72 hours must acquire a tourist visa in San Diego (available from travel agents, the Mexican Consulate, an immigration office at the border crossing, or the Automobile Club of Southern California.) Proof of nationality must accompany the visa. Non-US citizens should bring their passports and their green cards when crossing over.

US insurance is not valid in Mexico and it is definitely a wise move to obtain short-term insurance, obtainable at innumerable sales offices just north of the border.

Crossing into Mexico can be easy, with immigration officers at both sides often just waving you along. There are three major crossings: at busy **San Ysidro**, 18 miles (29 km) south of downtown San Diego, which is the gateway to Tijuana; at **Tecate** off State 94, where there is rarely a wait, although the border does tend to close in early in the evening; and at **Mexicali** (which is also Baja's capital), a dreary industrial city situated opposite the California town of Calexico, about 90 miles (145 km) to the east.

Because driving in Tijuana for those unfamiliar with the city (and the Spanish language) can be trouble-some, many drivers park in San Diego's San Ysidro, crossing into Tijuana via the elevated pedestrian walkway. Avoid leaving your car in the parking places of merchants as it will be towed away by police.

There's an all-day secure lot off the "Last Exit US parking" ramp – turn right at the stop sign to the Tijuana side. Cheap taxis and buses are also available.

Crossing Back: The return to California can be a bit more tense than the entry into Mexico, as US Border Patrol officers take far more interest in who's coming into the country (hence those passports and green cards). During busy American holiday periods, such as Independence Day (July 4) and Labor Day (early September), waiting up to two hours to cross back into the US is not uncommon.

Hitchhiking

In California, as elsewhere in the United States, hitchhiking is dangerous and unpredictable. Hitchhiking is illegal on all highways and interstates and on many secondary roads as well, and, because traffic is sparse in some regions, it can also be quite difficult.

However, if you do decide to hitch, it is best to do it from an exit ramp (if legal) or a highway rest stop rather than on the road itself. For long distances, it is advisable to make a sign clearly stating your destination. To find the safest situations, it is always worth checking ride services and college campus bulletin boards for posted ride shares.

TRANSPORTATION

ACCOMMODATIONS

EATING OUT

ACTIVITIES

A – Z

A CCOMMODATIONS

HOTELS, MOTELS, BED & BREAKFAST INNS

Hotels

California offers the complete spectrum of accommodations – from elegant European-style hotels to inexpensive motels that can be rented by the week.

In San Francisco, the most expensive hotels are generally located on Nob Hill, the Financial District and Union Square. These grand hotels are particularly well-suited to the international traveler, and many are attractive landmarks in their own right. In Los Angeles, the most expensive are situated Downtown and in Beverly Hills, with the best access to shopping and public transportation.

The concierge at most finer hotels will arrange theater tickets, tours, limousines with bilingual drivers and airline reservations.

There are also a large number of smaller hotels and hotel chains. These establishments usually offer all of the essential comforts without the high prices of the grand hotels.

Note: due to California's strict policy, most hotel and motel rooms are non-smoking. If smoking is important to you, check around before you book.

Motels

If you're traveling by car and don't plan on spending much time in your room, motels are the best solution. Whether located along busy Sunset Boulevard in Los Angeles or along the riverbank in a remote Northern California town, most motels provide parking space – at a premium in most of California – within just steps of your room.

Motel quality varies, but you can usually expect clean and simple accommodations. This is especially true for most of the national chains. A restaurant or coffee shop, swimming pool and sauna are often found on the motel premises.

Room facilities generally include a telephone, television and radio. Don't hesitate to ask the motel manager if you may inspect a room before agreeing to take it.

Other than their accessibility by auto, the attraction of motels is price. Motels in California cities range from $75 to $150 per night, double occupancy. They are less expensive in the outlying areas.

Motel Chains

Motel chains can be found all around California. Many chains have toll-free numbers available from other countries; check your local telephone directory. Toll-free telephone numbers within the US are usually indicated by 1-800 or 1-888.

BELOW: California has lovely B&Bs.

Best Western	1-800 528 1234
Comfort Inn	1-800 228 5150
Doubletree	1-800 222 8733
Embassy	1-800 362 2779
Holiday Inn	1-800 465 4329
La Quinta	1-800 531 5900
Marriott	1-888 236 2427
Motel 6	1-800 466 8356
Quality Inns	1-800 228 5151
Ramada	1-800 272 6232
Red Roof Inn	1-800 733 7663
Super 8	1-800 800 8000
Travelodge	1-800 255 3050
Vagabond	1-800 522 1555

Bed & Breakfast Inns

B&Bs are extremely popular throughout the United States, especially in New England and Northern California. Most cluster in such scenic areas as the Wine Country, Gold Country, North Coast and Monterey Peninsula. Situated in such beautiful rural settings, they do a thriving business with city dwellers in search of a romantic weekend retreat.

Converted from mansions and farmhouses with five to 15 rooms, these inns offer the traveler a highly individual experience; no two inns are alike, and, in most inns, no two rooms are alike. For those accustomed to the uniformity of hotels and motel chains, the inns provide a lovely alternative.

Many inns have shared bathrooms and only a few have televisions or telephones situated in the rooms. Most include breakfast with the price of the room, hence the name.

Prices vary greatly, but unlike in Europe, they tend to be fairly expensive. Call or write in advance – the inns are very popular on weekends and in summer. In fact, intimate inns are even popping up in large cities to compete with hotels.

TRANSPORTATION

ACCOMMODATIONS

ABOVE: camping for the day in the Russian River Valley, Northern California.

For B&B information, contact the **California Association of Bed & Breakfast Inns** (CABBI), 2715 Porter St, No. 104, Soquel, CA 95073. Tel: 831-464 8159; 1-800 373 9251, www.cabbi.com

Hostels

Some travelers may like to take advantage of California's chain of hostels. Hostels are clean, comfortable and very inexpensive (as low as $10 per night). Although suitable for people of all ages, they are definitely geared toward the young at heart. Beds are provided in dormitory-like rooms. Hostelers carry their own gear (silverware, sleeping bag, towel) and are expected to help clean up and perform other communal tasks. Hostels are closed 9.30am–4.30pm, so most guests fill their days with nearby outdoor activities.

Northern California has a chain of more than 20 hostels up and down the Pacific coast, from Jedediah Smith Redwoods State Park at the Oregon border down to John Little State Beach. All the hostels are along the shoreline; some are located inside old lighthouses. For urbanites, there are even hostels around Los Angeles.

For a **complete directory** of hostels by region, go to: www.hostels.com/en/us.ca.html
For lists of hostels area by area, try these numbers:
Central California Council, PO Box 2538, Monterey, CA 93942
Tel: 831-899 1252; www.westernhostels.org
Golden Gate Council, 425 Divisadero St, Room 307, San Francisco, CA 94117
Tel: 415-863 1444; www.norcalhostels.org

Los Angeles Council, 1434 Second St, Santa Monica, CA 90401
Tel: 310-393 3413; www.lahostels.org
San Diego Council, 739 Fourth Avenue, Suite 203, San Diego, CA 92101
Tel: 619-338 9981; www.sandiegohostels.org

Campgrounds

Public and private campgrounds are located in or near state and national parks. Most public campgrounds offer primitive facilities – a place to park, rest rooms and outdoor cooking. Private campgrounds are usually a little more expensive and offer additional facilities such as hook-ups, coin laundries, pools and restaurants. Most are busy from mid-June to September and are allotted on a first-come-first-served basis. If possible, make reservations.
National Park Service Reservation Center, tel: 1-800 365 CAVE; 1-800 436 PARK; www.recreation.gov
Easy-to-use site for checking facilities and making bookings.
California Department of Parks and Recreation
1416 9th St, Sacramento, CA 95814
Tel: 916-653 6995; www.parks.ca.gov

For information on specific campgrounds contact:
Buckhorn Campground, Angeles National Forest, above Cooper Canyon Falls. Sites for 38 small RVs and tents.
Tel: 818-899 1900.
Gaviota State Park, Between beach and mountains on the coast, 35 miles (56 km) west of Santa Barbara. Tents and small RVs.
Tel: 805-968 1033.

National Park Service, Pacific West Regional Office
One Jackson Center, 1111 Jackson St, Suite 700, Oakland, CA 94607
Tel: 510-817 1304; www.nps.gov
National Park Service, Department of the Interior
1849 C St NW, Washington DC, 20240
Tel: 202-208 4747; www.nps.gov
Palomar Mountain State Park, near Palomar Observatory and within easy reach of Lake Henshaw and the Anza-Borrego Desert State Park. Trail leads to Boucher Lookout with outstanding views. Tel: 1-800 444 7275.
Santa Rosa Island Campground, One of the uninhabited Channel Islands reached after a 3-hour boat ride from Ventura or Santa Barbara. Primitive facilities. No water or supplies available.
Tel: 1-800 365 2267.
Santa Catalina
The Santa Catalina Island Company operates the fully equipped campground **Hermit Gulch** about a mile from town (shuttle bus), close to the Botanical Garden and hiking trails. Reservations are required (tel: 310-510 8368). Other campgrounds include Two Harbors, Parson's Landing, Blackjack and Little Harbor.
Serrano Campground, San Bernardino National Forest. Situated amid the tall pine trees along Big Bear Lake, the site has showers, toilets, a dump station and full hookups for tents and RVs.
Tel: 877-444 6777.
USDA Forest Service, Pacific Southwest Regional Office, 1323 Club Drive, Vallejo, CA 94592
Tel: 707-562 USFS (8737); www.fs.fed.us

EATING OUT

ACTIVITIES

A – Z

ACCOMMODATIONS LISTINGS

NORTHERN CALIFORNIA

HOTELS

San Francisco

Hotel reservations may be made through services including San Francisco Reservations (tel: 1-800 737 2060; www.hotelres.com). The Convention and Visitors' Bureau can advise you regarding special needs or general information about their member hotels, motels, and inns, tel: 415-391 2000. Hotel chains like Hilton, Hyatt and Marriott offer toll-free telephone numbers for reservations, www.onlyinsanfrancisco.com

Abigail Hotel,
246 McAllister St, CA 94102
Tel: 415-626 6500;
Fax: 415-626 6580;
www.abigailhotel.com
Boutique hotel built in 1927. Uniquely decorated rooms and as it's located in Civic Center, is close to all attractions, including Union Square. Home to Millennium, a respected vegan/vegetarian restaurant. **$**

Adelaide Hostel and Hotel,
5 Isadora Duncan Lane (off Taylor between Geary and Post),
CA 94102
Tel: 415-359 1915;
Fax: 415-359 1940;
www.adelaidehostel.com;
e-mail: info@adelaidehostel.com
Small, casual hotel popular with Europeans. Old-World charm; perfect for the budget traveler. **$**

Campton Place,
340 Stockton St, CA 94108
Tel: 415-781 5555;
1-800 235 4300;
Fax: 415-955 5536;
www.camptonplace.com
Elegant, sophisticated and intimate hotel off Union Square housed in two early 20th-century buildings. Campton Place's award-winning restaurant is popular with business travelers. **$$$**

Cathedral Hill Hotel,
1101 Van Ness Ave,
CA 94109
Tel: 415-776 8200;
1-800 622 0855
Fax: 415-441 2841;
www.cathedralhillhotel.com;
e-mail:
concierge@cathedralhillhotel.com
Roof-top pool and garden patio; 24-hour fitness center; rooms have balconies or city views. Modern architecture and design. **$–$$**

Chancellor Hotel,
433 Powell St, CA 94102
Tel: 415-362 2004;
1-800 428 4748;
Fax: 415-362 1403;
www.chancellorhotel.com
A good-value family-owned hotel on Union Square, first opened in 1914. **$–$$**

Clarion Bedford Hotel,
761 Post St, CA 94109
Tel: 415-673 2600;
Fax: 415-563 6739;
www.hotelbedford.com
Reasonably priced, ideal Union Square location. Crushed Tomato's café and bar on premises. **$$**

Clift Hotel,
495 Geary St, CA 94102
Tel: 415-775 4700;
Fax: 415-441 4621;
www.clifthotel.com
Newly redesigned, a fusion of understated elegance and contemporary hipness. Home of Asia de Cuba restaurant and the Redwood Room. **$$$**

BELOW: the landmark Fairmont Hotel in San Francisco.

Fairmont Hotel,
950 Mason St, CA 94108
Tel: 415-772 5000;
1-800 344 3550;
Fax: 415-772 5013;
www.fairmont.com;
e-mail: sanfrancisco@fairmont.com
A San Francisco landmark, and one reason many people come to Nob Hill. Fine rooms, an elegant atmosphere and stunning city views. **$$$**

Grand Hyatt,
345 Stockton St, CA 94108
Tel: 415-398 1234;
1-800 233 1234;
Fax: 415-391 1780;
www.hyatt.com
With a lovely fountain in the garden, this hotel towers 36 stories above Union Square. **$$$**

Hilton & Towers San Francisco,
333 O'Farrell St, CA 94102
Tel: 415-771 1400;
1-800 445 8667;
Fax: 415-771 6807;
www.hilton.com
A pool, an exercise room, and five restaurants. One of the largest hotels in the city. **$$**

Holiday Inns,
Tel: 1-800 465 4329;
www.holiday-inn.com
Four large hotels; amenities vary according to property; most have swimming pools.
$–$$ depending on the location, amenities and property itself.

Hotel Bohème,
444 Columbus Ave, CA 94133
Tel: 415-433 9111;
Fax: 415-362 6292;
www.hotelboheme.com;
e-mail: info@hotelboheme.com
Touches like fringed lamps, retro fabrics, and Jerry Stoll's black and white photographs of the 1950s evoke the poetry of the Beatnik era in North Beach. All rooms have free Wi-fi.
$$

Hotel Griffon,
155 Steuart St, 0A 94105
Tel: 415-495 2100;
1-800 321 2201;
Fax: 415-495 3522;
www.hotelgriffon.com
Charming brownstone; attentive service; near Ferry Building farmers' market. Some rooms have Bay views. **$$–$$$**

Huntington Hotel Nob Hill Spa,
1075 California St,
CA 94108
Tel: 415-474 5400;
Fax: 415-474 6227;
www.huntingtonhotel.com
Popular with visiting dignitaries, celebrities and discriminating travelers who often request their favorite, (individually furnished) room. The epitome of understated elegance and one of the city's finest hotels. **$$$**

Hyatt Regency,
5 Embarcadero Center, CA 94111
Tel: 415-788 1234;
Fax: 415-398 2567;
www.hyattsf.com
Spectacular architecture: don't miss the triangular lobby atrium that soars for 170 ft (50 meters). **$$$**

Inn at the Opera,
333 Fulton St, CA 94102
Tel: 415-863 8400;
1-800 325 2708;
Fax: 415-861 0821;
www.innattheopera.com
A favorite resting spot for the performing artists who appear nightly in San Francisco's nearby arts centers. The atmosphere of a sumptuous private home; quiet and discreet. **$$**

King George Hotel,
334 Mason St, CA 94102
Tel: 415-781 5050;
1-800 288 6005;
Fax: 415-391 6976;
www.kinggeorge.com
Small, traditional rooms and afternoon tea; a favorite with British travelers. **$$$**

Marina Inn,
3110 Octavia St, CA 94123
Tel: 415-928 1000;
1-800 274 1420;
Fax: 415-928 5909;
www.marinainn.com
Lombard Street-area hotel that has more the feel of a countrified B&B than a city establishment. **$**

Mark Hopkins Intercontinental,
1 Nob Hill, CA 94108
Tel: 415-392 3434;
1-800 327 0200;
Fax: 415-421 3302;
www.markhopkins.net
Along with the Fairmont, Nob Hill's most famous establishment. The "Top of the Mark" restaurant and many rooms offer panoramic views. Neoclassical touches and lavish bathrooms are only two of the other attractions. **$$$**

The Maxwell Hotel,
386 Geary St, CA 94102
Tel: 415-986 2000;
1-800 553 1900;
Fax: 415-397 2447;
www.maxwellhotel.com
Well-located and within most people's budgets, owners have given this pleasant, well-located hotel a stylish, Art Deco look. Max's restaurant on the premises serves hearty deli fare. **$$**

Monticello Inn,
127 Ellis St, CA 94102
Tel: 415-392 8800;
1-866 778 6169;
Fax: 415-398 2650;
www.monticelloinn.com
Colonial-style flair right in the heart of the city, with an adjacent bar and grill. **$**

The Palace,
2 New Montgomery St, CA 94105
Tel: 415-512 1111;
Fax: 415-543 0671;
www.sfpalace.com
A historical landmark; home of the magnificent Garden Court Restaurant. **$$$**

Phoenix Hotel,
601 Eddy St, CA 94109
Tel: 415-776 1380;
1-800 248 9466;
Fax: 415-885 3109;
www.thephoenixhotel.com
Though the neighborhood is a bit dicey, this is where rock stars have been crashing since Bill Graham opened the Fillmore in the late Sixties. Today, it's the funky home of Bambuddha, one of the city's nightspots, and close to many other bars and clubs. Chill out the day after by lounging poolside with scensters from David Bowie to Norah Jones. **$**

Queen Anne Hotel,
1590 Sutter St, CA 94109
Tel: 415-441 2828;
1-800 227 3970;
Fax: 415-775 5212;
www.queenanne.com
The romance of a bygone era meets the comforts of the present in these individually appointed rooms in a restored Victorian building. **$–$$**

Renaissance Stanford Court,
905 California St, CA 94108
Tel: 415-989 3500;
1-800 468 3571;
Fax: 415-391 0513;
www.renaissancehotels.com
Ideally situated on the top of Nob Hill, where the cable cars cross. Two Tiffany-style glass doors grace the lobby. Lots of personal touches. **$$–$$$**

Hotel Rex,
562 Sutter St, CA 94102
Tel: 415-433 4434;
1-800 433 4434;
Fax: 415-433-3695;
www.thehotelrex.com
The decor is inspired by the literary salons of the 1920s. The lobby is a showpiece of period furnishings and fine antiquarian books. **$$**

Ritz-Carlton San Francisco,
600 Stockton St, CA 94108
Tel: 415-296 7465;
1-800 241 3333;
Fax: 415-291 0288;
www.ritzcarlton.com
Oil paintings and crystal chandeliers are two of the innovations that were added when a major hotel chain took over San Francisco's neoclassical Metropolitan Life Insurance Company building to create an "instant" landmark hotel. **$$$**

Royal Pacific Motor Inn,
661 Broadway, CA 94133
Tel: 415-781 6661;
1-800 545 5574;
Fax: 415-781 6688;
www.royalpacificmotorinn.com
No-frills motel in a lively location between North Beach and Chinatown. Finnish sauna, exercise room. **$**

San Francisco Fisherman's Wharf Marriott,
1250 Columbus Ave, CA 94133
Tel: 415-775 7555
Fax: 415-474 2099;
www.marriott.com
Two blocks from the attractions and bustle of Fisherman's Wharf. Great for both business travelers and families. Sauna and exercise room. **$$**

San Remo Hotel
2237 Mason St, CA 94133
Tel: 415-776 8688;
1-800 352 7366;
Fax: 415-776 2811;
www.sanremohotel.com
Built in 1906 after the earthquake, the San Remo served as a boarding house for sailors, poets and pensioners and a speakeasy during Prohibition. Today it remains a bargain for lodgers who want immaculate, well-situated rooms without telephones or TV. Some rooms share showers. The rooftop penthouse is a real San Francisco treat. **$**

Sir Francis Drake,
450 Powell St, CA 94102
Tel: 415-392 7755;
1-800-795 7129;
Fax: 415-391 8719;
www.sirfrancisdrake.com
Doormen are decked out in Beefeater costumes, and rooms are styled as if from an English country home. When the Drake was built in 1928, it contained the latest in innovations. Today, there's an Italian-style café, a bistro and an elegant lounge offering unparalleled city views and live music. **$$–$$$**

ABOVE: the Sir Francis Drake.

Hotel del Sol,
3100 Webster St, CA 94123
Tel: 415-921 5520;
877-433 5765;
Fax: 415-931 4137;
www.thehoteldelsol.com
This renovated 1950s motor lodge is cheery and conveniently located near the Marina district. Continental breakfast is served poolside. **$$**

Stanyan Park Hotel,
750 Stanyan St, CA 94117
Tel: 415-751 1000;
Fax: 415-668 5454;
www.stanyanpark.com
Listed on the National Register of Historic Places, near Golden Gate Park, Haight-Ashbury district and the UC Medical Center. Stylish rooms, some overlooking the park. Good continental breakfast. **$–$$**

Westin St Francis,
335 Powell St, CA 94102
Tel: 415-397 7000;
1-800-917 7458;
Fax: 415-774 0124;
www.westinstfrancis.com
A city landmark. Choose rooms in the original 1904 building or the more modern tower. Restaurateur Michael Mina's acclaimed restaurant of the same name is situated off the grand lobby. **$$$**

PRICE CATEGORIES

Prices categories are for a standard double room without breakfast:
$ = less than $150
$$ = $150–$225
$$$ = more than $225

Albion

Albion River Inn,
3790 N. Highway 1,
PO Box 100, CA 95410
Tel: 707-937 1919;
1-800 479 7944;
Fax: 707-937 2604;
www.albionriverinn.com
A romantic setting on the
Mendocino coast on 10
acres (4 hectares) of
secluded gardens and
headland bluffs. $$–$$$

Big Sur

Big Sur Lodge,
47225 Highway 1, CA 93920
Tel: 831-667 3100;
1-800 424 4787;
Fax: 831-667 3110
www.bigsurlodge.com
Big Sur architect Mickey
Muennig used the sea and
the mountains as a
backdrop to the lodge. Free
entry to nearby parks. $$
Deetjen's Big Sur Inn,
48865 Highway 1, CA 93920
Tel: 831-667 2377;
Fax: 831-667 0466;
www.deetjens.com
Cozy, wooden rooms and
cottages with rustic stoves
are tucked in among the
redwood groves of Castro
Canyon. The inn, built in
the 1930s by transplanted
Norwegian Helmuth
Deetjen, has attracted
everyone from bohemian
eccentrics and wayward
itinerants to actors from
Hollywood's golden era.
$–$$

Ventana Inn,
Highway 1, CA 93920
Tel: 831-667 2331;
1-800 628 6500;
Fax: 831-667 0573;
www.ventanainn.com
Nestled on a cliff
overlooking the dramatic
Pacific coastline, the
unique buildings offer
premiere lodgings for the
discriminating traveler. Spa
services and luxury suites
available. $$$

Marshall

Bleu Bay Beach Cottage,
22275 State Route 1,
CA 94940
Tel: 415-924 8250;
www.beachcottage.us;
e-mail: tflynn3@earthlink.net
A peaceful, homey retreat
cottage on Tomales Bay
with views of Point Reyes
National Seashore. Full
kitchen, hot tub and
adjacent sandy beach.
$$–$$$

Mendocino

Stanford Inn by the Sea,
44850 Comptche-Ukiah Rd, CA
95460
Tel: 707-937 5615;
1-800 331 8884;
www.stanfordinn.com;
e-mail: info@stanfordinn.com
Located on a hilltop
overlooking well-kept
gardens and Mendocino
Bay on a working organic
farm. Vegetarian
restaurant. $$$

Pescadero

**Costanoa Coastal Lodge
and Camp,**
2001 Rossi Road,
CA 94060
Tel: 650-879 1100;
Fax: 650-879 2275;
www.costanoa.com;
e-mail: costanoa@costanoa.com
A coastal lodge and camp
between SF and Santa Cruz
surrounded by wilderness
and secluded beaches.
Accommodations range
from no-frills campsites to
cabins (varying levels of
luxury), to the lodge itself
with full amenities. Spa
services. $–$$

San Simeon

Silver Surf Motel,
9390 Castillo Dr,
CA 93452
Tel: 805-927-4661;
1-800 621 3999
Fax: 805-927 3225
www.silversurfmotel.com
Affordable, friendly motel
halfway between San
Francisco and Los Angeles
on the coast. Beautiful
beaches and fabulous
Hearst Castle nearby. $

Yosemite National Park

The Ahwahnee,
Yosemite Valley, 95389.
Write to: Yosemite Reservations,
5410 East Home St, Fresno,
CA 98727
Tel: 559-252 4848;

Fax: 559-456 0542;
www.yosemitepark.com
Spectacular, historic lodge
with equally spectacular
views. Finely appointed
rooms, parlors and
cottages with massive
stone hearths and Native
American artwork. Booking
is up to a year in advance.
$$$
Yosemite Lodge,
Yosemite Valley, CA 95389
Tel: 559-252 4848;
www.yosemitepark.com
Glass-and-wood detailing
blend harmoniously with
rustic surroundings. The
closest property to
Yosemite Falls. Book up to
six months in advance
during summer, otherwise
several weeks ahead. $

Sequoia National Park

The Wuksachi Lodge,
Tel: 1-888 252 5757;
Fax: 559-565 4097;
www.visitsequoia.com
102-room lodge at 7,200 ft
(2,195 meters), in sight of
Mt Whitney. $$$

BED & BREAKFAST

San Francisco

Petite Auberge,
863 Bush St, CA 94108
Tel: 415-928 6000;
1-800 365 3004;
Fax: 415-673 7214;
www.jdvhotels.com
Gourmet breakfast buffet,
cozy parlor and French
provincial details. Good
value for money. Located
near Union Square. $$
Washington Square Inn,
1660 Stockton St, CA 94133
Tel: 415-981 4220;
1-800 388 0220;
Fax: 415-397 7242;
www.wsisf.com
Within walking distance of
Fisherman's Wharf,
Chinatown, the Financial
District; in North Beach. $$

Carmel

The Pine Inn,
Ocean Ave between Lincoln St and
Monte Verde St,
CA 93921

BELOW: the Stanford Inn in Mendocino overlooks the bay.

Tel: 831-624 3851;
1-800 228 3851;
Fax: 831-624 3030;
www.pine-inn.com
Built in 1889, this elegant inn exudes the charm of a former era. Situated in the heart of the village of Carmel, and just four blocks away from the city's lovely sandy beach. Try and get a room with a view of the ocean. **$$**

Humboldt County

Carter House Inns,
301 L St, Eureka,
CA 95501
Tel: 1-800 404 1390;
www.carterhouse.com
Four Victorian-era houses on Humboldt Bay on the North Coast, with marble fireplaces and jacuzzis in some rooms. Excellent restaurant and free afternoon wine (own label) and hors d'oeuvres. **$$–$$$**
The Gingerbread Mansion,
400 Berding St, Ferndale,
CA 95536
Tel: 707-786 4000;

1-800 952 4136;
www.gingerbread-mansion.com
A lavish Queen Anne-style Victorian house with afternoon tea, manicured gardens, gourmet breakfasts and clawfoot bathtubs in many of the prettily decorated guest rooms. **$$–$$$**

Monterey

Old Monterey Inn,
500 Martin St, CA 93940
Tel: 831-375 8284;
1-800 350 2344;
Fax: 831-375 6730;
www.oldmontereyinn.com
No expense has been spared to provide luxury accommodation here; you'll find plush feather beds and down duvets, elegant furnishings, wood-burning fireplaces and stained-glass windows. Massages and spa treatments are available if you need pampering, and horseback riding on the beach can be arranged if you need excitement. **$$$**

Napa

La Residence,
4066 Howard Lane, CA 94558
Tel: 707-253 0337;
1-800 253 9203;
Fax: 707-253 0382;
www.laresidence.com
This has been called one of Napa's most luxurious inns. Beautiful surroundings, a delightful pool, a wine-and-cheese reception every afternoon (free to guests), and in-room spa treatments are the perfect end to a hard day exploring the Napa Valley. **$$$**

Sonoma

The Gaige House,
13540 Arnold Dr, Glen Ellen CA 95442
Tel: 707-935 0237;
1-800 935 0237;
Fax: 707-935 6411;
www.gaige.com
Delightful bed & breakfast inn located in an elegant restored 1890s property in the Valley of the Moon. **$$$**

ABOVE: try the local wine when you stay at Kenwood.

The Kenwood Inn & Spa,
10400 Sonoma Highway,
Kenwood, CA 95452
Tel: 707-833 1293;
www.kenwoodinn.com
Surrounded by estate vineyards, the Kenwood Inn is the ultimate Wine Country retreat. The spa employs Kenwood's hooch with "vinotherapie" treatments using vine extracts. **$$$**

SOUTHERN CALIFORNIA

HOTELS

Los Angeles (Downtown)

Best Western Dragon Gate Inn,
818 N. Hill St, CA 90012
Tel: 213-617 3077;
Fax 213-680 3753;
www.bestwestern.com
Located in historic Chinatown, with 52 rooms, Asian decor, a shopping mall and an onsite Chinese herb and acupressure shop. Cable with HBO, wireless Internet and room service. Close to Union Station. **$**
Figueroa Hotel,
939 S. Figueroa St, CA 90015
Tel: 213-627 8971;
Fax: 213-689 0305;
www.figueroahotel.com;
e-mail: info@figueroahotel.com
A welcome retreat from Downtown's corporate hotels, the Figueroa is an

exotic addition, with a Moroccan decor, a cactus garden and atmospheric suites. There's also a pool, a jacuzzi, and restaurants. Great value. **$**
Los Angeles Marriott Downtown,
333 S. Figueroa St, CA 90071
Tel: 213-617 1133;
Fax: 213-613 0291;
www.marriott.com
On landscaped grounds, with a pool, near Music Center; luxurious. **$$**
Metro Plaza Hotel,
711 N. Main St, CA 90012
Tel: 213-680 0200;
Fax: 213-620 0200.
Laundromat, sauna, whirlpool, restaurant. **$**
Millennium Biltmore Hotel,
506 S. Grand Ave, CA 90071
Tel: 213-624 1011;
Fax: 213-612 1545;
www.millenniumhotels.com
e-mail: biltmore@mhrmail.com
A fabulous, luxurious historic landmark and not to be missed. Restaurants, pool, jacuzzi. **$$**

Miyako Hotel,
328 East 1st St, CA 90012
Tel: 213-617 2000;
Fax: 213-617 2700;
www.miyakoinn.com;
e-mail: reservation@miyakola.com
Lovely Asian hotel with karaoke bar and health spa. Laundromat, whirlpool, sauna, restaurant. **$**
The New Otani Hotel & Garden,
120 S. Los Angeles St,
CA 90012
Tel: 213-629 1200;
Fax: 213-622 0980;
www.newotani.com;
e-mail: comments@newotani.com
Next door to Little Tokyo with two shopping levels and a delightful Japanese garden. **$$**
Omni Los Angeles Hotel at California Plaza,
251 S. Olive St, CA 90012
Tel: 213-617 3300;
Fax: 213-617 3399;
www.omnihotels.com
Located in the California Plaza atop Bunker Hill, this luxurious hotel overlooks a

water court, adjoins the Museum of Contemporary Art and offers a health club, heated pool, sauna, Japanese fusion restaurant and a host of superb suites. **$$$**
The Standard Downtown LA,
550 S. Flower St, CA 90071
Tel: 213-892 8080;
Fax: 213-892 8686;
www.standardhotel.com
Hotelier André Balazs, of Hollywood's Chateau Marmont fame, opened Downtown's first style palace in a converted 12-story office building. One of the hippest places is the "destination" poolside bar on the roof. **$$$**

PRICE CATEGORIES

Prices categories are for a standard double room without breakfast:
$ = less than $150
$$ = $150–$225
$$$ = more than $225

Vagabond Inn,
3101 S. Figueroa St,
CA 90007
Tel: 213-746 1531;
1-800 522 1555;
Fax: 213-746 9106;
www.vagabondinn.com
Just steps from USC's campus and the Shrine Auditorium (home of the Emmy Awards), this on-the-cheap hotel caters to business travelers and families, with its free parking, high-speed internet access, heated pool, cable TV and pet-friendly rooms. **$**

Westin Bonaventure Hotel & Suites,
404 S. Figueroa St, CA 90071
Tel: 213-624 1000;
Fax: 213-612 4800;
www.westin.com
The Bonaventure has a distinctive circular interior and exterior, a pool, and a rooftop restaurant. There is a Hollywood Poster Gallery along the walk from the parking garage, and guests can ride the glass elevators that have appeared in movies. **$$$**

Wilshire Grand Los Angeles,
930 Wilshire Blvd, CA 90017
Tel: 213-688 7777;
Fax: 213-612 3989;
www.wilshiregrand.com
The closest hotel to the convention center has a pool, an exercise room, a coffee shop and four restaurants. **$$$**

Los Angeles (West Side)

Avalon Beverly Hills,
9400 W. Olympic Blvd,
Beverly Hills, CA 90212
Tel: 310-277 5221;
1-800 535 4715;
Fax: 310-277 4928;
www.avalonbeverlyhills.com
A selection of stylish rooms, suites and penthouse studios in three unique buildings around a beautifully illuminated pool. Highly regarded restaurant on the premises. **$$$**

Best Western Hollywood Hills Hotel,
6141 Franklin Ave, CA 90028.
Tel: 323-464 5181;
Fax: 323-962 0536;
www.bestwestern.com
Two blocks from Capitol Records and the Hollywood Vine Metro Station. Pool, coffee shop, cable with HBO, wireless Internet. **$**

Beverly Inn,
7701 Beverly Blvd, CA 90036
Tel: 323-931 8108;
Fax: 323-935 7103;
www.beverlyinn.com
A boutique motel near CBS TV City, Pan Pacific Park and the Farmers Market. Free covered parking and a pool. **$**

The Brentwood Inn,
12200 W. Sunset Blvd,
Hollywood, CA 90049
Tel: 310-476 9981;
Fax: 310-471 0768;
www.thebrentwood.com

This cozy hotel is in exclusive Brentwood. Built in 1947, there are 20 cute rooms with skylights and flat-screen TVs. Free parking, too. **$$**

Chamberlain West Hollywood,
1000 Westmount Dr,
West Hollywood, CA 90069
Tel: 310-657 7400;
Fax: 310-854 6744;
www.chamberlainwesthollywood.com
Suites, kitchens, rooftop pool, jacuzzi, sauna, laundromat, tiny gym. **$$**

Holiday Inn Express Century City,
10330 W. Olympic Blvd, Century City, CA 90064
Tel: 310-553 1000;
Fax: 310-277 1633;
www.hiexpress.com
All rooms with whirlpool. **$$**

Hollywood Roosevelt Hotel,
7000 Hollywood Blvd,
CA 90028
Tel: 323-466 7000;
Fax: 323-462 8056;
www.hollywoodroosevelt.com;
e-mail: ecarrillo@thompsonhotels.com
Legendary landmark hotel with all the Art Deco trimmings. Its palm-shaded pool and sleek steakhouse make this a modern-day, happening scene. **$$$**

Hotel Bel Air,
701 Stone Canyon Rd,
Bel Air, CA 90077
Tel: 310-472 1211;
Fax: 310-476 5890;
www.hotelbelair.com
Deluxe and seductive, a long-standing movie-star hideaway in landscaped grounds and secluded canyon, complete with elegant suites. Eight lucky guests sit at Table One. **$$$**

Hyatt West Hollywood,
8401 Sunset Blvd,
West Hollywood, CA 90069
Tel: 323-656 1234;
1-800 233 1234;
Fax: 323-650 7024;
www.hyatt.com
Famous rock 'n roll hotel near LA's hottest clubs. The rooftop pool on "the Strip" is always a scene. **$$–$$$**

The London West Hollywood,
1020 N. San Vicente Blvd,
West Hollywood, CA 90069
Tel: 310-854 1111;
Fax: 310-854 0926;
www.thelondonla.com

Formerly the deluxe Wyndham Bel Age, the newly renovated hotel is a sexy, sophisticated addition to the Sunset Strip. Innovative design, fine dining, a full service spa and expert concierge service. **$$$**

Maison 140,
140 Lasky Dr,
Beverly Hills, CA 90212
Tel: 310-281 4000;
1-800 432 5444
Fax: 310-281 4001;
www.maison140beverlyhills.com
This chic hotel was once a boarding house run by Lillian Gish. **$$$**

Mondrian Los Angeles,
8440 Sunset Blvd,
West Hollywood, CA 90069
Tel: 323-650 8999;
Fax: 323-650 5215;
www.mondrianhotel.com
This chic, Philippe Starck-designed hotel is a popular rendezvous for people in the movie industry. Have a cocktail in the Skybar. **$$$**

Los Angeles (Coastal)

The Cadillac Hotel,
8 Dudley Ave, Venice, CA 90291;
Tel: 310-399 8876;
Fax: 310-399 4536;
www.thecadillachotel.com
Art Deco spot on the boardwalk with a roof sundeck. **$$**

Comfort Inn,
2815 Santa Monica Blvd, Santa Monica, CA 90404
Tel: 310-828 5517;
Fax: 310-829 6084;
www.choicehotels.com
Not far from Santa Monica Pier; heated pool. **$**

Fairmont Miramar Hotel,
101 Wilshire Blvd, Santa Monica, CA 90401
Tel: 310-576 7777;
Fax: 310-458 7912;
www.fairmont.com
Lush retreat above the ocean big with celebs. **$$$**

Foghorn Harbor Inn,
4140 Via Marina,
Marina del Rey, CA 90292
Tel: 310-823 4626;
Fax: 310-578 1964;
www.foghornhotel.com
Value near beach. **$**

The Hotel California,
1670 Ocean Ave,
Santa Monica, CA 90401
Tel: 310-393 2363;

BELOW: a suite in LA's fabulous, secluded Hotel Bel Air.

1-866 571 0000;
Fax: 310-393 1063;
www.hotelca.com
Dating from 1948, this
small, vintage hotel has
ocean views, tropical murals
and free Internet access. $$
**Loews Santa Monica
Beach Hotel**,
1700 Ocean Ave,
Santa Monica, CA 90401
Tel: 310-458 6700;
1-800 235 6397;
Fax: 310-458 6761;
www.loewshotels.com
Sleek hotel with terrific
Pacific views. $$$
Malibu Beach Inn,
22878 Pacific Coast Highway,
Malibu, CA 90265
Tel: 310-456 6444;
Fax: 310-456 1499;
www.malibubeachinn.com
Near the pier; some rooms
have fireplaces. $$
Oceana Santa Monica,
849 Ocean Ave,
Santa Monica, CA 90403
Tel: 310-393 0486;
1-800 777 0758;
Fax: 310-458 1182;
www.hoteloceana.com;
e-mail: @hoteloceana.com
Mediterranean-villa like,
across from the ocean.
Pool, laundromat, Pacific
views. $$$
**Ramada Limited Marina
del Rey**,
3130 Washington Blvd,
Marina del Rey, CA 90292
Tel: 310-821 5086;
Fax: 310-821 6167;
www.ramada.com
A few blocks from the
beach and boardwalk. $
**Santa Monica Pico
Travelodge**,
3102 Pico Blvd,
Santa Monica, CA 90405
Tel: 310-450 5766;
Fax: 310-450 8843;
www.travelodge.com
Kitchenettes, laundromat
and a pretty good (free)
breakfast. A bargain. $
Shangri-La Hotel,
1301 Ocean Ave.
Santa Monica, CA 90401
Tel: 310-394 2791;
Fax: 310-451 3351;
www.shangrila-hotel.com
Art Deco landmark
opposite Palisades Park;
kitchenettes. $$
**Shutters Hotel on the
Beach**,
1 Pico Blvd, Santa Monica,
CA 90405

Tel: 310-458 0030;
1-800 334 9000;
Fax: 310-458 4589;
www.shuttersonthebeach.com
Cozy, low-key retreat on the
beach; classy and full of
artworks. $$$
Viceroy Santa Monica,
1819 Ocean Ave,
Santa Monica, CA 90401
Tel: 310-260 7500;
1-800 670 6185;
Fax: 310-260 7515;
www.viceroysantamonica.com
Urban retreat on the beach
with sauna, whirlpool. $$

Los Angeles (Universal City)

**Hilton Los
Angeles/Universal City**,
555 Universal Hollywood Dr,
CA 91608
Tel: 818-506 2500;
1-800 445 8667;
Fax: 818-509 2058;
www.hilton.com
Near Universal Studios;
pool, whirlpool, exercise
room. $$
Sheraton Universal Hotel,
333 Universal,
Hollywood Dr, CA 91608
Tel: 818-980 1212;
1-800 325 3535;
Fax: 818-985 4980;
www.sheraton.com
Actually located on Universal
Studios lot; whirlpool,
exercise room. $$$

Anaheim

Disneyland Hotel,
1150 Magic Way, CA 92802
Tel: 714-956 6582.
Pools, spa, tennis courts,
restaurants and a Peter
Pan "relaxing" area. $$$
**Disney's Grand Californian
Hotel**,
1600 South Disneyland Dr,
CA 92803
Tel: 714-635 2300;
1-800 225 2024;
Fax: 714-300 7300.
Craftsman-style resort built
as part of the California
Adventure. Pool, spa,
restaurants. $$$
Jolly Roger Inn,
640 W. Katella Ave, CA 92802
Tel: 714-782 7500;
Fax: 714-772 2308;
www.jollyrogerhotel.com
Cocktail lounge, spacious
guest rooms, shuttle to
Disneyland. $

Cambria

The Blue Whale Inn,
6736 Moonstone Beach Dr,
CA 93428
Tel: 805-927 4647;
1-800 753 9000;
Fax: 805-927 3852;
www.bluewhaleinn.com
Gourmet breakfasts to
start the day and
spectacular sunsets to
round it off in this Central
Coast inn north of Morro
Bay. Afternoon tea with
delicious home-made cakes
and biscuits, too. $$$
Olallieberry Inn,
2476 Main St,
CA 93428
Tel: 888-927 3222;
Fax: 805-927 0202;
www.olallieberry.com
A stylish 1870s home with
gourmet breakfasts. $$
White Water Inn,
6790 Moonstone Beach Dr,
CA 93428
Tel: 805-927 1066;
1-800 995 1715;
Fax: 805-927 0921;
www.whitewaterinn.com
Very small and pretty, with
a nice exclusive feel; hot
tub, some rooms with
jacuzzis. $$

Long Beach

**Guest House International
Hotel Long Beach**,
5325 E. Pacific Coast Highway,
CA 90804
Tel: 562-597 1341;
1-800 990 9991;
Fax: 562-597 1664;
www.guesthouselb.com
Pool, deli-restaurant. $
Long Beach Marriott,
4700 Airport Plaza Dr,
CA 90815
Tel: 562-425 5210;
1-800 228 9290;
Fax: 562-425 2744;
www.marriot.com
Pools, sauna, whirlpool,
exercise room. $$

Los Alamos

The 1880 Union Hotel,
362 Bell St, Box 616,
Los Alamos, CA 93440
Tel: 805-344 2744;
Fax: 805-344 3125;
www.unionhotelvictmansion.com
Unique theme rooms in an
elegant Victorian structure;
well worth the trip. $$–$$$

ABOVE: a spa – the ultimate
California experience.

Palm Springs

Ingleside Inn,
200 W. Ramon Rd,
CA 92264
Tel: 760-325 0046;
Fax: 760-325 0710;
www.inglesideinn.com;
e-mail: contact@inglesideinn.com
Greta Garbo slept here;
garden, antiques, pool,
restaurant. $$$
La Mancha Villas,
400 N. Avenida Caballeros,
CA 92263
Tel: 760-320 0398;
Fax: 760-320 7155;
www.lamanchavillas.com
Attractively furnished villas,
pool, sauna, putting green,
lighted tennis courts,
croquet. $$$
La Quinta Resort & Club,
49–499 Eisenhower Dr,
La Quinta, CA 92253
Tel: 760-564 4111;
1-800-598-3828;
Fax: 760-564 5768;
www.laquintaresort.com;
e-mail: resinquiry@laquintaresort.com
Twenty miles (32 km) from
Palm Springs; numerous
swimming pools and spas,
tennis courts and seven
restaurants. $$$
Riviera Resort & Spa,
1600 N. Indian Canyon Dr,
CA 92262
Tel: 760-327 8311;

Fax: 760-327 4323;
www.psriviera.com
Near the Aerial Tramway;
tennis courts, pools,
supervised children's
camp. **$$$**
Royal Sun Inn,
1700 S. Palm Canyon Dr.,
CA 92264
Tel: 760-327 1564;
1-800 619 4786
Fax: 760-323 9092;
www.royalsuninn.com;
e-mail: royalsun@royalsuninn.com
Pool, sauna, restaurants
adjoining premises, free
breakfast. **$**
Shilo Inn Suites,
1875 N. Palm Canyon Dr,
CA 92262
Tel: 760-320 7676;
Fax: 760-320 9543;
www.shiloinns.com
Landscaped grounds,
pool, sauna, exercise
room. **$**
Viceroy Palm Springs,
415 S. Belardo Rd,
CA 92262
Tel: 760-320 4117;
www.viceroypalmsprings.com
Poolside pavilions,
terraced villas and nicely
furnished studios, some
with fireplaces. **$$**
Villa Royale Inn,
1620 Indian Trail,
Palm Springs, CA 92264
Tel: 760-327 2314;
Fax: 760-322 3794;
www.villaroyale.com;
e-mail: info@villaroyale.com
Suites decorated in
styles of different
countries, charming
courtyards, pool. **$$**

Paso Robles

The JUST Inn,
justin Vineyards & Winery,
11680 Chimney Rock Rd,
CA 93446
Tel: 1-800 726 0049;
Fax: 805-237 4152;
www.justinwine.com
Ultimately romantic and far
off the beaten path of the
Central Coast, this inn
consists of four sumptuous
suites secluded among the
vines of Justin Winery. **$$$**
Paso Robles Inn,
1103 Spring St, CA 93446
Tel: 805-238 2660;
Fax: 805-238 4707;
www.pasoroblesinn.com
A fantastic getaway with
mineral spa rooms, lush
gardens, a historic
ballroom and a popular
steakhouse. **$**

Pismo Beach

Rose Garden Inn,
230 Five Cities Dr,
CA 93449
Tel: 805-773 1841;
Fax: 805-773 1944.
Just off US 101.
Beach views, near shops. **$**
Sandcastle Inn,
100 Stimson Ave,
CA 93449
Tel: 805-773 2422;
1-800 822 6606;
Fax: 805-773 0771;
www.sandcastleinn.com
Contemporary design; on
the beach; whirlpool;
sundecks with great views
of the pier. **$$**

Riverside

**The Mission Inn Hotel &
Spa**,
3649 Mission Inn Ave,
CA 92501
Tel: 951-784 0300;
Fax: 951-683 1342;
www.missioninn.com;
e-mail: concierge@missioninn.com
Historic hostelry popular
with presidents and movie
stars. Unique pastiche of
architectural styles. **$$$**

San Diego

Bahia Resort Hotel,
998 W. Mission Bay Dr,
CA 92109
Tel: 858-488 0551;
www.bahiahotel.com
This beachfront resort has
over 300 rooms, water
sports, pool, children's
activities and moonlight
cruises on the *Bahia Belle*.
$$
Balboa Park Inn,
3402 Park Blvd, CA 92103
Tel: 619-298 0823;
Fax: 619-294 8070;
www.balboaparkinn.com;
e-mail: info@balboaparkinn.com
Near the zoo; bar, in-room
jacuzzi, free breakfast. **$**
**Hilton San Diego
Mission Valley**,
901 Camino del Rio S.
CA 92108
Tel: 619-543 9000;
1-800 445 8667;
Fax: 619-543 9358;
www.hilton.com
Pool, whirlpool, exercise
room. **$$**
**Holiday Inn San Diego
Downtown**,
1617 1st Ave, CA 92101
Tel: 619-239 9600;
Fax: 619-233 6228;
www.ichotelsgroup.com
Close to Interstate 5; pool,
laundromat. **$$**
Hotel del Coronado,
1500 Orange Ave, Coronado,
CA 92118
Tel: 619-435 6611;
Fax: 619-522 8262;
www.hoteldel.com;
e-mail: delinquiries@hoteldel.com
This world-famous Victorian-
era landmark is situated on
its own beach. Sumptuous
and grand, the Del has
tennis courts, pools and
restaurants galore. The
hotel "starred" in the movie
Some Like It Hot. **$$$**

La Jolla Beach Travelodge,
6750 La Jolla Blvd, CA 92037
Tel: 858-454 0716;
1-800 255 3050;
Fax: 858-454 1075;
www.travelodge.com
Jacuzzi and swimming pool,
with a good restaurant
opposite. **$**
The Lodge at Torrey Pines,
11480 N. Torrey Pines Rd,
La Jolla, CA 92037
Tel: 858-453 4420;
1-800-656 0087;
www.lodgetorreypines.com
Craftsman-type mansion on
ocean bluff. Meticulously
furnished. Near golf course.
$$$
Manchester Grand Hyatt,
Harbor Dr. and Market Pl,
CA 92101
Tel: 619-232 1234;
1-800 233 1234;
Fax: 619-233 6464;
www.hyatt.com
Pool, sauna, tennis courts,
exercise room. **$$$**
**Paradise Point Resort &
Spa**,
1404 Vacation Rd,
CA 92109
Tel: 858-274 4630;
1-800 344 2626;
www.paradisepoint.com
Bungalows in spacious
landscaped grounds on
Mission Bay; pools, tennis
courts, boat rentals. **$$**
Quality Inn Airport,
2901 Nimitz Blvd, CA 92106
Tel: 619-224 3655;
1-800 695 8284;
Fax: 619-224 4025;
www.choicehotels.com
Near airport, zoo and
SeaWorld; pool, coffee
shop. **$**
**Ramada Gaslamp
Convention Center**,
830 Sixth Ave, CA 92101
Tel: 619-531 8877;
Fax: 619-231 8307;
www.ramada.com
Near Gaslamp Quarter;
harbor-view rooftop, lobby
bar and grill. **$**
**San Diego Marriott
Gaslamp Quarter**,
660 K St, CA 92101
Tel: 619-696 0234;
Fax: 619-231 8199;
www.marriott.com
Sauna, whirlpool, exercise
room, laundromat. **$$**
Town and Country Resort,
500 Hotel Circle N, CA 92108
Tel: 619-291 7131;
www.towncountry.com

BELOW: the Victorian-era Hotel del Coronado in San Diego.

Landscaped grounds with pools, restaurants and coffee shops. **$**

US Grant Hotel,
326 Broadway, CA 92101
Tel: 619-232 3121;
Fax: 619-239 9517;
www.usgrant.net;
e-mail: usgranthotel@usgrant.net
Historic Downtown hotel near shopping; exercise room, restaurant. **$$**

The Westgate Hotel,
1055 2nd Ave, CA 92101
Tel: 619-238 1818;
Fax: 619-557 3737;
www.westgatehotel.com
Lovely interiors and furnishings, exercise room, restaurant. **$$**

The Westin Horton Plaza,
910 Broadway Circle, CA 92101
Tel: 619-239 2200;
Fax: 619-239 0509.
Pool, saunas, lighted tennis courts, health club. **$$**

The Westin San Diego,
400 West Broadway, CA 92101
Tel: 619-239 4500;
www.starwoodhotels.com
A stunning green cluster of geometric towers with spectacular views of San Diego Bay, ergonomic work chairs, a fitness center, an outdoor pool and upscale contemporary cuisine. **$$$**

San Luis Obispo

Madonna Inn,
100 Madonna Rd, CA 93405
Tel: 805-543 3000;
Fax: 805-543 1800;
www.madonnainn.com;
e-mail: info@madonnainn.com
Hotel well known for its eccentricity and bizarre decor. Rooms come dressed up in Western, Hawaiian or Austrian styles. **$$**

Travelodge Downtown,
345 Marsh St, CA 93401
Tel: 805-543 6443;
Fax: 805-545 0951;
www.travelodge.com
Near Downtown; pool, laundry. **$**

Santa Barbara

El Encanto Hotel & Garden Villas,
1900 Lasuen Rd, CA 93103
Tel: 805-687 5000;
Fax: 805-687 3903;
www.elencantohotel.com
Part of the Orient Express

group, this gorgeous in-town hotel has a restaurant, pool and tennis courts. Recently restored. **$$$**

Fess Parker's Doubletree Resort,
633 E. Cabrillo Blvd, CA 93103
Tel: 805-564 4333;
www.fpdtr.com
Across from beach in grounds; pool, sauna, putting green. **$$$**

The Franciscan Inn,
109 Bath St, CA 93101
Tel: 805-963 8845;
Fax: 805-564 3295;
www.franciscaninn.com
At the beach; health club, pool, complimentary breakfast. **$**

Harbor View Inn,
28 W. Cabrillo Blvd, CA 93101
Tel: 805-963 0780;
Fax: 805-963 7967;
www.harborviewinnsb.com
On the beach opposite Stearns Wharf; pool, whirlpool, adjacent restaurant. **$$–$$$**

Inn by the Harbor,
433 W. Montecito, CA 93101
Tel: 805-963 7851;
Fax: 805-962 9428;
www.sbhotels.com;
e-mail: harbor@sbhotels.com
Close to the beach; pool, kitchenettes, laundromat. **$**

Inn of the Spanish Garden,
915 Garden St, CA 93101
Tel: 805-564 4700;
Fax: 805-564 4701;
www.spanishgardeninn.com
Mediterranean-style complex with pool and courtyard; 23 spacious, elegant rooms and covered parking. **$$**

Hotel Mar Monte,
1111 E Cabrillo Blvd, CA 93103
Tel: 805-963 0744;
www.hotelmarmonte.com
Across from beach; pool, whirlpool, health club. **$$**

Sandpiper Lodge,
3525 State St, CA 93105
Tel: 805-687 5326;
Fax: 805-687 2271;
www.sandpiperlodge.com
North end of Midtown; pool, jacuzzi, nearby coffee shop. **$**

San Ysidro Ranch,
900 San Ysidro Lane, CA 93108
Tel: 805-969 5046;
Fax: 805-565 1995;
www.sanysidroranch.com
Luxury resort with a celebrated history: John F.

Kennedy brought his bride Jackie here on their honeymoon. **$$$**

Secret Garden Inn,
1908 Bath St, CA 93101
Tel: 805-687 2300;
Fax: 805-687 4576;
www.secretgarden.com;
e-mail: garden@secretgarden.com
Main house and cottages in pleasantly landscaped grounds; some rooms with hot tubs. **$$**

The Upham,
1404 De La Vina St, CA 93101
Tel: 805-962 0058;
Fax: 805-963 2825;
www.uphamhotel.com;
e-mail: innkeeper@uphamhotel.com
Last of the great, old Santa Barbara hotels (founded 1871) with all the charm and style you'd expect. Beautifully furnished garden bungalows. **$$$**

Villa Rosa Inn,
15 Chapala St, CA 93101
Tel: 805-966 0851;
www.villarosainnsb.com
At the beach; pool, spa. **$$**

Santa Catalina Island

The Santa Catalina Island Company,
(www.visitcatalinaisland.com) offers various bargain packages, including round-trip transportation, two nights' accommodation, and three tours.

El Terado Terrace,
230 Marilla Ave, CA 90704
Tel: 310-510 0831;
www.elterado.com;
e-mail: info@elterado.com
A mini-suite hotel near the bottom of Marilla Avenue. On a hill above the harbor, some rooms have great views. **$$**

La Paloma Cottages,
Tel: 310-510 1505;
Fax: 310-510 2424;
e-mail: lapaloma@catalinaisp.com
Self-contained properties at the top of Metropole near the golf course. **$$**

Snug Harbor Inn,
108 Sumner Ave CA 90704
Tel: 310-510 8400;
Fax: 310-510 8418;
www.snugharbor-inn.com;
e-mail: info@snugharborinn.com
Six lovely and luxurious bay-view rooms situated in the century-old former Hotel Monterey. **$$$**

Zane Grey Pueblo Hotel,
199 Chimes Tower Rd,
CA 90704
Tel: 310-510 0966;
Fax: 310-510 1340;
www.zanegreypueblohotel.com;
e-mail: zanegrey@catalinaisp.com
This hilltop hotel was once the home of famed novelist Zane Grey and now has a heated pool, courtesy taxi service and airy rooms. **$$**

Solvang

Royal Scandinavian Inn,
400 Alisal Rd, Box 30
CA 93464
Tel: 805-688 8000;
Fax: 805-688 0761;
www.royalscandinavianinn.com
Close to wineries and a golf course. **$**

Svendsgaards Danish Lodge,
1711 Mission Dr,
CA 93463
Tel: 805-688 3277;
Fax: 805-686 5616.
Pool, whirlpool, kitchenettes. **$**

Ventura

Bella Maggiore Inn,
67 S. California St, CA 93001
Tel: 805-652 0277;
Fax: 805-648 5670.
A 1925 landmark near the beach; may be haunted. **$**

Vagabond Inn,
756 E. Thompson Blvd,
CA 93001
Tel: 805-648 5371;
1-800 522 1555;
Fax: 805-648 5613.
Pool, whirlpool, coffee shop on the premises. **$**

PRICE CATEGORIES

Prices categories are for a standard double room without breakfast:
$ = less than $150
$$ = $150–$225
$$$ = more than $225

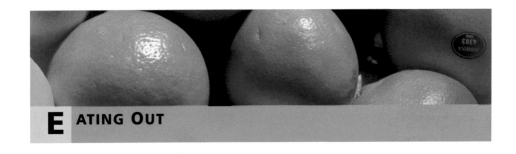

E ATING OUT

RECOMMENDED RESTAURANTS, CAFES & BARS

Choosing a Restaurant

California is a food-lover's delight, and has the statistics to prove it. There are more restaurants in San Francisco, per capita, than in any other US city, and it's been estimated that Southern Californians dine out on average two or three times a week. Although the most prevalent ethnic food you'll encounter is Mexican, there is an endless variety of other foods, as well as classic American cuisine, and "California" cuisine. Plus the best local wine in the country, of course.

The following list is a mere sampling of some of the notable restaurants across the state.

RESTAURANT LISTINGS

AROUND SAN FRANCISCO

San Francisco

Balboa Cafe,
3199 Fillmore
Tel: 415-921 3944.
Among the city's finest California cooking: order warm salads, perfect pasta, hamburgers and fresh fish. **$$**
Boulevard,
1 Mission St
Tel: 415-543 6084.
This stylish, elegant brasserie has views of the bay and serves generous portions, artfully presented. The wood-oven specialties like organic chicken with porcini mushrooms are standouts. **$$$**

Fournou's Ovens,
Stanford Court Hotel,
905 California
Tel: 415-989 1910.
Order from the oven – a succulent roast rack of lamb, fine fowl or other meats. There's also an award-winning wine list. **$$$**
Greens,
Fort Mason, Building A
Tel: 415-771 6222.
Gourmet vegetarian restaurant with views of the marina and the Golden Gate. Reservations two weeks in advance, and they're hard to come by. Closed for Sunday dinner and Monday lunchtime. **$$**

Herbivore,
2 San Francisco Locations
531 Divisadero St
Tel: 415-885 7133
983 Valencia St
Tel: 415-826 5657.
Fresh-pressed juices, teas and live (raw) food. A real vegan Californian experience with creative, substantial and good, affordable food. **$**
Juicy Lucy,
703 Columbus Ave
Tel: 415-786-1285
Groovy café and organic juice bar where good vibes abound. Opt for a wheat-grass tonic or treat yourself to a freshly squeezed juice combo packed with anti-

oxidents served in a ceramic bowl. **$**
Julius' Castle,
1541 Montgomery St
Tel: 415-392 2222.
Contemporary French with an Italian accent and a magnificent view overlooking the bay. **$$–$$$**
La Rondalla,
901 Valencia St
Tel: 415-647 7474.
Inexpensive Mexican food served until 1.30am to a lively neighborhood crowd. Closed all day Monday, cash only. **$**
Le Colonial,
20 Cosmo Place
Tel: 415-931-3600

Exceptional French-Vietnamese cuisine with delicately balanced flavors in a swanky locale frequented by society types. The specialty cocktails and crispy spring roll appetizers alone are worth a visit. **$$–$$$**

Mama's,
1701 Stockton St
Tel: 415-362 6421.
Just plain good food. It's jammed on weekends, so try it during the week. Closed Monday. **$$**

Masa's,
648 Bush St
Tel: 415-989 7154.
Consistently one of the finest French restaurants in town. Coats and ties are required, reservations recommended. Closed Monday. **$$$$**

Osome,
3145 Fillmore
Tel: 415-931 8898.
Excellent sushi bar plus usual range of cooked Japanese food. Closed for lunch on weekends. **$$**

L'Osteria del Forno,
519 Columbus Ave
Tel: 415-982 1124.
Ample, affordable and flavorful Italian at a spot that captures the spirit of North Beach. **$**

Plouf,
40 Belden Place
Tel: 415-986 6491
This seafood bistro in a narrow European-style pedestrian alley with outdoor tables serves heavenly, heaped bowls of steamed mussels prepared eight different ways. **$$**

Postrio,
545 Post St
Tel: 415-776 7825.
If you haven't had a chance to eat in one of renowned chef Wolfgang Puck's restaurants, now is the time. **$$$**

Slanted Door,
1 Ferry Building
Tel: 415-861-8032.
Chef Charles Phan's masterful take on Viet-namese wins over the foodies; so does the bay view, through the floor-to-ceiling windows. **$$–$$$**

Sushi on North Beach,
745 Columbus Ave
Tel: 415-788 8050.
This friendly, family-owned Japanese restaurant serves deliciously creative rolls along with the standard favorites. Lunch specials are a serious bargain and good-sized cuts of extremely fresh fish, plus an extensive sake list, set it apart from the others. **$–$$**

Zuni,
1658 Market St
Tel: 415-552 2522.
Simply cooked California cuisine made from fresh local ingredients. Closed Monday. **$$**

Bay Area

Café Rosso & Bianco,
473 University Ave, Palo Alto
Tel: 650-752-0350.
A casual Italian eatery owned by director Francis Ford Coppola. The focal point is the wine bar, where selections from Coppola's own winery are always available. **$$**

Chez Panisse,
1517 Shattuck Ave, Berkeley
Tel: 510-548 5525.
One of the most famous restaurants in the country, and where "California cuisine" is said to have started. Restaurant downstairs open Monday–Saturday for dinner with set menu only. **$$$$**
Café upstairs open for lunch and dinner, Monday–Saturday. **$$$**
Make reservations to each place weeks in advance.

Lark Creek Inn,
234 Magnolia Ave, Larkspur
Tel: 415-924-7766.
Inside a Victorian home, celebrity chef/restaurateur Bradley Ogden delivers seasonal fresh ingredients and American fare in a delightful setting. Enjoy a selection from the vast California-only wine list as you dine beneath the redwoods. **$$$–$$$$**

Yoshi's,
510 Embarcadero West, Oakland
Tel: 510-238-9200.
This classy Japanese place on Jack London Square doubles as one of the Bay Area's best jazz venues. Superfresh sushi makes the perfect date night, but Sunday matinees are kid friendly – as are the *udon* noodles. Call for reservations. **$$–$$$**

Monterey/Big Sur

Casanova,
Fifth Ave near San Carlos Carmel
Tel: 831-625 0501.
Emphasis is on seafood served with light sauces, but there are also veal, lamb and beef selections. Breakfast, lunch, dinner and Sunday brunch in a French cottage setting. **$$**

Nepenthe,
Hwy 1, Big Sur
Tel: 831-667 2345.
Spectacular view of waves crashing 800 ft (244 meters) below, homemade soups and enormous chef's salads. Tourists and locals mingle comfortably at this legendary café. **$$**

Sierra Mar,
Hwy 1, Big Sur
Tel: 831-667 2800.
The glass-walled restaurant overlooking the sea serves up some of the classiest cuisine around. **$$$**

Ventana,
State Hwy 1, Big Sur
Tel: 831-667 2331.
A luxurious resort set back in the woods with an award-winning restaurant called Cielo. **$$$–$$$$**

PRICE CATEGORIES

Prices are for a meal for two people, without wine.
$ = less than $30
$$ = $30–$60
$$$ = $60–$100
$$$$ = more than $100

NORTHERN CALIFORNIA

Eureka

Café Marina,
601 Startare
Woodley Island at the
Eureka Marina
Tel: 707-443 2233.
Serves very fresh scampi, scallops and sole. If fish is not your fare, there are scrumptious sandwiches and Italian dishes. Breakfast, lunch and dinner. **$**

Hurricane Kate's,
511 Second St, Eureka
Tel: 707-444 1405.
A creative, eclectic menu that changes frequently and features world fusion cuisine, wood-fired specialties, and signature cocktails. Soups are divine and homemade. **$–$$**

Samoa Cookhouse,
Off Hwy 101 across the Samoa Bridge
Tel: 707-442 1659.
Breakfast includes orange juice, scambled eggs, pancakes, sausages, hash browns and coffee. Hefty lunches and dinners start with soup, salad and plenty of bread, and end with apple pie. **$**

High Sierra/ Yosemite

Ahwahnee,
Yosemite National Park
Tel: 209-372 1489.
The Grande Dame of hotels in breathtaking Yosemite Valley serves classy, healthy California cuisine in its cathedral-like dining room. **$$$$**

Erna's Elderberry House,
48688 Victoria Lane
(Hwy 41), Oakhurst
Tel: 559-683 6800.
Elegant French country inn hidden in the forest. Stunning interior design mingles with classic European cuisine. Far from cheap but worth the trip. Reservations are recommended. **$$$$**

Lake Tahoe

Rosie's Café,
571 North Lake Blvd, Tahoe City
Tel: 530-583 8504.

Breakfast, lunch and dinner are served at this downhome restaurant that oozes charm. **$**

The Soule Domain,
9983 Stateline Rd, Crystal Bay
Tel: 530-546 7529.
A creative, eclectic menu with American, French and Asian influences served in a romantic log cabin setting. **$$**

North Coast

Albion River Inn,
3790 N. Hwy 1, Albion
Tel: 707-937 1919.
Chic food in a beautiful setting; award-winning wine list. **$$$–$$$$**

Boonville Hotel,
State Hwy 128, Boonville
Tel: 707-895 2210.
California cooking to the core – fresh, simple and sensitively prepared. All the food has been grown or raised right near the hotel. Closed Tuesday and Wednesday. **$$$$**

Cafe Beaujolais,
961 Ukiah St, Mendocino
Tel: 707-937 5614.
A really cozy atmosphere. Beautifully prepared dishes with fresh ingredients. **$$**

Ledford House,
3000 N Hwy 1, Albion
Tel: 707-937 0282.
A rustic little house overlooking the sea. Locally grown food is always cooked to order. Dinner only; closed Monday and Tuesday. **$$**

Manka's Inverness Lodge,
30 Callendar Way, Inverness
Tel: 415-669 1034.
Seasonal cuisine featuring wild game in a rustic-chic

former sportsman's lodge. A cult favorite among coastal Bay Area foodies. **$$$$**

St Orres,
36601 State Hwy 1, in Gualala, below Mendocino
Tel: 707-884 3303.
A beautiful restaurant emphasizing North Coast cuisine in a Russian-style hotel. Also serves Sunday brunch. **$$$**

Station House Cafe,
11180 Hwy 1, Point Reyes Station
Tel: 415-663 1515.
Fresh, well-cooked food in a warm, busy atmosphere. A perfect stop after a day's hiking on Point Reyes Peninsula. **$–$$**

Vladimir's,
12785 Sir Francis Drake Ave, Inverness
Tel: 415-669 1021.
Immense plates of rib-sticking Czech fare like chicken paprikash, red cabbage and strudel have been served in this cozy European-style pub for more than 40 years. **$$**

Sacramento

Hong Kong,
501 Broadway
Tel: 916-442 7963.
Good Chinese food from a variety of regions in a converted Western barbecue place that still has the wagon-wheel light fixtures. Closed Wednesday. **$$**

Wakano Ura,
2217 10th St
Tel: 916-448 6231.
An upstairs place in the Japanese district that can be noisy with revelers,

although the fun soon becomes infectious. **$$**

The Waterboy,
2000 Capitol Ave
Tel: 916-498 9891.
Seasonal and good French-Italian food. **$$**

Zelda's,
1415 21st St
Tel: 916-447 1400.
Deep-dish pizza is a specialty here. **$**

San Joaquin Valley

The Ripe Tomato,
5064 North Palm, Fresno
Tel: 559-225 1850.
Quail and venison are standard menu items; typical specials include duck with apricot-garlic sauce, veal with oysters and mushrooms in vermouth, and lamb with pesto sauce. Closed Sunday, Monday. **$$$**

The Vintage Press,
216 North Willis, Visalia
Tel: 559-733 3033.
Fresh food with a European flair. Open Sunday for brunch only. **$$–$$$**

San Jose

Émile's,
545 S. Second St, San Jose
Tel: 408-289 1960.
French contemporary and Swiss cuisine. Dinner only; closed Monday. **$$**

Henry's Hi-Life,
301 W. Saint John St
San Jose
Tel: 408-295 5414.
Good barbecued food at reasonable prices. Open for lunch and dinner, closed for lunch Saturday–Monday. **$$**

La Forêt,
21747 Bertram Road, San Jose
Tel: 408-997 3458.
On the site of the first adobe hotel in California (built in 1848), this charming old house is graced with tuxedo-clad waiters, French-Italian entrées, fresh mussels and clams, and tempting desserts. Dinner and Sunday brunch; closed Monday. **$$–$$$**

Original Joe's,
301 S. First St, San Jose
Tel: 408-292 7030.

Home of the famous "Joe's Special" – a tasty sandwich of spinach, ground beef, mushrooms, onions and scrambled eggs. **$**

Paolo's Continental Restaurant,
333 W. San Carlos St
San Jose
Tel: 408-294 2558.
Good service and great pastas. Closed Sunday. **$$**

Wine Country

Auberge du Soleil,
180 Rutherford Hill Rd, Rutherford
Tel: 707-963 1211.
Wine Country cuisine with fresh food and a view of the vineyards. **$$$$**

Calistoga Inn Restaurant and Brewery,

1250 Lincoln Ave, Calistoga
Tel: 707-942 4101.
Casual, friendly service, large portions and excellent food. **$$**

The French Laundry,
6640 Washington St,
Yountville
Tel: 707-944 2380.
A true Wine Country gem in a beautiful building serving award-winning cuisine. Call months in advance for reservations, and save money for months in order to sample the 9-course tasting menu. **$$$$**

Hydro Bar & Grill,
1403 Lincoln Ave, Calistoga
Tel: 707-942 9777.
Over 20 microbrews and California cuisine in a breezy café atmosphere. **$$**

Martini House,
1245 Spring St, St Helena
Tel: 707-963 2233.
A two-story bungalow with rustic yet genteel decor and top-notch seasonal Californian cuisine. Try the chef's tasting menu. **$$$**

The Swiss Hotel,
18 W. Spain St, Sonoma
Tel: 707-938 2884.
Located on the beautiful and historic Sonoma Plaza, the cozy, low-ceilinged bar is a favorite among locals. Homemade pastas and wood-fired pizza are house specialties, served on the garden patio or in the elegant dining room. **$$**

Zazu,
3535 Guerneville Rd, Santa Rosa
Tel: 707-523 4814.

A husband-and-wife chef team bring their individual styles to the table and the result is a refreshing mix of rustic Italian and American/Californian cuisine with an emphasis on seasonal fresh produce and creative combinations. **$$**

SOUTHERN CALIFORNIA

Los Angeles

Aunt Kizzy's Back Porch,
4325 Glencoe Ave,
Marina del Rey
Tel: 310-578 1005;
www.auntkizzys.com
Actors and athletes favor the ambience (and the fried chicken). **$**

Barney's Beanery,
8447 Santa Monica Blvd,
West Hollywood
Tel: 323-654 2287;
www.barneysbeanery.com
A newspaper-sized menu offering more different beer labels than you can shake a stick at, plus tables for a friendly game of pool. Barney's is casual, funky and famous locally. **$**

Café Latte,
6254 Wilshire Blvd
Tel: 323-936 5213.
California cuisine; fresh sausages. **$$**

Café Pinot,
700 W. 5th St, Downtown
Tel: 213-239 6500;
www.patinagroup.com
Delicious food in an unlikely elevated glass box adjoining the Central Library. **$$$**

California Pizza Kitchen,
207 S. Beverly Dr, Beverly Hills
Tel: 310-275 1101;
www.cpk.com
One of a chain – "the

People's Spago" says one critic. **$**

Campanile,
624 South La Brea Ave
Tel: 323-938 1447;
www.campanilerestaurant.com
First-rate California-Mediterranean cooking with the fantastic bread from the bakery next door. Closed Sunday dinner. **$**

Canter's Delicatessen, Restaurant and Bakery,
419 North Fairfax Ave
Tel: 323-651 2030;
www.cantersdeli.com
Famous large and lively deli with classic 1950s interior. Open around the clock. **$**

Cicada,
617 S. Olive St
Tel: 213-488 9488.
Classy eatery in the plush surroundings of Downtown's Oviatt Building. Fabulous Northern Italian food for a well-heeled crowd. **$$$**

Dar Maghreb,
7651 Sunset Blvd, Hollywood
Tel: 323-876 7651;
www.darmaghrebrestaurant.com
This lushly decorated restaurant offers a solid Moroccan menu. Open for dinner only. **$$**

Gaucho Grill,
11754 San Vicente Blvd,
Brentwood
Tel: 310-447 7898;
www.gauchogrillrestaurant.com

Various mixed-grill combinations are good choices at this modestly priced Argentine hideway. **$**

The Gumbo Pot,
6333 W. 3rd St
Tel: 323-933 0358;
www.thegumbopotla.com
One of many great eating places in the Farmers Market. Open daily until 9pm; market closes slightly earlier at weekends. **$**

Kate Mantilini,
9101 Wilshire Blvd, Beverly Hills
Tel: 310-278 3699.
In a distinctive-looking building, this popular late-night spot serves until 1.30am or later every night but Sunday. Open for breakfast, lunch and dinner. **$$**

The Malibu Inn Bar & Restaurant,
22969 Pacific Coast Hwy, Malibu
Tel: 310-456 6060;
www.malibu-inn.com
Unpretentious eating spot long familiar to Hollywood stars whose pictures line the walls. **$**

Mel's Drive-In,
1660 N. Highland Ave, Hollywood
Tel: 323-465 3111;
wwwmelsdrive-in.com
In the shadow of the Hollywood & Highland Center, this classic diner entices tourists, natives and night owls alike.

Though not the original Mel's featured in *American Graffiti*, this one still has the charm of those innocent days. **$**

Musso & Frank Grill,
6667 Hollywood Blvd, Hollywood
Tel: 323-467 7788.
A traditional American menu presented in an old-fashioned Hollywood hangout, where writers like Ernest Hemingway and Raymond Chandler used to dine. **$$$**

Nate 'n Al,
414 N. Beverly Dr Beverly Hills
Tel: 310-274 0101;
www.natenal.com
Sandwiches and other specialties are always superb at Beverly Hills' long-famous deli. **$**

The Original Pantry Café,
877 S. Figueroa
Tel: 213-972 9279;
www.pantrycafe.com
Always crowded, inexpensive Downtown landmark that's been around even longer than former mayor Richard Riordan,

PRICE CATEGORIES

Prices are for a meal for two people, without wine.
$ = less than $30
$$ = $30–$60
$$$ = $60–$100
$$$$ = more than $100

who bought the place to stop its demolition. **$**

Philippe the Original,
1001 N. Alameda St, Downtown
Tel: 213-628 3781;
www.philippes.com
A block north of stylish Union Station is this busy, low-key eatery, known since 1908 for its famous French dip sandwich. **$**

Porterhouse Bistro,
8635 Wilshire Blvd, Beverly Hills
Tel: 310-659 1099;
Fax: 310-659 2099;
www.porterhousebistro.com
Specializing in steak, the bistro offers a daily *prix-fixe* menu that includes two beverages, warm bread, a light salad, a delectable entrée and a dessert. **$$$**

Sidewalk Café,
1401 Ocean Front Walk, Venice
Tel: 310-399 5547;
www.thesidewalkcafe.com
The best place on the Venice boardwalk from which to watch the non-stop action. **$**

Spago,
176 N. Canon Dr, Beverly Hills
Tel: 310-385 0880;
Fax: 310-385 9690;
www.wolfgangpuck.com
Among LA's most famous restaurants. From his renowned pizzas to his delectable desserts, owner and chef Wolfgang Puck delights. Reservations required. **$$$$**

The Stinking Rose,
55 N. La Cienega Blvd,
Beverly Hills
Tel: 310-652 7673;
www.thestinkingrose.com
California-Italian cuisine with lots of garlic. **$$**

Woody's Bar-B-Que,
3446 W. Slauson Ave
Tel: 323-294 9443.

This is the best in LA, according to some barbecue aficionados. **$**

Yamashiro,
1999 North Sycamore Ave
Tel: 323-466 5125;
www.yamashirorestaurant.com
Some claim Yamashiro has the best view in Los Angeles. Surrounded by Japanese gardens, this is a lovely place for dinner (not open for lunch) or just a drink. **$$$**

Anaheim Area

Acapulco Mexican Restaurant,
1535 W. Katella Ave, Orange
Tel: 714-639 9550;
www.acapulcorestaurants.com
Award-winning Mexican food not far from the Angel Stadium and Disneyland. **$$**

The Catch,
1929 S. State College Blvd
Tel: 714-935 0101;
www.catchanaheim.com
Steak and seafood. **$$**

The Cellar,
305 North Harbor Blvd, Fullerton
Tel: 714-525 5682;
www.cellardining.com
Superb French cuisine and expansive wine cellar just 4 miles (6.4 km) from Disneyland. Closed Sunday. **$$$**

Five Crowns,
3801 East Coast Hwy,
Corona del Mar
Tel: 949-760 0331.
Award-winning food served in a beautiful two-story building modeled after Ye Olde Bell, England's oldest inn. **$$**

Koisan Japanese Cuisine,
1132 E. Katella Ave, Orange
Tel: 714-639 2330.
Traditional Japanese food

served with a background of kabuki music. **$$$**

National Sports Grill,
450 N. State College Blvd, Orange
Tel: 714-935 0300;
www.nationalsportsgrill.com
This branch in Orange of a national chain offers dozens of TV monitors, four giant screens, pool tables, 50 different beers and an extensive menu. **$$**

Plaza Garibaldi,
301 N. Tustin Ave, Santa Ana
Tel: 714-758 9014.
Mariachi singers, fiery tango dancers, Inca flutes, and other entertainment accompanies the Mexican cuisine. **$$$**

Tandoor Cuisine of India,
1132 E. Katella Ave, Orange
Tel: 714-538 2234.
There are 70 spiced and tasty dishes on the menu; many of the ingredients are made on the premises. **$$$**

Huntington Beach

Chimayó at the Beach,
315 Pacific Coast Hwy,
Huntington Beach
Tel: 714-374 7273;
Fax: 714-374 7263;
www.culinaryadventures.com
Tropical seaside joint serving an eclectic seafood menu that includes raw oysters, sushi, curried mussels, lobster tacos and "voodoo shrimp." **$$**

Good Mood Food Café,
5930 Warner Ave,
Huntington Beach
Tel: 714-377 2028;
www.goodmoodfood.com
Chef Ursula Horaitis combines her European heritage with the benefits of raw food. Creative dishes include zucchini pasta and olive pâté crostinis. **$**

Long Beach

Belmont Brewing Co,
25 39th Place
Tel: 562-433 3891;
www.belmontbrewing.com
Brew pub with good dishes and a view of the *Queen Mary* cruiseliner. **$**

L'Opera,
101 Pine Ave
Tel: 562-491 0066;
www.lopera.com

A romantic Italian spot with tasty veal and fettucine. **$$**

Newport Beach

The Crab Cooker,
2200 Newport Blvd
Tel: 949-673 0100;
www.crabcooker.com
Grilled seafood on paper plates, reasonable prices; no reservations. **$$**

21 Oceanfront Restaurant,
2100 W. Oceanfront
Tel: 949-673 2100;
www.21oceanfront.com
Across from the Newport Beach Pier, this opulent restaurant offers prime steaks and what some believe is the best seafood in Orange County. **$$$$**

Palm Springs

The Cheesecake Factory,
The River at Rancho Mirage
71-800 Hwy 111, Rancho Mirage
Tel: 760-404 1400;
www.thecheesecakefactory.com
The extensive menu ranges from avocado egg-rolls (spring rolls) and cajun jambalaya pasta to an assortment of luscious cheesecakes. **$$**

Elmer's,
1030 East Palm Canyon Dr.
Tel: 760-327 8419;
www.elmers-restaurants.com
Twenty varieties of pancakes and waffles, fine steaks and seafood for dinner. Can become very crowded on weekend mornings. **$**

Kobe Japanese Steak House,
Hwy 111 at Frank Sinatra Dr,
Rancho Mirage
Tel: 760-324 1717;
www.koberanchomirage.com
Hibachi-style steak and chicken in a replica of a 300-year-old Japanese country inn. **$$$**

Las Casuelas Terraza,
222 South Palm Canyon Dr.
Tel: 760-325 2794;
www.lascasuelasterraza.com
Mexican-style cuisine on a pleasant outdoor patio. **$**

Pasadena

Babita's Mexican Cuisine,
1823 S. San Gabriel Blvd,
San Gabriel
Tel: 626-288 7265.

This inexpensive menu blends Mexican and French cuisine, such as lamb-shank *mixiote* (maguey leaf) and rice-pudding brûlée. **$$**
Twin Palms,
101 W. Green St;
Tel: 626-577 2567;
www.twin-palms.com
Since 1994, this Pasadena favorite has presented New American cuisine and a variety of martinis amid smooth jazz on a palm-shaded patio. **$$$**

Redondo Beach

Aimee's Bistro,
800 S. Pacific Coast Hwy
Tel: 310-316 1081;
www.aimeesbistro.com
Shrimp and salmon are favorites, as well as the tasty desserts, all prepared in a French manner. **$$**
Chez Melange,
Palos Verdes Inn,
1716 Pacific Coast Hwy
Tel: 310-540 1222;
www.chezmelange.com
A wide variety of cuisines including Italian, Chinese and even Cajun, is on the extensive menu. **$$**

San Diego Area

Bali Hai Restaurant,
2230 Shelter Island Dr
Tel: 619-222 1181;
www.balihairestaurant.com
Opened in 1953, this lively joint was also the first Tiki temple erected on Shelter Island. Hawaiian and Polynesian cuisine. **$$**
Buca di Beppo San Diego,
705 6th Ave
Tel: 619-233 7272;
Fax: 619-233 3707;
www.bucadibeppo.com
Celebrated national chain, known for its kitschy decor, family-sized portions and classic Italian cuisine. **$$**
Casa Guadulajara,
4105 Taylor St
Tel: 619-295 5111;
Located in the Bazaar del Mundo in Old Town; reliable Mexican food and great margaritas. **$**
Croce's Restaurant & Jazz Bar,
802 Fifth Ave
Tel: 619-233 4355;
www.croces.com

Dedicated to the late folk musician Jim Croce, this fixture in the Gaslamp Quarter combines inventive pasta, seafood and poultry dishes with live music and memorabilia. **$$$**
Gringo's Cantina,
4474 Mission Blvd
Tel: 858-490 2877;
www.gringoscantina.com
A local favorite in the heart of Pacific Beach, with dramatic architecture, award-winning margaritas and contemporary Mexican cuisine. **$$**
The Marine Room,
2000 Spindrift Dr, La Jolla
Tel: 858-459 7222;
www.ljbtc.com
Located in the beach and tennis club, at high tide the waves crash just outside the windows. **$$**
The Oak Room,
Pala Casino, Resort & Spa,
35008 Pala Temecula Road, Pala
Tel: 760-510 5100;
www.palacasino.com
A world-class steakhouse, not far from gaming tables, live entertainment and a health spa. **$$$**

San Fernando Valley

Art's Delicatessen & Restaurant,
12224 Ventura Blvd, between Laurel Canyon Blvd and Whitsett Ave, Studio City
Tel: 818-762 1221.
Where "every sandwich is a work of art." **$**
Bamboo Inn,
14010 Ventura Blvd, between Woodman and Hazeltine avenues, Sherman Oaks
Tel: 818-788 0202.
A good neighborhood place for Chinese cuisine. **$$**
The Castaway,
1250 Harvard Rd, Burbank
Tel: 818-848 6691;
www.castawayrestaurant.com
A Burbank landmark for over 40 years, this seafood and steak restaurant has breathtaking views of the city. **$$$**
Dr Hogly Wogly's Tyler Texas BBQ,
8136 N. Sepulveda Blvd,
(one block south of Roscoe Blvd),
Van Nuys
Tel: 818-780 6701;
www.hoglywogly.com
LA's top-rated ribs. **$**

The Great Greek,
13362 Ventura Blvd,
Sherman Oaks
Tel: 818-905 5250;
www.greatgreek.com
Boisterous restaurant/club with Greek cuisine and the familiar plate-breaking, dancing waiters, etc. **$$**
Karl Strauss Brewing Company,
Universal CityWalk, Universal City
Tel: 818-753 BREW;
www.karlstrauss.com
Microbrewery serving salads, burgers, ribs and steaks. **$$**
Mistral,
13422 Ventura Blvd
(Between Woodman and Coldwater Canyon avenues), Sherman Oaks
Tel: 818-981 6650.
Good food in the valley version of a French bistro. **$$**
Smoke House,
4420 Lakeside Dr, Burbank
Tel: 818-845 3731;
www.smokehouse1946.com
Ribs, chicken, and unforgettable garlic and cheese bread are favorites of the crowd from the nearby studios. **$$**
Sushi Nozawa,
11288 Ventura Blvd, Studio City
Tel: 818-508 7017.
Japanese, and good with it. **$$$**

Santa Barbara

Bay Café,
131 Anacapa St
Tel: 805-963 2215;
www.sbbaycafe.com
The Bay has some of the best seafood around. **$$**
Fresco at the Beach,
901 East Cabrillo Blvd
Tel: 805-963 0111.
California cuisine in a beautiful, if noisy spot. Great views of the ocean. **$$**

Galanga Thai,
507 State St
Tel: 805-963 6799.
Thai eatery with outrageous decor and inexpensive soups, curries and duck dishes. **$**
Jade,
3132 State St
Tel: 805-563 2007.
A friendly place offering California cuisine. **$**
Playa Azul Café,
914 Santa Barbara St
Tel: 805-966 2860.
Mexican food near the Presidio. **$$**
Sage & Onion,
34 E. Ortega St
Tel: 805-963 1012;
www.sageandonion.com
A charming restaurant near the Presidio, with an impressive wine list, inventive surf-and-turf and elegant decor. **$$$**
The Wine Cask,
813 Anacapa St
Tel: 805-966 9463;
www.winecask.com
Choose from among the hundreds of wines in the adjoining wine shop to accompany the delicious California cuisine served at the Wine Cask. **$$$**
Zia Café,
532 State St
Tel: 805-962 5391.
Authentic Southwestern cuisine, offering spicy salsa, tasty margaritas and honey-drizzled *sopaipillas* (fried bread). **$**

PRICE CATEGORIES

Prices are for a meal for two people, without wine.
$ = less than $30
$$ = $30–$60
$$$ = $60–$100
$$$$ = more than $100

A CTIVITIES

THE ARTS, NIGHTLIFE, FESTIVALS AND EVENTS, TOURS, SPORTS AND SHOPPING

THE ARTS

Theater

San Francisco

Actors' Theatre,
533 Sutter St
Tel: 415-345 1287;
www.actorstheatresf.org
Often does classics by such
luminaries as Tennessee Williams
and other innovators. Thursday–
Sunday. An intimate, fun setting.
**American Conservatory Theater –
Geary Theater (ACT),**
415 Geary St
Tel: 415-749 2228;
www.act-sfbay.org
Every kind of material.
Asian American Theater Company,
690 Fifth St, Suite 211
Tel: 415-543 5738;
www.asianamericantheater.org
Known for innovative Asian themes
and casts.

BELOW: the Hollywood Bowl.

Curran Theater,
445 Geary St
(between Mason and Taylor)
Tel: 415-551 2000;
www.shnsf.com
The Eureka,
215 Jackson
Tel: 415-788-7469.
Golden Gate Theater,
1 Taylor Street
Tel: 415-551 2000.
The Magic Theatre,
Fort Mason, Building D
Tel: 415-441 8822;
www.magictheatre.org
Innovative and known for premiering
plays by Michael McClure and Sam
Shepard.

Los Angeles

Groundlings Theater, 7307 Melrose
Ave (tel: 323-934 4747;
www.groundlings.com), is a long-
established venue and now under
challenge from the breakaway **Acme
Comedy Theatre** (tel: 323-525 0202;
www.acmecomedy.com). But, in addition
to the dozens of tiny houses, there
are also the better-known **Mark Taper
Forum** (tel: 213-628 2772); and
Ahmanson (tel: 213-628 2772) in
the Music Center (www.musiccenter.org)
at 135 N. Grand; and the **Geffen
Playhouse,** (tel: 310-208 6500;
www.geffenplayhouse.com).
   Repertory can be enjoyed at the
Theatre West, 3333 Cahuenga Blvd
W., Hollywood (tel: 323-851 4839;
www.theatrewest.org). Another theater
with a regular schedule is the
Pantages, 6233 Hollywood Blvd (tel:
323-468 1716). Further afield are
the **South Coast Repertory,** 655
Town Center Dr, Costa Mesa (tel:
714-708 5555; www.scr.org), and the
Pasadena Playhouse, 39 S. El
Molino Ave (tel: 626-356 7529;
www.pasadenaplayhouse.org).

San Diego

Don Powell Theatre,
5500 Campanile Dr, Performing Arts
Plaza, San Diego State University
Tel: 619-594 6884;
theatre.sdsu.edu
A 500-seat theater in SDSU's School
of Theatre, Television and Film,
featuring zany musicals and modern
adaptations. The nearby **Experimental Theatre** presents classic and
contemporary plays, plus performances from the San Diego Asian
American Repertory Theatre.
La Jolla Playhouse,
2910 La Jolla Village Dr, La Jolla
Tel: 858-550 1010; 858-550 1070;
www.lajollaplayhouse.org
An award-winning regional theater,
with three main venues and bold,
eclectic programs.
Lyceum Theatre,
79 Horton Plaza, Downtown
Tel: 619-544 1000; 619-231 3586;
www.sandiegorep.com
Home to the innovative San Diego
Repertory Theatre since 1986 and
witness to over 40 world premieres.
The premises also house a two-level
visual art gallery.
The Old Globe,
1363 Old Globe Way, Balboa Park
Tel: 619-234 5623; 619-231 1941;
www.theoldglobe.org
Classic and contemporary
productions on three stages: the
580-seat Old Globe Theatre, the 225-
seat Cassius Carter Centre Stage,
and the 612-seat outdoor Lowell
Davies Festival Theatre.
**Stephen and Mary Birch North Park
Theatre,**
2891 University Ave, North Park
Tel: 619-239 8836;
www.birchnorthparktheatre.net
Built in 1928, this vibrant 730-seat
theater features performances by the
Lyric Opera San Diego.

Concerts and Operas

San Francisco

Audium,
1616 Bush St in the Civic Center area
Tel: 415-771 1616;
www.audium.org
Presents contemporary and
precedent-setting kinds of music.
This is the first theater of sound
exploration, experimenting with
169 speakers which move music
around you in a kind of sculpture.
Cash only.

Golden Gate Park Band,
Music Concourse, Golden Gate Park
Tel: 415-831 5500
Each Sunday April to October, 1pm.
Pack a picnic and enjoy a traditional
brass band, free.

San Francisco Conservatory of Music,
50 Oak St,
Tel: 415-864 7326 (a 24-hour tape
recording lists music activities);
www.sfcm.edu
Offers professional chamber music
as well as student recitals. With
graduates like Isaac Stern to its
credit, it is regarded as the best
West Coast music school.

San Francisco Opera,
Van Ness Ave at Grove St in the Civic
Center area
Tel: 415-864 3330;
www.sfopera.com
Features internationally renowned
stars of the opera world. Having
entered its seventh decade of annual
seasons, ten operas are presented
each year in repertory. Standing-room
tickets can be purchased two hours
before the performance.

San Francisco Symphony,
Davies Symphony Hall, Van Ness Ave
at Grove St in the Civic Center Area
Tel: 415-864 6000;
www.sfsymphony.org
The San Francisco Symphony plays a
summer pops series, a Beethoven
Festival and the Mostly Mozart
Festival each year in addition to its
regular season.

Los Angeles

The Frank Gehry-designed **Walt
Disney Concert Hall** is the premier
concert venue in the city. It's the
home of the Los Angeles Philharmonic
(www.laphil.com). The nearby **Music
Center** complex also has concerts.
The June to September season at the
Hollywood Bowl (www.hollywoodbowl.com)
sees nightly concerts: jazz, classical
and pop. Park free at specific lots
and take the round-trip bus or the
Bowlbus from four different locations. For more information and
reservations, call the Music Center
line, tel: 213-972 7211. Ask about
free morning rehearsals.

Los Angeles also has regular
concerts at the **Greek Theatre** (tel:
323-665 5857; www.greektheatrela.com)
in Griffith Park and performances on
summer Sundays in Warner Center
Park, Woodland Hills. Call the Valley
Cultural Center (www.valleycultural.org)
for schedules. Santa Clarita's summer
concerts take place in **Old Orchard
Park** (tel: 661-255 4910); in Thousand
Oaks, in **Conejo Community Park**
(tel: 805-495 2163).

Dorothy Chandler Pavilion,
135 N. Grand Ave, Downtown
Tel: 213-972 7211/972 7483;
www.musiccenter.org
Part of the Music Center complex, the
building is richly appointed with marble
walls and chandeliers.

The Wilshire Ebell Theatre,
4401 W. Eighth St
Tel: 323-939 1128;
www.ebellla.com
This Spanish-designed venue was built
in 1924 and often plays host to the
Los Angeles Opera Theater, in addition
to regular theatrical productions.

The Wiltern,
Wilshire Blvd and Western Ave
Tel: 213-380 5005.
Built in 1930 and now a protected
Art Deco landmark, the Wiltern is
also a refurbished venue for rock
concerts and musical events.

San Diego

California Center for the Arts,
340 N. Escondido Blvd, Escondido
Tel: 760-839 4138;
800-988 4253;
www.artcenter.org
Situated on a 12-acre (5-hectare)
campus in downtown Escondido,
adjacent to historic Grape Day Park,
the center consists of a 1,500-seat
concert hall, a 400-seat theater, a
visual arts museum, as well as art
and dance studios. Since 1994, the
center has hosted pop, blues,
classical and holiday concerts, as
well as opera performances.

Copley Symphony Hall,
750 B St, Downtown
Tel: 619-235 0804;
www.sandiegosymphony.com
Opened in 1929 as the fabulous Fox
Theatre, Copley Symphony Hall is
now home to both the San Diego
Symphony and the San Diego Youth
Symphony.

The Neurosciences Institute,
10640 John Jay Hopkins Dr, north of
UC San Diego in La Jolla
Tel: 858-626 2000;
www.nsi.edu
Chamber music ensembles, brass
quintets, the San Diego Master
Chorale and others present their
musical talents within the institute's
Performing Arts Auditorium.

ABOVE: San Francisco music venue.

**Poway Center for the Performing
Arts**,
15498 Espola Rd, Poway
Tel: 858-748 0505;
www.powayarts.org
Besides theater and dance, the
center hosts R&B concerts, the San
Diego Symphony and other well-
known musical acts.

Spreckels Organ Pavilion,
Balboa Park
Tel: 619-702 8138;
www.sosorgan.com
On Sunday afternoons, music lovers
flock to this outdoor stage for free
organ concerts.

Ballet and Dance

San Francisco

San Francisco Ballet,
Tel: 415-861 5600;
www.sfballet.org
After more than seven decades, the
company is still delighting audiences.
Well-known for traditional
choreography and consistently
excellent productions, the San
Francisco Ballet was the first in the
country to perform the *Nutcracker
Suite* as a Christmas event.
Performances are held at the San
Francisco Opera House, Van Ness
and Grove in the Civic Center area.
Tickets may be purchased through
BASS or at the box office for
performances at the Opera house.

ODC Dance,
Tel: 415-863 6606;
www.odcdance.org
Known nationally for its
entrepreneurial savvy and artistic
innovation, ODC was the first modern-
dance company in America to build
its own resident facility. The ever-
popular company does over 120
performances a year.

Los Angeles

The Music Center,
135 N. Grand Ave
Tel: 213-972 7211;
www.musiccenter.org
A venue for traveling ballet companies
and modern-dance troupes.
The Shrine Auditorium,
649 W. Jefferson Blvd
Tel: 213-748 5116;
www.shrinela.com
The Shrine has recently completed a
massive renovation and hosts
several televised award shows.
UCLA Royce Hall,
Westwood
Tel: 310-825 2101.
Famous ballet companies share this
center with modern-dance
performances.
The **Wiltern** (tel: 213-380 5005);
the **Veterans Wadsworth Theatre**
(tel: 310-825 2101); the **Pasadena
Civic Auditorium**; and Glendale's
Alex Theatre (tel: 818-243 ALEX;
www.alextheatre.org) also stage dance
concerts semi-regularly. For specific
listings, consult the Sunday Calendar
section of the *Los Angeles Times*.

San Diego

Casa del Prado Theater,
Balboa Park
Tel: 619-239 0512;
www.balboapark.org
This 650-seat theater offers diverse
performances from San Diego Civic
Youth Ballet and San Diego Civic
Dance Arts. Also host to the annual
Celebrate Dance Festival.
**Mandell Weiss Center for the
Performing Arts,**
9500 Gilman Dr, University of
California San Diego, La Jolla
Tel: 858-534 4574; 858-534 3791;
theatre.ucsd.edu
Students present innovative dance
performances in four spaces, shared
with the La Jolla Playhouse.
San Diego Civic Theatre,
1100 Third Ave, Downtown
Tel: 619-570 1100; 619-615 4000;
www.sdcivic.org
Ballet performances, Irish dancing
and Broadway musicals.

Listings Publications

For concerts, shows, festivals,
and celebrations in Northern
California, check out "Datebook"
in the *San Francisco Chronicle* or
the *SF Weekly*. Listings for more
specialized events appear in
smaller local papers. For Southern
California, check the "Calendar"
section of the *Los Angeles Times*
or a current copy of *LA Weekly* or
Los Angeles Magazine.

NIGHTLIFE

California's cities have a vibrant
nightlife, with pulsing dance clubs,
funky blues venues and first-rate
comedy clubs. But clubs appear and
disappear; although most listed here
are long-standing joints, it's always
advisable to consult up-to-date listings
in local newspapers and magazines.
Because cover charges, dress codes,
reservation policies and show times
vary from place to place, you should
always call ahead for details.

Clubs

San Francisco

1015 Folsom,
1015 Folsom St
Tel: 415-431 1200;
www.1015.com
DJs and electronic music.
El Rio,
3158 Mission St
Tel: 415-282 3325;
www.elriosf.com
Salsa, world beat, and DJs.
The EndUp,
401 6th St
Tel: 415-357 0827;
www.theendup.com
After-hours house music and dancing.

Los Angeles

The Derby,
4500 Los Feliz Blvd, Los Feliz
Tel: 323-663 8979;
www.clubderby.com
Made famous by the film *Swingers*,
this is *the* place to jitterbug and
groove to live concerts.
The Mayan,
1038 S. Hill St, Downtown
Tel: 213-746 4674;
www.clubmayan.com
This 1920s-era movie theater is a
multi-tiered dance club with exotic
decor and dramatic lighting.
The Roxy Theatre,
9009 Sunset Blvd, West Hollywood
Tel: 310-278 9457;
www.theroxyonsunset.com
Live music and famous neighboring
clubs lure trendy shakers to this
historic joint on the Sunset Strip, as
legendary for its modern rock
performances as for its celebrity
guests, who have ranged from John
Lennon to today's tabloid stars.
The Viper Room,
8852 Sunset Blvd, West Hollywood
Tel: 310-358 1881;
www.viperroom.com
With the vibe of a 1920s-era Harlem
jazz club, the Viper continues to host
famous rock acts, while DJs entice
partygoers onto the dance floor.

San Diego

The Bitter End,
770 5th Ave, Gaslamp Quarter
Tel: 619-338 9300;
www.thebitterend.com
Situated in a historic building that
dates back to 1874, this popular,
sophisticated nightclub offers three
levels of fun – a main bar with billiard
tables, a dance hall and an elegant
VIP lounge. Famous for its signature
"black martini."
Jimmy Love's,
672 5th Ave, Gaslamp Quarter
Tel: 619-595 0123;
www.jimmyloves.com
Occupying two floors of the 125-year-
old "Old City Hall" building, this
restaurant and nightclub hosts live
jazz, blues, dance and disco bands
every night of the week.
Stingaree,
454 6th Ave, Gaslamp Quarter
Tel: 619-544 9500;
www.stingsandiego.com
Situated within a historic warehouse
in San Diego's former Red Light
District, this popular tri-level celebrity
hangout features a waterfall, a fire
pit and rooftop cabanas.

Music Venues

San Francisco

Boom Boom Room,
1601 Fillmore St
Tel: 415-673 8000;
www.boomboomblues.com
Blues, blues, and more blues.
Café du Nord,
2170 Market St
Tel: 415-861 5016;
www.cafedunord.com
Swing, jazz, eclectic, spoken word.
The Fillmore,
1805 Geary at Fillmore St
Tel: 415-346 6000;
www.thefillmore.com
Major headline acts; legendary venue
that is part of SF's musical history.
Great American Music Hall,
859 O'Farrell Street
Tel: 415-885 0750;
www.musichallsf.com
Live music; food most nights.

Los Angeles

The Cowboy Palace Saloon,
21635 Devonshire St, Chatsworth
Tel: 818-341 0166;
www.cowboypalace.com
For over 30 years, this honky-tonk
has showcased live Country &
Western music every night.
Harvelle's,
1432 4th St, Santa Monica
Tel: 310-395 1676;
www.harvelles.com
Since 1931, this moody, sexy room
has invited guests to drink, dance

ABOVE: wile away the blues in sunny California.

and listen to the hottest jazz, blues, soul and burlesque.

House of Blues Sunset Strip,
8430 Sunset Blvd, West Hollywood
Tel: 323-848 5100;
www.hob.com
The funky stage attracts famous rock and blues acts, and the gospel brunch lures the locals.

Knitting Factory Hollywood,
7021 Hollywood Blvd, Hollywood
Tel: 323-463 0204;
www.knittingfactory.com
Young night owls converge here for live jazz and punk.

Troubadour,
9081 Santa Monica Blvd, West Hollywood
Tel: 310-276 6168;
www.troubadour.com
Live rock bands have been jamming at this legendary venue since 1957.

Whisky A Go-Go,
8901 Sunset Blvd, West Hollywood
Tel: 310-652 4202;
www.whiskyagogo.com
A famous history and rockin' bands continue to entice dancers to this LA landmark, opened in 1964.

San Diego

4th & B,
345 B St, Downtown
Tel: 619-299 2583;
www.4thandb.com
Recently renovated, San Diego's premier live music venue hosts everything from hip-hop dynamos to punk rock legends. Managed by the House of Blues.

Belly Up Tavern,
143 S. Cedros Ave, Solana Beach
Tel: 858-481 8140;
www.bellyup.com
Consistently voted San Diego's best live music venue, this long-standing club entices a diverse selection of good musicians, from Stevie Wonder to Dr John.

The Casbah,
2501 Kettner Blvd, Little Italy
Tel: 619-232 4355;
www.casbahmusic.com
With an enclosed smoking patio, pool tables and live bands at least six nights a week, this venue tempts music lovers of all varieties.

Humphrey's Backstage Music Club,
2241 Shelter Island Dr, Shelter Island
Tel: 619-224 3577;
www.humphreysbythebay.com
Overlooking the San Diego Bay, this outdoor venue lures jazz, soul and rock legends to the stage behind Humphrey's restaurant.

Comedy and Magic

San Francisco

Cobb's Comedy Club,
915 Columbus Ave
Tel: 415-928 4320;
www.cobbscomedyclub.com

Punch Line Comedy Club,
444 Battery St (up the stairs)
Tel: 415-397 7573;
www.punchlinecomedyclub.com

Purple Onion,
140 Columbus Ave (down the stairs)
Tel: 415-956 1653;
www.purpleonioncomedy.com

Los Angeles

The Comedy & Magic Club,
1018 Hermosa Ave, Hermosa Beach
Tel: 310-372 1193;
www.comedyandmagicclub.com
Jay Leno, host of *The Tonight Show*, regularly tests out new material here.

The Comedy Store,
8433 Sunset Blvd, West Hollywood
Tel: 323-650 6268;
www.thecomedystore.com
Once the site of legendary nightclub Ciro's, this club has featured comic greats like Eddie Murphy, Richard Pryor and George Carlin.

The Ice House Comedy Club,
24 Mentor Ave, Pasadena
Tel: 626-577 1894;
www.icehousecomedy.com
Since the 1970s, this comedy club has hosted famous stand-up comedians, from Lily Tomlin to Billy Crystal, as well as ambitious amateurs. The complex includes two showrooms, a restaurant and an outdoor patio.

Improv Olympic West,
6366 Hollywood Blvd, Hollywood
Tel: 323-962 7560;
www.iowest.com
The West Coast branch of the famous Chicago venue offers improvisational shows and classes.

Laugh Factory,
8001 Sunset Blvd, Hollywood
Tel: 323-656 1336;
www.laughfactory.com
With branches in Long Beach and New York, too, this famous comedy club often surprises patrons with its all-star shows.

The Magic Castle,
7001 Franklin Ave, Hollywood
Tel: 323-851 3313;
www.magiccastle.com
Housed in a fanciful Victorian mansion, the world's most famous club for magicians showcases some of the globe's most legendary performers. Since it's a private club, only members, their friends and guests of the nearby Magic Castle Hotel are allowed inside.

Magicopolis,
1418 4th St, Santa Monica
Tel: 310-451 2241;
www.magicopolis.com
This classy venue presents shows that blend elements of magic, illusion and laughter.

San Diego

The Comedy CO-OP,
11211 Sorrento Valley Rd, Sorrento Valley
Tel: 888-567 4464;
www.comedycoop.org
Patrons can bring in any outside food or drink; visiting comedy troupes will bring the laughs.

The Comedy Store La Jolla,
916 Pearl St, La Jolla
Tel: 858-454 9176;
www.thecomedystore.com
A recent extension of LA's famous comedy club.

National Comedy Theatre,
3717 India St, Midtown
Tel: 619-295 4999;
www.nationalcomedy.com
Appropriate for all ages, these 90-minute improvisational comedy shows pit two teams against each other, with the winner decided by the rowdy audience.

Festivals and Events

Here are just a few of the most popular festivals and events in California.

January

Buick Invitational, San Diego,
Tel: 619-281 4653;
www.buickinvitational.com
Annual golf tournament.
Miss L.A. Chinatown Pageant,
Downtown Los Angeles
Tel: 213-617 0396;
www.lachinesechamber.org
San Diego Boat Show,
Tel: 858-274 9924;
www.discoverboating.com
SF Sketchfest, San Francisco
www.sfsketchfest.com
Sketch comedy groups from all over the United States converge to crack you up.
Southwest Arts Festival, Indio
Tel: 760-347 0676;
www.southwestartsfest.com
Tournament of Roses Parade and Rose Bowl Football Game, Pasadena
Tel: 626-449 4100;
www.tournamentofroses.com
Whale Watching, Ventura
Tel: 1-800 333 2989;
www.venturausa.com

February

Chinese New Year
Large celebrations in San Francisco, Los Angeles and San Diego. Call local tourist bureaus for information.
Clam Chowder Cook-Off, Santa Cruz
Tel: 831-423 5590;
www.beachboardwalk.com
Teams work on their recipes for tasting and prizes.
National Date Festival, Indio
Tel: 760-863 8247;
www.datefest.org
Arabian Nights pageant; camel and ostrich races.
San Diego Brazil Carnaval,
Downtown San Diego
Tel: 619-224 4684;
www.brazilcarnival.com
San Francisco Independent Film Festival,
www.sfindie.com
Screening of the best indie films and videos from the Bay Area and beyond.
Santa Barbara International Film Festival,
Tel: 805-963 0023;
www.sbfilmfestival.org
Sex Tour, San Francisco Zoo
Tel: 415-753 7165;
www.sfzoo.org
The San Francisco Zoo hosts a Valentine's Day Sex Tour showcasing the mating and courtship rituals of the animals.

March

Blessing of the Animals,
Olvera Street, Los Angeles;
www.olverastreet.com
Historical Easter event.
Celebration of the Whales, Oxnard
Tel: 805-985 4852.
Saint Patrick's Day,
Parades and celebrations, San Francisco, Los Angeles and San Diego (17th).
Snow Festival, Tahoe
Tel: 530-583 7167;
www.tahoesnowfestival.com
Ten days of winter fun.

April

Apple Blossom Festival, Sebastopol
Tel: 707-823 3032;
www.sebastopol.org
Cherry Blossom Festival,
San Francisco
Tel: 415-563 2313.
An annual tradition in Japantown.
Fallbrook Avocado Festival,
Tel: 760-728 5845;
www.fallbrookca.org
Festival of Books,
UCLA Campus, Los Angeles
Tel: 800-LATIMES;
www.latimes.com
Joshua Tree National Park Arts Festival, Twentynine Palms
Tel: 760-367 5525;
www.joshuatree.org
San Francisco International Film Festival, San Francisco
Tel: 415-561 5000;
www.sffs.org
Toyota Grand Prix, Long Beach
Tel: 888-82 SPEED;
www.gplb.com

May

ING Bay to Breakers, San Francisco
Tel: 415-359 2707.
70,000 costume-clad runners converge on the world's largest footrun, from Ferry Building to Ocean Beach.
Carlsbad Village Faire, Carlsbad
Tel: 760-945 9288;
www.kennedyfaires.com
California's largest one-day street fair.
Carnaval San Francisco,
Tel: 415-920 0125;
www.carnavalsf.com
Mardi Gras, Brazilian-style.
Catalina Island Rugby Festival,
Tel: 310-LARUGBY;
www.larugby.com
Cinco de Mayo, San Francisco, Los Angeles, San Diego and Santa Barbara (5th)

Ethnic Food Fair, Balboa Park, San Diego
Tel: 619-234 0739;
www.sdhpr.org
Fiesta Hermosa!, Hermosa Beach
Tel: 310-376 0951;
www.fiestahermosa.com
Jazz Jubilee, Sacramento
Tel: 916-372 5277;
www.sacjazz.com
Largest Dixieland festival.
Jumping Frog Jubilee, Angels Camp
Tel: 209-736 2561.
Accompanying the amphibians contest is a rodeo and county fair.
Long Beach Lesbian and Gay Pride Celebration, Long Beach
Tel: 562-987 9191;
www.longbeachpride.com
Strawberry Festival, Garden Grove
Tel: 714-638 0981;
www.strawberryfestival.org
Kinetic Grand Championship,
Arcata to Ferndale, Humboldt County
Tel: 707-499 0643;
www.kineticgrandchampionship
Transportation meets art at this three-day race; participants ride human-powered sculptures over a 38-mile (61-km) course.

June

California Music Awards, Oakland
www.californiamusicawards.com
Haight-Ashbury Street Fair,
San Francisco
Tel: 415-863 3489;
www.haightashburystreetfair.org
Lesbian and Gay Pride Parade,
San Francisco
Tel: 415-864 3733;
www.sfpride.org
Living History Celebration,
San Juan Bautista
Tel: 831-623 4526;
www.san-juan-bautista.ca.us
Dressing up like in the old days.
Los Angeles Film Festival,
Tel: 310-432 1208;
www.lafilmfest.com
National Shakespeare Festival,
San Diego, The Old Globe
Tel: 619-234 5623;
www.oldglobe.org
North Beach Festival, San Francisco
Tel: 415-989 2220;
www.sfnorthbeach.org
Ojai Music Festival, Ojai
Tel: 805-646 2094;
www.ojaifestival.org
Bluegrass, Cajun, rockabilly.
Playboy Jazz Festival, Hollywood Bowl, Los Angeles
Tel: 323-850 2050;
www.playboy.com
San Diego County Fair,
Tel: 858-793 5555;
www.sdfair.com
Exhibits, rides, games and food.

ABOVE: Santa Claus arrives at the Chinese Theatre in Hollywood.

Temecula Valley Balloon and Wine Festival,
Tel: 951-676 6713;
www.tvbwf.com

July

Boat Parade and Fireworks Show,
Bass Lake
Tel: 559-642 3676.
Comic-Con International, San Diego
Tel: 619-491 2475;
www.comic-con.org
Fortuna Rodeo, Fortuna
Tel: 707-725 3959;
www.fortunarodeo.com
The world's biggest chili cook-off, live music, junior rodeo and penny scramble.
Fourth of July.
Celebrations and fireworks throughout the state.
Gilroy Garlic Festival, Gilroy
www.gilroygarlicfestival.com
Tel: 408-842 1625.
Lambtown USA Festival,
Dixon, Solano County
Tel: 707-678 2650;
www.lambtown.com
Cook-off with entertainment.
Pageant of the Masters,
Laguna Beach
Tel: 949-494 1145;
www.foapom.com
Long-standing festival with its hugely popular attraction – live depictions of famous artworks.
Sawdust Art Festival,
Tel: 949-494 3030;
www.sawdustartfestival.org
Laguna Beach's traditional arts and crafts festival.
US Open Sandcastle Competition,
Imperial Beach
Tel: 619-424 6663;
www.usopensandcastle.com
A two-day sandcastle-building contest for both serious contenders and curious onlookers.

August

California State Fair, Sacramento
Tel: 916-263-FAIR;
www.bigfun.org
Livestock, food, music, entertainment.
International Surf Festival,
Hermosa, Manhattan and Redondo beaches;
www.surffestival.org
Exhibition surfing. Call beach-city tourist bureaus for information.
Nihonmachi Street Fair,
Japantown, San Francisco
Tel: 415-771 9861;
www.nihonmachistreetfair.org
Lion dancers, Taiko drummers, Japanese arts and crafts.
Nisei Week, Little Tokyo, Los Angeles
Tel: 213-687 7193;
www.niseiweek.org
One of the country's oldest Japanese-American festivals.
Old Spanish Days Fiesta,
Santa Barbara
Tel: 805-962 8101;
www.oldspanishdays-fiesta.org
Folk dancing, market, carnival, rodeo and parade.
Orange County Classic Jazz Festival,
Costa Mesa
Tel: 888-215 6222;
www.oc-classicjazz.org
Sunset Junction Street Festival,
Los Angeles
Tel: 323-661 7771;
www.sunsetjunction.org

September

Chocolate Fest, Ghirardelli Square, San Francisco
Tel: 415-775 5500;
www.ghirardellisq.com
Desserts, plus an ice-cream sundae-eating contest.
KJAZZ Blues Festival, Long Beach
Tel: 562-985 5566;
www.jazzandblues.org

Lobster Festival, San Pedro
Tel: 310-798 7478;
www.lobsterfest.com
Los Angeles County Fair, Pomona
Tel: 909-623 3111;
www.lacountyfair.com
Monterey Jazz Festival, Monterey
Tel: 831-373 3366;
www.montereyjazzfestival.org
Oktoberfest, Big Bear Lake
Tel: 909-585 3000;
www.bigbearevents.com
Weekends between mid-September and the end of October.
Sausalito Art Festival, Sausalito
Tel: 415-331 3757;
www.sausalitoartfestival.org
S.F. Comedy Day,
www.comedyday.com
Free five-hour comedy celebration in SF's Golden Gate Park.
Watts Towers Day of the Drum Festival, Los Angeles
Tel: 213-847 4646.

October

Art and Pumpkin Festival,
Half Moon Bay
Tel: 650-726 9652.
California Avocado Festival,
Carpinteria
Tel: 805-684 0038;
www.avofest.com
Exotic Erotic Ball, Cow Palace, Daly City, San Francisco
Tel: 415-567-BALL
www.exoticeroticball.com
The largest indoor masquerade ball in the world.
Fleet Week, San Diego and San Francisco
Tel: 650-599 5057; 650-599 5057;
www.fleetweeksandiego.org; fleetweek.us
Contests, air shows and ship tours in honor of the US military.
Golf Cart Parade, Palm Desert
Tel: 760-346 6111;
www.golfcartparade.com

Decorated golfcarts, marching bands.
Hollywood Film Festival,
Tel: 310-288 1882;
www.hollywoodawards.com
A glittering festival that kicks off the
awards season, which culminates in
the Oscars.
**Pasadena Heritage's Craftsman
Weekend**,
Tel: 626-441 6333.
Lectures, exhibits and tours of
beautiful homes.
Sandcastle Contest, Newport Beach
Tel: 949-729 4400;
www.newportbeach.com
S.F. Jazz Festival,
Tel: 415-398 5655
www.sfjazz.org
Runs from mid-Oct to late-Nov.

November

Death Valley '49ers Encampment,
Death Valley
Tel: 760-852 4524;
www.deathvalley49ers.org
Fiddlers contest, art shows and a
trek through the hot, hot valley.
Doo Dah Parade, Pasadena
Tel: 626-205 4029;
www.pasadenadoodahparade.info
Outrageous fall parade.
Mother Goose Parade, El Cajón
Tel: 619-444 8712;
www.mothergooseparade.org
**San Diego Thanksgiving Dixieland
Jazz Festival**,
Tel: 619-297 5277;
www.dixielandjazzfestival.org
Village Faire, Carlsbad
Tel: 760-945 9288;
www.kennedyfaires.com
The state's largest one-day fair.
Weed Show, Twentynine Palms
Tel: 760-367 3445.

December

December Nights, San Diego
Tel: 619-239 0512;
www.balboapark.org
Lighted Boat Parades, Marina del
Rey and San Diego. Call local tourist
bureaus for information.
Parade of Lights, Oxnard
Tel: 805-985 4852;
www.channelislandsharbor.org
Sawdust Art Festival, Laguna Beach
Tel: 949-494 3030;
www.sawdustartfestival.org
Tamale Festival, Indio
Tel: 760-342 6532;
www.tamalefestival.net
Tamale eating and juggling contests.

TOURS

Adventure Bus (tel: 888-737 5263;
www.adventurebus.com) offers
inexpensive transportation through
much of California departing from
Salt Lake City and Las Vegas.
Destinations include Yellowstone
and the southwestern national
parks, plus other trips, stopping
at scenic spots en route.
Architours,
Tel: 323-294 5821;
www.architours.com;
e-mail: info@architours.com
Various Los Angeles tours visit works
by Frank Lloyd Wright and Richard
Neutra, as well as restaurants and
other facilities of architectural merit.
FOOT!
Tel: 415-793-JEST (5378)
www.foottours.com
Fun, informative, interactive walking
tours that allow for personal and

memorable experiences. Guides are
professional comedians who share
their love and knowledge of San
Francisco with you.
**Mangia! North Beach – History,
Food and Culture Tours**,
e-mail: gaw@sbcglobal.net
Learn about the Italian heritage of
the neighborhood, taste truffles and
focaccia, and enjoy a three-course
lunch with *SF Chronicle* food
columnist GraceAnn Walden. Named
one of the 100 best things about
San Francisco by *Gourmet* magazine.
Reservations necessary.
Old Town Trolley Tours,
Tel: 619-298 8687;
www.trolleytours.com
Vibrant green-and-orange trolleys,
driven by spirited conductors, take
visitors to San Diego's most popular
sites, including Old Town, the San
Diego Harbor Seaport Village, Petco
Park, the Gaslamp Quarter, the Hotel
del Coronado, the San Diego Zoo and
Balboa Park.
San Francisco City Guides,
Tel: 415-557 4266;
www.sfcityguides.org
Nearly 70 free architectural and
history tours by trained volunteers
are offered all year long. Tours cover
topics from the murals of Mission to
the mansions of Pacific Heights and
everything in between.
Starline Tours,
Tel: 1-800 959 3131;
www.starlinetours.com;
e-mail: info@starlinetours.com
An assortment of LA sightseeing
tours, from movie stars' homes to
the delights of Disneyland.
Victorian Home Walk,
Tel: 415-252 9485;
www.victorianwalk.com
Go where buses can't. Learn about
San Francisco architecture and
history from long-time residents.
Most days at 11am a tour leaves
from the old lobby of the Westin St
Francis on Powell and Geary in Union
Square. No reservations required.
Warner Bros Studios V.I.P. Tour,
Tel: 818-846 1403
For two colorful hours, small groups
of movie lovers can ride through this
famous Burbank lot, visiting such
classic sets as the Walton family
home and Errol Flynn's Sherwood
Forest as well as sound stages and
post-production labs.
Wok Wiz Walking Tours,
Tel: 650-355 9657
www.wokwiz.com
SF's Chinatown history, culture and
folklore lectures during an insider's
view of the largest Chinatown outside
of China. The daily tour includes a
seven-course dim-sum lunch.
Reservations required.

Whale Watching

Spring and fall are the seasons for
whale-spotting. The **American
Cetacean Society** is among the
many groups that organize trips to
see some of the thousands of
magnificent 40-ton (36-tonne)
California gray whales on their
10,000-mile (16,100-km)
migration from Alaska to South
America. Traveling 80–100 miles
(130– 160 km) per day, some of
these mammals can be seen from
high spots along the coast –
particularly from the Palos Verdes
Peninsula – and around the
Channel Islands. Other whale-
watching options are Point Reyes
Lighthouse at the Point Reyes
National Seashore, north of San
Francisco; organized boats from
Santa Cruz Harbor (tel: 831-423

1213); **Sea Landing** in Santa
Barbara (tel: 805-963 3564); and
Redondo Sport Fishing (tel: 310-
372 2111) in Redondo Beach.
Seals and sea lions are also
plentiful in the islands to which
Island Packers (tel: 805-642
1393) run trips and about which
the **Channel Islands National Park**
(tel: 805-658 5730) can provide a
wealth of information. In addition,
snowy plovers and cormorants are
found on San Miguel; kestrels,
larks and owls on Santa Barbara;
and brown pelicans, who nest
between May and August, on
Anacapa, the closest island to the
mainland. For information about
Santa Cruz, the largest island of
the group, call the helpful **Nature
Conservancy** (tel: 949-263 0933).

SPORTS

Spectator Sports

Baseball

California possesses some of the finest teams in professional baseball; the season runs from April–October. In Southern California, the Los Angeles Dodgers play at Dodger Stadium; the Anaheim Angels play at Angel Stadium; and the San Diego Padres play at PETCO Park. In Northern California, the San Francisco Giants play at AT&T Park, and the Oakland Athletics (known as the As) play in McAfee Coliseum.

Basketball

The regular National Basketball Association (NBA) season runs from October through April, with championship play-offs continuing in June. The Los Angeles Lakers, who are almost always a league powerhouse, and the LA Clippers play at the popular Staples Center Downtown, and the Golden State Warriors play at Oracle Arena in Oakland. In Sacramento, the Kings play at ARCO Arena.

Football

The National Football League (NFL) season begins in September and ends in December, with pre-season games in August and post-season play-offs in January. San Diego's Chargers play at San Diego Qualcomm Stadium. The Rose Bowl is held annually on New Year's Day between the best team in the Pac-10 conference and the best team in the Big Ten. This popular event – with a great parade – is held at the Rose Bowl Stadium in Pasadena, which seats over 100,000 people, but it is still difficult to get seats. In Northern California, the San Francisco 49ers play at Monster Park, and the Oakland Raiders play at McAfee Coliseum in Oakland.

Hockey

California has two professional hockey teams, the Los Angeles Kings, who play at the 19,000-seat Staples Center, 1111 S. Figueroa St, Downtown, and the younger San Jose Sharks, who play at HP Pavilion. The hockey season runs October–April.

Soccer

Soccer has been steadily gaining interest in the US. From April to October, the Los Angeles Galaxy, starring David Beckham, faces other US teams in the Home Depot Center.

Participant Sports

Ballooning

Temecula in the Wine Country north of San Diego is one of the most popular ballooning areas. **D&D Ballooning**, tel: 1-800 510 9000; www.hotairadventures.com **Lake Tahoe Balloons**, tel: 1-800 872 9294; www.laketahoeballoons.com **Balloons above the Valley** in Napa, tel: 1-800 464 6824; www.balloonrides.com

Cycling

Organized weekend and six-day bicycle adventures, which include accommodations, operate in the Napa and Sonoma valleys and other parts of the state from travel company "Backroads," (tel: 1-800 462 2848; www.backroads.com). **Mammoth Mountain Bike Park** (tel: 1-800 228 4947) offers 90 miles (145 km) of cycling trails and stunt tracks perfect for enthusiasts.

Golf Courses

San Francisco Area
Half Moon Bay Golf Links, 2 Miramontes Point Rd, Half Moon Bay, tel: 650-726 4438; www.halfmoonbaygolf.com **Harding Park Golf Course**, Harding Rd and Skyline Blvd, San Francisco, tel: 415-661 1865; www.harding-park.com **Lincoln Park Golf Course**, 34th Ave and Clement St, San Francisco, tel: 415-221 9911; www.lincolnparkgc.com **Pasatiempo Golf Course**, 20 Clubhouse Rd, Santa Cruz, tel: 831-459 9155; www.pasatiempo.com **Tilden Park Golf Course**, Grizzly Peak Blvd and Shasta Road, Berkeley, tel: 510-848 7373.

Monterey Peninsula
The Links at Spanish Bay, 2700 17-Mile Dr, Pebble Beach, tel: 1-800 654 9300; www.pebblebeach.com **Pacific Grove Municipal Golf Links**,

77 Asilomar Blvd, Pacific Grove, tel: 831-648 5775; www.cipg.ca.us/golf **Pebble Beach Golf Links**, 17-Mile Dr, Pebble Beach, tel: 1-800 654 9300; www.pebblebeach.com **Poppy Hills Golf Course**, 3200 Lopez Rd, Pebble Beach, tel: 831-622 8239; www.ncga.org **Spyglass Hill Golf Course**, Stevenson Dr. and Spyglass Hill Rd, Pebble Beach, tel: 1-800 654 9300; www.pebblebeach.com

Greater Los Angeles Area
Brookside Golf Course, 1133 N. Rosemont Ave, Pasadena, tel: 626-795 0631. **Griffith Park Golf Courses**, 4730 Crystal Springs Dr, Los Angeles, tel: 323-664 2255. **Industry Hills Golf Club**, 1 Industry Hills Pkwy, Industry Hills, tel: 626-810 4653; www.hgolfclub.com **Rancho Park Golf Course**, 10460 W. Pico Blvd, Los Angeles, tel: 310-838 7373.

San Diego Area
Balboa Park Municipal Golf Course, 2600 Golf Course Dr, San Diego, tel: 619-570 1234. **Mission Bay Golf Course**, 2702 N. Mission Bay Dr, San Diego, tel: 858-581 7880. **Pala Mesa Golf Resort**, 2001 State 395, Fallbrook, tel: 760-728 5881; www.palamesa.com **Rancho Bernardo Inn Golf Resort and Spa**, 17550 Bernardo Oaks Dr, tel: 858-675 8500; www.ranchobernardoinn.com

Santa Barbara Area
Alisal Golf Course, 1054 Alisal Rd, Solvang, tel: 805-688 6411; www.alisal.com **La Purisima Golf Course**, 3455 State 246, Lompoc, tel: 805-735 8395; www.lapurisimagolf.com **Ojai Valley Inn and Country Club**, 905 Country Club Rd, Ojai, tel: 805-646 2420; www.ojairesort.com

Palm Springs Area
Indian Wells Golf Resort, 44–500 Indian Wells Lane, Indian Wells, tel: 760-346 4653; www.golfresortatindianwells.com **La Quinta Resort and Club**, 49–499 Eisenhower Dr, La Quinta, tel: 760-564 5729; www.laquintaresort.com **Mission Hills Country Club**, 34–600 Mission Hills Dr, Rancho Mirage, tel: 760-770 9496. **PGA West**, 56150 PGA Blvd, La Quinta, tel: 760-564 5729; www.pgawest.com

Skiing

Lake Tahoe Area

Alpine Meadows, Alpine Meadows Rd off State 89 between Truckee and Tahoe City, tel: 530-583 4232/800-441 4423; www.skialpine.com

Boreal, Castle Peak exit off Interstate 80 at Soda Springs, tel: 530-426 3666; www.borealski.com

Heavenly, Ski Run Blvd off US-50, South Lake Tahoe, tel: 775-586 7000; www.skiheavenly.com

Homewood, State 89, 6 miles (10 km) south of Tahoe City, tel: 530-525 2992; www.skihomewood.com

Northstar-at-Tahoe, State 267 Between Truckee and Kings Beach, tel: 530-562 1010; 1-800-GONORTH; www.skinorthstar.com

Squaw Valley USA, Squaw Valley Rd off State 89, 5 miles (8 km) north of Tahoe City, tel: 530-583 6985; 1-800 403 0206; www.squaw.com

Central Sierra

Badger Pass, Glacier Point Rd in Yosemite National Park off State 41, tel: 209-372 8430; www.yosemiterentals.combadger.htm

Dodge Ridge, off State 108, 32 miles (50 km) east of Sonora, tel: 209-965 3474; www.dodgeridge.com

Kirkwood, State 88 at Carson Pass, 35 miles (56 km) south of South Lake Tahoe, tel: 209-258 6000; www.kirkwood.com

Mount Reba/Bear Valley, State 4, 52 miles (84 km) east of Angels Camp, tel: 209-753 2301. www.bearvalley.com

Sierra Ski Ranch, off US 50, 12 miles (19 km) west of South Lake Tahoe, tel: 530-659 7453. www.sierratahoe.com

Sierra Summit, State 168, 64 miles (102 km) northeast of Fresno at Huntington Lake, Big Creek, tel: 559-233 3330; www.sierrasummit.com

Water Activities

Rafting expeditions are organized near Yosemite and Tahoe and throughout the Sierras by many companies including: **Arta River Trips** (tel: 1-800-323-2782); **Earthtrek Expeditions** (tel: 1-800 229 8735); and Whitewater Voyages (tel: 800-400 RAFT).

Kern River Tours (tel: 760-379 4616; www.kernrivertours.com) operates out of Lake Isabella, three hours north of LA. **Aqua Adventures Kayak Center** in San Diego and **Paddle Power Inc** (tel: 949-675 1215), of Newport Beach offer kayak lessons and rentals. **Cass' Sailing School** (tel: 415-332 6789) in Sausalito organizes boats in the Bay area.

ABOVE: San Francisco's fabulous Neiman Marcus store in Union Square.

SHOPPING

Northern California

From elegant malls to farmers' markets, Northern California offers a wide array of shopping opportunities. In San Francisco alone, there are 20 distinct shopping areas. The best known is probably **Union Square**, where most of the large, prestigious department stores are located, including Neiman Marcus, Macy's and Saks. A block away is **Maiden Lane**, a cute pedestrian street with boutiques, stationery stores and outdoor cafés. **The Galleria**, a collection of specialty shops, restaurants and services housed under a vaulting glass dome, modeled after Milan's Galleria Vittorio Emmanuelle, is nearby. The **Westfield San Francisco Centre** recently expanded to 170 stores, adding Bloomingdales, a movie theater and an upscale food court. In **SoMa**, look for good souvenirs in the galleries and art shops, plus check out **Metreon** (www.metreon.com), a huge entertainment complex combining shops, restaurants and theaters.

Visitors will also find lots of shopping around **Fisherman's Wharf**. The shopping area extends from **Pier 39** to **Ghirardelli Square** and includes the **Cannery**, the **Anchorage** and a host of street vendors. Once a cargo wharf, Pier 39 now offers two levels of shops, restaurants, amusements and free outdoor entertainment by some of the city's best street performers. Both the Cannery and Ghirardelli Square are converted factories. The Cannery was once a Del Monte peach-canning plant, and Ghirardelli housed a chocolate

factory. The Anchorage, a colorful, modern shopping complex, is also located along the Northern Waterfront. Along with specialty shops and galleries, each complex offers entertainment and breathtaking views across to Alcatraz, the Golden Gate Bridge and the bay.

The **Embarcadero Center** (www.embarcaderocenter.com) is also located on the waterfront, east of Pier 39 near the Financial District. Spread out over four complexes between Sacramento and Clay streets, it combines numerous shops, restaurants and nightclubs.

Other shopping areas in San Francisco tend to reflect the character of its neighborhood. They include Columbus Avenue and Grant Street in North Beach (**Little Italy**), Grant Street in **Chinatown**, **Castro** Street between 20th and Market and between Market and Church, **Haight Street** along the Golden Gate Park Panhandle, **Union Street** and **Chestnut Street** in the Marina, **Sacramento Street** in Presidio Heights (for high-end shopping and consignment stores), **Hayes Street** between Laguna and Octavia, Valencia in between 16th and 24th streets, and the **Japan Center**.

In the **East Bay**, visitors will find a distinct collegiate shopping atmosphere along vendor-laden Telegraph Avenue in Berkeley; and small neighborhoods of specialty shopping in Berkeley's famous "Gourmet Ghetto" along Shattuck Avenue and Oakland's Rockridge district along College Avenue. 4th Street in Berkeley is one of the better shopping destinations in the East Bay. The Powell Street Exit in Emeryville is

Where the Stars Shop

A trip down West Hollywood's **Melrose Avenue** is a must. Some of LA's best people-watching goes on here, and there are plenty of little cafés to serve as rest stops. Those into avant-garde high fashion can go to **Maxfield** near Robertson and Melrose, an austere temple of haute style, where stars like Jack Nicholson, Robin Williams and a host of rock 'n' rollers find labels like Gaultier, vintage Hermes and Prada. For a change of pace, you might want to browse among one of the city's best known collections of metaphysical and philosophical books at the **Bodhi Tree Bookstore** in the 8500 block of Melrose, where a three-story-high bodhi tree provides a shady reading spot in the backyard.

ABOVE: shop for inexpensive cigars in Tijuana and Southern California.

a big draw to big retail chains and the massive IKEA. Other locations in the Bay Area boasting boutiques, restaurants and specialty stores include Solano Avenue in Albany, Piedmont Avenue and Jack London Square in Oakland, University Avenue in Palo Alto, Stanford's toned-down "Telegraph Avenue" and the entire business district of Sausalito.

Southern California

For intrepid shoppers, Southern California is right up there with the big guns like Paris, New York and Hong Kong. Of course, the glitziest shopping street is Los Angeles' famous **Rodeo Drive**. While Rodeo has become smething of a tourist trap, with more people window-shopping than buying, there are still some terrific, world-class shops along the drive, with names like Chanel, Armani, Cartier, Louis Vuitton and Bottega Veneta.

Rodeo Drive's luxurious amenities were increased by 40 percent with the addition of another street, **Two Rodeo** (or **Via Rodeo**), a curving, cobble-stoned walkway lined with top-name stores like Tiffany, Baracci, Versace and Porsche, whose classy emporiums feature elegant colonnades and copper-toned roofs. A parking lot with free valet parking feeds shoppers right into the middle of the street.

Although such trendy shopping streets as **La Brea Avenue** off Melrose and Santa Monica's **Montana Avenue** will not lose their luster, a thriving newcomer is Venice's **Abbott Kinney Boulevard** (named after the visionary developer who created Venice at the turn of the 20th century). Palm trees set off art galleries, vintage clothing and jewelry stores.

Even more recently, the **Silver Lake** district – centered on Vermont Avenue and Sunset Boulevard – has become a trendy area, full of fashion boutiques and street vendors.

For mall-lovers, Southern California is a shopper's Valhalla. The mind reels at the number of mega-malls dotted throughout the region: **Westfield**, **Century City**, **Beverly Center**, **Westfield Topanga**, **Westfield Fashion Square**, **Paseo Colorado** and **Fashion Island** are just a few.

One of the Southland's most famous landmarks, the outstanding former Uniroyal tire plant beside the Santa Ana Freeway in the City of Commerce, has re-emerged as the **Citadel Outlets** (www.citadeloutlets.com), an enticing shopping plaza whose 80 or so stores spread around a tree-flanked courtyard.

You might, however, want to concentrate your energies on the **South Coast Plaza** (www.southcoastplaza.com) in Costa Mesa (just a stone's throw from Newport in Orange County), a shopping tour-de-force. South Coast Plaza is huge and almost all the 300 stores are first-rate: J Crew (of mail-order fame), Armani, a Metropolitan Museum of Art gift store, Christian Dior, Yves Saint-Laurent, Cartier, Chanel, Pottery Barn and a Disney store to name just a few, as well as a wide range of eateries in all price brackets.

In Santa Barbara, **El Paseo Mall** on State Street is host to gifts and clothes stores as well as galleries and restaurants. The city's biggest shopping mall is also on State Street, called **La Cumbre Plaza**. Two attractive, Spanish-style malls are **La Arcada Court** and **Paseo Nuevo** (www.sbmall.com), the latter anchored by Nordstrom and Macy's.

Because of its upscale nature, the shopping in Palm Springs, centered around **Palm Canyon Drive**, ranges from trendy art galleries and vintage furniture stores to wine emporiums and fine-jewelry boutiques.

Yet another era is evoked by San Diego's **Gaslamp Quarter**, a 16-block, 38-acre (15-hectare) district recom-mended for arts-and-crafts browsers. In addition to that city's **Seaport Village** (www.seaportvillage.com) and the multi-level **Horton Plaza** is nearby **Mission Valley**, which has two shopping malls housing around 350 stores. San Diego is also just a short distance away from the Mexican bor-der town of **Tijuana**, where there are loads of souvenirs, low prices and the enticement of shopping for a day in a different country.

In California, there is a sales tax of 7.25 percent on most items, which is

Clothing Sizes

This table gives a comparison of American, Continental and British clothing sizes. It is always advisable to try on any article before buying, however, as sizes may vary.

Women's Dresses/Suits

American	Continental	British
6	38/34N	8/30
8	40/36N	10/32
10	42/38N	12/34
12	44/40N	14/36
14	46/42N	16/38
16	48/44N	18/40

Women's Shoes

American	Continental	British
4½	36	3
5½	37	4
6½	38	5
7½	39	6
8½	40	7
9½	41	8
10½	42	9

Men's Suits

American	Continental	British
34	44	34
–	46	36
38	48	38
–	50	40
42	52	42
–	54	44
46	56	46

Men's Shirts

American	Continental	British
14	36	14
14½	37	14½
15	38	15
15½	39	15½
16	40	16
16½	41	16½
17	42	17

Men's Shoes

American	Continental	British
6½	39	6
7½	40	7
8½	41	8
9½	42	9
10½	43	10
11½	44	11

always assessed at the cash register, so prices rarely reflect the final total. To further complicate matters, various cities and counties levy an additional sales tax, usually approved by voters to raise money to meet an urgent need. Residents of Los Angeles, for example, voted to increase the local sales tax to 8.25 percent in order to raise money to accelerate repairs after a devastating earthquake in the San Fernando Valley.

A HANDY SUMMARY OF PRACTICAL INFORMATION, ARRANGED ALPHABETICALLY

Admission Charges

Most large museums have reasonably moderate entrance fees – typically $7 to $15 for the first visit. Smaller art galleries tend to be free. Special exhibitions usually cost extra, but many museums have free general admission on certain days each month or once a week in the evenings. Some attractions, like LA's Getty Center, are always free. Plays, concerts and sporting events are often expensive, as are theme park tickets. You can sometimes get free tickets to live TV shows, especially sitcoms, if you call in advance.

Budgeting for your Trip

San Francisco and Los Angeles tend to be more expensive than other parts of California, although exclusive resorts for skiing or spa holidays are more expensive still. If you're looking for a hotel room with an acceptable minimum level of comfort, cleanliness and facilities, a reasonable starting point for the price of a double room is $85 in budget-class hotels; upping your budget from there to at least $150

will make a significant difference in quality. For between $150 and $300 a whole range of hotels opens up, from bland business traveler places to hip little boutique hotels. Beyond this, and certainly beyond $350, you're moving into deluxe territory; though you don't really arrive at "discreet hideaway for celebrities" status until $700 and above.

Food costs range from $3–10 for a perfectly acceptable hot dog, burrito or Asian delicacy, to $50 for a two or three-course meal at a cute California-cuisine type restaurant. Expect to pay $100+ at a fine restaurant.

Getting around by public transportation can cost as little as $3–5 a day. Car rentals cost $40 or more per day.

Business Hours

Standard business hours are 9am–5pm weekdays. Most department stores open at 10am and many stores, especially those in shopping malls, stay open until 9pm. San Francisco, Los Angeles and San Diego have a number of 24-hour restaurants. A few supermarkets and convenience stores also open around the clock. Bank hours usually run

from 9am–5pm, although some stay open until 6pm. Some branch offices keep Saturday morning hours. However, most banks are equipped with 24-hour automated tellers on the outside of their buildings, and, if you have an ATM card, you can use these machines for simple transactions at your convenience. Be careful at night.

Keep in mind that, during public holidays, post offices, banks, government offices and many private businesses are closed.

Children

Because of the weather and the number of world-famous theme parks, the Golden State is a good place to bring kids. Hotels are usually accommodating, allowing kids to stay in parents' rooms for only a nominal charge. The official website of the California State Tourism Commission, www.visit california.com, has a separate link for families. Called "Fun Spots," the pages include tips on traveling with youngsters, family discounts and even games to play. Go to: www.cafunspots.com.

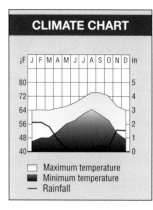

CLIMATE CHART

iF J F M A M J J A S O N D in

- ☐ Maximum temperature
- ■ Minimum temperature
- — Rainfall

C limate

Northern California: San Francisco's climate is typical of the Northern California coast. Daytime temperatures average in the mid-50s Fahrenheit (12–14° Celsius) and drop as much as 10°F (6°C) at night. Average temperatures are significantly higher in the South Bay and inland valleys. In fact, in the Sacramento and San Joaquin valleys, summer temperatures often reach the 90s F (32–37°C). Summers tend to be warm and dry. Winters are generally rainy; temperatures rarely go below freezing along the coast.

Do note that San Francisco can be chilly and foggy during the summer months, even though the sun might be shining just over the bridge in the Bay Area. If you plan to visit the city itself, wait until the fall, when the weather is often perfect.

Southern California: one of the few places in the world where you can ski in the morning and surf in the afternoon. It is not uncommon for the temperature to vary by 30–40°F (17–22°C) as you travel from mountains to deserts to the beach. The change of seasons is not as dramatic as it is elsewhere. The winters are mild, with a rainy season that lasts from January through March. In the summer months, the humidity is usually low, so discomfort is rare. The famous LA smog is at its worst in August and September.

Consulates and Embassies

Australia: 625 Market Street, San Francisco. Tel: 415-536-1970 Also: 2049 Century Park East, Century City (Los Angeles). Tel: 310-229 4800.
Canada: 555 Montgomery, San Francisco. Tel: 415-834-3180 Also: 550 S. Hope Street, Los Angeles. Tel: 213-346 2700.
Great Britain: 1 Sansome Street, San Francisco. Tel: 415-617-1300 Also: 11766 Wilshire Boulevard, Los Angeles. Tel: 310-481 0031.
Ireland: 100 Pine Street, San Francisco. Tel: 415-392-4214 Also: 751 Seadrift Drive, Huntington Beach (Los Angeles). Tel: 714-658 9832.
New Zealand: no SF address. Tel: 415-399-1255. Also: 2425 Olympic Boulevard, Santa Monica (Los Angeles). Tel: 310-566 6555.
South Africa: 6300 Wilshire Blvd, Suite 600, Los Angeles. Tel: 323-651-0902

Crime and Safety

Like places all over the world, California's cities have dangerous neighborhoods. Common sense is an effective weapon. Do not walk alone at night. Keep a careful eye on belongings – lock valuable possessions in a safe. Never leave your car unlocked. Never leave children by themselves.

If you are driving, never pick up anyone you don't know. Always be wary of who is around you. If you have trouble on the road, stay in the car and lock the doors, turn on your hazard lights and leave the hood up

Electricity

The standard electric current in the United States is 110 volts, requiring a converter and an adaptor plug for European appliances. Many hotel bathrooms have plugs for electric shavers that work on either current.

in order to increase visibility and alert police cars.

Hotels usually warn that they do not guarantee the safety of belongings left in the rooms. If you have any valuables, you may want to lock them in the hotel safe.

Customs Regulations

Whether or not there is anything to declare, all people entering the country must go through US Customs. This can be a time-consuming process, but, in order to speed things up, be prepared to open your luggage for inspection and try to keep the following restrictions in mind:
● There is no limit to the amount of money you can bring in with you. If the amount exceeds $10,000, however, you must fill out a report.
● Anything you have for your own personal use may be brought in duty- and tax-free.
● Adults are allowed to bring in one quart (1 liter) of alcohol for personal use.
● You can bring in gifts valued at less than $800 duty- and tax-free. Anything over $800 is subject to duty charges and taxes.
● Dogs, cats and other animals may be brought into the country with certain restrictions. For details, contact the US consulate nearest you or write to the Department of Agriculture.
● Automobiles may be driven into the US if they are for the personal use of the visitor, family and guests.

US Customs & Border Protection, 1300 Pennsylvania Avenue NW, Washington, DC 20229, tel: 202-344 1000, www.cbp.gov.

D isabled Travelers

For more than a decade, California has had legislation requiring public buildings and most public transportation to be accessible to the disabled. There are also some special concessions: Greyhound buses allow a disabled person plus a companion to travel for one fare plus a half-fare (tel: 1-800 752 4841) and the railway system, Amtrak, offers discounted

Emergency Numbers

In the case of an emergency, dial **911** from any telephone for the police, fire department or ambulance service.

tickets and accessible rooms. For more information, call 1-800 872 7245.

Access-able Travel Source is a company offering travel and adventure tours for the disabled. Tel: 303-232 2979 or www.access-able.com.

E ntry Requirements

Foreign travelers to the US must have a passport, and depending on where they are arriving from, a visa or a health record. Exempt from the visa rules are: Canadian citizens; certain European nationals; and certain government officials. Due to recent security alterations, non-US citizens may be required to produce photo ID when traveling within the country, so always have photocopies of your passport at hand.

Any person who enters the US can visit Mexico or Canada for a short period and still be re-admitted to the States without needing a new visa. Visas can be obtained from any US embassy. If a visitor loses their visa while in the country, a new one may be obtained from the embassy of the visitor's home country. Extensions are granted by various service centers of the Bureau of Citizenship and Immigration Services, tel: 1-800 870-3676, www.uscis.gov.

G ay and Lesbian Travelers

San Francisco is one of the world's most welcoming places for gay men and lesbians. The best source for up-

to-date information on new clubs, shows, films, events and gay news are the free newspapers, notably the *Bay Times* and the *Bay Area Reporter (BAR)* found in cafés or street-corner boxes. **The Center**, at 1800 Market Street, www.sfcenter.org, has become a vital nexus for the LGBT (lesbian, gay, bisexual and transgender) community and has numerous flyers and listings for events. **The Women's Building**, www.womensbuilding.org, houses various non-profit organizations and you'll find newspapers, bulletin board postings and information here too. Two free weekly news-papers, the *Bay Guardian* and *SF Weekly*, have useful listings and information as well.

In Los Angeles, **West Hollywood** contains Southern California's largest homosexual population, and sponsors LA's annual Gay Pride Parade. Visit www.visitwesthollywood.com for more information. Also check out the website www.oneinstitute.org for details about the **ONE National Gay & Lesbian Archives** (909 W. Adams Boulevard, tel: 213-741 0094), the world's largest research library on gay, lesbian, bisexual and transgendered issues.

H ealth and Medical Care

There is nothing cheap about being sick in the United States. It is essential to have adequate medical insurance and to carry an identification card or policy number at all times.

In the event that you need medical assistance, consult the local *Yellow Pages* for the physician or pharmacist nearest you. In large cities, there is usually a physician referral service number listed. If you need immediate attention, go to a hospital emergency room.

Hospitals

San Francisco: some of the larger hospitals with 24-hour emergency services are:
the **California Pacific Medical Center,** with buildings at 3700 California Street, 3898 California Street, 2333 Buchanon Street, and the **Davies Medical Center** (at Castro and Deboce streets). Main telephone number and information, tel: 415-387-8700. 24-hour medical services are also provided at the **San Francisco General Hospital**, 1001 Potrero Ave, tel: 415-206-8000.
Los Angeles: some of the most central hospitals are: **California Hospital Medical Center**, 1401 S. Grand Avenue (Downtown), tel: 213-748 2411.

Cedars-Sinai Medical Center, 8700 Beverly Boulevard (Beverly Hills), tel: 310-423 3277
LAC+USC Medical Center, 1200 N. State Street (East LA), tel: 323-226 2622
Saint John's Health Center, 1328 22nd Street (Santa Monica), tel: 310-829 5511
UCLA Medical Center, 10833 Le Conte Avenue (West LA), tel: 310-825 8518

I nternet

You should be able to find internet cafés in all major cities and larger towns, but be warned they are not nearly as commonplace as in Europe. Most public libraries have free terminals, and FedEx Kinko's, a national chain, rents out space on terminals, scanners and printers by the minute or by the hour. The company has many locations throughout the state. Check the *Yellow Pages* for details.

If you've brought your own laptop computer and want to find a café or relaxing spot with wireless connection, check out California locations on www.wififreespot.com/ca.html Some cafés will ask you to pay a minimal service fee for use of their wireless router. Others, like Starbucks, require that you buy an account (daily or monthly) with their preferred service.

Most hotels have dataports in their guestrooms; the more expensive or hip premises offer wireless and high speed internet connections and even a laptop to support it. Even modest hotels tend to have at least one computer for the use of guests.

M aps

In San Francisco, if you find yourself confused and mapless, look for a MUNi bus shelter, which often has a detailed map of the city, including a close-up map of Downtown. The Rand-McNally store on Market Street at the corner of 2nd Street sells maps of the major cities of the world. Some corner shops and gas stations also sell maps.

Tourists can receive a variety of Los Angeles maps from **MTA** (transportation maps; tel: 800-266 6883), **LA INC.** (tel: 213-689 8822) and individual visitor bureaus. In addition, the **Automobile Club of Southern California** (tel: 213-741 3686), with various branches in the area, offers assorted street maps of LA plus maps of California and Mexico. It's worth joining if you plan

Public Holidays

- **New Year's Day** January 1
- **Martin Luther King Jr's Birthday** Third Monday in January, near January 15
- **Presidents' Day** Third Monday in February
- **Easter Sunday**
- **Memorial Day** Last Monday in May
- **Independence Day** July 4
- **Labor Day** First Monday in September
- **Veterans' Day** November 11
- **Thanksgiving Day** Fourth Thursday in November
- **Christmas Day** December 25

to drive within Los Angeles, because the cost of being towed away once by traffic wardens could be less than the annual membership fee.

Insight Flexi Map: San Francisco and *Insight Flexi Map: Los Angeles* are laminated, easy-to-fold maps that combine detailed cartography with pictures and essential information.

Media

Television & Radio

Television and radio are invaluable sources of up-to-the-minute information about weather, road conditions and current events. Television and radio listings are published in local newspapers. Sunday papers usually have a detailed weekly guide to events and activities.

Newspapers & Magazines

San Francisco has two major daily newspapers, the *San Francisco Chronicle* (www.sfgate.com) in the morning and the *San Francisco Examiner* (www.examiner.com) in the afternoon. The weekend edition of the *Chronicle* includes special sections, such as "Datebook," which highlights the area's sports, entertainment and cultural events. Other papers in Northern California include the *Sacramento Bee*, the *San Jose Mercury-News* and the *San Francisco Bay Guardian*.

The website www.sfstation.com is a hip site that keeps up to date with events and activities.

The *Los Angeles Times* (www.latimes.com) is one of the most widely read papers in the country. There are several editions, and there is probably no better local entertainment section than the *Times'* Sunday "Calendar" section.

Other large daily papers are San Fernando Valley's *The Daily News*, *The San Diego Union-Tribune* and the *Orange County Register*.

Los Angeles Magazine, *Palm Springs Life*, *San Diego*, *Santa Barbara* and *Orange Coast* are monthly regional magazines that carry feature articles on Southern California culture, as well as listings of restaurants and current events.

The website www.la.com describes area attractions, spas, hotels, eateries, clubs and shops, and lists most local events.

Some of the free local weekly newspapers are excellent sources of up-to-the-minute information on what's going on in a particular town. Check out the *LA Weekly* in Los Angeles, the *East Bay Express* in the East Bay, the *San Francisco Bay Guardian* and *SF Weekly* in San Francisco.

Money

Cash: Most banks belong to a network of ATMs (automatic teller machines) which dispense cash 24 hours a day.

Credit cards: Not all credit cards are accepted at all places, but most places accept either **Visa**, **American Express** or **MasterCard**. Major credit cards can also be used to withdraw cash from ATMs. (Look for an ATM that uses one of the banking networks indicated on the back of your credit card, such as Plus, Cirrus and Interlink.) There will be a charge.

Traveler's Checks: Since visitors may face problems changing foreign currency, it is better to use American-dollar traveler's checks. When lost or stolen, most traveler's checks can be replaced and they are accepted in most stores, restaurants and hotels. Banks readily cash large traveler's checks, although be sure to take along your passport.

Postal Services

Post offices open between 7 and 9am and usually close at 5pm, Monday–Friday. Many are also open for a few hours on Saturday morning. Post offices are closed all day on Sunday. If you don't know where you will be staying in any particular town, you can receive mail by having it addressed to General Delivery at the main post office in that town. You must pick up General Delivery mail in person and show proper identification. You can buy stamps in most convenience stores, alhough you may have to buy a book of stamps.

Senior Travelers

Senior citizens (over 65 for men, over 62 for women) are entitled to many benefits, including reduced rates on public transportation and for entrance to museums. Seniors who want to be students should write to **Elderhostels**, 80 Boylston Street, Suite 400, Boston, MA 02116, Massachusetts, for information on places that provide both accommodation and classes. The Bay Area has a number of Elderhostel locations. **Access-able Travel Source** is a company offering travel and adventure tours for seniors. Tel: 303-232 2979 or www.access-able.com.

Smoking

California's famed tolerance is not extended towards smokers. State law bans smoking in bars, clubs, restaurants, within 25 feet (7.5 meters) of playgrounds and sandboxes, and within 20 feet (6 meters) of all public buildings.

In San Francisco, smoking is prohibited in all city-owned parks, plazas and public sports facilities. Even some public beaches in Southern California have made cigarettes illegal; look for signs on the sand to see if you can light up. You may find it difficult to reserve a smoking room in a hotel, so be sure to check at the time of booking, and be prepared to shop around.

Student Travelers

With a current school ID, a student traveler can take advantage of discounts at some museums, movie theaters and public transportation. Check out colleges in the summer for dormitory accommodation.

TRANSPORTATION

ACCOMMODATIONS

EATING OUT

ACTIVITIES

A – Z

Telephones and Faxes

Telephones: with the growing popularity of cell phones, coin-operated telephones are not as common as before, but can usually be found in hotels, gas stations and often in lighted booths on street corners.

To place a long-distance call, dial 1+area code+local number. Be sure to have plenty of change with you.

If you are having problems, dial "0" for the operator from any phone. Another indispensable number is for information assistance, which can provide telephone listings. For information, dial 411 or 1+area code+555 1212. For a toll-free number directory, dial 1-800 555 1212. Make use of toll-free numbers when possible (toll-free telephone numbers within the US are indicated by 1-800, 855, 866, 877 or 888). When making personal calls, take advantage of lower long-distance rates after 7pm on weekdays and during weekends.

Cell phones: to use your GSM cellular phone in the US, you must have a tri-band phone and contact your service provider before you leave to set up international roaming. It may be cheaper to just bite the bullet and buy a US-issue phone.

Telephone codes: with the proliferation of cell phones, modems and fax lines, California has been forced to divide, then subdivide its existing telephone exhanges. Although every effort has been made to keep the telephone prefixes listed here up to date, it's a good idea to check with the operator if you're in doubt.

Information

Fax machines: although email and cell phones have replaced the need for many faxes, machines can be found in most hotels, motels and convenience stores.

Tipping

Just as in other parts of the country, service personnel in California rely on tips for a large part of their income. In most cases, 15–20 percent is the going rate for waiters and bartenders, 15 percent for taxi drivers. The accepted rate for baggage handlers at airports and hotels is around $1 per bag. For overnight stays, it is not necessary to tip the chambermaid. For longer stays, the rule of thumb is to leave a minimum tip of one or two dollars per night stayed in the room. A doorman expects to be tipped at least $1 for unloading your car or for other services.

Tourist Information Offices

General information on visiting the Golden State is available from **California Tourism**, PO Box 1499, Sacramento, CA 95812 Tel: 1-800 862 2543; www.visitcalifornia.com
Anaheim/Orange County Visitor and Convention Bureau, 800 W Katella Ave, Anaheim, CA 92802 Tel: 714-765 8888; www.anaheimoc.org
Berkeley Convention and Visitors Bureau, 2015 Center St, Berkeley, CA 94704 Tel: 510-549 7040; 1-800 847 4823; www.visitberkeley.com
Beverly Hills Conference and Visitors Bureau, 239 South Beverly Drive, Beverly Hills, CA 90212 Tel: 310-248 1015; 1-800 345 2210; www.beverlyhillsbehere.com
Buena Park Convention and Visitors Office, 6601 Beach Blvd, Suite 200, Buena Park, CA 90621 Tel: 714-562 3560; www.visitbuenapark.com
Catalina Island Chamber of Commerce, 1 Green Pier, Avalon, CA 90704 Tel: 310-510 1520; www.catalina.com; e-mail: info@visitcatalina.org
Hollywood Visitor Information Center, 6801 Hollywood Blvd at Hollywood and Highland, Hollywood,

Time Zones

California is situated entirely in the Pacific Time Zone, which is two hours behind Chicago, three hours behind New York and eight hours behind Greenwich Mean Time. On the second Sunday in March, the clock is moved ahead one hour for Daylight Savings Time. On the first Sunday in November, the clock is moved back one hour to return to Standard Time.

CA 90028 Tel: 323-467 6412; www.greaterlosangeles.com
Lake Tahoe Incline Village and Crystal Bay Visitors' Bureau, 969 Tahoe Blvd, Incline Village, NV 89451 Tel: 1-800-GOTAHOE; www.gotahoe.com
Lake Tahoe Visitors' Authority, 169 Highway 50 Stateline, NV 89449 Tel: 1-800-AT-TAHOE; www.bluelaketahoe.com
Long Beach Area Convention and Visitors Bureau, 1 World Trade Center, 3rd floor, Long Beach, CA 90831 Tel: 562-436 3645; 1-800 452 7829; www.visitlongbeach.com
Los Angeles Area Chamber of Commerce, 350 South Bixel, Los Angeles, CA 90017 Tel: 213-580 7500; www.lachamber.org; e-mail: info@lachamber.org
Los Angeles Convention and Visitors Bureau, 685 South Figueroa St, Los Angeles, CA 90017 Tel: 213-689 8822; www.greaterlosangeles.com
Monterey County Convention and Visitors' Bureau, 150 Olivier St, Monterey, CA 93942 Tel: 831-649 1770; 888-221-1010; www.montereyinfo.org
Napa Valley Conference and Visitors' Bureau, 1310 Napa Town Center, Napa, CA 94559 Tel: 707-226 7459; www.napavalley.com
Palm Springs Desert Resort Communities Convention and Visitors Authority, 70–100 Highway 111, Rancho Mirage, CA 92270 Tel: 760-770 9000; 1-800 417 3529; www.giveintothedesert.com

Sacramento Convention and Visitors' Bureau,
1608 I St, Sacramento, CA 95814
Tel: 916-264 7777;
www.sacramentocvb.org

San Diego International Visitor Information Center,
1040⅓ West Broadway,
San Diego, CA 92101
Tel: 619-236 1212;
www.sandiego.org;
e-mail: sdinfo@sandiego.org

San Diego North Convention and Visitors Bureau,
360 North Escondido Blvd,
Escondido, CA 92025
Tel: 760-745 4741;
1-800 848 3336;
www.sandiegonorth.com;
e-mail: info@sandiegonorth.com

San Francisco Chamber of Commerce,
235 Montgomery St, 12th Floor,
San Francisco, CA 94104
Tel: 415-392 4520;
www.sfchamber.com

San Francisco Convention & Visitors' Bureau,
900 Market St,
San Francisco, CA 94102
Tel: 415-391 2000;
www.onlyinsanfrancisco.com

San Luis Obispo County Visitor and Conference Bureau,
811 E1 Capitan Way, Suite 200,
San Luis Obispo, CA 93401
Tel: 805-541 8000;
1-800 634 1414;
www.sanluisobispocounty.com;
e-mail: info@sanluisobispocounty.com

San Jose Convention and Visitors' Bureau,
408 Almaden Blvd,
San Jose, CA 95110
Tel: 1-800 SAN JOSE;
www.sanjose.org

Santa Barbara Conference and Visitors Bureau,
1601 Anacapa St,
Santa Barbara, CA 93101
Tel: 805-965 3021/966 9222/
1-800 927 4688/676 1266;
www.santabarbaraca.com;
e-mail: tourism@santabarbaraca.com

Santa Cruz County Conference and Visitors Council,
1211 Ocean St,
Santa Cruz, CA 95060
Tel: 1-800 833 3494;
www.scccvc.org
e-mail: comments@santacruz.org

Sonoma County Tourism Bureau,
420 Aviation Blvd, Suite 106
Santa Rosa, CA 95403
Tel: 707-522 5800
www.sonomacounty.com

Sonoma Valley Vistors' Bureau,
453 First St East, Sonoma, CA 95476
Tel: 707-996 1090
www.sonomavalley.com

ABOVE: San Francisco can be chilly during the summer months, so dress in layers.

Ventura Visitors and Convention Bureau,
89C South California St,
Ventura, CA 93001
Tel: 805-648 2075;
www.ventura-usa.com;
e-mail: tourism@ventura-usa.com

Yosemite and Sierra Visitors' Bureau,
41969 Hwy 41, Oakhurst, CA 93644
Tel: 559-683 4636;
www.go2yosemite.net

U seful Addresses

California has 13 Welcome Centers situated throughout the state to assist visitors. The centers provide maps, brochures and helpful on-the-spot advice. For more information and precise driving directions, go to: www.VisitCWC.com

Anderson (Shasta Cascade),
1699 Hwy 273, south of Redding on I-5. Tel: 530-365 1180.
Arcate (North Coast), 1635 Heindon Rd. Tel: 707-822 3619.
Auburn (Gold Country), 13411 Lincoln Way. Tel: 530-887 2111.
Barstow (Deserts), 2796 Tanger Way, Suite 100. Tel: 760-253 4782.
Merced (Central Valley), 710 W. 16th St, Suite A. Tel: 209-384 2791.
Oceanside (San Diego), 928 North Coast Hwy. Tel: 760-721 1101.
Oxnard (Central Coast), 1000 Town Center Dr., Suite 135. Tel: 805-385 7545.
Pismo Beach (Central Coast), 333 Five Cities Drive, Suite 100, in the Prime Outlets. Tel: 805-773 7924.
San Bernardino, 159 Hospitality Lane. Tel: 1-800 867 8366.
San Francisco, Pier 39, Building P. Tel: 415-981 1280.

Santa Ana (Orange County), 2800 N. Main St, Suite 112, MainPlace. Tel: 714-667 0400.
Santa Rosa (North Coast), 9 Fourth St in the downtown area. Tel: 1-800 404 7673.
Yucca Valley (Deserts), 56711 29 Palms Hwy. Tel: 760-365 5464.

W eights and Measures

The US uses the Imperial system of weights and measures. Metric is rarely used. Below is a conversion chart:

1 inch	=	2.54 centimeters
1 foot	=	30.48 centimeters
1 mile	=	1.609 kilometers
1 sq. mile	=	2.59 sq. kilometers
1 quart	=	0.946 liter
1 ounce	=	28.35 grams
1 pound	=	0.454 kilograms
1 yard	=	0.9144 meters
1 acre	=	0.4047 hectare

What to Wear

Northern California: With the exception of the finer restaurants, jackets, ties and formal dresses are unnecessary. San Francisco is famous for its fog and breezy hilltops, so bring along a sweater or jacket, even if it is warm when you first step out.

Southern California: Dress in Southern California is casual and few restaurants require jackets and ties for men. Unless you are visiting the mountains, heavy clothing is unnecessary. Wool sweaters or lightweight overcoats are sufficient for winter evenings, and a light jacket is adequate for summer evenings. Expect rain in winter and springtime.

If you are planning to go to the mountains or desert, pack accordingly.

FURTHER READING

General

Back Roads to the California Coast: Scenic Byways and Highways to the Edge of the Golden State, by Earl Thollander and Herb McGrew. Sasquatch Books, 2002.
Behind the Mask of Innocence, by Kevin Brownlow. Alfred A Knopf, 1990.
California: A Guide to the Golden State, by the Federal Writers Project. Hastings House, 1939.
California Coastal Access Guide, by the California Coastal Commission.
California Politics: The Fault Lines of Power, Wealth, and Diversity, by Edgar Kaskla. CQ Press, 2007.
California Southern Country, by Carey McWilliams. Duell, Sloan Pearce, 1946.
Coast Walks, by John Mckinney. Olympus Press, 1999
Cruel Justice: Three Strikes and the Politics of Crime in America's Golden State, by Joe Domanick. University of California Press, 2004.
A Guide to Architecture in Los Angeles and Southern California, by Gebhard and Winter.
Los Angeles A–Z: an Encyclopedia of City & Country, by Dale & Leonard Pitt. University of California Press, 1997.
My California: Journeys by Great Writers. Angel City Press, 2004.
The Real Oscar, by Peter H. Brown. Arlington House, 1991.
Southern California: An Island on the Land, by Carey McWilliams. Peregrine Smith, 1946.
Street Gallery: Guide to 1000 Los Angeles Murals, by Robin J. Dunkitz. RJD Enterprise, 1993.
Take Sunset Boulevard, by Barbara and Rudy Marinacci. Presidio Press, 1980.
Tales from the Hollywood Raj, by Sheridan Morley. Viking Press, NY 1983.
Tales of the City, by Armistead Maupin. Perennial, 1989.
Travelers' Tales San Francisco, True Stories of Life on the Road, edited by James O'Reilly, Larry Habegger & Sean O'Reilly, 2002.
The Underground Guide to San Francisco, by Jennifer Joseph. Manic D Press, 2002.

A Very Good Year: The Journey of a California Wine from Vine to Table, by Mike Weiss. Gotham, 2005.
The War Between the State: Northern California vs. Southern California, by Jon Winokur. Sasquatch Books, 2004.

People and Places

All the Stars in Heaven: Louis B. Mayer's MGM, by Gary Carey. E.P. Dutton, 1981.
Baseball in San Diego: From Padres to Petco, by Bill Swank. Arcadia Publishing, 2004.
California Vieja: Culture and Memory in a Modern American Place, by Phoebe S. Kropp. University of California Press, 2006.
The Great Movie Stars: The Golden Years, by David Shipman. Crown, 1970.
Hollywood Interrupted: Insanity Chic in Babylon – The Case Against Celebrity, by Andrew Breitbart and Mark Ebner. John Wiley & Sons, 2004.
Homicide Special: A Year with the LAPD's Elite Detective Unit, by Miles Corwin. Henry Holt & Company, 2004.
Life and Good Times of William Randolph Hearst, by John Tebbel. EP Dutton, 1952.
The Life of Raymond Chandler, by Frank McShane. EP Dutton, 1976.
Los Angeles Stories, Great Writers on the City, edited by John Miller. Chronicle Books, 1991.
Mark Twain's San Francisco, edited by Bernard Taper. Heyday Books, 2003.
Movie Star Homes: The Famous to the Forgotten, by Judy Artunian. Santa Monica Press, 2004.
Santa Barbara Celebrities: Conversations from the American Riviera, by Cork Millner. Santa Barbara Press, 1989.
Day Hikers Guide to California State Parks, by John Mckinney. Olympus Press, 1998
The Los Angeles Watts Towers, by Bud & Arloa Goldstone. The Getty Institute, 1997.
This is Hollywood, by Ken Schessler. Universal Books.
Venice of America, by Jeffrey Stanton. Donahue Publications, 1987.

Geography and Natural History

California Wildlife Reviewing Guide, by Jeanne L Clarke. Falcon Press, 1996.
Finding Fault in California: An Earthquake Tourist's Guide, by Susan Elizabeth Hough. Mountain Press Publishing, 2004.
Introduction to Air in California, by David Carle. University of California Press, 2006
Natural Los Angeles, by Bill Thomas. Harper and Row, 1989.
Malibu Diary: Notes from an Urban Refugee, by Penelope O.Malley. University of Nevada Press, 2004.
Wildly Successful Plants: Northern California, by Pam Peirce. Sasquatch Books, 2004.

History

Agrarian Dreams: The Paradox of Organic Farming in California, by Julie Guthman. University of California Press, 2004.
California: A History, by Kevin Starr. Modern Library, 2007.
The California Gold Rush and the Coming of the Civil War, by Leonard L. Richards. Knopf, 2007.
A Companion to California, by James Hart. Oxford University Press, 1978.
The Days of the Great Estates, by David F. Myrick. Trans-Angelo Books, 1990.
Filming in San Diego: Hollywood's Backlot 1898–2002. San Diego Historical Society, 2002.
The Golden Game: The Story of California Baseball, by Kevin Nelson. Heyday Books, 2004.
History of the San Fernando Valley, by Frank M. Keffner. Stillman, 1934.
Hollywood: The First Hundred Years, by Bruce T. Torrence. New York Zoetrope, 1982.
Los Angeles Two Hundred, by David Lavender. Harry N. Abrams, 1980.
The Times We Had: Life with William Randolph Hearst, by Marion Davis. Bobbs Merrill, 1975.
Whitewashed Adobe: The Rise of Los Angeles and the Remaking of Its Mexican Past, by William Deverell. University of California Press, 2004.

ART & PHOTO CREDITS

INDEX

Numbers in italics refer to photographs

Getting Around Los Angeles

```
0 ————————————————— 5 miles
0 ————————————————— 5 km
```